ADDITIVE REPRESENTATIONS OF PREFERENCES

THEORY AND DECISION LIBRARY

General Editors: W. Leinfellner and G. Eberlein

Series A: Philosophy and Methodology of the Social Sciences
Editors: W. Leinfellner (Technical Universtiy of Vienna)
G. Eberlein (Technical University of Munich)

Series B: Mathematical and Statistical Methods
Editor: H. Skala (University of Paderborn)

Series C: Game Theory, Mathematical Programming and Operations Research
Editor: S. H. Tijs (University of Nijmegen)

Series D: System Theory, Knowledge Engineering and Problem Solving
Editor: W. Janko (University of Vienna)

SERIES C: **GAME THEORY, MATHEMATICAL PROGRAMMING AND OPERATIONS RESEARCH**

Editor: S. H. Tijs (University of Nijmegen)

Editorial Board

H. Keiding (Copenhagen), J.-F. Mertens (Louvain-la-Neuve), H. Moulin (Blacksburg), B. Peleg (Jerusalem), T. E. S. Raghavan (Chicago), J. Rosenmüller (Bielefeld), A. Roth (Pittsburgh), D. Schmeidler (Tel-Aviv), R. Selten (Bonn).

Scope

Particular attention is paid in this series to game theory and operations research, their formal aspects and their applications to economic, political and social sciences as well as to socio-biology. It will encourage high standards in the application of game theoretical methods to individual and social decision making.

For a list of titles in this series, see final page.

ADDITIVE REPRESENTATIONS OF PREFERENCES

A New Foundation of Decision Analysis

by

PETER P. WAKKER
Department of Mathematical Psychology,
University of Nijmegen, The Netherlands

KLUWER ACADEMIC PUBLISHERS
DORDRECHT / BOSTON / LONDON

Library of Congress Cataloging in Publication Data

Wakker, Peter P.
Additive representations of preferences : a new foundation of decision analysis / Peter P. Wakker.
p. cm. -- (Theory and decision library. Series C, Game theory, mathematical programming, and operations research)
"Rewritten version of the author's Ph.D. dissertation at the Department of Economics of the University of Brabant"--P.
Bibliography: p.
Includes index.
ISBN 0-7923-0050-5
1. Decision-making--Mathematical models. I. Title. II. Series.
QA402.5.W325 1989
658.4'03'3--dc19 88-26783
CIP

ISBN 0-7923-0050-5

Published by Kluwer Academic Publishers,
P.O. Box 17, 3300 AA Dordrecht, The Netherlands.

Kluwer Academic Publishers incorporates
the publishing programmes of
D. Reidel, Martinus Nijhoff, Dr W. Junk and MTP Press.

Sold and distributed in the U.S.A. and Canada
by Kluwer Academic Publishers,
101 Philip Drive, Norwell, MA 02061, U.S.A.

In all other countries, sold and distributed
by Kluwer Academic Publishers Group,
P.O. Box 322, 3300 AH Dordrecht, The Netherlands.

Printed in The Netherlands

CONTENTS

ACKNOWLEDGEMENTS

The results in this book were obtained while the author held positions at the Department of Mathematics of the University of Leiden, the Department of Mathematics of the University of Nijmegen, the Department of Statistical Methods of the Netherlands Central Bureau of Statistics, and the Nijmegen Institute of Cognition and Information technology (NICI) of the University of Nijmegen. For the latter position financial support was given by the Royal Netherlands Academy of Arts and Sciences.

The book is a rewritten version of the author's Ph.D. dissertation at the Department of Economics of the University of Brabant; it would not have been written without the encouragements of Professor S.H. Tijs. Supervisors for the dissertation were Professor P.H.M. Ruys, Professor D. Schmeidler, and Professor S.H. Tijs. Further the dissertation received comments of Dr. J.A.M. Potters and Dr. H.J.M. Peters. The rewritten parts in the book have received comments of Professor Th. Bezembinder, Dr. H.J.M. Peters, and Dr. J.A.M. Potters.

Many parts of the book have, in earlier forms, been published in journals. Comments of anonymous referees have contributed to improvements of the book.

PREFACE, PREVIEW, AND GUIDE LINES FOR USE

Preface

In decision theories the assumption is usually made that a decision maker maximizes some quantitative goal function. Depending on the context, such a function may be called a profit function, utility function, representing function (this will be our term), etc., and is usually assumed to possess certain desirable properties, such as continuity, concavity, etc.

The purpose of this monograph is to show a way to make the above-mentioned assumption operational. To this end, choice behaviour of the decision maker is taken as observable primitive. In Chapter I we shall give the conditions under which choice behaviour can be represented by a preference relation. In the following chapters this preference relation will then be taken as primitive, particularly in the formulation of the 'representation theorems' given there.

After specification of the presupposed context, these representation theorems state the equivalence of (usually) two statements. The first statement, numbered (i), is theoretical. It says that a representing function, with certain desirable properties, exists. The second statement, numbered (ii), is formulated in empirical terms. It **characterizes** statement (i), i.e., gives the conditions for the preference relation, necessary and sufficient for the truth of statement (i). So, representation theorems 'translate' theoretical statements into empirical statements. They give the criteria for verification/justification, or falsification/criticism, of the assumption that the desired representing function, described in statement (i), exists. After the representation theorems usually so-called 'uniqueness results' are given in 'Observations'. The proofs of the representation theorems do not only show the existence of representing functions, but also, mainly through the process described in section III.5, indicate how to construct the (quantitative) representing functions from the qualitative information contained in the preference relation.

The main subject in this monograph is decision making under uncertainty. In particular representations of subjective expected utility maximization will be given, without use of the tool of lotteries (i.e., without using objective probabilities), in Chapters IV and V. Subjective expected utility maximization is notorious for the many vivid discussions about its appropriateness. The first well-known representation theorems for (subjective) expected utility maximization, the one in von Neumann&Morgenstern (1944) and the one in Savage(1954) (see our section A2), have had great influence in the economic literature, and have stirred the statistical literature because of their profound implications for the foundations of statistics. We think discussions of subjective expected utility are best understood when embedded in the more general framework of 'measurement' theory, i.e., the general theory about quantitative representations of qualitative phenomena. In Chapter VII we will show that also classical results concerning risk aversion can be obtained without use of lotteries. Thus the book gives a new behavioural foundation to decision analysis which does not need lotteries. A recent account of decision analysis, keeping use of mathematical tools to a minimum, and built on long practical experience, is given in von Winterfeldt&Edwards(1986). That reference, like this book, concentrates on expected utility maximization, and supplies general information not available in this book. We further give one of the new approaches to decision making under uncertainty/risk, deviating from expected utility, in Chapter VI. Here again the aim has been to show that lotteries can be dispensed with.

It is common use in economic analyses that scientists, using subjective expected utility without lotteries available, for a justification refer to Savage(1954). We are however not aware of an economic analysis in which actually the restrictive conditions of Savage(1954) are verified. The restrictive condition of our set-up, continuity of utility (see Theorems IV.2.7 and V.6.1), usually is satisfied.

It should be emphasized that representation theorems as such are not only useful for advocates of the use of some special kind of representing functions, but just as well give the tools for criticisms. For instance, Allais(1953a) used the independence condition of von Neumann&Morgenstern, and the sure-thing principle of Savage, to criticize expected utility. We aim to be neutral by 'selling our weapons to both sides'.

The theorems of Savage(1954), and von Neumann&Morgenstern(1944), (and Anscombe&Aumann,1963) apply to special circumstances, where the state space is well structured, or where many lotteries, with known probability distributions, are available. Such special circumstances are usually not present in economic contexts. The main purpose of this monograph is to provide representation theorems for subjective expected utility maximization under special circumstances (continuity) which usually àre present in economic contexts.

We have avoided the use of differentiability conditions, and restricted ourselves to continuity conditions. Firstly, this leads to logically stronger results. Secondly, the difficulties with continuity, sketched in section III.1, hold a fortiori for differentiability. Thirdly, and mainly, the continuity approach leads to directly testable conditions, whereas 'rate-of-substitution-like' conditions as emerging from the differentiability approach are not directly testable.

Preview

First, in Chapter 0, we give some elementary definitions. Section 0.2 gives the elementary results from topology used in this book. Then, in Chapter I, preference relations are related to choice behaviour by means of the 'revealed preference' approach, originating from consumer demand theory. In order to achieve maximal operationality, we define our 'revealed preference' relations in a way slightly different from the way most usual in the literature; the characterization theorems are derived with the aid of these revealed preference relations. For intuitive purposes, choice behaviour in our view is a more appropriate primitive for decision theory than a preference relation. Hence in Chapter I the 'paradigm' of decision theory is discussed in terms of choice behaviour. We shall give our preferred interpretations of the entities occurring in decision theory, interpretations which have led to the set-up of this book. This should not deter readers with other views from the remainder of the book, since the representation theorems in following chapters can be studied independently of the views expressed in Chapter I.

In Chapter I we do not yet assume that any structure (other than the trivial set-theoretic structure) is observable on the set of alternatives. So apart from the choices made, the only information about alternatives which is used is whether two alternatives are identical or not. In following chapters, more and more structure on the set of alternatives will be imposed. Chapter II will assume a Cartesian-product-structure available, according to which we can completely describe an alternative by a list of 'attributes' (coordinates). Chapter III will add a (connected separable) topology, according to which it can be said whether or not alternatives come close to each other; etc. Finally, in sections VII.6 and VII.7, we will meet the most-structured case, the case where the set of alternatives is a Euclidean space. The primary reason to consider spaces, more general (so with simpler structures!) than Euclidean spaces, is not the mathematician's desire for generality at the cost of accessibility. The primary reason is to increase applicability. With the exception of sections VII.6 and VII.7, all of our work is applicable to decision situations where no physical quantification of the alternatives is available. This makes our work useful already at the stage of decision making where quantifications are not yet available, but are to be introduced.

The set-up of this monograph shows the reduction of complicated statements such as 'the decision maker does/should maximize subjective expected utility with continuous utility, risk aversion, and nonincreasing risk aversion', as we shall meet in sections VII.6 and VII.7, to simple statements in terms of choice making, as we shall start with in Chapter I.

In Chapter II the structure is introduced which will be most important in this monograph: The set of alternatives is assumed to be a Cartesian product. Each coordinate of an alternative describes a relevant aspect. For making his decisions, the decision maker is to weigh the advantages and disadvantages of the several aspects against each other, and combine them into a decision. The Cartesian product structure plays a central role, thus our work finds application, in many fields of science. Section II.1 gives some examples, amongst them decision making under uncertainty. Section II.4 introduces a way to derive comparisons of tradeoffs of coordinates from the preference relation on the alternatives. It will make possible transparent formulations of conditions for the preference relation in the remainder of the book. It is the key idea by means of which this book obtains the classical results of decision analysis without needing lotteries as a tool.

In Chapter III topological structure is introduced. We assume that the set of alternatives is endowed with a connected (and separable; compare Remarks A3.1 and

III.7.1) product topology. From then on, in all our main theorems, the preference relation will be continuous and complete (either by assumption, or as a consequence of other assumptions). Section III.1 gives some comments on the fact that the conditions of continuity and completeness are of a technical nature, and are not fully operational. In sections III.4 to III.6 we characterize the existence of continuous additive representations. Section III.5 gives a fully elaborated derivation of the construction of additive representations. This derivation aims to preserve full mathematical rigidity, while being accessible to readers without high-level mathematical background. The price to pay for this is the large number of pages that the exposition takes. The large number of pages, and the presentation and layout of the proof, should help to *minimize* the time and effort of the reader needed to understand the derivation.

In Chapter IV a further structural assumption is added: It is assumed that all factor sets in the Cartesian product are identical. (This assumption will be dropped only in sections VII.1 to VII.4.) Theorem IV.2.7 gives the central result of this monograph, a characterization of subjective expected utility maximization by means of a new condition for the preference relation: The preference relation should not reveal contradictory tradeoffs. Let us, for the moment, take for granted the, in economic contexts common, assumptions of transitivity, completeness and continuity of the preference relation. Then Theorem IV.2.7 shows that subjective expected utility maximization can be justified (, or verified, or criticized, or falsified) if and only if the nonrevelation of contradictory tradeoffs can be. This is all obtained under the assumption that the state space is finite. The adaptation to infinite state spaces will be given in Chapter V. Theorem IV.2.7 is central because the preceding results can be considered preparations for it, and the following results extensions.

In the remainder of Chapter IV, and in Chapters V and VI, several generalizations of Theorem IV.2.7 are obtained. Also applications to contexts other than decision making under uncertainty are given. For instance, we give, for dynamic contexts, an alternative characterization of a representation characterized before by Koopmans(1972). The main result of Chapter V, Theorem V.6.1, adapts the results of Chapter IV to infinite state spaces. This is done both for finitely additive and for countably additive probability measures. Chapter VI extends Theorem IV.2.7 to 'capacities', i.e. 'nonadditive probability measures'. These were introduced in decision making under uncertainty by Schmeidler (1984a,b). Our contribution to Schmeidler's work is like the contribution of Theorem IV.2.7 to the theorem of Anscombe&Aumann(1963): We replace the restrictive assumption that many lotteries are available by the restrictive assumption that utility is continuous. Besides the motives like those for other chapters, there was a further motivation for Chapter VI: In Schmeidler's work the auxiliary lotteries are dealt with accordancing to the axioms of von Neumann&Morgenstern, so that one still is restricted to the additive approach to risk. By means of our work this restriction can be removed, so that a general nonadditive attitude, both towards uncertainty and towards risk (for the latter see Yaari(1987a)), is no longer excluded. The reason to include Chapter VI in a book on additive representations is that the nonadditive results in this Chapter are derived from the additive results as laid down in Chapter III.

In Chapter VII a further structure on the set of alternatives is added: A mixture-structure. Again, the most well-known examples are convex subsets of linear spaces. We use this structure to define, and characterize, *concave* additive representing functions, by means of 'nonincreasing derived tradeoffs'. Such (representing) functions are prominent in mathematical programming, consumer and producers theory, and decision making under uncertainty, in the latter to characterize risk aversion. Still, to the best of our knowledge, no other characterization is available in the literature.

In sections VII.6 and VII.7 we assume that the factor sets are convex subsets of the set of real numbers. Real numbers may for instance indicate amounts of money. Thus here the alternative sets of this monograph, endowed with most structure, occur. It is then shown that assumptions on (nonincreasing) risk aversion, current in economic literature, simplify the characterization of subjective expected utility maximization in a way which, at least to the author, was a surprise.

The appendix gives some results which are of use for this monograph, but did not fit in well at other places. Section A1 gives some elementary results from analysis, section A2 gives simple presentations of the main classical characterizations of subjective expected utility, finally section A3 gives a list of Remarks.

The research which led to the main results of this book started with a trial to extend the characterization of expected utility maximization, as obtained by de Finetti(1974, Chapter 3; see our Theorem A2.1) for the special case of linear utility by means of 'coherence', to the case of concave utility. This led to the 'concavity assumption' (VII.3.1), a condition which did not suffice to give expected utility yet. Then the question what should be added to give expected utility led to the condition called 'cardinal coordinate independence' (see section IV.2).

Guide lines for use

Primarily this book deals with mathematical questions in decision theory. It is self-contained in the sense that proofs of results are omitted only when these results are side results, not needed for the sequel, and available elsewhere in the literature. Elementary knowledge of analysis and set-theory will suffice to understand the main results. For understanding of details the elementary results of topology, given in section 0.2, will be needed, and a willingness to pursue abstract trains of thought. Chapter V requires knowledge of integration theory for the main results, and knowledge of measure theory for details. Fishburn(1972) is a concise and accessible collection of elementary mathematical results used in decision theory, starting with set theory.

We have gathered many references to related works. This indicates relatedness between many diverse fields of science nowadays. The references will however not always be of interest to every reader. Hence they are usually listed as numbered notes in the 'Reference-Notes' just before the references at the end of the book. Reference to the number of such a note is made by a superindex[rf..] on the proper place in the text.

Only very essential references are given immediately in the text. Sometimes the last section in a Chapter is devoted to a discussion of literature and history concerning the topic of the chapter.

The format of the main representation theorems has been explicated at the beginning of the Preface. We have as much as possible formulated the representation theorems in such a way that the reader can understand them without consulting other parts of the text, except the Subject Index and the references to the text therein. Directly above the main representation theorems the facts are listed which are needed for understanding. The main representation theorems have been listed in Remark A3.3 in the Appendix.

The figure on the following page illustrates the dependencies of the several sections and chapters in this book.

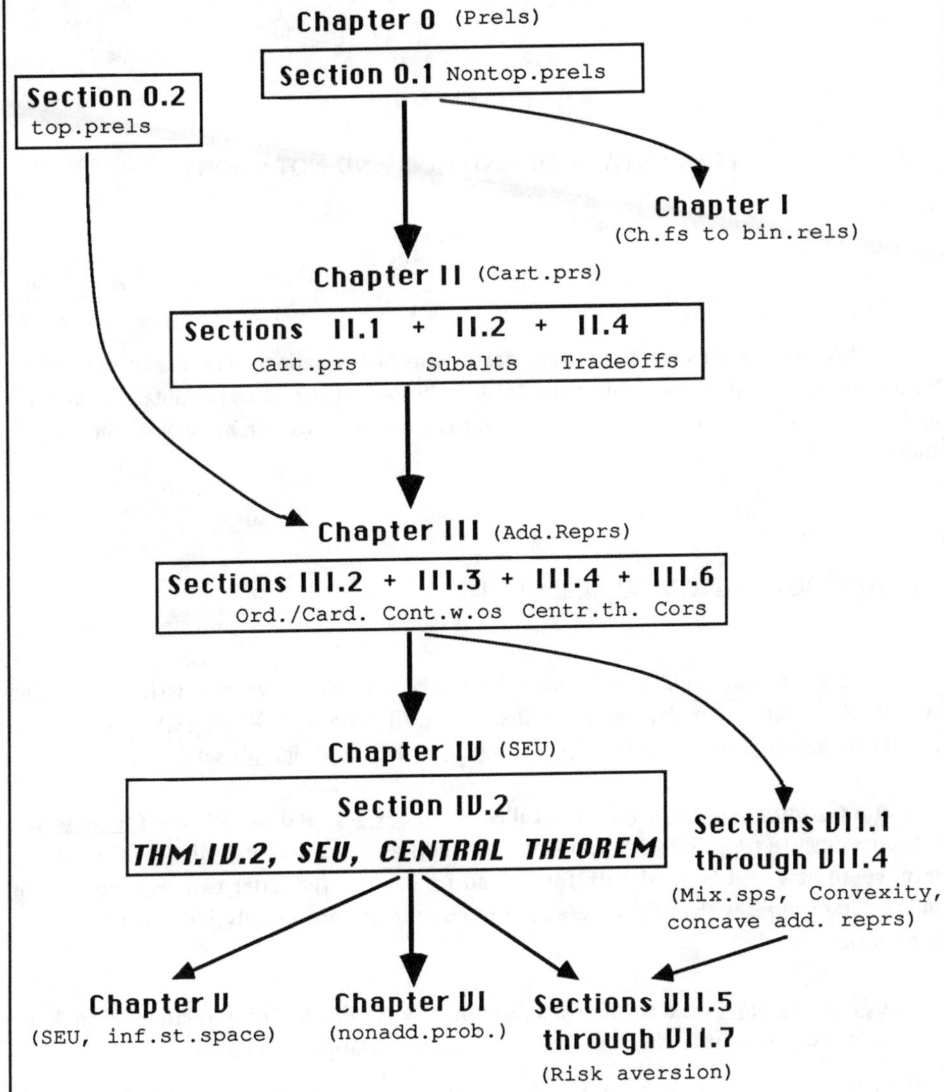

FIGURE (The set-up of the book). An arrow from section(s) A to section/chapter B indicates that B depends on A, hence on everything upon which A depends.

CHAPTER 0

ELEMENTARY DEFINITIONS AND NOTATIONS

In this chapter we give elementary definitions and notations. The reader familiar with them may wish to skip this chapter, or only look at the standard notations at the end of section 0.1, and may in case of doubt consult this chapter by way of the Subject Index.

0.1. NONTOPOLOGICAL PRELIMINARIES

The signs $\subset$ and $\supset$ will also be used for trivial subsets, so we may write $A \subset A$ and $A \supset \emptyset$. For a set X, 2^X denotes the collection of all subsets of X. By $(x_j)_{j=1}^n$ we denote the ordered sequence $(x_1,\ldots,x_n)$, by $\{x_j\}_{j=1}^n$ the ('unordered') set $\{x_1,\ldots,x_n\}$.

In a *Cartesian product* $\prod_{i\in I}\Gamma_i$, I is called the **index set**, and the Γ_i's are **factor sets**. For an element $(x_i)_{i\in I}$ of such a Cartesian product, x_i is the i-th **coordinate** of x. The term coordinate will be used both for x_i, and for i, so in the latter case as synonym for index. Other indexes than those referring to coordinates are usually indicated by superscripts.

A *binary relation* on a set X is a subset of $X \times X$. For a binary relation $\succcurlyeq$ on X we usually write $x \succcurlyeq y$ instead of $(x,y) \in \succcurlyeq$. A binary relation $\succcurlyeq$ on X is :

(a) **transitive**	if:	$[(x \succcurlyeq y \ \& \ y \succcurlyeq z) \Rightarrow (x \succcurlyeq z)]$	for all $x,y,z \in X$,
(b) **complete**	if:	$[(x \succcurlyeq y) \text{ or } (y \succcurlyeq x)]$	for all $x,y \in X$,
(c) **reflexive**	if:	$[x \succcurlyeq x]$	for all $x \in X$,
(d) **irreflexive**	if:	$[\text{not } (x \succcurlyeq x)]$	for all $x \in X$,
(e) **symmetric**	if:	$[(x \succcurlyeq y) \Rightarrow (y \succcurlyeq x)]$	for all $x,y \in X$,
(f) **asymmetric**	if:	$[(x \succcurlyeq y) \Rightarrow (\text{not } y \succcurlyeq x)]$	for all $x,y \in X$,
(g) **antisymmetric**	if:	$[(x \succcurlyeq y \ \& \ y \succcurlyeq x) \Rightarrow (x = y)]$	for all $x,y \in X$.

Throughout this monograph $\succ$ denotes the **asymmetric part** of $\succcurlyeq$; i.e., [x $\succ$ y] if and only if [x $\succcurlyeq$ y and not y $\succcurlyeq$ x]. By $\approx$ we denote the **symmetric part** of $\succcurlyeq$; i.e., [x $\approx$ y] if and only if [x $\succcurlyeq$ y and y $\succcurlyeq$ x]. We write x $\preccurlyeq$ y for y $\succcurlyeq$ x, and x $\prec$ y for y $\succ$ x. If a binary relation $\succcurlyeq$ is endowed with indexes, then without further mention $\succ$, $\approx$, $\preccurlyeq$, and $\prec$, when endowed with the same indexes, are defined analogously.

A **weak order** $\succcurlyeq$ is transitive and complete. Hence it is also reflexive, its symmetric part is an **equivalence relation** (i.e., is transitive, reflexive, and symmetric), its asymmetric part is transitive, irreflexive, and asymmetric, and finally we have x $\succcurlyeq$ y if and only if not y $\succ$ x. A binary relation is **trivial** if x $\succcurlyeq$ y for all x,y; it is the **identity (relation)** if [x $\succcurlyeq$ y] <=> [x = y]. Of course the identity can also be considered as a function. A pair of elements x,y of X is **incomparable (with respect to** $\succcurlyeq$) if neither x $\succcurlyeq$ y nor y $\succcurlyeq$ x.

Let $\succcurlyeq$ be a binary relation on a Cartesian product $\prod_{i\in I}\Gamma_i$. Let, for every $i \in I$, $\geq_i$ be a binary relation on Γ_i. Then $\succcurlyeq$ is **weakly monotonic (with respect to** $(\geq_i)_{i\in I}$) on a set $E \subset \prod_{i\in I}\Gamma_i$ if, for all x, y $\in$ E, x $\succcurlyeq$ y whenever [$x_i \geq_i y_i$ for all i], and **strongly monotonic** on E if, for all x, y $\in$ E, x $\succ$ y whenever [$x_i \geq_i y_i$ for all i and $x_i >_i y_i$ for at least one i]. 'On $\prod_{i\in I}\Gamma_i$' is usually omitted. If $\Gamma_i \subset \mathbb{R}$ then usually without further mention it is assumed that $\geq_i$ is the usual ordering $\geq$.

We call an element $x \in X$ **maximal** [respectively **minimal**] (with respect to $\succcurlyeq$) on $E \subset X$ if there is no $y \in E$ such that y $\succ$ x [respectively y $\prec$ x].

In Chapter I we shall deal with *choice functions*. A **choice function** C is a function from a collection Δ of subsets of a set X, to 2^X, such that $\emptyset \neq C(\Delta) \subset D$ for all $D \in \Delta$. Of course this implies $\emptyset \notin \Delta$. Often we omit brackets, and write for instance C{a,b} instead of C({a,b}).

An *interval* G is a subset of $\mathbb{R}$ that is convex (i.e., for all $\mu,\nu \in G$ and $0 \leq \lambda \leq 1$, $\lambda\mu + (1-\lambda)\nu \in G$), and that may be open, closed, or half-open, bounded or unbounded, both from the left and/or from the right. By $[\mu,\nu]$ we denote the interval $\{\lambda \in \mathbb{R} : \mu \leq \lambda \leq \nu\}$, by $]\mu,\nu[$ the interval $\{\lambda \in \mathbb{R} : \mu < \lambda < \nu\}$; $[\mu,\nu[$ and $]\mu,\nu]$ are analogous. A **nondegenerate interval** is an interval with more than one, so infinitely many, elements. $\mathbb{R}_+ = \{\mu \in \mathbb{R} : \mu \geq 0\}$, $\mathbb{R}_{++} = \{\mu \in \mathbb{R} : \mu > 0\}$.

Now let G be an arbitrary subset of $\mathbb{R}$, and let $\varphi : G \to \mathbb{R}$. Then φ is **strictly increasing** if, for all $\mu > \nu$ in G, $\varphi(\mu) > \varphi(\nu)$; φ is **strictly decreasing** if, for all $\mu > \nu$ in G, $\varphi(\mu) < \varphi(\nu)$. Further φ is **nondecreasing** if, for all $\mu > \nu$, $\varphi(\mu) \geq \varphi(\nu)$, and φ is **nonincreasing** if, for all $\mu > \nu$, $\varphi(\mu) \leq \varphi(\nu)$. The terms 'increasing' and 'decreasing' will not be used. The function φ is **convex** if, for all $0 \leq \lambda \leq 1$, and μ,ν, and $\lambda\mu + (1-\lambda)\nu$ in G,

$$\varphi(\lambda\mu + (1-\lambda)\nu) \leq \lambda\varphi(\mu) + (1-\lambda)\varphi(\nu) .$$

The function φ is **concave** if $-\varphi$ is convex; and φ is **affine** if it is both convex and concave. The function φ is affine if and only if there exist real σ,τ such that

$\varphi : \mu \mapsto \tau + \sigma\mu$. Note that we also allow $\sigma = 0$. Further φ is **positive affine** if σ above is positive, i.e. $\sigma > 0$. Affine functions are often called linear in the literature. We shall call a function $\varphi : \mathbb{R} \to \mathbb{R}$ **linear** only if it is affine and assigns value 0 to the argument 0. The function φ is **quasiconvex** if, for all $0 \le \lambda \le 1$, and μ,ν, and $\lambda\mu + (1-\lambda)\nu$ in G,

$$\varphi(\lambda\mu + (1-\lambda)\nu) \le \max\{\varphi(\mu),\varphi(\nu)\} .$$

The function φ is **quasiconcave** if $-\varphi$ is quasiconvex. A convex function is quasiconvex, a concave function is quasiconcave.

Next we give some *measure-theoretic* definitions, used mainly in Chapter V. Halmos(1950) is an extensive treatment of measure theory. A collection Σ of subsets of a set I is an **algebra** if $I \in \Sigma$ and for all $A,B \in \Sigma$ also A^c and $A \cup B \in \Sigma$. Then also $\emptyset \in \Sigma$, and Σ is intersection-closed. Σ is a **σ-algebra** if furthermore, for all $(A_j)_{j=1}^{\infty} \in \Sigma$, $\cup_{j=1}^{\infty} A_j \in \Sigma$.

A **probability measure** on an algebra Σ is a function $P : \Sigma \to [0,1]$ such that $P(I) = 1$ and P is **finitely additive**, i.e., for all disjoint $A,B \in \Sigma$, $P(A \cup B) = P(A) + P(B)$. Then also $P(\emptyset) = 0$. Note that we do not assume 'σ-additivity'. P is **σ-additive** (or **countably additive**) if, for any sequence $(B_m)_{m=1}^{\infty}$ of mutually disjoint events, with $B = \cup_{m=1}^{\infty} B_m$ in Σ, we have $P(B) = \sum_{m=1}^{\infty} P(B_m)$. It is well-known that a probability measure P is σ-additive if and only if, for any $(A_j)_{j=1}^{\infty} \in \Sigma$ with $A_{m+1} \subset A_m$ for all m and $\cap_{m=1}^{\infty} A_m = \emptyset$, $\lim_{m\to\infty} P(A_m) = 0$. This is seen by substituting $A_m := B \setminus (\cup_{k=1}^{m} B_k)$, or $B_m := A_m \setminus A_{m+1}$. If I is finite, say $I = \{1,...,n\}$, then we usually assume, without further mention, that $\Sigma = 2^I$. Note that then the probability measure P is completely determined by $(p_j)_{j=1}^{n}$, with $p_j := P(\{j\})$ for all j.

The **Lebesgue measure** on (subsets of) $\mathbb{R}$ is the function ('measure') which assigns to each interval its length, and which, loosely spoken, is extended in a natural way to the **Borel-σ-algebra**, i.e., the smallest σ-algebra containing all intervals (; it contains every subset of $\mathbb{R}$ one will meet in applications). More details are provided in Halmos(1950). Finally, an **ordered partition** $\pi = (A_1,...,A_m)$, or **partition** for short, of a set I is a finite sequence of disjoint subsets of I, with union I. We do not exclude $A_j = \emptyset$ for some j's.

Some *standard notations* in this monograph are the following. X is a nonempty set, elements of which are called **alternatives**; alternatives are usually denoted by x,y,v,w,s,t,z, and sometimes by a,b,c,d. Usually a binary relation $\succcurlyeq$, called **preference relation**, is present on X. Then $x \succcurlyeq y$ is pronounced as: 'x is weakly preferred to y', or 'x is at least as good as y'; $x \succ y$ is pronounced as 'x is strictly preferred to y', or 'x is strictly better than y'; $x \approx y$ is pronounced as 'x is equivalent to y' (even though in general $\approx$ does not have to be an equivalence relation; in our main results it will be an equivalence relation though), or 'x and y are equally good'. In Chapters II to VII, X is a Cartesian product $\prod_{i \in I} \Gamma_i$, and with the exception of Chapter V, I is the finite set $\{1,...,n\}$.

Often all Γ_i's are equal to a set Γ; then we also write $\alpha,\beta,\gamma,\delta$, and sometimes μ,ν,σ,τ, for elements of Γ. Subsets of I are usually denoted by A,B,C,D. By E,F,G,H we usually denote subsets of Γ, or of X. Real numbers are usually denoted by Greek characters $\lambda,\mu,\nu,\sigma,\tau$, or sometimes by a,b,c,d.

Further one-element sets will often be denoted as their elements, with braces omitted, so as i instead of {i}.

0.2. TOPOLOGICAL PRELIMINARIES

In this section we give, mostly without proofs, the elementary definitions and results of topology used in this book. More advanced results on topology can be found in Kelley(1955).

Let X be a set, and T a collection of subsets of X. T is a **topology (on** X) if T contains $\emptyset$ and X, and contains any finite intersection and arbitrary union of its elements. We then call (X,T) a **topological space**. Elements of T are called **open**, complements of elements of T are **closed**. The most common example of a topological space is $\mathbb{R}$ endowed with the **Euclidean** topology, i.e., the topology containing all sets which are a union of intervals $]\mu,\nu[$. A topology T' is **coarser** than T, or T is **finer** than T', if $T' \subset T$. For $E \subset X$ the collection of sets of the form $F \cap E$ with $F \in T$ is a topology on E, it is called the **restriction of** T **to** E. The **Euclidean topology** on $\mathbb{R}^m$ is the topology of all sets which are a union of open spheres, i.e., spheres without 'boundary'. Restrictions of Euclidean topologies are also called **Euclidean topologies**.

If (X,T) and (Y,T') are topological spaces then a map $f : X \to Y$ is **continuous** if for every $H \in T'$ we have $f^{-1}(H) \in T$. The composition of two continuous maps is again continuous. Most of the usual functions from $\mathbb{R}$ to $\mathbb{R}$ are continuous; also finite sums, differences, products, and maxima and minima of continuous functions to $\mathbb{R}$ are continuous. If Y above is $\mathbb{R}$ (endowed with the Euclidean topology) then for continuity of f it is sufficient that, for all $\mu \in \mathbb{R}$, the sets $\{x \in X : f(x) > \mu\}$ and $\{x \in X : f(x) < \mu\}$ are open. Analogously to this a binary relation $\succcurlyeq$ on X is **continuous** if $\{x : x \succ y\}$ and $\{x : x \prec y\}$ are open for all y. By taking complements one sees that a weak order $\succcurlyeq$ is continuous if and only if $\{x : x \succcurlyeq y\}$ and $\{x : x \preccurlyeq y\}$ are closed for all y. The **order topology** of a binary relation $\succcurlyeq$ is the coarsest topology containing all sets of the form $\{y \in X : y \succ x\}$ and $\{y \in X : y \prec x\}$, so the smallest topology with respect to which $\succcurlyeq$ is continuous.

A topological space is **(topologically) connected** if the only sets which are both open and closed are $\emptyset$ and X. This holds if and only if there do not exist open nonempty subsets G,H of X such that $G \cap H = \emptyset$ and $G \cup H = X$, which holds if and only if there do not exist closed nonempty subsets G,H of X such that $G \cap H = \emptyset$ and $G \cup H = X$. $\mathbb{R}$ (as always, endowed with the Euclidean topology) is connected; the proof of this result is not very simple. A subset of $\mathbb{R}$ is connected if and only if it is convex, so if and only if it is an interval. Any convex subset of $\mathbb{R}^m$ is connected. Since the image of a connected space under a continuous map is again connected, the image of a connected space under a continuous function to $\mathbb{R}$ is an interval. This result is important for the work in this book. Conversely, a topological space is connected whenever the image of every continuous function of the topological space to $\mathbb{R}$ is an interval. X is **arcwise connected** if, for every $x,y \in X$, there exists an **arc** from x to y, i.e., a continuous function $\varphi : [0,1] \to X$ with $\varphi(0) = x$, $\varphi(1) = y$. If X is arcwise connected, then it is connected. A set $E \subset X$ is **dense** if it intersects every nonempty open set. A topological space is **(topologically) separable** if it contains a countable dense subset. $\mathbb{R}$ is topologically separable, and so is any subset of $\mathbb{R}$ and of $\mathbb{R}^m$.

If X is a Cartesian product $\prod_{i\in I}\Gamma_i$, and every Γ_i is endowed with a topology T_i, then the **product topology** on X is the smallest topology containing all subsets of X of the form $E_i \times (\prod_{j\neq i}\Gamma_j)$ with $i \in I$, $E_i \in T_i$. An elementary result is the following lemma. It shows, for any fixed $z_{A^c} \in \prod_{i\in A^c}\Gamma_i$, continuity of the natural injection from $\prod_{i\in A}\Gamma_i$ into $\{z_{A^c}\} \times \prod_{i\in A}\Gamma_i$.

LEMMA 0.2.1. *Suppose* $E \subset X = \prod_{i\in I}\Gamma_i$ *is open [respectively closed] with respect to the product topology on* X. *Let* $A \subset I$, $z \in X$. *Then the set*

$\{x_A \in \prod_{i\in A}\Gamma_i$: E *contains the element* v *of* X *with* $v_i = x_i$ *for all* $i \in A$, $v_i = z_i$ *for all* $i \notin A\}$

is open [respectively closed] with respect to the product topology on $\prod_{i\in A}\Gamma_i$.

PROOF. Let E be open (the case where E is closed follows from this by taking complements). Let G be the set as defined above. Let $x_A \in G$. There must exist open sets E_i, for all $i \in I$, with $E_i \neq \Gamma_i$ for only finitely many i, such that v, as defined above, is in $\prod_{i\in I}E_i$, and such that the latter is a subset of E. We see that $x_A \in \prod_{i\in A}E_i \subset G$. Only finitely many E_i's being different from Γ_i, $\prod_{i\in A}E_i$ is an open neighbourhood of x_A within G.

□

For a subset E of X, the **topological interior** of E, **int**(E), is the largest open subset of E.

CHAPTER I

FROM CHOICE FUNCTIONS TO BINARY RELATIONS

I.1. CHOICE FUNCTIONS, THEIR USE, AND INTERPRETATIONAL COMPLICATIONS

The following simple example of a choice problem will illustrate several questions to be addressed in the sequel.

I.1.1. EXAMPLE

Suppose a person, the 'decision maker', is in a fruit-store, and has to decide whether to buy nothing (n), a banana (b), or a pear (p). The decision maker prefers buying a pear to buying a banana, (so he chooses p from {b,p}), because pears are more juicy than bananas. Further it is his custom to buy a banana if only bananas are available (so to choose b from {b,n}), because bananas look nice. Apparently p is preferred to b, and b to n. Hence the first inclination is to buy a pear (so to choose p from {b,n,p}).

However, not sure about his true motives, the decision maker strongly imagines what his choice would be from {n,p}. There is no doubt: It would be n, the decision maker would not buy the pear, he does not like pears enough. The viewpoint of the decision maker is: 'If from {b,n,p} I would actually choose p (in accordance with the first inclination described above), then from {n,p} I should also choose p (the decision maker wants to satisfy 'IIA', see Definition I.2.8.); still I am sure I would choose n from {n,p}. Something is wrong!' An introspection follows, and the conclusion is that the choice of b from {b,n} was not truly motivated. On second thought the decision maker rather chooses n from {b,n}. So now n is preferred to b; as before, n is preferred to p. Finally, n is chosen from {b,n,p}.

In the example the decision maker, for making his decision in the actual choice situation with {b,n,p} available, used thought experiments in which hypothetical choice situations were considered (compare section I.1.3). He made comparisons between (his choices in) these several situations, and wanted his choices to be 'consistent'. When a violation of a consistency condition (e.g., IIA) was discovered, the decision maker rearranged his decisions to get IIA satisfied. The rearrangement was based on 'introspection', in which the decision maker reconsidered his needs, information, etc.; on this process we had no more to say. In the exposition sometimes the notion of 'preference' was used; Corollary I.2.12 shows that, if IIA is accepted as a consistency condition to be satisfied, then indeed the terminology of preferences can be used to determine how to choose.

I.1.2. ELEMENTARY FORMALIZATIONS AND SOME ASSUMPTIONS

We study models for situations where from some nonempty set D of **(available) alternatives**, a decision maker chooses exactly one element. (This will be modified in subsection I.1.5, to simplify work.) The decision maker is usually assumed to be a single person. But also the decision maker may be an animal, a computer, an extraterrestrial being, a respondent, a firm, a society, etc. It is intended that the decision maker is completely *free*[rf1] to choose the alternative which he wants. In the example D was {b,n,p}. In several special contexts there are special terms for alternatives, such as: Options, prospects, acts, securities, allocations, strategies, commodity bundles, tests, estimators, responses, etc. If there is a possibility 'choosing nothing', then we just represent this by an element of D, such as n above. An important stage in decision making is to find out what the set of available alternatives is[rf2] . We assume that this stage has already been dealt with.

We shall not use sequential models. If analogous, or other, choice situations will (repeatedly) occur, and have significance for the one choice situation presently considered, then this significance should appear in the appropriate places, such as in descriptions and valuations of the alternatives. We neither assume, nor exclude, repetitions; only they are not central in our study.

I.1.3. THOUGHT EXPERIMENTS

Although our work is intended to be applicable if the decision maker precisely once has to choose one element from one set D, this one choice is not enough to build a meaningful theory. To show the meaning of entities such as preference relations and utility functions, more choice situations must be considered, at least as thought experiments, and comparisons between them must be made. This is in fact what we do by working with choice functions, (and with binary relations, considered as representations for choice functions). It is very useful to imagine what would have happened if some actual problem at hand would have been different in this or that respect, to compare it to other analogous problems, and to base a model on this. This is common practice in science, it discloses the essential *parameters* of the problem. As an example of the use of thought experiments, let us consider the derivation of the laws of the lever, in 'De Aequiponderantibus', by Archimedes of Syracuse. He argued that the splitting up of a weight in two equal shares, subsequently placed at a same distance on either side of the original weight, should not affect equilibrium. Mach(1883, section I.II.3) states that the involved experiments in such cases can be considered to be thought experiments; one reason is that actual ('metrical') experiment will always deviate somewhat. In decision theories conditions which compare choices in different choice situations are sometimes called consistency conditions. In the example of subsection I.1.1, not only the actual choice situation with available alternatives {b,n,p} is considered, but also situations with available alternatives {b,n}, {b,p}, {n,p}, and comparisons between these situations are made. If p is not chosen from {n,p}, then p should neither be chosen from {b,n,p}, so was supposed there. From the reasoning used here, and Corollary I.2.12, one may conclude that the preference relation of the decision maker, a weak order, is an essential *parameter*[rf3].

In this chapter we shall concentrate on choice situations that differ from the actual one with respect to the set of available alternatives. Usually in a hypothetical choice situation the set of available alternatives, D', is a subset of D, the one for the actual situation.

As usual in science, a 'ceteris paribus' assumption must be made. We assume that the (hypothetical) cause, restricting D to D', does not change other relevant exogeneous aspects of the situation. For instance, in subsection I.1.1 the restriction of {b,n,p} to {b,n} (say the fruit-store has no pears in store) should not change the person that the decision maker is, his desires, his knowledge, etc. The condition of IIA (see Definition I.2.8) may be considered a concrete expression of the ceteris paribus condition in the above example. The supposed changes are described accurately, but the relevant things that should not be changed remain, at least in part, unspecified. The more science proceeds, the more can be said about the 'relevant things' to be controlled for the ceteris paribus condition.

Let us compare the above to classical particle mechanics. Newton's second law, $F = m.a$ (F force, m mass, a acceleration), is intended to be applicable in every single situation. Essential for its significance are comparisons to (hypothetical) analogous situations such as: If some (hypothetical) cause would make F twice as large, then also acceleration a should become twice as large. The ceteris paribus condition should anyway entail that m is kept constant. From Mach(1883, section II.III.8, page 240; see also Mach,1896, page 425) we quote on the meaning of mass: 'Strictly viewed, however, we are concerned with precisely as many properties, and there is no other function left for *matter* save that of representing the constancy of connection of the several properties of bodies, of which *mass* is *one* only'. I.e., mass is a 'theoretical' quantity. From section II.V.3 of Mach(1883) we quote, on the definition of mass: 'My definition is the outcome of an endeavor to establish *the interdependence of phenomena* ....' (Italics from original.) Not always does the doubling of F as mentioned above have to be a hypothetical experiment. Sometimes it really can be achieved in an experiment. Such an experiment is a different event, happening at another time and/or place. Not only is F doubled, and also a; there is an infinity of other differences. These must then, by a ceteris paribus assumption, be assumed to concern irrelevant matters[rf4].

Similarly, for our work the other considered choice situations are not always only thought experiments. And similarly, they may really have occurred, or have been achieved in experiments. Still we use the term thought experiment, to avoid any possible confusion with *repetitions* of choice situations. Comments on differences between thought experiments as used by us, and repetitions as used in Camacho's utility theory, are given in section I.3. Our interest in this difference stems from the view that it is one of the differences between 'subjective' probabilities as obtained in our Theorem IV.2.7, and 'objective' probabilities as obtained for instance from repetitions of tosses of a coin. Further consideration of the difference between subjective and objective probabilities is not the aim of this monograph.

For the derivation of mathematical results it is often convenient to use infinite sets of alternatives (usually endowed with a topology) such as $\mathbb{R}^m_+$. Continuity assumptions can then be made to simplify the technical work and to give convenient uniqueness results. Thus hypothetical[rf5] alternatives, which were not present in the actual set of available alternatives D, but which have informative properties, are introduced. Then the set X of all considered alternatives contains more elements than only the alternatives which are actually available in the set D. Of course consideration of hypothetical alternatives implies consideration of hypothetical choice situations.

Also it will sometimes be of use to assume that other exogeneous aspects of the choice situation can be varied. For instance, for the binary relations $\succcurlyeq_i$, to be introduced in Chapter II, it is useful to imagine that certain coordinates of the alternatives can be ignored. This may be because a consumer is completely satisfied with respect to the 'commodities' corresponding to these coordinates; or because the extra information is obtained that the 'states of nature', corresponding to these coordinates, are untrue.

I.1.4. NORMATIVE AND DESCRIPTIVE APPLICATIONS

All results in this monograph can as well be used for 'normative' applications as for 'descriptive' applications. In **normative** applications one deals with situations where it must be determined how decisions can be made in a good way. Let us discuss here how for instance Theorem IV.2.7 in the sequel can be used normatively. We shall take for granted the decision-theoretic frame-work within which the theorem is formulated. The theorem gives (in statement (ii) there) **characterizing**, i.e. necessary and sufficient, conditions for the maximization of continuous subjective expected utility. One will be convinced that it is good to maximize continuous subjective expected utility, if and only if one is convinced that it is good to satisfy the characterizing conditions. One can convince other people that continuous subjective expected utility should be maximized, if and only if one can convince them that the characterizing conditions should be satisfied. Note that one then has not yet answered the question of how to choose the probabilities and utilities involved in subjective expected utility. The theorems and proofs of this monograph may help to gain insight into that question, but at least partly the answering of the question will be based on matters (sometimes called subjective) which are not revealed by the models adopted in our analysis. Obviously, one can criticize the use of continuous subjective expected utility if and only if one can criticize the characterizing conditions.

In descriptive applications one uses models to describe actual decisions of people, and to gain insight into these. Whether the decisions are wise or not is not a matter of primary interest. Let us see how Theorem IV.2.7 can be used here. Decisions of a person can be (perfectly) described by means of continuous subjective expected utility if and only if the characterizing conditions are not violated by these decisions. So these conditions give the criteria for verification or falsification of the hypothesis of continuous subjective expected utility maximization.

The difference between normative and descriptive applications is not so large as may appear at first sight. Normative work will be most useful if it will be applied by actual decision makers, and descriptive work will only describe decisions which are at least wise enough to make some sense. 'Prescriptive' approaches, and 'advisory' approaches, can be considered normative approaches with special attention to actual applicability by nonperfect persons. Usually in normative applications the probabilities and utilities are determined first, next by means of these the decisions are determined. In descriptive applications usually first decisions are observed, next probabilities and utilities are derived from these. The probabilities and utilities may then be used to predict future decisions.

When discussing a result we sometimes use terminology of descriptive applications, and sometimes of normative applications. This choice is often arbitrary, and does not mean that we exclude other applications. Our main intended application is normative.

Mutatis mutandis everything said above for Theorem IV.2.7 applies as well to any other theorem of this monograph, whether uncertainty is considered or not[rf6].

I.1.5. THE PRELIMINARY-CHOICE-PROBLEM

For theoretical purposes it is convenient to consider the case where the decision maker may choose a nonempty subset from D, instead of just one element. Such a choice is called a preliminary choice, or just choice if no confusion will arise. Thus for a choice function C, the C(D)'s may contain more than one element. The interpretation is that the decision maker would be willing to choose, from D, any element contained in C(D), and no element from D\C(D). His actually chosen alternative is one arbitrary element from D, say $C_f(D)$[rf7].

We shall be interested in C(D), and shall represent this in the sequel. This meets the, admitted, problem that not C(D), but only $C_f(D)$, is observable. In normative applications of representation results the consequences of this 'preliminary-choice-problem' are not serious. A representation yielding the prescription to choose an alternative from C(D), without specifying which one, is not seriously deficient, because it does not matter which element is chosen. All elements of C(D) are equally good.

Far more serious are the consequences of the preliminary-choice-problem for descriptive applications. It can never be falsified from observed choices that the decision maker was completely indifferent (i.e., C(D) = D for all choice situations D) and made all his choices arbitrarily. Here is a subject for further investigation, to derive 'sensible' preference relations from observed choices $C_f(D)$, and to find out to what degree the choices must have been arbitrary[rf8].

A way to circumvent the problem of preliminary choice is to simply communicate with the decision maker, and ask him what his C(D)'s are. This approach falls outside the scope of this monograph. We base our representations solely on choice behaviour[rf9]. Another way to circumvent the problem may be to assume that the decision maker's choice behaviour in several choice situations can be observed repeatedly, with indeed the decision maker choosing exactly one element every time; the decision maker will, governed by chance, choose every time one arbitrary element from C(D). After sufficiently many observations we can be almost sure that all elements from C(D) have been chosen at least once, so have been observed.

I.2. FROM CHOICE FUNCTIONS TO BINARY RELATIONS, AND TO REPRESENTING FUNCTIONS

In this section we indicate how to represent choice functions by binary ('preference') relations.

I.2.1. THE CONGRUENCY CONDITION

Let X be the nonempty set of all considered **alternatives**, $\Delta \subset 2^X \backslash \{\emptyset\}$ the nonempty collection of all considered **choice situations**. For $D \in \Delta$, elements of D are **available alternatives (with respect to** D). We assume that $C : \Delta \to 2^X$ is a choice function. C(D), the **choice set for** D, contains exactly those elements of D which the decision maker is willing to choose from D. Elements of C(D) are called **chosen alternatives (from** D).

An example can be found in consumer demand theory. There the decision maker is a consumer, $X = \mathbb{R}^\ell_+$, alternatives are commodity bundles, choice situations are budget sets, the choice function is the demand (multi)function, and the choice set is the demand set.

DEFINITION I.2.1. A binary relation $\succcurlyeq$ on X **represents** C if for all $D \in \Delta$:

$$C(D) = \{x \in D : x \succcurlyeq y \text{ for all } y \in D\} .$$

We have in mind that the binary relations, occurring in following chapters, represent choice functions. These binary relations will often be called preference relations. They may be interpreted to reflect the decision maker's opinion about the alternatives. If one wants to make a distinction between the decision maker's mere opinion, and the decision maker's (dispositional) choice behaviour, one may prefer the term choice relation for the binary relations as interpreted by us. As the interpretation of the binary relations is immaterial for the mathematical work of the following chapters, we adopt the most customary term, i.e., preference relation[rf10].

The following definition shows a way to derive binary relations from choice functions. Such derived binary relations are called revealed preference relations.

DEFINITION I.2.2 (see Figure I.2.1). We write

xRy if : [there is a $D \in \Delta$ such that $x \in C(D)$, $y \in D$] or [$x = y$] ,

xPy if : [there is a $D \in \Delta$ such that $x \in C(D)$, $y \in D \setminus C(D)$] ,

xEy if : [there is a $D \in \Delta$ such that {$x \in C(D)$ and $y \in C(D)$}] or [$x = y$] .

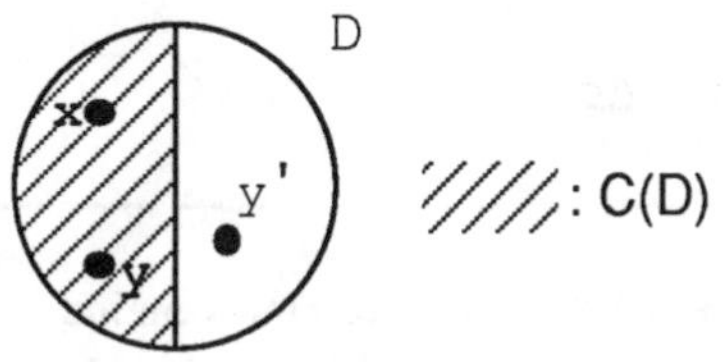

The preferences xEy, xRy, xRy', (even) xPy', yEx, yRx, yRy', and (even) yPy' are revealed. While the choice situation D does not reveal other preferences, it may in general very well be that other choice situations reveal further preferences between x,y, and y', such as possibly xPy, y'Rx, etc.

FIGURE I.2.1 (Revealed preferences).

The above definition does not forbid occurrence of both xRy and yPx. In Example I.1.1, the decision maker originally considered C{b,n} = b, C{b,p} = p, C{b,n,p} = p, and C{n,p} = n. The last two choices reveal pPn, and nRp (even nPp)[rf11].

We say that one binary relation $\succcurlyeq$ **extends** another binary relation $\succcurlyeq'$, if, for all x,y, $x \succcurlyeq' y$ implies $x \succcurlyeq y$. The definition below gives extensions of the directly revealed preference relations.

DEFINITION I.2.3. We write $x\bar{R}y$ if there exists a finite sequence $(x^0,x^1,\ldots,x^m)$ such that $x^0 = x$, $x^m = y$, and x^jRx^{j+1} for all $0 \le j \le m-1$. We write $x\bar{P}y$ if a sequence $(x^j)_{j=0}^{m}$ as above exists with, furthermore, x^jPx^{j+1} for at least one $0 \le j \le m-1$. Finally, we write $x\bar{E}y$ if $x\bar{R}y$ and $y\bar{R}x$.

So $\bar{R}$ is the smallest transitive extension of R, $\bar{P}$ and $\bar{E}$ are transitive extensions of P, respectively E, but usually not the smallest.

DEFINITION I.2.4 (See Figure I.2.2, with $x^0=x$, $x^n=y$). The choice function C is <u>congruent</u> if :

for all $x,y \in X$: $[x\bar{R}y \Rightarrow \text{not } yPx]$.

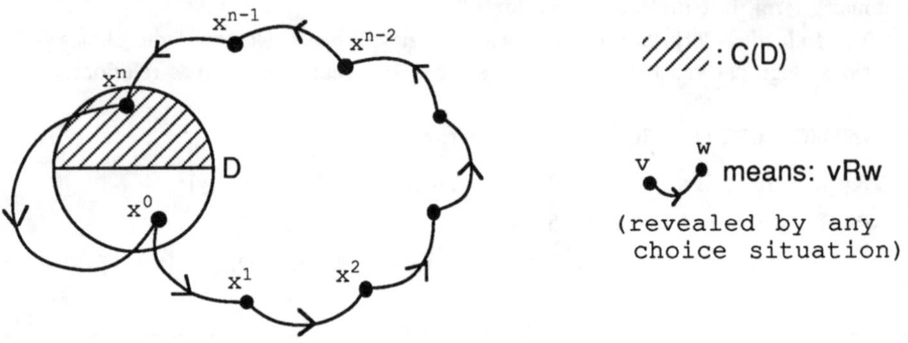

FIGURE I.2.2 (<u>A violation of congruency</u>). If x^jRx^{j+1} for all j, then x^nPx^0 violates congruency.

The congruency condition, and the main result (i) <=> (ii) below, were first obtained by Richter(1966, Theorem 1)[rf12]. The equivalence (i) <=> (iii) is remarkable, in showing that at the present state of analysis transitivity is the crucial condition, and completeness does not add a restriction to transitivity. This is less so in the presence of further behavioural conditions; see section III.1 for a further discussion. Statement (v) below shows that $\bar{R}$ can be taken for the transitive binary relation of statement (iii). Statement (iv) shows the usual relations between weak preference, strict preference, and equivalence. Statement (vi) is of use in the reference note rf11.

THEOREM I.2.5. *For the choice function* C *the following two statements are equivalent* :

(i) **There exists a weak order $\succcurlyeq$ representing C.**

(ii) **C is congruent.**

Further the following four statements are equivalent to the above two statements :

(iii) **There exists a transitive binary relation $\succcurlyeq'$ representing C.**

(iv) **$\bar{R}$ represents C, $\bar{P}$ is the asymmetric, $\bar{E}$ the symmetric part of $\bar{R}$.**

(v) **$\bar{R}$ represents C.**

(vi) **$\bar{P}$ is the asymmetric part of $\bar{R}$.**

Furthermore, the binary relation $\succcurlyeq$ in (i), and the smallest reflexive extension of the binary relation $\succcurlyeq'$ in (iii), are extensions of $\bar{R}$, their asymmetric parts are extensions of $\bar{P}$, and their symmetric parts are extensions of $\bar{E}$.

PROOF. For a first nontrivial implication, (iii) => (ii), suppose that (iii) holds. Let $x^0Rx^1R...Rx^m$. Then $x^0 \succcurlyeq' x^1 \succcurlyeq' ... \succcurlyeq' x^m$. By transitivity $x^0 \succcurlyeq' x^m$, and, if $x^m \succcurlyeq' y$ for all y in a set D, then $x^0 \succcurlyeq' y$ for all y in D. So if $x^m \in C(D)$ and $x^0 \in D$, then $x^0 \in C(D)$. Hence x^mPx^0 is impossible. Congruency is established.

To derive a second nontrivial implication, (ii) => (v), suppose that congruency holds. Let D be an arbitrary set. Obviously, if $x \in C(D)$, then xRy for all $y \in D$, so obviously $x\bar{R}y$ for all $y \in D$. Conversely, if $x\bar{R}y$ for all $y \in D$, then yPx for no y in D, so that $x \in C(D)$ is the only possibility. (v) follows.

The implication (v) => (iii) is direct. We conclude that (ii), (iii), and (v) are equivalent. Also it is trivial that (i) implies these statements.

Let us next derive the nontrivial implication (iii) => (i). Say (iii) holds. It straightforwardly follows from the Lemma of Zorn (see Kelley,1955) that among the transitive binary relations which represent C, there must be 'maximal' ones in the sense that they cannot be extended properly. So for (i) it suffices to show that noncomplete transitive binary relations, representing C, can be extended properly. So say $\succcurlyeq'$ of (iii) is not complete. We extend it. Say neither $x \succcurlyeq' y$, nor $y \succcurlyeq' x$. We extend $\succcurlyeq'$ to $\tilde{\succcurlyeq}$ by simply defining $x \tilde{\approx} y$ ($x \tilde{\succ} y$ or $x \tilde{\prec} y$ could just as well be taken) and by then setting, for transitivity :

$v \tilde{\succcurlyeq} w$ whenever: [$v \succcurlyeq' w$, or $v \succcurlyeq' x$ & $y \succcurlyeq' w$, or $v \succcurlyeq' y$ & $x \succcurlyeq' w$].

Transitivity of $\tilde{\succcurlyeq}$ follows from an elementary consideration of all possible cases, as follows. Suppose $a \tilde{\succcurlyeq} b \tilde{\succcurlyeq} c$. Say $a \succcurlyeq' x \tilde{\approx} y \succcurlyeq' b$ ($a \succcurlyeq' b$ is simpler, $a \succcurlyeq' y \tilde{\approx} x \succcurlyeq' b$ is symmetric). We have [$b \succcurlyeq' c$, or $b \succcurlyeq' x$ & $y \succcurlyeq' c$, or $b \succcurlyeq' y$ & $x \succcurlyeq' c$]. In the first case $a \succcurlyeq' x \tilde{\approx} y \succcurlyeq' b \succcurlyeq' c$, so by transitivity of $\succcurlyeq'$, $a \succcurlyeq' x \tilde{\approx} y \succcurlyeq' c$, and $a \tilde{\succcurlyeq} c$ follows. In the second case $a \succcurlyeq' x \tilde{\approx} y \succcurlyeq' c$, so $a \tilde{\succcurlyeq} c$. In the third case $a \succcurlyeq' x \succcurlyeq' c$, so $a \succcurlyeq' c$, i.e. $a \tilde{\succcurlyeq} c$. Transitivity holds.

Finally, we show that $\tilde{\succcurlyeq}$ represents C. The only thing that could go wrong is that there were D and $x \in D$ with $x \tilde{\succcurlyeq} y$ for all $y \in D$, but not $x \in C(D)$ because for some $y \in D$ not $x \succcurlyeq' y$. Then for any $y \in C(D)$ we would have $y \succ' x$ and $x \tilde{\succcurlyeq} y$ so not $y \tilde{\succ} x$. So it suffices to show that $\tilde{\succ}$ extends $\succ'$. For this it suffices to check that we have introduced new preferences $v \tilde{\succcurlyeq} w$ (where not $v \succcurlyeq' w$) only for pairs v,w which were incomparable with respect to $\succcurlyeq'$, i.e., for which neither $w \succcurlyeq' v$; in that case $v \tilde{\succcurlyeq} w$ has not 'destroyed' a $w \succ' v$. As an example, if $v \succcurlyeq' x$ & $y \succcurlyeq' w$ and also $w \succcurlyeq' v$, then $y \succcurlyeq' x$ by transitivity of $\succcurlyeq'$, contradicting incomparability of x and y. Other cases are symmetric.

Apparently (iii) implies (i), so that equivalence of (i), (ii), (iii), and (v) is established.

Before dealing with (iv) and (vi), we first derive the furthermore-statement. By the definition of R, $\succcurlyeq$ of (i) and the reflexive extension of $\succcurlyeq'$ of (iii) are extensions of R. By transitivity they are extensions of $\bar{R}$. Hence their symmetric parts extend $\bar{E}$.

Now suppose $x\bar{P}y$. To prove is that $x \succ y$ and $x \succ' y$. Let $x = x^0Rx^1...Rx^jPx^{j+1}R...Rx^m = y$. We write $\succcurlyeq^*$ both for $\succcurlyeq$ of (i) and for the reflexive extension of $\succcurlyeq'$ of (iii). It follows that $x^i \succcurlyeq^* x^{i+1}$ for all $0 \leq i \leq m-1$, so that $x^k \succcurlyeq^* x^\ell$ for all $0 \leq k < \ell \leq m$, in particular $x \succcurlyeq^* y$. Were now $y \succcurlyeq^* x$, then by transitivity $x^k \approx {}^*x^\ell$ for all $0 \leq k \leq \ell \leq m$, contradicting x^jPx^{j+1}. So $x \succ^* y$, and $\succ^*$ must extend $\bar{P}$.

For the demonstration of (vi) => (ii), suppose xPy. Then $x\bar{P}y$, so by (vi) not $y\bar{R}x$, and (ii) follows.

For (i) => (vi), first note that by (i), $x\bar{P}y$ implies, by the furthermore-statement, that not $y\bar{R}x$. Since $x\bar{P}y$ => $x\bar{R}y$ always holds true, [$x\bar{P}y$] => [$x\bar{R}y$ and not $y\bar{R}x$] follows.

To establish the reversed implication, suppose that [$x\bar{R}y$ and not $y\bar{R}x$]. Then $x = x^0Rx^1...Rx^m = y$ can be arranged. To prevent $y = x^mRx^{m-1}R...Rx^0 = x$, there must be a j such that not $x^{j+1}Rx^j$. For this j, x^jPx^{j+1}. It follows that $x\bar{P}y$. (vi) is established, and with it the equivalence of (vi), (i), (ii), (iii), (v).

Of course (iv) => (v) is direct. For (v) => (iv), note that $\bar{E}$ by definition is the symmetric part of $\bar{R}$, and that (v) implies (vi).

□

I.2.2. OTHER CONDITIONS FOR CHOICE FUNCTIONS

The characterization by means of congruency, obtained in Theorem I.2.5, was completely general. In this subsection we consider some conditions for choice functions, simpler than congruency. By relating them to congruency we show that, under certain restrictions, they imply the existence of a representing weak order[rf13].

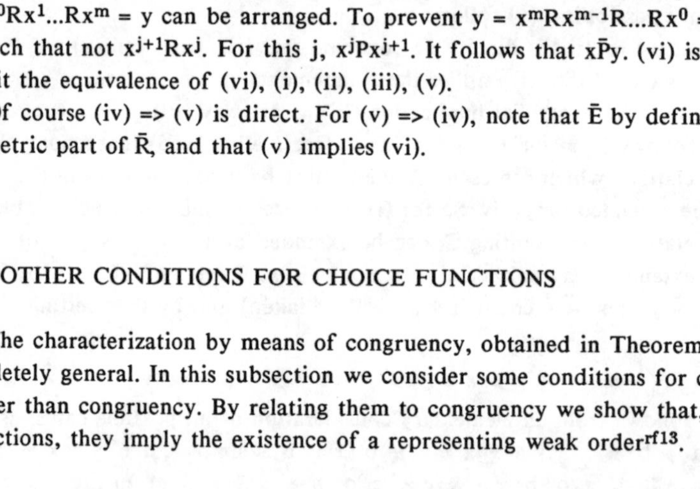

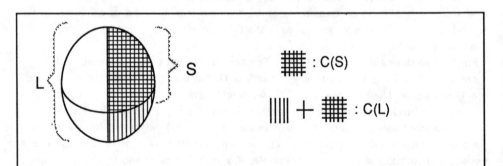

FIGURE I.2.3 (Independence of irrelevant alternatives (IIA)). Let S⊂L. If the choice set C(L) of the ('large') set L intersects the ('small') set S, then C(S)=C(L)∩S.

DEFINITIONS[rf14] for a choice function C.

I.2.6. C satisfies the **strong axiom of revealed preference** (**SARP**) if no sequence $(x^j)_{j=0}^{m}$ exists such that x^jPx^{j+1} for all $0 \le j \le m-1$, and x^mPx^0.

I.2.7. C satisfies the **weak axiom of revealed preference** (**WARP**) if, for all alternatives x,y : [xRy => not yPx].

I.2.8 (See Figure I.2.3.). C satisfies **independence of irrelevant alternatives** (**IIA**) if for all S, L $\in \Delta$ with $S \subset L$: $[C(L) \cap S = \emptyset$ or $C(L) \cap S = C(S)]$.

LEMMA I.2.9. *Congruency implies SARP, WARP, and IIA. WARP implies IIA.*

PROOF. Congruency forbids the existence of $(x^j)_{j=0}^{m}$, $(D^j)_{j=0}^{m}$, such that $x^j \in C(D^{j+1})$, $x^{j+1} \in D^{j+1}$ for all $0 \le j \le m-1$, and $x^m \in C(D^0)$, $x^0 \in D^0\backslash C(D^0)$. SARP forbids this only for the special case that $x^{j+1} \in D^{j+1}\backslash C(D^{j+1})$ for all $0 \le j \le m-1$. WARP forbids it only for the special case that m = 1. IIA can be seen to forbid it only for the special case that m = 1 and furthermore $D^0 \subset D^1$ or $D^1 \subset D^0$.

□

LEMMA I.2.10. *If* C(D) *contains exactly one element for all* $D \in \Delta$, *then SARP implies congruency.*

PROOF. Assume that SARP holds, and let C(D) contain exactly one element for all $D \in \Delta$. Let $x^0Rx^1...Rx^mPx^0$. We derive a contradiction. We may assume that $x^0 \neq x^1... \neq x^m$. (For instance, if $x^j = x^{j+1}$, then replace $x^jRx^{j+1}Rx^{j+2}$ by x^jRx^{j+2}, etc.) Since C(D) contains only one element for all $D \in \Delta$, we must now have $x^0Px^1...Px^mPx^0$. This contradicts SARP.

□

LEMMA I.2.11. *If* Δ *contains all two-and three-point subsets of* X, *or if* Δ *is union-closed, then IIA implies congruency.*

PROOF. Assume that IIA holds, and let $x^0Rx^1...Rx^m$. We prove that *not* x^mPx^0. As in the proof of the above lemma, we may assume $x^j \neq x^{j+1}$ for all $0 \le j \le m-1$. Hence $D^1,...,D^m$ exist such that $x^j \in C(D^{j+1})$, $x^{j+1} \in D^{j+1}$ for all $0 \le j \le m-1$. If $x^m = x^0$, or not x^mRx^0, then also not x^mPx^0. So let us assume that $x^m \neq x^0$ and x^mRx^0; i.e., D^0 exists with $x^m \in C(D^0)$, $x^0 \in D^0$. For [not x^mPx^0] we must show that $x^0 \in C(D^0)$.

First we prove this for the case that Δ contains all two- and three-point subsets of X. Since $\{x^j,x^{j+1}\} \subset D^{j+1}$, by IIA: $x^j \in C\{x^j,x^{j+1}\}$ for all $0 \le j \le m-1$. We may suppose $D^{j+1} = \{x^j,x^{j+1}\}$ for all $0 \le j \le m-1$; and, analogously, $D^0 = \{x^0,x^m\}$. For m = 1 everything follows. For $m \ge 2$, consider the nonempty set $C\{x^0,x^1,x^2\}$. If it contains x^2, then by IIA and $\{x^1,x^2\} \subset \{x^0,x^1,x^2\}$ it also contains x^1. If it contains x^1, then by IIA and $\{x^0,x^1\} \subset \{x^0,x^1,x^2\}$ it also contains x^0. So, by a 'domino-argument', the nonempty set $C\{x^0,x^1,x^2\}$ must contain x^0. By IIA, $x^0 \in C\{x^0,x^2\}$ and $x^0Rx^2R...Rx^m$. Analogously we see that $x^0 \in C\{x^0,x^j\}$ for $j = 3,4,...,m$. Since $\{x^0,x^m\} = D^0$, $x^0 \in C(D^0)$.

Next we prove $x^0 \in C(D^0)$ for the case that Δ is union-closed. Consider, for $m\geq 2$, the nonempty set $C(D^1 \cup D^2)$. If there is $y^2 \in D^2$ such that $y^2 \in C(D^1 \cup D^2)$, then by IIA and $D^2 \subset D^1 \cup D^2$, $x^1 \in C(D^1 \cup D^2)$. So always there is $y^1 \in D^1$ such that $y^1 \in C(D^1 \cup D^2)$. By IIA and $D^1 \subset D^1 \cup D^2$ always $x^0 \in C(D^1 \cup D^2)$. Analogously (substitute $D^1 \cup ... \cup D^{j-1}$ for D^1, D^j for D^2, x^{j-1} for x^1 above, etc.) we obtain $x^0 \in C((D^1 \cup D^2 \cup ... \cup D^{j-1}) \cup D^j)$ for $j = 2,3,...,m$, and, also for $m=1$, $x^0 \in C((D^1 \cup ... \cup D^m) \cup D^0)$. Since $D^0 \subset (D^1 \cup ... \cup D^m \cup D^0)$, by IIA: $x^0 \in C(D^0)$.

□

COROLLARY I.2.12[rf15]. *If* Δ *contains all two-and three-point subsets of* X, *or if* Δ *is union-closed, then the following four statements are equivalent* :

(i) There exists a representing weak order for C.

(ii) C is congruent.

(iii) C satisfies WARP.

(iv) C satisfies IIA.

If C(D) *contains exactly one element for every* $D \in \Delta$, *then the following three statements are equivalent* :

(v) There exists a representing weak order for C.
(vi) C is congruent.
(vii) C satisfies SARP.

PROOF. By the previous theorems and lemmas in this section.

□

In the following chapters we shall work with binary relations, intended to represent a choice function, and often called preference relations. Note that binary relations do not specify the domain of the choice function. Also note that representing weak orders, as in (i) of Theorem I.2.5, do not have to be uniquely determined. Hence conditions, characteristic for such a weak order, do not have to be characteristic for the choice function[rf16]. If Δ is rich enough, for instance contains all two-point subsets of X, then the representing binary relation $\succcurlyeq$ in (i) of Theorem I.2.5 equals $\bar{R}$ (even R) of (v) there, and is uniquely determined.

I.2.3. REPRESENTING FUNCTIONS

The major part of this book will take preference relations as given, and will derive 'representing functions' for these. A function V <u>represents</u> $\succcurlyeq$ if $V : X \rightarrow \mathbb{R}$ and, for all alternatives x,y :

$$[x \succcurlyeq y] \iff [V(x) \geq V(y)]. \qquad \text{(I.2.1)}$$

As usual we shall feel free to use for V terms such as (quantitative) representation. In decision theory the term utility function is the most usual one for a representing function. We shall however need that term for a somewhat different notion in decision making under uncertainty, see Definition IV.2.1. If (I.2.1) holds for all x,y from a subset G of X, then we say that V **represents** $\succcurlyeq$ **on** G.

If a preference relation $\succcurlyeq$ represents a choice function C, and a function V represents the preference relation, then we have, for all $D \in \Delta$:

$$C(D) = \{x \in D : V(x) \geq V(y) \text{ for all } y \in D\} .$$

It is directly verified that a representing function can exist for the preference relation $\succcurlyeq$ only if $\succcurlyeq$ is a weak order. For a finite set X, a representing function exists for $\succcurlyeq$ if and only if $\succcurlyeq$ is a weak order. (Let the representation assign 1 to the lowest $\approx$-equivalence class, 2 to the second-lowest $\approx$-equivalence class, etc.) For infinite X this no longer holds true, as can be inferred from the lexicographic order on $\mathbb{R}^2$ (the collection $\{]V(\alpha,0),V(\alpha,1)[: \alpha \in \mathbb{R}\}$ would yield an uncountable number of disjoint nondegenerate intervals). It is known that there exists a representing function for a preference relation $\succcurlyeq$ if and only if $\succcurlyeq$ is a weak order that further has a countable 'perfectly dense' subset G in the sense that for every $x \succ y$ there is an element $e \in G$ such that $x \succcurlyeq e \succcurlyeq y$[rf17].

It would be desirable to formulate conditions for the existence of functions to be maximized, not in terms of the 'intermediate' preference relations, but directly in terms of choice functions. We have not pursued this[rf18].

I.3. COMPARISON WITH OTHER SET-UPS (OR: WHAT WE DO NOT DO)

In Luce&Suppes(1965) a distinction is made between 'probabilistic' (= 'stochastic') and 'algebraic' approaches. In probabilistic approaches there is randomness in the choices of the decision maker, for example the decision maker chooses (C(D) =) x from D with probability 1/3 and (C(D) =) y from D with probability 2/3. Our approach is algebraic, the decision maker's choices do not involve random mechanisms[rf19]. Neither do we take account of the effects of measurement errors, and a possible randomness in observed choices caused by such measurement errors. Hence no goodness-of-fit considerations will occur in this monograph.

Also there is no randomness or uncertainty concerning the *alternatives* that result from the decision maker's choices. The decision maker can choose any available alternative he wants, and then be sure to obtain this alternative. Still we do consider uncertainty in the sequel, in fact that will be the major subject of this monograph. The uncertainty, made explicit and studied by us in the sequel, will concern what 'consequence' will result from an alternative, see Example II.1.1 in the sequel. There may be further, 'implicit', uncertainty in such consequences. We neither assume, nor exclude, the existence of such uncertainty, only it is not central in our study. In this respect our approach deviates from the approach of Savage(1954), who assumes that in the basic model all relevant uncertainty has been made explicit in the 'state space'[rf20]. As an illustration, suppose that a decision maker can choose a bet in a boxing-match, yielding \$3 if boxer 1 wins, and \$–7 (i.e., a loss) if boxer 2 wins or if the match is a tie. Then in other approaches the amounts of money \$3 and \$–7 may be called alternatives, and the decision maker may be considered to be uncertain about which alternative will result from his choice. In the set-up of this monograph the bet is an alternative, the amounts of money \$3 and \$–7 are consequences (or 'coordinates', see section II.1 and Example II.1.1). We do not exclude or assume the existence of uncertainty about what will result from a consequence '\$3'; only such uncertainty will not be central in our study.

Our set-up is ordinal in the sense that everything in the sequel will be derived solely from the preference relation of the decision maker on the set of alternatives (where the preference relation again is derived from the choice function), and structure of the set of alternatives. Nothing cardinal-like has been introduced 'from outside'. No strength of preference relation is presupposed. Also no addition-like operation on alternatives is used. For example, we do not use repetitions.

A typical thought experiment for the repetitions approach, as for instance in Shapiro(1979) or Camacho(1980)[rf21] is as follows. Let $D_1 = \{b,n\}$, $D_2 = \{b,p\}$, $D_3 = \{n,p\}$. It is now assumed that the decision maker has to deal with *all* three of these choice situations, and for instance he must choose between two 'possibilities'. The first is that he obtains b from D_1, p from D_2, p from D_3. The second is that he obtains n from D_1, p from D_2, n from D_3. Then the first possibility can be denoted as $b \tilde{+} p \tilde{+} p$, or $b \tilde{+} (2\tilde{\times}p)$, the second as $n \tilde{+} p \tilde{+} n$, or $(2\tilde{\times}n) \tilde{+} p$. Here $\tilde{+}$ and $\tilde{\times}$ are formal operations. One sees that here not in each one of the choice situations D_1, D_2, D_3, the decision maker is free to choose. If the decision maker wants to choose b from D_1, then he must choose the first possibility, hence p from D_3. In our set-up, to the contrary, the decision maker in each single situation is free to choose what he thinks best there. For instance, if in the transitivity assumption we assume that choices b from D_1 and p from D_2 should imply the choice p from D_3, then all these choices are intended to agree with the decision maker's freedom of choice in each single situation.

We will not consider the complications of 'bounded rationality' (the decision maker has only bounded calculation capacity and for that reason cannot consider all relevant aspects of complicated decision situations)[rf22], and we do not consider the modeling complications of finding out what in a decision situation are the available alternatives.

Finally, we do not use lotteries on alternatives[rf23].

CHAPTER II

CARTESIAN PRODUCT STRUCTURE

II.1. CARTESIAN PRODUCT STRUCTURE, EXAMPLES

In this section we introduce on X, the set of alternatives, the main structure of interest in this monograph. **We shall assume throughout the sequel that X is a Cartesian product $\prod_{i \in I} \Gamma_i$, with I an index set. We shall nearly always, with Chapter V excepted, assume that I is a finite set {1,...,n}, for** $n \in \mathbb{N}$. Many definitions and results of this chapter are as well applicable to infinite index sets I.

The idea is that every alternative is described by a list of properties, indexed by I. For instance, alternative $x = (x_1,x_2,x_3,x_4)$ may describe a car, where x_1 is the maximum speed, x_2 the price, x_3 a description of what the car looks like, x_4 the fuel consumption. For alternatives x,y, $x \succcurlyeq y$ means that x is thought at least as good as y. Let us emphasize that no physical quantification of the coordinates is needed for our work. Indeed, what the car looks like may be described in nonquantitative terms.

In applications, one of the central matters is to find an appropriate list of properties, to be indexed by I[rf1]. The list should be large enough to contain all relevant aspects of the alternatives, and small enough to be tractable. Also, in our set-up, each property should have meaning on its own. If in the above example it were impossible to give a meaningful description of x_3, what the car looks like, independent of maximum speed, price, and fuel consumption, then the list of indexed properties used above would not be well-suited for our purposes. Throughout this monograph we shall assume that the Cartesian product structure has already been obtained.

For many fields of science the Cartesian product structure is a central matter of study. We concisely list some examples[rf2] :

EXAMPLE II.1.1. Decision making under uncertainty
Here x is an **act**, I a **state space**, $i \in I$ a **(possible) state (of nature)**. Exactly one state is the true state, the others are untrue. Act x yields **consequence** x_i if i is the true state. The decision maker is uncertain about which of the states is true. Usually in this context $\Gamma_i = \Gamma_1 =: \Gamma$ for all i. The set Γ is called the **consequence space**.

As an example one may think of a horse race. Of, say, (n =) 3 participating horses exactly one will win. Here i indicates the 'possible state of nature' that the i-th horse will win, i = 1,2,3. $\Gamma_i = \mathbb{R}$ for all i, indicating money. An example of an act is $x = (5,-3,-1)$, indicating an act (or 'gamble', as the usual term in this context is) which will leave the decision maker with $x_1 = \$5$ if the first horse will win, $x_2 = \$-3$ if the second horse will win, and $x_3 = \$-1$ if the third horse will win. If the decision maker chooses the gamble (act) x, then he is uncertain about which amount of money (= consequence) x_j will result from this, since he is uncertain about which horse will win the race (i.e., which state is true). See Savage(1954), or Drèze(1987,Chapter 1).

EXAMPLE II.1.2. Consumer theory
Here x is a **commodity bundle**, i indicates a kind of **commodity**, $x_i \in \mathbb{R}_+$ the amount of commodity i in x; $x \succcurlyeq y$ means that a **consumer** (i.e., the decision maker) thinks x is at least as good as y. See Katzner(1970).

EXAMPLE II.1.3. Producers theory
Here x is an **input vector**, i indicates a production factor, x_i is the input (rate) of production factor i. $V : \prod_{i \in I}\Gamma_i \to \mathbb{R}$ is a **production function**, assigning to every x the (maximally attainable, one-dimensional) output V(x). $x \succcurlyeq y$: x gives at least as much output as y. See Shephard(1970).

EXAMPLE II.1.4. Dynamic applications
Here x is a consumption/production path, stream of income, etc. Every i indicates a **point of time**, x_i is the consumption/production/income at point of time i. See Koopmans(1972).

EXAMPLE II.1.5. Welfare theory
Here x is an **allocation** or social situation, I is a society or group of agents/players, every $i \in I$ is an **agent**/player, and x_i indicates the wealth or utility for agent i under allocation x. See Harsanyi(1955).

EXAMPLE II.1.6. Price indexes
Here every i indicates a good or service, x_i is the price of good or service i at the time, or in the place, described by x. Here a **price index** V, assigning to every x a measure for the level of prices, is usually the primitive. $x \succcurlyeq y$: the level of prices in time or place x is at least as high as that in y. See Fisher(1927b).

In Examples II.1.3 and II.1.6 it is custom to take a quantitative (representing) function V as primitive, instead of $\succcurlyeq$. The relation between such quantitative representations, and $\succcurlyeq$, is the central topic of this monograph[rf3,rf4,rf5].

Most of this monograph will deal with Example II.1.1. Let us shortly, without discussion, mention here some intuitive assumptions which underlie our work for decision making under uncertainty, in addition to those mentioned in Sections I.1 and I.3[rf6]. These assumptions are prerequisites for the 'CI-condition' (see next section), which will be assumed everywhere in this book, except in Chapter VI. Firstly it is intended that the decision maker has not any influence on which state of nature is the true state[rf7]. Secondly, the consequences should model everything relevant for the future of the decision maker in the case that the consequence obtains. So if one makes use of the set-up of Example II.1.1, and describes what the consequences are, then these descriptions of the consequences should be complete enough to justify that use[rf8]. The assumption of section I.1.2 that it is only the free will of the decision maker to determine which act is chosen should for instance entail that the choice of act is not influenced by which state of nature is the true state; the choice of act of the decision maker can neither serve as a signal giving information to the decision maker about which state is true[rf9].

II.2. ALTERNATIVES, SUBALTERNATIVES, AND PREFERENCES BETWEEN THEM

For $A \subset I$, x_A denotes the element of $\prod_{i\in A}\Gamma_i$ with i-th coordinate x_i, for all $i \in A$. If an alternative x is given, and one considers x as a map from I to $\cup_{i\in I}\Gamma_i$, assigning x_i to every $i \in I$, then x_A can be considered to be the restriction of x to A. We call x_A a **subalternative**; its **length** is $|A|$. Of course $x_{\{i\}} = x_i$, and $x_I = x$; coordinates and alternatives are special forms of subalternatives. Let x_{-A} denote the element of $\prod_{i\notin A}\Gamma_i$ with i-th coordinate x_i, for all $i \notin A$. For $x,y \in \prod_{i\in I}\Gamma_i$, $x_{-A}y_A$ denotes the alternative with i-th coordinate x_i for all $i \notin A$, and with i-th coordinate y_i for all $i \in A$. The most-used example of this notation, with as usual i for {i}, is :

$x_{-i}v_i$ is (x with x_i replaced by v_i) .

The above notation makes explicit the i-th coordinate. Thus the notations $x_{-i}v_i$ and $x_{-i}w_i$ immediately show that the two alternatives differ only with respect to their i-th coordinate. For $i \neq j$ an analogous notation, simplifying $(x_{-i}v_i)_{-j}w_j$, is :

$x_{-i,j}v_i,w_j$ is (x with x_i replaced by v_i and x_j by w_j).

We say, for a subset A of I, and a subset E of $\prod_{i\in I}\Gamma_i$, that A is **inessential on** E (**with respect to** $\succcurlyeq$) if $x_{-A}v_A \approx x_{-A}w_A$ for all $x_{-A}v_A$ and $x_{-A}w_A$ in E. The opposite of inessential is **essential**. If $\succcurlyeq$ is a weak order, then A is essential on E if and only if $x_{-A}v_A \succ x_{-A}w_A$ for some $x_{-A}v_A$ and $x_{-A}w_A$ in E. Then the coordinates of A cannot be ignored for the preferences within E. If E is the entire set $\prod_{i\in I}\Gamma_i$, then we usually omit 'on $\prod_{i\in I}\Gamma_i$'. Mostly A will be a one-coordinate-set {j}, often denoted as j.

LEMMA II.2.1. *Suppose* $\approx$ *is an equivalence relation. Let* $x_j = y_j$ *for all essential* j. *Then* $x \approx y$. *Further* $\succcurlyeq$ *is trivial if and only if no coordinate is essential.*

PROOF. Let $x_j = y_j$ for all essential j. If no coordinate is inessential then x = y, so $x \approx y$ by reflexivity of $\approx$. Now let there be k inessential coordinates, say {1,...,k}, with k > 0. Then

$$x \approx (x_{-1}y_1) \approx (x_{-1,2}y_1,y_2) \approx \ldots \approx (x_{-\{1,\ldots,k\}}(y_1,\ldots,y_k) = y.$$

By transitivity of $\approx$ we get $x \approx y$. From this also follows that $\succcurlyeq$ is trivial whenever all coordinates are inessential. Conversely, if $\succcurlyeq$ is trivial, then $x_{-j}v_j \approx x_{-j}w_j$ for all $x_{-j}v_j$, $x_{-j}w_j$ so that every coordinate j is inessential.

□

The above lemma shows that inessential coordinates may just as well be suppressed. In the sequel we will sometimes do so. The conditions for binary relations introduced below will be assumed, or implied by other assumptions, throughout this monograph, with the exception of Chapter VI.

DEFINITION II.2.2. The binary relation $\succcurlyeq$ on $\prod_{i\in I}\Gamma_i$ satisfies **independence of equal subalternatives** if, for all alternatives x,y,v,w and all $A \subset I$,

$$[x_{-A}v_A \succcurlyeq y_{-A}v_A] \iff [x_{-A}w_A \succcurlyeq y_{-A}w_A] .$$

For the idea of the above definition suppose it is satisfied. Then, in a preference, an identical pair of subalternatives may be replaced by any other identical pair of subalternatives, without affecting the preference. (In the above definition the identical pair of subalternatives v_A,v_A is replaced by the identical pair of subalternatives w_A,w_A.) For finite Cartesian products there is a simpler, equivalent, formulation for independence of equal subalternatives.

DEFINITION II.2.3 (see Figure II.2.1). The binary relation $\succcurlyeq$ on $\prod_{i\in I}\Gamma_i$ satisfies **independence of equal coordinates**, or shortly **coordinate independence** (**CI**) if, for all $i \in I$, x, $y \in \prod_{i\in I}\Gamma_i$, and v_i, $w_i \in \Gamma_i$:

$$[x_{-i}v_i \succcurlyeq y_{-i}v_i] \iff [x_{-i}w_i \succcurlyeq y_{-i}w_i]$$

Also we then say that $\succcurlyeq$ *is* CI.

So, if two alternatives have a common coordinate, then by CI the preference is unaffected when that coordinate is changed into any other common coordinate. (In the above definition the common coordinate v_i is changed into the common coordinate w_i.) CI is the restriction of independence of equal subalternatives to the case where the involved subalternatives are coordinates. Hence independence of equal subalternatives

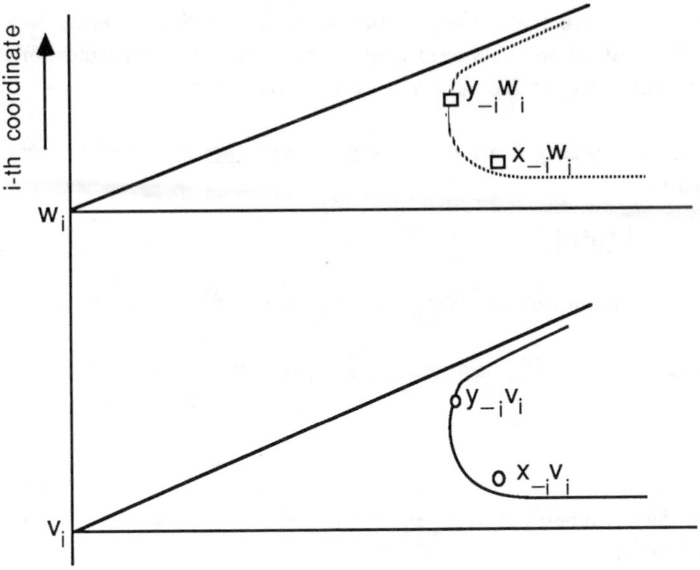

FIGURE II.2.1. (Coordinate independence (CI)). If $x_{-i}v_i$ is preferred to the (equivalence class going through) $y_{-i}v_i$, then $x_{-i}w_i$ should be preferred to the equivalence class going through $y_{-i}w_i$. This is easily seen to imply that the equivalence classes in parallel planes are parallel.

implies CI. But also CI implies independence of equal subalternatives for finite Cartesian products $\prod_{i \in I}\Gamma_i$, as is seen as follows: If in a preference $x_{-A}v_A \succcurlyeq y_{-A}v_A$ we find on the left and right side an identical subalternative v_A, then, by CI, we may replace, one by one, every pair of identical coordinates v_i,v_i for $i \in A$, by the pair w_i,w_i, without affecting the preference by any one of these replacements. Thus, after $|A|$ replacements, we end up with all of v_A,v_A replaced by w_A,w_A, resulting in the preference $x_{-A}w_A \succcurlyeq y_{-A}w_A$. So we have :

OBSERVATION II.2.4. *A binary relation $\succcurlyeq$ on a finite Cartesian product satisfies independence of equal subalternatives if and only if it satisfies CI.*

□

Independence of equal subalternatives when restricted to equal subalternatives of length n−1, is so much weaker than full-strength-independence of equal subalternatives, that its characteristics are rather different. Hence we shall introduce a term, 'weak separability', for that restriction. This term is not consistent with the further terminology in this monograph, but is by far the most usual one in the literature.

DEFINITION II.2.5. The binary relation $\succcurlyeq$ is **weakly separable** if, for all alternatives x, y, v, w, and coordinates $i \in I$,

$$[v_{-i}x_i \succcurlyeq v_{-i}y_i] \iff [w_{-i}x_i \succcurlyeq w_{-i}y_i] .$$

The following binary relations on the Γ_i's are mainly useful if $\succcurlyeq$ is weakly separable.

DEFINITION II.2.6. For all i, x_i, y_i we write $x_i \succcurlyeq_i y_i$ if there exists an alternative v such that

$$v_{-i}x_i \succcurlyeq v_{-i}y_i .$$

With, as usual, $\succ_i$ the asymmetric part of $\succcurlyeq_i$, $\approx_i$ the symmetric part, and $\preccurlyeq_i$ and $\prec_i$ 'reversed' binary relations, we have :

LEMMA II.2.7. *Let* $\succcurlyeq$ *be a weakly separable weak order. Then for all* i, x_i, y_i :

$[x_i \succcurlyeq_i y_i] \iff [v_{-i}x_i \succcurlyeq v_{-i}y_i$ *for all alternatives* v] .

$\succcurlyeq_i$ *is a weak order.*

$[x_i \succ_i y_i] \iff$ [*there exists an alternative* v *such that* $v_{-i}x_i \succ v_{-i}y_i] \iff$ $[v_{-i}x_i \succ v_{-i}y_i$ *for all alternatives* v] .

$[x_i \approx_i y_i] \iff$ [*there exists an alternative* v *such that* $v_{-i}x_i \approx v_{-i}y_i] \iff$ $[v_{-i}x_i \approx v_{-i}y_i$ *for all alternatives* v] .

$\succcurlyeq$ *is weakly and strongly monotonic with respect to* $(\succcurlyeq_j)_{j=1}^{n}$.

□

The derivation of these results is straightforward, and left to the reader. They are so intimately related to weak separability that in the sequel we may say **by weak separability**, when applying one of the above results.

II.3. ADDITIVE REPRESENTATIONS

This monograph will consider 'additive representations' for preference relations. In short, a function V on $\prod_{i \in I}\Gamma_i$ is **additive** if it can be written as a sum of coordinate functions, $V : x \mapsto \sum_{j=1}^{n} V_j(x_j)$. We shall sometimes use functions defined only on subsets, hence introduce the following somewhat more complicated terminology.

Let $E \subset \prod_{i \in I} \Gamma_i$. $V : E \to \mathbb{R}$ is **additive** (**on** E) if there exist, for $j = 1,...,n$, $E_j \subset \Gamma_j$ and functions $V_j : E_j \to \mathbb{R}$, such that $V : x \mapsto \sum_{j=1}^{n} V_j(x_j)$. If V is an additive representation for $\succcurlyeq$ (on $E \subset \prod_{i \in I} \Gamma_i$) then the functions V_j as above are called **additive value functions** (on $E \subset \prod_{i \in I} \Gamma_i$). If $E = \prod_{i \in I} \Gamma_i$, then 'on $\prod_{i \in I} \Gamma_i$' is mostly omitted.

One way to obtain additive representations goes in two stages. In the first stage one formulates conditions which will give a representation whatsoever. In the second stage one then adds the conditions that will guarantee the possibility of choosing the representation additive. Indeed this has been the most usual approach in economic literature. In this monograph we will follow a different approach. We shall, following Krantz,Luce,Suppes&Tversky(1971) (hereafter abbreviated KLST), obtain an additive representation 'in one stroke'. As it turns out the structure and conditions, needed anyhow in the second stage above, are also of use in the first stage. In particular we will, like KLST, find with our one-stroke approach that the condition of topological separability, assumed by Debreu(1960, Theorem 3) and used by him in the first stage, can be dispensed with (see Remark III.7.1). Hence the derivation of general representations without additivity-restriction will not receive much attention in this monograph. The phenomenon that 'one-stroke' approaches may have advantages can also be inferred from Corollary VII.7.3 in the sequel. There we shall find that adding conditions of risk-aversion to expected utility facilitates the very derivation of expected utility.

Next let us briefly sketch the characterization of additive representations for the case where $\prod_{i \in I} \Gamma_i$ is finite. The result itself will not be used in the sequel, but is given for its importance, and for its role in the appreciation of results in the sequel. It is assumed now that $\succcurlyeq$ is a weak order. Suppose we have a list of m + 1 weak preferences with at least one, say the last, strict :

$$\begin{array}{ccc}
(x_1^1,...,x_n^1) & \succcurlyeq & (y_1^1,...,y_n^1) \\
(x_1^2,...,x_n^2) & \succcurlyeq & (y_1^2,...,y_n^2) \\
\vdots & & \vdots \\
(x_1^m,...,x_n^m) & \succcurlyeq & (y_1^m,...,y_n^m) \\
(x_1^0,...,x_n^0) & \succ & (y_1^0,...,y_n^0)
\end{array}$$

with every $z_j \in \Gamma_j$ occurring equally often to the left of the preferences (so in the column of x_j's), as to the right of the preferences (so in the column of y_j's). (I.e., there exist permutations π_j on $\{0,...,m\}$ such that $y_j^i = x_j^{\pi_j(i)}$ for all j,i.) Suppose there would exist additive value functions V_j for $\succcurlyeq$. Then because of the preferences the sum of $V_j(x_j^i)$'s $(i = 0,...,m,\ j = 1,...,n)$, the 'left-sum', should be greater than the 'right-sum' of $V_j(y_j^i)$'s $(i = 0,...,m,\ j = 1,...,n)$. However, because every term $V_j(z_j)$ occurs equally often in the left-sum as in the right-sum, the two sums should be equal: Contradiction. Thus a necessary condition for the existence of an additive representation is that lists of preferences as above do not occur.

This condition turns out to be also sufficient for the existence of additive value functions, if $\prod_{i\in I}\Gamma_i$ is finite[rf10]. For the interested reader we give a very concise sketch of the proof, based on the separating hyperplane theorem.

Concise Sketch of Proof. For notational convenience we assume that, for all alternatives z and coordinates $i \neq j$, $z_i \neq z_j$; this can be accomplished e.g. by writing (z_i,i) instead of z_i. Consider the formal linear space with as basis the set $\cup_{j=1}^{n}\Gamma_j$. We identify every $x \in \prod_{i\in I}\Gamma_i$ with $\sum_{j=1}^{n}x_j$, i.e., with the vector with ones for the coordinates corresponding to the x_j's, zero otherwise. Let C^+ be the convex cone generated by $\{x-y : x \succcurlyeq y\}$, and C^{--} the convex hull of $\{x-y : x \prec y\}$. Additive value functions $(V_j)_{j=1}^{n}$ for $\succcurlyeq$ correspond with a hyperplane (through the origin, by reflexivity) separating the sets C^+ and C^{--} with C^{--} not intersecting the hyperplane, such that the hyperplane has a vector V as normal where V has $V_i(x_i)$ as coordinate corresponding to x_i for all i and x_i, and C^+ is on the same side of the hyperplane as the vector V. By the separating hyperplane theorem, additive value functions do *not* exist if and only if the sets C^+ and C^{--} intersect. It can be seen that an element $\sum_{i=1}^{k}\lambda_i(a^i-b^i)$ from C^+ ($a^i \succcurlyeq b^i$ for all i), equal to an element $\sum_{j=1}^{\ell}\mu_j(c^j-d^j)$ from C^{--} ($c^j \prec d^j$ for all j), can always be chosen so that all λ_i and μ_j are rational. We can multiply the two sums with a natural number N so large that all $N\lambda_i$ and $N\mu_j$ are natural numbers. From that we obtain the list of preferences as above, the first $\sum_{i=1}^{k}N\lambda_i$ preferences $x^h \succcurlyeq y^h$ of the form $a^i \succcurlyeq b^i$ (each preference $a^i \succcurlyeq b^i$ occurs $N\lambda_i$ times), the last $\sum_{j=1}^{\ell}N\mu_j$ preferences $x^h \succcurlyeq y^h$ of the form $d^j \succcurlyeq c^j$ (each preference $d^j \succcurlyeq c^j$ occurs $N\mu_j$ times). The preferences of the second form in fact are strict. Since the μ_j's are weights in a convex combination, not all $N\mu_j$'s can be zero. Hence we have at least one strict preference $d^j \succ c^j$; this can be taken for $x^0 \succ y^0$.

□

For complete binary relations the requirement that, only for some fixed m, a list of preferences as above should not exist, is equivalent to what KLST(section 9.2) call m^{th}-order cancellation. For complete binary relations one can further derive :

Transitivity is the special version of second-order cancellation with all the π_j-permutations above the same; this implies *all* cancellation axioms for which the π_j-permutations as above are the same.

Coordinate independence is first-order cancellation.

In this monograph we shall deal with additive representations under the topological restrictions common in the literature. These restrictions will greatly facilitate characterizations since they call on no more than one or two special cases of the above 'cancellation' axioms (see Remark III.7.6). To some this may show the usefulness of simplifying structural conditions such as continuity[rf11]. Others may interpret this as a danger of continuity, the danger to mask essential intuitive aspects. With only a theorem as Theorem III.6.6 in the sequel at hand, one, when checking a finite amount of data for additive representability, will not easily get the idea to test the data for more complicated cancellation axioms. Analogously, with at hand only representation theorems for subjective expected utility such as our Theorem IV.2.7, or the representation result in Savage(1954), one will not easily get the idea to test data for the very complicated 'polynomial' conditions for subjective expected utility as provided by Shapiro(1979)[rf12].

II.4. COMPARISONS OF TRADEOFFS DERIVED FROM ORDINAL PREFERENCES

This section shows a way to derive comparisons of tradeoffs of coordinates from preferences on alternatives, using a tradeoff idea from multi-attribute utility theory. One may interpret these comparisons of tradeoffs as comparisons of 'strengths of preferences on coordinates'. In view of the controversial history of strengths of preferences, some may dispute the content validity of such strengths of preferences. The view may be held that even if strengths of preferences are empirically meaningful, then still they do not have to coincide with the notion defined below. In our view at least in some contexts, such as the (controversial) case of decision making under uncertainty, strengths of preferences as below are 'as good' as other notions of strengths of preferences. The reason for us to choose the term tradeoff instead of strength of preference, is linguistic: Terminologies, to be introduced in the sequel, are more convenient, in particular concerning pronunciation.

DEFINITION II.4.1 (see Figure II.4.1)[rf13]. For the binary relation $\succcurlyeq$ on $\prod_{i \in I}\Gamma_i$ we write :

$x_iy_i \succ_i^{**} v_iw_i$ if :

there exist alternatives a and b such that

$a_{-i}x_i \succcurlyeq b_{-i}y_i$ and

not $a_{-i}v_i \succcurlyeq b_{-i}w_i$.

In section III.5 and Chapter VII we shall sometimes write $[x_i;y_i] \succ_i^{**} [v_i;w_i]$ for $x_iy_i \succ_i^{**} v_iw_i$.

One may say that the pair b_{-i},a_{-i} has been used as a 'measuring rod' to compare the tradeoff x_iy_i with the tradeoff v_iw_i. For an intuitive elucidation, suppose for simplicity that x_i is better than y_i (i.e., $x_i \succ_i y_i$) and that v_i is better than w_i. Let us start with the second ('non')preference [not $a_{-i}v_i \succcurlyeq b_{-i}w_i$]. This suggests that the positive argument for the left alternative against the right alternative, to obtain v_i instead of w_i on coordinate i, does not outweigh the (apparently) negative argument, yielded by the remaining coordinates. And [$a_{-i}x_i \succcurlyeq b_{-i}y_i$] suggests that the positive argument, to obtain x_i instead of y_i, does, to the contrary, outweigh that negative argument. The above definition interprets this to mean that it has been revealed from $\succcurlyeq$ that the value of the tradeoff of x_i for y_i exceeds that of v_i for w_i. Lemmas II.4.3 and II.4.5 further

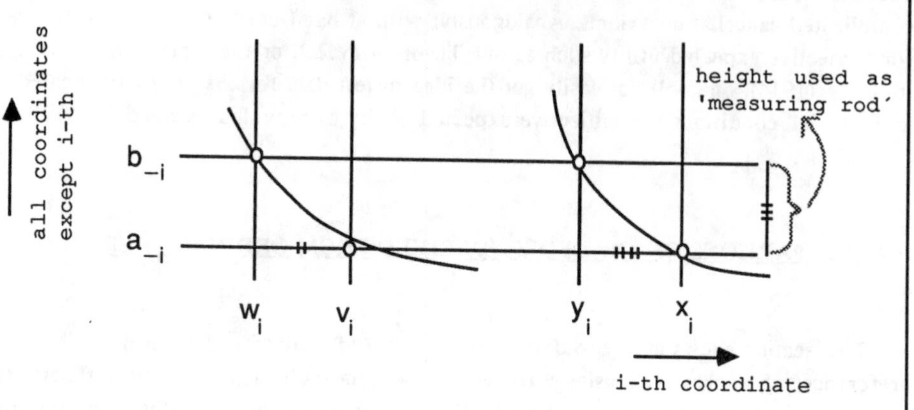

FIGURE II.4.1 (Comparisons of tradeoffs). The height $[b_{-i};a_{-i}]$ is used as 'measuring rod' to establish the 'revealed comparison of tradeoffs' $x_iy_i \succ_i^{**} v_iw_i$. I.e., the 'difference' between x_i and y_i is at least as large as that between b_{-i} and a_{-i}, which is larger than that between v_i and w_i.

illustrate the meaning of the above condition, and of the following, analogous, definition. We use one asterisk less than above to indicate that $\succ_i^{**}$ need not be the asymmetric part of $\succcurlyeq_i^*$ as introduced below; we shall even see (e.g., in Example III.6.7) that $\succ_i^{**}$ itself does not have to be asymmetric. Compare also Definition II.4.4 below.

DEFINITION II.4.2. For the binary relation $\succcurlyeq$ on $\prod_{i\in I}\Gamma_i$ we write :

$x_iy_i \succcurlyeq_i^* v_iw_i$ if :

There exist alternatives a,b such that

$a_{-i}x_i \succcurlyeq b_{-i}y_i$ and

$a_{-i}v_i \preccurlyeq b_{-i}w_i$.

In Chapter VII we shall sometimes write $[x_i;y_i] \succcurlyeq_i^* [v_i;w_i]$ for $x_iy_i \succcurlyeq_i^* v_iw_i$.

The introduced relations $\succ_i^{**}$ and $\succcurlyeq_i^*$, 'directly revealed from $\succcurlyeq$', can be considered to be quarternary relations on Γ_i. Alternatively, they can be considered to be binary relations, on the set Γ_i^2, and that is what we shall do in the sequel. These binary relations $\succ_i^{**}$ and $\succcurlyeq_i^*$ do not have to satisfy conditions such as transitivity or completeness, even if $\succcurlyeq$ does satisfy these conditions. The study of specific conditions for $\succ_i^{**}$ and $\succcurlyeq_i^*$ is not our present purpose. We shall only use these binary relations on Γ_i^2 as tools to find useful conditions for the preference relation $\succcurlyeq$, and to obtain transparent formulations for these conditions. When studied for their own interest it may be natural to extend the 'directly revealed' comparisons of tradeoffs $\succ_i^{**}$ and $\succcurlyeq_i^{*}$ to 'indirectly revealed' comparisons of tradeoffs through the conditions of transitivity, 'reversibility' ($x_iy_i \succ_i^{**} s_it_i \Rightarrow t_is_i \succ_i^{**} y_ix_i$, same for $\succcurlyeq_i^{*}$), and 'concatenation' ($x_iy_i \succ_i^{**} s_it_i$ & $y_iz_i \succcurlyeq_i^{*} t_iv_i \Rightarrow x_iz_i \succ_i^{**} s_iv_i$)[rf14]. See also the Counterexample (3) in section VII.4. Note that reversibility has the natural implication that $x_iy_i \succ_i^{**} v_iw_i$ if there exist alternatives a and b such that [not $a_{-i}x_i \preccurlyeq b_{-i}y_i$] and [$a_{-i}v_i \preccurlyeq b_{-i}w_i$]. We might just as well have chosen this 'dual' definition instead of the one above, or taken both notions together. Then only minor details in formulations and proofs in the sequel would have to be adapted.

As an second illustration of the above definitions we give a reformulation of coordinate independence. CI holds if and only if, for no i, x_i, y_i, and alternatives a,b, simultaneously [$a_{-i}x_i \succcurlyeq b_{-i}x_i$] and [not $a_{-i}y_i \succcurlyeq b_{-i}y_i$]. So :

LEMMA II.4.3. *CI holds if and only if* :

$$x_ix_i \succ_i^{**} y_iy_i \text{ for no } x_i, y_i.$$

□

The binary relations $\succ_i^{**}$ and $\succcurlyeq_i^{*}$ will not always be useful, or in accordance with the interpretation of comparisons of tradeoffs as we gave above. Consider the following definition, describing a phenomenon which one will want to exclude when working with $\succ_i^{**}$ and $\succcurlyeq_i^{*}$:

DEFINITION II.4.4. We say that coordinate i <u>reveals contradictory tradeoffs (with respect to</u> $\succcurlyeq$) if there exist x_i, y_i, v_i, and w_i such that simultaneously

$$[x_iy_i \succ_i^{**} v_iw_i] \text{ and } [v_iw_i \succcurlyeq_i^{*} x_iy_i] . \quad (II.4.1)$$

Somewhat more accurate would be a terminology like 'contradictory orderings/ comparisons of tradeoffs' instead of 'contradictory tradeoffs'. We prefer the above terminology for its tractability. The following result gives a condition sufficient to guarantee that no coordinate reveals contradictory tradeoffs. It will be used in Chapter III, and further illustrates the above definitions.

LEMMA II.4.5. *Let there exists an additive representation* $V : z \mapsto \sum_{j=1}^{n} V_j(z_j)$ *for* $\succcurlyeq$. *Then* :

$$x_iy_i \succ_i^{**} v_iw_i \Rightarrow V_i(x_i) - V_i(y_i) > V_i(v_i) - V_i(w_i) , \quad (II.4.2)$$

$$x_iy_i \succcurlyeq_i^{*} v_iw_i \Rightarrow V_i(x_i) - V_i(y_i) \geq V_i(v_i) - V_i(w_i) . \quad (II.4.3)$$

Consequently, if there exists an additive representation for $\succcurlyeq$, *then no coordinate reveals contradictory tradeoffs.*

PROOF. Suppose that $x_iy_i \succ_i^{**} v_iw_i$. We derive (II.4.2). There exist alternatives a and b such that

$$[a_{-i}x_i \succcurlyeq b_{-i}y_i] \text{ and } [\text{not } a_{-i}v_i \succcurlyeq b_{-i}w_i] \, . \tag{II.4.4}$$

This implies that

$$\Sigma_{k\neq i}V_k(a_k) + V_i(x_i) \geq \Sigma_{k\neq i}V_k(b_k) + V_i(y_i)$$

and

$$\Sigma_{k\neq i}V_k(a_k) + V_i(v_i) < \Sigma_{k\neq i}V_k(b_k) + V_i(w_i) \, .$$

We rewrite these two inequalities as

$$V_i(x_i) - V_i(y_i) \geq \Sigma_{k\neq i}(V_k(b_k)-V_k(a_k))$$

and

$$V_i(v_i) - V_i(w_i) < \Sigma_{k\neq i}(V_k(b_k)-V_k(a_k)) \, ,$$

which implies

$$V_i(x_i) - V_i(y_i) > V_i(v_i) - V_i(w_i) \, .$$

(II.4.2) is established. (II.4.3) is derived analogously. (II.4.2) and (II.4.3) together imply that no coordinate can reveal contradictory tradeoffs.

□

Theorem III.6.6 will show that, for a (connected-topology-) continuous weak order, the condition that no coordinate reveals contradictory tradeoffs is not only necessary for additive representability, but also sufficient. This shows that the binary relations $\succ_i^{**}$ and $\succcurlyeq_i^{*}$ will primarily be of use for additively representable preference relations.

The further definitions of 'revealed tradeoffs' and 'revealed contradictory tradeoffs', to be introduced in following chapters, and built forth upon the above definitions, will be listed in Remark A3.2. A final comment on our use of the term tradeoff. Say n=2, $\Gamma_1=\Gamma_2=\mathbb{R}$, x=(2,3), y=(1,4), and $x \succ y$. Then in multiattribute utility theory the term tradeoff is used for the exchange of the 'gain' $[x_1;y_1]$ for the loss $[x_2;y_2]$, which may be called a (favourable) tradeoff. We use, differently, the term tradeoff for $[x_1;y_1]$, i.e., the simple receipt of x_1 instead of y_1, and we might call the tradeoff $[x_1;y_1]$ 'more favourable' than the tradeoff $[y_2;x_2]$. For simultaneous use, the version of multiattribute utility theory might be called 'tradeoff between coordinates'.

II.5. CONDITIONS RELATED TO COORDINATE INDEPENDENCE, AND HISTORY

A condition for preference relations, related to CI, was introduced in Sono(1945, 1961) and Leontief(1947a, 1947b) in terms of the derivatives of a (presupposed), representing function. See also Samuelson(1947, pp. 174–180). These formulations required the 'rate of substitution' between two coordinates to be independent of the other coordinates. Already Fleming(1952), for the context of welfare theory, formulated independence of equal subalternatives in terms of a (presupposed, representing) function, but without using derivatives. He did use derivatives in his proof. KLST mention Fisher(1927a, p. 175 ff) as an early place where the basic idea of CI can be recognized. At least the idea of 'weak separability' can be recognized there.

In Debreu(1960) CI was formulated in its present, more appealing, form, in terms of the preference relation, again without differentiability assumptions. Before, Savage(1954) had formulated the 'sure-thing principle' (a more or less informal principle, captured by his postulates P2 and P3) for decision making under uncertainty. The postulate P2, as formulated in section 2.7 there, is identical with the condition of independence of equal subalternatives, thus fully captures the idea of CI. Let us note here that the formulation of P2 in the end pages of Savage(1954), in the intended presence of postulate P1 ($\succcurlyeq$ is a weak order), is not correct, as was pointed out by Fishburn, and corrected in the second edition of 1972 of 'The Foundations of Statistics'. Already Samuelson(1952) recognized the relatedness of the independence conditions, commonly used in decision making under risk/uncertainty, with the independence conditions used in other fields.

The sure-thing principle can be seen to underlie the 'likelihood principle' in statistics. The likelihood principle says that the value of a statistical decision (e.g., to reject a null hypothesis), given observed values of random quantities, should be independent of what the statistician planned to decide, had the observed values of the random quantities been different. If this principle is accepted in statistics the consequences are rather devastating. 'Power' and 'size', and all statistical techniques based on these, then have to be discarded, and the classical statistical model does not give more support than the application of the formula of Bayes. The major part of a statistical decision is then shifted to the choice of 'prior probabilities' and 'loss functions', matters outside the (classical) statistical model, and for that reason often called 'subjective'. See Berger&Wolpert(1984) and Edwards(1972) for more information on the likelihood principle. The sure-thing principle can be considered the adaptation to decision making under uncertainty of the 'independence condition' as formulated by von Neumann&Morgenstern(1944) for the context of decision making under risk (where alternatives are lotteries). For a discussion of the appropriateness of the conditions of the sure-thing principle, and/or von Neumann&Morgenstern independence, see Samuelson (1952) and Machina(1982a). McClennen(1983) gives a classification of the usual arguments for the conditions, and opposes to each of them. Wakker(1988b), inspired by McClennen(1983), adds a nonaversion-of-information argument for the conditions.

Kahneman&Tversky(1979) describe the 'isolation effect' as follows: 'In order to simplify the choice between alternatives, people often disregard components (= coordinates) that the alternatives share, and focus on the components that distinguish them'. This can be taken as another description of CI.

Debreu, and some other authors, have used the term (preferential) independence for CI. A further usual term is (strong/strict) separability. Katzner uses the term additivity. For an extensive study of generalizations, and many economic applications of CI, see Blackorby,Primont&Russell(1978).

Gorman(1976, p. 212, 224) argues for the importance of conditions like CI in economic theory, as this enables us to partition a complex decision problem into a number of simpler subproblems, in the following way (where we shall consider consumer theory whit coordinates referring to commodities) :

> First the set I of all commodities is separated into subgroups of commodities, such as the subgroup of clothes, the subgroup of foods, etc.; next within each subgroup it is determined what is optimal there. Finally the optimal results within subgroups are aggregated into an 'overall' decision.

Analogously CI allows a consumer to determine how much money to spend on each subgroup of commodities, without yet having determined how the money will be spent within the subgroups, and to determine how to spend an amount of money within a subgroup of commodities without considering how money is spent within other subgroups of commodities. Also Van Praag(1975, section 4) describes this, and relates CI to the 'consistency' condition used in a theorem of Kolmogorov in probability theory to obtain a simultaneous distribution for a family of 'subdistributions' (see Feller,1966, Theorem IV.6.1). In fact CI is so strong that it allows the above procedures for every possible separation into subgroups.

Lazimy(1986) develops an algorithm to solve multiple criteria problems in which tradeoffs between coordinates are determined while the other coordinates are kept fixed. This again presupposes CI as underlying assumption.

One further context in which we met an analogue of CI is in the modeling of sequential decision situations by means of decision trees. A well-known principle here is 'backwards induction'. It states that an optimal solution can be obtained by first finding in several subtrees what is optimal there, and by next aggregating these optimal solutions in subtrees into an overall optimal solution. An elaboration of the relatedness of backwards induction with CI has been provided in Burks(1977, Chapter 5). The 'invariance axiom' there says that same decision sub-trees, occurring in different decision trees, should be treated identically. In the presence of the second axiom (trees with same normal forms should be treated identically) invariance is equivalent to the sure-thing principle, see page 277/278 there. LaValle&Wapman(1986) show a related thing for decision making under risk.

In bargaining game theory related conditions are 'consistency' as in Peters(1986) (see also Young,1987a,b for the division of money), or 'Multilateral Stability' as in Lensberg (1987). Loosely formulated, these conditions say the following. Suppose a group of people has to 'bargain' about which alternative to choose from a set of available alternatives. Suppose firstly a subgroup of these people is satisfied. Then the result of the bargaining between the remainder of the group should depend only on the alternatives still available to them, and should be independent of the level at which the subgroup has been satisfied. In Lensberg(1987) and Peters(1986) these conditions are used to characterize bargaining solutions, such as the Nash solution, which can be seen to maximize additive functions. Lensberg(1987) refers to many related conditions. For social choice and welfare theory the condition is discussed, under the name SE, by Deschamps&Gevers(1978).

CHAPTER III

ADDITIVE REPRESENTATIONS

III.1. INTRODUCTION

In this chapter we introduce topological structure, and use this to obtain additive representations under continuity assumptions. As before, the set of alternatives is a Cartesian product $\prod_{i \in I}\Gamma_i$. As always (with Chapter V excepted) I is the finite set {1,...,n}. Furthermore, we shall from now on assume that every Γ_i is a connected and separable topological space. A reader not interested in general topology may simply assume that Γ_i is a convex subset of a Euclidean space, e.g. Γ_i is $\mathbb{R}_+^{m_i}$, or $\mathbb{R}$. Then all topological assumptions in the sequel are satisfied, and can be ignored. $\prod_{i \in I}\Gamma_i$ will always be endowed with the product topology, hence is connected (see Kelley, 1955, Chapter 3, problem 0) and separable too. The condition of topological separability has been added only for simplicity of presentation. It can nearly always be omitted (see Remarks A3.1 and III.7.1). The crucial assumption is connectedness.

It suffices for connectedness that any alternative can be transformed into any other alternative by a process of gradual changes (a 'continuous' process). Then the set of alternatives satisfies 'arcwise connectedness', which is known to imply connectedness. A further way to gain intuition for the meaning of topological connectedness is through the observation that a topological space is connected if and only if every continuous function from it to $\mathbb{R}$ has an interval as image, so that this image has no 'holes'.

As before, in all the main results the preference relation $\succcurlyeq$ will be transitive. Furthermore $\succcurlyeq$ will from now on be continuous in our main results, either as explicit assumption, or as consequence of other assumptions, and $\succcurlyeq$ will be complete. The remainder of this section discusses the appropriateness of continuity and completeness.

In section I.1.3 we indicated that $\prod_{i \in I}\Gamma_i$ would sometimes contain hypothetical alternatives, not present in actual situations. In the set-up of Chapters I and II it was not harmful to let $\prod_{i \in I}\Gamma_i$ be 'too' large. We could always let the preference relation ignore the redundant part of $\prod_{i \in I}\Gamma_i$, by letting every alternative of the redundant part be incomparable to every other alternative, or be adding only those preferences with redundant alternatives involved that are necessary to maintain conditions such as monotonicity, reflexivity, transitivity. Since we, from now on, shall deal with complete preference relations, 'ignoring by incomparability' is no longer possible.

A consequence of our topological assumptions is that, if not all alternatives are equivalent, then $\prod_{i\in I}\Gamma_i$ must be uncountable. (This follows from the Remark III.3.8, combined with the fact that the set Y there is separable, if countable.) This fact, together with the above-mentioned implication of completeness by which 'ignoring' no longer is possible, shows a serious restriction of the set-up of this and following chapters, be it that this set-up is very customary in the literature.

Some people may object against completeness because they want the decision maker to have the right, for a pair of alternatives, simply not to choose between them. This is not the objection we have in mind. In our set-up the decision maker simply must make a choice in every actual decision situation. (An option 'choosing nothing', if available, is simply formalized as an alternative in our set-up). Our objection against completeness is that many choice situations are not actual, but hypothetical, and that it is unrealistic to suppose that the decision maker is confronted with very many, some unrealistic, choice situations. Still the theory, through the assumption of completeness, is built upon all such choice situations[rf1].

There is some redundancy in the assumptions of transitivity, completeness, and continuity with respect to a connected topology. Schmeidler(1971) shows that transitivity of $\succcurlyeq$, and continuity (defined appropriately for noncomplete binary relations) with respect to a connected topology *imply* completeness or symmetry of $\succcurlyeq$. Sonnenschein (1965) gives conditions under which completeness and continuity imply transitivity. Also the theorems in this chapter indicate the restrictiveness of completeness and continuity; Theorem III.4.1, in particular for three or more essential coordinates, is usually conceived as a surprisingly strong result.

Instead of our topological approach KLST use an 'algebraic' approach. In this book we have chosen the topological approach because it is more known, hence more easily accessible[rf2].

III.2. ORDINAL AND CARDINAL REPRESENTATIONS

Usually we shall not only be interested in the *existence* of a(n array of) function(s) having certain properties, (such as being representing, continuous, additive, or whatever a context requires), but we shall also be interested in uniqueness results, i.e., in finding the entire class of functions having the involved properties. We use the following terminologies. A function V is **ordinal (with respect to** some properties) [respectively **continuously ordinal (with respect to** some properties)] if the class of all functions having these properties consists of all strictly increasing [respectively continuous strictly increasing] transformations of V. The function V is **cardinal (with respect to** some properties) if the class of all functions having these properties consists of all positive affine transformations of V. Obviously such transformations are continuous and strictly increasing. An array of functions $(V_j)_{j=1}^n$ is **jointly cardinal (with respect to** some properties) if the class of all arrays of functions $(W_j)_{j=1}^n$ having these properties, consists of those $(W_j)_{j=1}^n$, for which real τ_j, $j = 1,...,n$, and a positive σ exist such that $W_j = \tau_j + \sigma V_j$ for all j.

To give examples, we define $V : \mathbb{R}^2 \to \mathbb{R}$ by $V : (x_1,x_2) \mapsto x_1 + x_2$, and we let $\succcurlyeq$ on $\mathbb{R}^2$ be represented by V. In the examples we shall use theorems, given in the sequel; the reader should take these theorems for granted, and still understand the examples. V is ordinal with respect to the property of being representing, as is easily derived from the observation $V(x) \geq V(y) \Leftrightarrow x \succcurlyeq y \Leftrightarrow W(x) \geq W(y)$, for any representing function W. V is continuously ordinal with respect to the properties of being continuous and representing, as follows from Observation III.3.6′. V is cardinal with respect to the properties of being continuous, representing, and additive, as can easily be derived from Observation III.6.6′. Finally, with $V_1, V_2 : \mathbb{R} \to \mathbb{R}$ being identity, (V_1,V_2) is jointly cardinal with respect to the properties of being continuous and of being additive value functions, again by Observation III.6.6′.[rf3]

III.3. <u>CONTINUITY OF WEAK ORDERS</u>

The definition of continuity of binary relations has been given in section 0.2. The lemma below supplements Lemma II.2.7. Again we shall often say <u>by weak separability</u> when in fact we use this lemma.

LEMMA III.3.1. *Let $\succcurlyeq$ be a weakly separable continuous weak order. Then every $\succcurlyeq_i$ is a continuous weak order.*

PROOF. By Lemma II.2.7 every $\succcurlyeq_i$ is a weak order. Let z be an arbitrary fixed alternative. The set $\{x_i \in \Gamma_i : x_i \succcurlyeq_i y_i\} = \{x_i \in \Gamma_i : z_{-i}x_i \succcurlyeq z_{-i}y_i\} = \{x_i \in \Gamma_i : z_{-i}x_i \in C\}$, with C the closed set $\{w \in \prod_{j\in I}\Gamma_j : w \succcurlyeq z_{-i}y_i\}$. By Lemma 0.2.1 the set $\{x_i \in \Gamma_i : x_i \succcurlyeq_i y_i\}$ must be closed. Analogously the set $\{x_i \in \Gamma_i : x_i \preccurlyeq_i y_i\}$ is closed. Continuity of $\succcurlyeq_i$ follows. □

Next we make explicit the topological assumption that we shall mostly use in the sequel. The requirement of topological separability in fact is needed only for the case of exactly one essential coordinate (see Remarks A3.1 and III.7.1)[rf4].

ASSUMPTION III.3.2 (<u>Topological Assumption</u>). Every set Γ_j is a connected separable topological space, e.g. $\mathbb{R}_+^m$, or $\mathbb{R}$. The Cartesian product $\prod_{i\in I}\Gamma_i$ is endowed with the product topology.

The main consequence of our continuity assumptions will be 'restricted solvability'. We say $\succcurlyeq$ satisfies **restricted solvability** if, for every $x_{-i}a_i \succcurlyeq y \succcurlyeq x_{-i}c_i$, there exists b_i such that $x_{-i}b_i \approx y$. Absence of such a b_i may be interpreted as a 'hole' in Γ_i, which by connectedness should be precluded.

LEMMA III.3.3. *Suppose the topological assumption III.3.2 holds. Let* $\succcurlyeq$ *be a continuous weak order. Then* $\succcurlyeq$ *satisfies restricted solvability.*

PROOF. Let $x_{-i}a_i \succcurlyeq y \succcurlyeq x_{-i}c_i$. Let $G := \{v_i \in \Gamma_i : x_{-i}v_i \succcurlyeq y\}$, and $H := \{w_i \in \Gamma_i : x_{-i}w_i \preccurlyeq y\}$. Then $a_i \in G$ and $c_i \in H$, so G and H are nonempty. By Lemma 0.2.1 G and H are closed. Their union is Γ_i. By connectedness of Γ_i, $G \cap H \neq \emptyset$. Take $z \in G \cap H$.

□

REMARK III.3.4. The only implication of continuity of $\succcurlyeq$ used in the proof above is **sectional continuity**. It requires closedness of all **sections**, i.e., sets of the form $\{a_i : x_{-i}a_i \succcurlyeq y\}$ or $\{c_i : x_{-i}c_i \preccurlyeq y\}$, and is derived from continuity by application of Lemma 0.2.1. It implies continuity of every $\succcurlyeq_i$, but is stronger than that; the lexicographic order on $\mathbb{R}^2$ ($(x_1,x_2) \succcurlyeq (y_1,y_2)$ if $x_1 > y_1$ or $x_1 = y_1$ and $x_2 \geq y_2$) has every $\succcurlyeq_i$ ($= \geq$) continuous, but the section $\{a_1 : (a_1,-1) \succcurlyeq (0,0)\} = \mathbb{R}_{++}$ is not closed.

The following lemma will be needed for topological details in many proofs in the sequel. It further reflects the idea that connectedness guarantees the absence of 'holes'. The first statement will mostly be applied to $\succcurlyeq_i$ instead of $\succcurlyeq$.

LEMMA III.3.5. *Suppose the topological assumption III.3.2 holds. Let* $\succcurlyeq$ *be a continuous weak order. Then :*

If $x \succ z$, *then there exists a* y *such that* $x \succ y \succ z$.

Now let $\succcurlyeq$ *further be weakly separable. Then :*

If $x_{-i}v_i \succ y$, *and* $z_i \prec_i v_i$, *then there exists a* w_i *such that* $z_i \prec_i w_i \prec_i v_i$ *and* $x_{-i}w_i \succ y$.

If $x_{-i}v_i \prec y$, *and* $z_i \succ_i v_i$, *then there exists a* w_i *such that* $z_i \succ_i w_i \succ_i v_i$ *and* $x_{-i}w_i \prec y$.

PROOF. For the first statement we take y from $\{s : s \prec x\} \cap \{s : s \succ z\}$, which by connectedness and continuity is nonempty.

For the second statement we take w_i from

$$[\{s_i : x_{-i}s_i \succ y\} \cap \{s_i : s_i \succ_i z_i\}] \;\cap\; [\{s_i : s_i \prec_i v_i\}] ,$$

where nonemptiness of this set remains to be derived. By continuity of $\succcurlyeq$ and Lemma 0.2.1 the first set between braces is open. By Lemma III.3.1 the second and third set between braces are open. So the two sets between [...] square brackets are open. They are nonempty, the first containing v_i, the second z_i. Their union is Γ_i, since by weak separability any $s_i \succcurlyeq_i v_i$ is contained in the first and second set between braces. Nonemptiness follows from connectedness.

The third statement is analogous.

□

If we apply the last two results of the above lemma, then we shall often say that 'we choose w_i between v_i and z_i **close enough to** v_i', or '**so close to** v_i **that** ...'. The following well-known result of Debreu(1954, 1964) will be used throughout the sequel to deal with the case of exactly one essential coordinate. This in fact is the case where the Cartesian product structure is of no interest. This case is somewhat outside the main interest of this monograph; hence no proof will be given[rf5].

THEOREM III.3.6. *Let Y be a connected separable topological space. For a binary relation $\succcurlyeq'$ on Y the following two statements are equivalent* :

(i) **There exists a continuous representing function $\varphi : Y \to \mathbb{R}$.**

(ii) **The binary relation $\succcurlyeq'$ is a continuous weak order.**

OBSERVATION III.3.6′ (Uniqueness result for Theorem III.3.6). *The function φ in (i) above is continuously ordinal.*

□

For the sake of easy reference we write out the following corollary of the above theorem.

COROLLARY III.3.7. *Suppose the topological assumption III.3.2 holds. Let at most one coordinate be essential. For the binary relation $\succcurlyeq$ on $\prod_{i\in I}\Gamma_i$ the following two statements are equivalent* :

(i) **There exist continuous additive value functions $(V_j)_{j=1}^{n}$ for $\succcurlyeq$.**

(ii) **The binary relation $\succcurlyeq$ is a continuous weak order.**

Furthermore, the V_j's in (i) are continuously ordinal, and $\succcurlyeq$ in (ii) is CI.

PROOF SKETCH. Note that inessential coordinates j do not affect the preferences. To them constant additive value functions V_j can, and must, be assigned, e.g. V_j constant zero. If no coordinates are essential then everything of the Lemma follows. If one coordinate is essential, then the inessential coordinates, not affecting preferences, may as well be suppressed. Then the corollary, apart from the statement about CI, straightforwardly reduces to Theorem III.3.6 and Observation III.3.6′. That $\succcurlyeq$ in (ii) satisfies CI follows from (i), and the observation that

$$x_{-i}\alpha \succcurlyeq y_{-i}\alpha \iff \sum_{j\neq i}V_j(x_j) \geq \sum_{j\neq i}V_j(y_j) \iff x_{-i}\beta \succcurlyeq y_{-i}\beta.$$

□

REMARK III.3.8. Suppose that the binary relation $\succcurlyeq$ in Theorem III.3.6 is nontrivial, so that the representing function is not constant. Then the image of this function, being connected, must be a nondegenerate interval. Its domain must be uncountable.

III.4. THE CENTRAL THEOREM ON ADDITIVE REPRESENTATIONS

In this section we present the 'central theorem' of additive representations. The proof of the central theorem will be given in section III.5. In section III.6 (and section III.7) reformulations and variations of the theorem will be given.

III.4.1. RELATED WORKS AND MOTIVATION

The literature provides many excellent derivations of additive representations (see section III.8). Hence a motivation for the derivation in this book is in order. Some derivations, such as in Keeney&Raiffa(1976), or French(1986, Chapter 4), are easily accessible and appealing, but do not elaborate details (mainly topological details). Or derivations require a study of results from advanced mathematical theories, such as web theory in Debreu(1960), functional equations in Katzner(1970) and Blackorby,Primont& Russell(1978, elaborating Gorman,1968), group theory in KLST and Fuhrken&Richter (1988), or the theory of mean groupoids as in Vind(1986a). Somewhere in between are the derivations in Koopmans(1972) and Fishburn(1970). The latter two give a good impression of the ideas of additive representations, and of the way to make the proofs rigid, but do not elaborate many (topological) details, and make some simplifying structural assumptions[rf6]. It is our experience that there is need for a self-contained, and fully elaborated proof, which is easily accessible to readers without high-level mathematical training. Providing such a proof has been our aim. We shall preserve full mathematical rigidity. Details will be omitted only for being straightforward, never for being tedious.

We have striven for generality, so that specific results needed in particular applications are most easily available. An advantage of generality in proofs is that generality guarantees exclusion of roundabout operations dealing with irrelevant structures[rf7].

There is one aspect in which the proof for the case of exactly two essential coordinates differs from the case of three or more essential coordinates (Steps 3.1 and 3.2 in section III.5). This has usually led to a separated treatment of these two cases in the literature. It is our experience that this repels readers. Hence we have chosen one simultaneous proof for both cases. Only when we arrive at the aspect where the two cases differ (at Steps 3.1 and 3.2), we will temporarily separate the two cases. Then, once this aspect has been taken care of for each case separately, we will again continue the proof in a unified way. Thus we simultaneously show the unity in additive representations, and enable a reader only interested in one of the two cases not to bother about the other case. Leaving out of consideration the approaches which use functional equations and hence are rather different from our approach, we are not aware of a place in the literature where the case of three or more essential coordinates is treated like we do in Step 3.2; i.e., fully independent from the case of two essential coordinates. In the literature the case of three or more essential coordinates is always based on the two-coordinate case, mainly by *deriving* from CI the 'hexagon condition' (defined below), or a related condition. The direct derivation for the case of three or more coordinates as in Step 3.2 is, in our view, more efficient, and simpler than the very derivation of the hexagon (or a related) condition from CI.

A further motivation for our approach, with the construction of the grid as mainly in Stage 2, is that this approach gives a good impression of the way to construct an additive representation from actual data, or the way to construct it in a session where an analyst is consulted by a practical decision maker[rf8].

The price to pay for our approach is the large number of pages needed to lay it down. This should not mean that the time and effort, needed for the reader to get access to the proof presented here, should be large. To the contrary, besides mathematical rigidity and generality, minimization of time and effort for the reader has been our prime aim. Further, our presentation of the derivation, spitting it up in many stages and steps, should make it easy for the reader to skip details outside his interest, and thus to quickly see the structure of the derivation and its main ideas. A reader interested in getting an impression of the intuitive aspects of the derivation, without interest in details[rf9], may consult the sketch of the proof given in the next subsection, or proceed as follows. First he consults the proof, without the elaborations, from Step 1.1 to Step 2.2. This will take about 2/3 page of reading. Next, if he wants to know more about the construction of the additive representation, he may consult the first two paragraphs of the comment of Stage 5, the comment of Step 6.1, and formula (III.5.5). This will take about 1/3 page of reading. If he wants to know more about the role of the CI and the hexagon conditions he may consult Stage 3 and its comment, at his choice either Step 3.1, its comment, and the elaboration of the case $z_1 > 0$ and $z_2 > 0$, or Step 3.2, its comment, and Case 3.2.1. Either choice takes about 2/3 page of reading. The work in Stage 3 is the most important intuitive part of the proof. Outside this stage no other implication of CI (and the hexagon condition) than weak separability has been used.

III.4.2. THE HEXAGON CONDITION AND THE THEOREM

One condition, not yet defined, will be needed for the central theorem; see Figure III.4.1. For $n = 2$ we say that $\succcurlyeq$ satisfies the **hexagon condition** if, for all x_1, y_1, v_1, a_2, b_2, c_2 we have :

$$\left[\begin{array}{l}(y_1,a_2) \approx (x_1,b_2) \;\;\&\;\; (v_1,a_2) \approx (y_1,b_2) \;\;\& \\ (y_1,b_2) \approx (x_1,c_2)\end{array}\right]$$

$$\Rightarrow \qquad [(v_1,b_2) \approx (y_1,c_2)] \,.$$

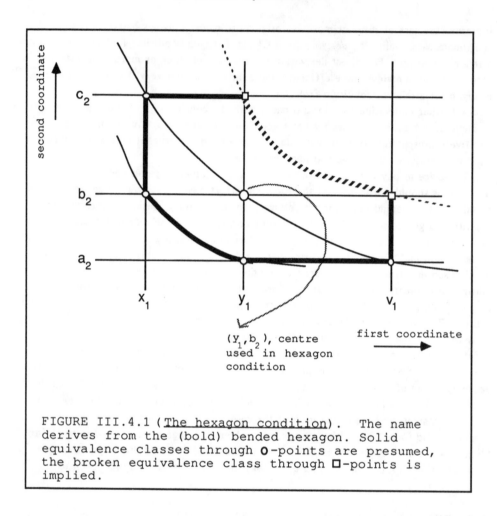

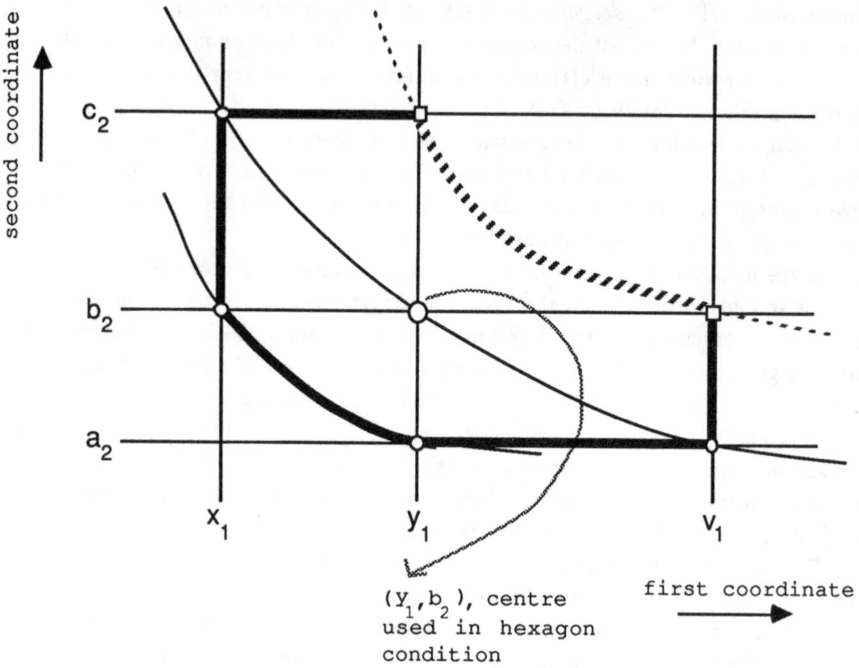

FIGURE III.4.1 (The hexagon condition). The name derives from the (bold) bended hexagon. Solid equivalence classes through o-points are presumed, the broken equivalence class through □-points is implied.

Symmetry of coordinates 1 and 2 in the condition follows by interchanging the second and third equivalence in the condition. We think the best way to justify (or criticize) the hexagon condition is analogous to the justification of the stronger condition of triple cancellation (see section III.6, in particular Lemmas III.6.1 and III.6.2), through the non-revelation of contradictory tradeoffs, see Lemma III.6.4. Also the derivation of the proof of Lemma III.6.3 (left to the reader) will be clarifying. If $n \neq 2$, but there are exactly two essential coordinates, then we say that $\succcurlyeq$ satisfies the **hexagon condition** if the hexagon condition is satisfied after deletion of the inessential coordinates. As a preparation for Step 3.1 in the proof of the following theorem let us comment some more on the hexagon condition. When we derive an equivalence as the fourth above from the other three equivalences, we sometimes say: '**The equivalence** $(v_1,b_2) \approx (y_1,c_2)$ **follows from** the

hexagon condition with centre (y_1,b_2)'. The case where $x_1 \prec_1 y_1 \prec_1 v_1$ and $a_2 \prec_2 b_2 \prec_2 c_2$ (as chosen in Figure III.4.1; see also Figure III.5.3.b) will sometimes be called the North-East hexagon condition. The case where $x_1 \succ_1 y_1 \succ_1 v_1$ and $a_2 \succ_2 b_2 \succ_2 c_2$, is sometimes called the **South-West hexagon condition**, see Figure III.5.3.c (then interchange notations x and v and a and c). Also we shall use in Step 3.1 in the proof below a 'South-East' and 'North-West' version of the hexagon condition. These two versions in general do not have to be implied by the hexagon condition, but under the conditions as holding in the proof below can be derived from the hexagon condition.

THEOREM III.4.1. (Central theorem for additive representations). *Suppose the topological assumption III.3.2 holds. Let at least two coordinates be essential. Let $\succcurlyeq$ be a continuous CI weak order on $\prod_{i \in I}\Gamma_i$, satisfying the hexagon condition if exactly two coordinates are essential. Then there exist jointly cardinal continuous additive value functions $(V_j)_{j=1}^n$ for $\succcurlyeq$.*

SKETCH OF PROOF THROUGH FIGURES OF THE NEXT SECTION (say $\Gamma = \mathbb{R}$, and $\succcurlyeq$ is monotonic). (An elaborated proof will be given in the next section.) Figure III.5.1 suggests how, after an arbitrary choice of w^0 and $w_1^1 \succ_1 w_1^0$, the coordinates can be found for which the additive value functions are integer-valued; these coordinates constitute a 'grid'. Then, for the case of two dimensions, Figure III.5.2 shows how 'tradeoffs' between different coordinates are so that on the grid indeed the functions $(V_j)_{j=1}^n$ are additive value functions. Figure III.5.5 suggests the same for three (or more) dimensions. Figure III.5.6.b shows a point $w_1^{1/2}$ by means of which the density of the grid can be doubled, to include all coordinates with value z/2 (z an integer) for the involved additive value function. An infinite repetition of this doubling will give a dense grid, containing all coordinates with a binary value for the involved additive value function. Limit-taking will then give an additive representation on the entire space. □

III.5. PROOF OF THE CENTRAL THEOREM

Above Definition II.2.5 we pointed out that weak separability is implied by CI. In the sequel we shall refer to weak separability instead of CI whenever we use no more implications of CI than weak separability.

STAGE 1. THREE SIMPLIFYING ASSUMPTIONS

A reader looking for least-time-consuming access to this proof may skip Steps 1.2 and 1.3 below. The adaptation of the proof to the case without these assumptions (if not taken for granted) is trivial and immediately obvious, and will take less time than the study of the elaborations (presented somewhat concisely) of these assumptions. (Mainly will the choice of the coordinates w^{z}_{j} in the construction of the grid in Step 2.2 no more be unique; then one simply chooses any coordinate satisfying the required equivalences.) One reason for us to add the assumptions of Steps 1.2 and 1.3 is that their derivation has its own interest, related assumptions often being made in the literature. The second reason is that, after establishment of these assumptions, the remainder of the proof can be interpreted to be the embedding of $\prod_{i\in\{1,\ldots,n\}}\Gamma_i$ in $\mathbb{R}^n$; this to us is an appealing interpretation; it will be useful for readers interested only in the gist of the proof.

Step 1.1. **We may assume that all coordinates are essential.**

Elaboration. Inessential coordinates j, by Lemma II.2.1, do not affect the preference relation. For them the function V_j must be constant. We can set $V_j \equiv 0$ for such coordinates, and ignore them in the sequel.

Step 1.2. **We may assume that the topology on every Γ_i is the order topology of $\succcurlyeq_i$.**

Comment. Thus the $\approx_i$-equivalence classes 'topologically are single points'.

Elaboration. We replace the topologies on the Γ_i's by the order topologies with respect to the $\succcurlyeq_i$'s.

By Lemma III.3.1 these are coarser than the original topologies, hence are connected and separable too.

Continuity of $\succcurlyeq$ with respect to the 'new' product topology is not trivial, but is not needed either. (It can be obtained as a corollary of Theorem III.4.1.) The only implication of continuity of $\succcurlyeq$ with respect to the product topology that we need in the proof (and in the proof of Lemmas III.3.1, III.3.3 and III.3.5) is sectional continuity. We derive closedness of the section $\{s_i : x_{-i}s_i \succcurlyeq y\}$. Closedness is direct if the section equals $\varnothing$ or Γ_i, so suppose it does not. Then there are v_i and w_i such that $x_{-i}v_i \succcurlyeq y \succ x_{-i}w_i$, and by restricted solvability there is t_i with $x_{-i}t_i \approx y$. By weak separability the section equals the set $\{s_i : s_i \succcurlyeq_i t_i\}$. This indeed is closed with respect to the order topology of $\succcurlyeq_i$. Analogously $\{s_i : x_{-i}s_i \preccurlyeq y\}$ is closed.

The proof as given below will then give the additive value functions, continuous with respect to the order topologies, so a fortiori continuous with respect to the stronger original topologies.

Step 1.3. **We may assume that every $\succcurlyeq_i$ is antisymmetric.**

Comment. Antisymmetry means that $x_i \approx_i y_i$ only if $x_i = y_i$. So we completely 'treat the $\approx_i$-equivalence classes as single points'.

Elaboration. We replace every set Γ_i of coordinates x_i by the set Γ_i' of equivalence classes $x_i' = \{v_i \in \Gamma_i : v_i \approx_i x_i\}$.

By repeated application of Lemma II.2.7, [$x_i \approx_i y_i$ for all i] implies [$x \approx y$]. Hence we can define $\succcurlyeq'$ on $\prod_{i\in I}\Gamma_i'$ by

$(x_1',...,x_n') \succcurlyeq' (y_1',...,y_n')$ iff $(x_1,...,x_n) \succcurlyeq (y_1,...,y_n)$,

the particular choice of x_i, y_i from x_i' respectively y_i' being immaterial.

Like $\succcurlyeq$, $\succcurlyeq'$ can be seen to be a CI weak order, it preserves essentiality of coordinates, and, if there are exactly two essential coordinates, then $\succcurlyeq'$ satisfies the hexagon condition.

Further the order topologies of the $\succcurlyeq_i'$'s are connected since an open and closed nonempty nontrivial subset E_i' of Γ_i' would correspond with the open and closed nonempty nontrivial subset E_i of Γ_i, consisting of the union of all $\approx_i$-equivalence classes contained in E_i'. Separability of the order topologies is straightforward (and according to Remark III.7.1 in the sequel is not needed). Sections remain closed.

So the remainder of the proof can be carried out for $\succcurlyeq'$, giving additive value functions $(V_j')_{j=1}^n$ for $\succcurlyeq'$, continuous with respect to the order topologies with respect to the $\succcurlyeq_j'$'s. Defining $V_j : x_j \mapsto V_j'(x_j')$ then gives additive value functions for $\succcurlyeq$, continuous since e.g. $\{x_j : V_j(x_j) < \alpha\}$ is the union of the $\approx_j$-equivalence classes x_j''s contained in the open set $\{x_j' \in \Gamma_j' : V_j'(x_j') < \alpha\}$, hence is open too.

In the sequel we shall often use antisymmetry without explicit mention.

STAGE 2. CONSTRUCTING A GRID WITH 'CENTRE' w^0, AND 'MESH' $[w_1^1;w_1^0]$

Comment. For the actual construction of additive representations this is the main stage. We construct a grid of points 'at equal distance'. (I.e., in terms of tradeoffs, the tradeoff of one 'initial' point for, say, its left neigbour is equally large at each 'initial' point.)

Step 2.1. The centre and the mesh.

Comment. We take a starting point w^0, the 'centre' of the grid ($V_j(w_j^0) = 0$ will be set in the sequel for all j), and a $w_1^1 \succ_1 w_1^0$, where the 'mesh' $[w_1^1;w_1^0]$ will determine the distance between neighbouring points of the grid; it is the unit of measurement. (We shall set $V_1(w_1^1) = 1$.) The mesh is taken so small that for every $j \neq 1$ there is a w_j^1 such that $w^0{}_{-j}w_j^1 \approx w^0{}_{-1}w_1^1$.

Elaboration. By essentiality we can take w_j^0, v_j^1 for every j such that $v_j^1 \succ_j w_j^0$. Let i be such that $w^0{}_{-i}v_i^1 \preccurlyeq w^0{}_{-j}v_j^1$ for all j. We set $w_i^1 := v_i^1$, and by restricted solvability we can for all j take w_j^1 such that $w^0{}_{-j}w_j^1 \approx w^0{}_{-i}w_i^1$.

CONVENTION FOR NOTATION. In the sequel we shall often leave out from notation coordinates which are identical to those from w^0; thus we may write (v_i^1,v_j^2) for $(w^0{}_{-i,j}v_i^1,v_j^2)$, or (w_1^z,w_2^0) for $(w^0{}_{-1,2}w_1^z,w_2^0)$.

Step 2.2. Construction of the grid.

Comment. We use the equivalence (III.5.1) below (so the mesh $[w_1^1;w_1^0]$ as 'measuring rod') to define points $w_j^{z_j}$ for all $j \neq 1$ and positive and negative z_j's. (III.5.2) will treat

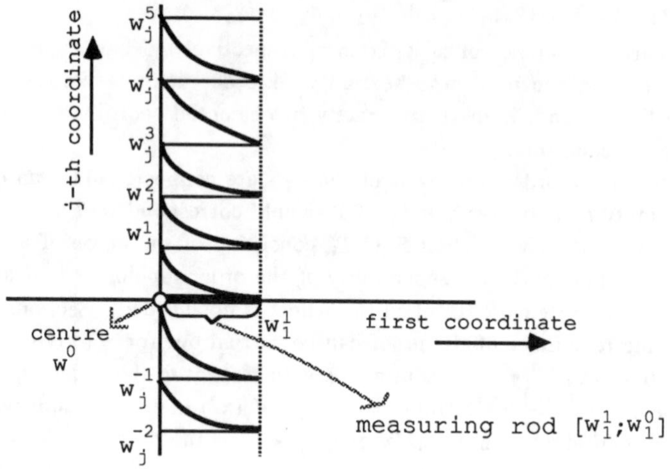

FIGURE III.5.1.a (Construction of j-th coordinates of grid-points, for $j \neq 1$). Curves indicate equivalence classes. We use $[w_1^1;w_1^0]$ as 'measuring rod' to peg out the coordinates w_j^z. After setting $V_1(w_1^0)=0$, $V_1(w_1^1)=1$, the construction will imply $V_j(w_j^z)=z$ for all z.

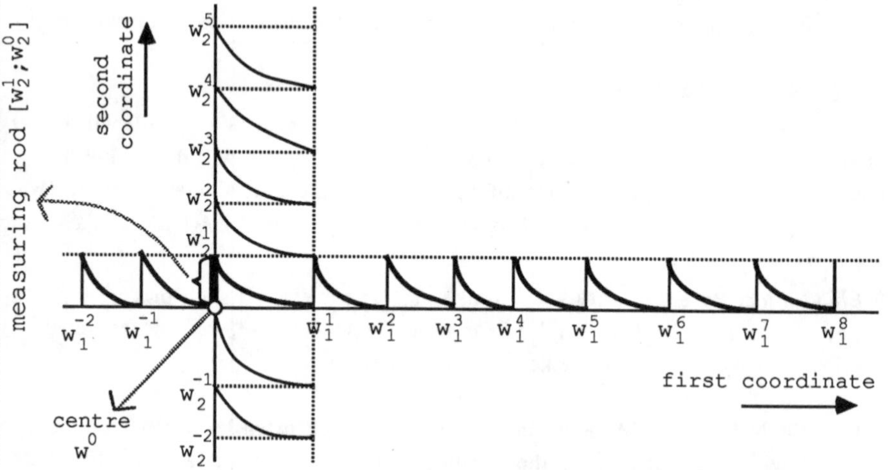

FIGURE III.5.1.b (Construction of first coordinates of grid-points). Curves indicate equivalence classes. Now $[w_2^1;w_2^0]$ is used as 'measuring rod' to peg out the coordinates w_1^z. From $V_2(w_2^0)=0$ and $V_2(w_2^1)=1$ it follows that $V_1(w_1^z)=z$ for all z.

coordinate 1 analogously.

Elaboration. For every $j = 2,...,n$ we define (see Figure III.5.1.a), by induction with respect to z,

$$w^z_j \text{ is such that } (w^0_1, w^z_j) \approx (w^1_1, w^{z-1}_j) \quad \text{(III.5.1)}$$

for positive natural z. (This will imply $V_j(w^z_j) = z$, as we shall see in the sequel.) Either this gives an infinite sequence, or there is a $z - 1 \in \mathbb{N}$ such that no w^z_j exists to satisfy (III.5.1). In the latter case, because of restricted solvability, no x_j can exist such that $(w^0_1, x_j) \succcurlyeq (w^1_1, w^{z-1}_j)$.

Also we use (III.5.1) for every j to define, inductively, w^{z-1}_j for *negative* integers $z - 1$. (Again $V_j(w^z_j) = z$ will be implied.) Again this either gives an infinite sequence, or it stops at a certain z, in which case by restricted solvability no x_j exists such that $(w^0_1, w^z_j) \succcurlyeq (w^1_1, x_j)$.

Completely analogously (see Figure III.5.1.b), we use the equivalences

$$(w^z_1, w^0_2) \approx (w^{z-1}_1, w^1_2) \quad \text{(III.5.2)}$$

to define points w^z_1 for positive and negative z. So for defining the w^z_1's on the first coordinate we have used as 'measuring rod' $[w^1_2; w^0_2]$. A set of alternatives of the form $(w^{z_1}_1, ..., w^{z_n}_n)$ as constructed above is called a grid with centre w^0, and mesh $[w^1_1, w^0_1]$.

STAGE 3. CHECKING THE GRID

Comment. For understanding of the intuitively most important conditions in the theorem (CI and the hexagon condition) this stage is the central one. The hexagon condition, and CI apart from its implication of weak separability, are used nowhere outside this stage.

This stage will show that the grid constructed above indeed gives the right way to derive the functions V_j; i.e., that **defining** :

$$V_j : w^{z_j}_j \mapsto z_j$$

gives additive value functions on the constructed grid. First we shall show that, for any $i \neq j$, and any alternative $w = (w^{z_1}_1, ..., w^{z_n}_n)$ in the grid,

$$(w_{-i,j} w^{z_i+1}_i, w^{z_j}_j) \approx (w_{-i,j} w^{z_i}_i, w^{z_j+1}_j) \quad \text{(III.5.3)}$$

whenever the involved alternatives exist. I.e., a 'tradeoff of size 1 between coordinates i and j' (V_i decreased by 1, V_j increased by one) does not lead to another equivalence class.

Step 3.1. (III.5.3) for the case of two (essential) coordinates (Can be skipped by readers interested only in the case of three or more (essential) coordinates.)

Comment. To show is $(w^{z_1+1}_1, w^{z_2}_2) \approx (w^{z_1}_1, w^{z_2+1}_2)$. This will essentially use the hexagon condition. The reader may figure out this step from Figures III.5.2 and III.5.3b without consultation of the elaboration below, for the most characteristic case $z_1 > 0$ and $z_2 > 0$.

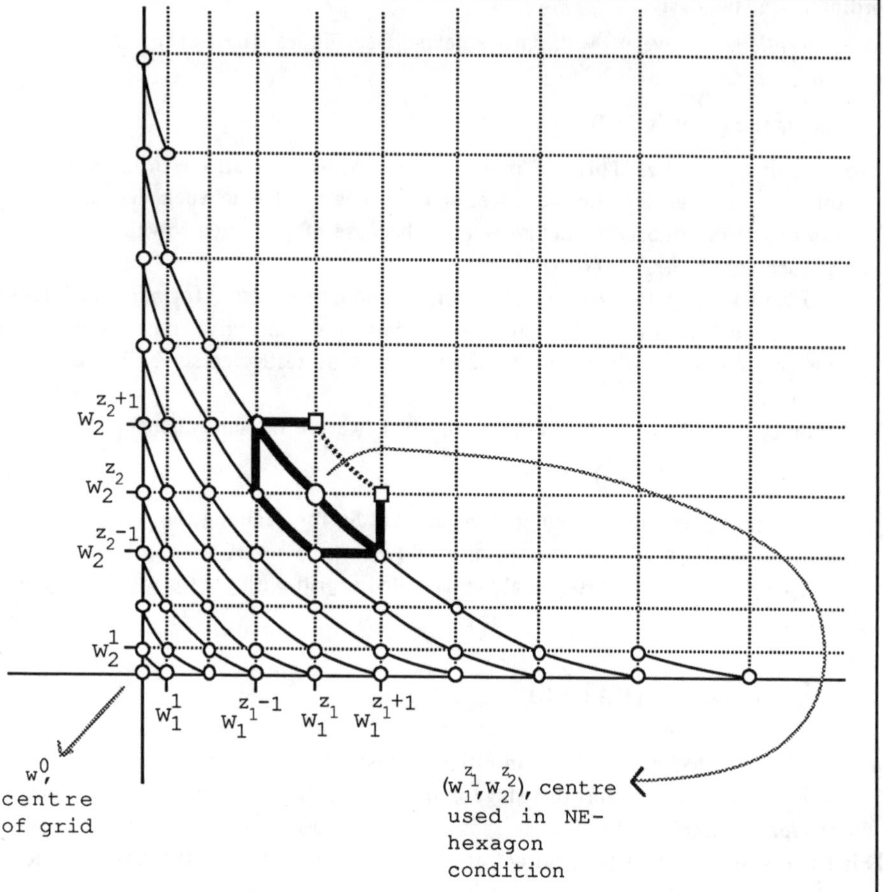

FIGURE III.5.2 (Step 3.1); the case $z_1>0$ and $z_2>0$. Curves indicate equivalence classes. The solid curves through O-points are presumed by the induction hypothesis, or follow from the definition of the grid-coordinates. The broken equivalence class through □-points is implied by the (NE-)hexagon condition.

Elaboration. If $z_1 = 0$ or $z_2 = 0$ then the equivalence follows from the very definition of the coordinates of the grid. Let us consider now the case where $z_1 > 0$ and $z_2 > 0$. Below the remaining cases will be dealt with in an analogous way. Induction Hypothesis(m): (III.5.3) (say i = 1, j = 2) holds true for all $z_1 \geq 0$,

$z_2 \geq 0$ with $z_1 + z_2 \leq m$. The induction hypothesis holds true for $m = 1$, as we saw before. Now suppose it proved for arbitrary $m > 0$. Then for $z_1 + z_2 = m + 1$, $z_1 > 0$ and $z_2 > 0$ ($z_1 = 0$ or $z_2 = 0$ has been established above) the equivalence follows from the 'North-East' hexagon condition with centre $(w^{z_1}_1, w^{z_2}_2)$.

Analogously for the case $z_1 < 0$ and $z_2 < 0$, the case $z_1 > 0$ and $z_2 < 0$, and the case $z_1 < 0$, $z_2 > 0$, (III.5.3) is proved by induction with respect to $|z_1| + |z_2|$, with respectively the South-West hexagon condition with centre $(w^{z_1+1}_1, w^{z_2+1}_2)$, the South-East hexagon condition with centre $(w^{z_1}_1, w^{z_2+1}_2)$, and the North-West hexagon condition with centre $(w^{z_1+1}_1, w^{z_2}_2)$, where the latter two still have to be defined and established. That will be done in the remainder of this step.

We shall define and derive the South-East version (see Figure III.5.3.d), the North-West version (see Figure III.5.3.a) being analogous; see Figure III.5.4.a. We suppose $x_1 \prec_1 y_1 \prec_1 v_1$ and $a_2 \prec_2 b_2 \prec_2 c_2$, $(x_1,c_2) \approx (y_1,b_2)$, $(x_1,b_2) \approx (y_1,a_2)$, $(y_1,c_2) \approx (v_1,b_2)$. The **South-West hexagon condition** requires that now $(y_1,b_2) \approx (v_1,a_2)$.

Let for contradiction $(y_1,b_2) \prec (v_1,a_2)$ (the analogous case $(y_1,b_2) \succ (v_1,a_2)$ will be considered below). Then by restricted solvability there exists a w_1 between y_1 and v_1 such that $(w_1,a_2) \approx (y_1,b_2)$. But then, by the North-East hexagon condition with (y_1,b_2) as centre, $(w_1,b_2) \approx (y_1,c_2)$, whereas by weak separability $(w_1,b_2) \prec (v_1,b_2)$. This gives contradiction.

Analogously, if $(y_1,b_2) \succ (v_1,a_2)$, then we will find an alternative 'above' (v_1,a_2) which is equivalent to (y_1,b_2). By the South-West hexagon condition we then find an alternative 'above' (y_1,a_2) equivalent to (x_1,b_2). By weak separability this contradicts $(x_1,b_2) \approx (y_1,a_2)$.

The South-East hexagon condition has been established.

Step 3.2. (III.5.3) for the case of three or more (essential) coordinates (Can be skipped by readers interested only in the case of two (essential) coordinates.)

Comment. This case is easier to deal with because, for tradeoffs between two coordinates, now a third coordinate is available to provide a measuring rod to serve as intermediary. The reader may, without consultation of the elaboration below, figure out formula (III.5.4) from Figure III.5.5 (see page 58), observing the intermediary role of $[w^1_1; w^0_1]$.

Elaboration. By CI, (III.5.3) for general z_k's follows from (III.5.3) for the special case where $z_k = 0$ for all $k \neq i$, $k \neq j$. So when deriving (III.5.3) in the sequel we shall assume that $z_k = 0$ for all $k \neq i$, $k \neq j$. For the cases below note that (III.5.3) is symmetric in i and j. Also note that in our measurement procedure coordinate 1 was given a special role, in providing a measuring rod for all other coordinates; coordinate 2 played a special role in providing the measuring rod for coordinate 1. This explains the splitting of cases below.

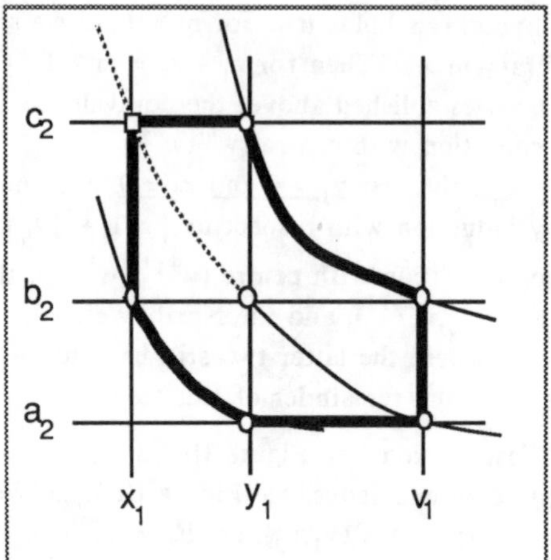

FIGURE III.5.3.a (<u>The North-West hexagon condition</u>).

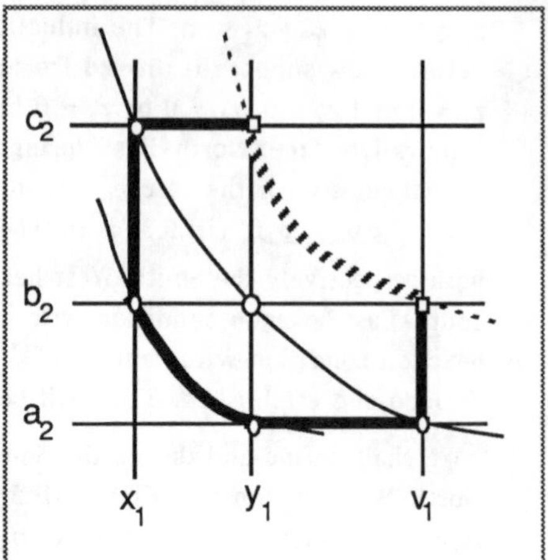

FIGURE III.5.3.b (<u>The North-East hexagon condition</u>).

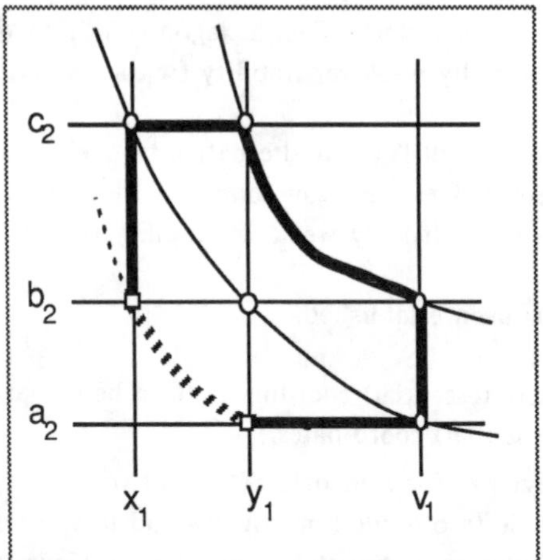

FIGURE III.5.3.c (<u>The South-West hexagon condition</u>).

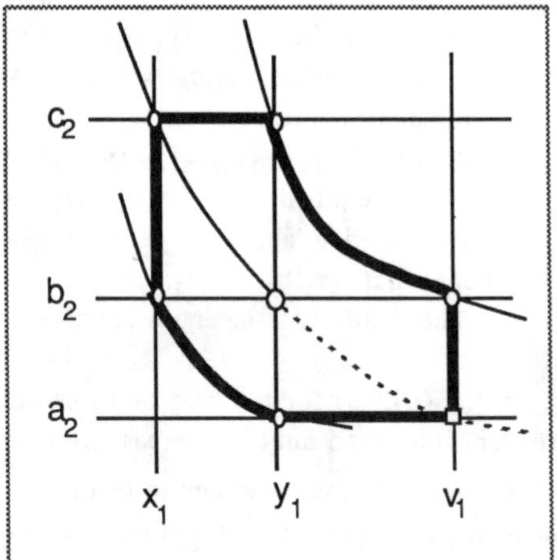

FIGURE III.5.3.d (<u>The South-East hexagon condition</u>).

FIGURE III.5.3 (<u>Four kinds of hexagon conditions</u>). Solid equivalence classes through o-points are presumed, the broken equivalence class through the □-point(s) is implied. In the text it is indicated that The North-East and South-West hexagon conditions are just special versions of the ('general') hexagon condition, whereas the other two conditions are different.

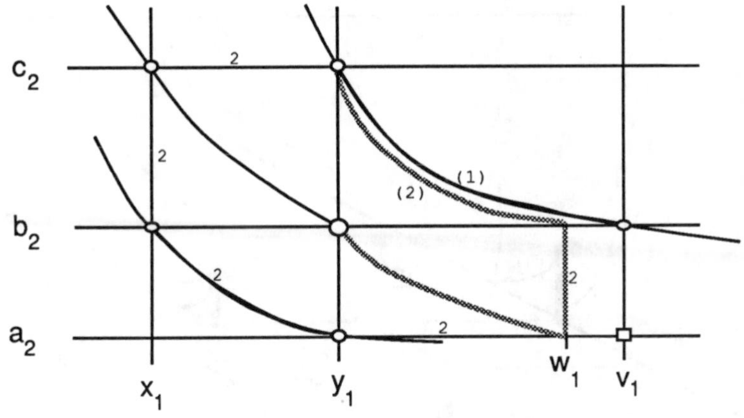

FIGURE III.5.4.a (<u>Deriving the South-East hexagon condition from the North-East hexagon condition</u>); a contradiction is suggested for the case where $(y_1, b_2) \prec (v_1, a_2)$. Then the grey equivalence class numbered (2), implied by the North-East hexagon condition (see the bended hexagon numbered 2) contradicts the given equivalence class numbered (1).

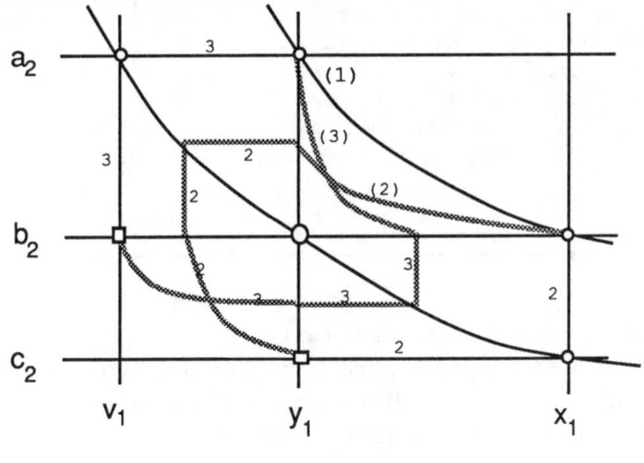

FIGURE III.5.4.b (<u>Deriving the South-West hexagon condition from the North-East hexagon condition</u>); a violation of the South-West hexagon condition leads to a contradiction. Either the equivalence class numbered (2) on the bended hexagon numbered 2, or the equivalence numbered (3) on the bended hexagon numbered 3, contradicts the given equivalence class numbered (1).

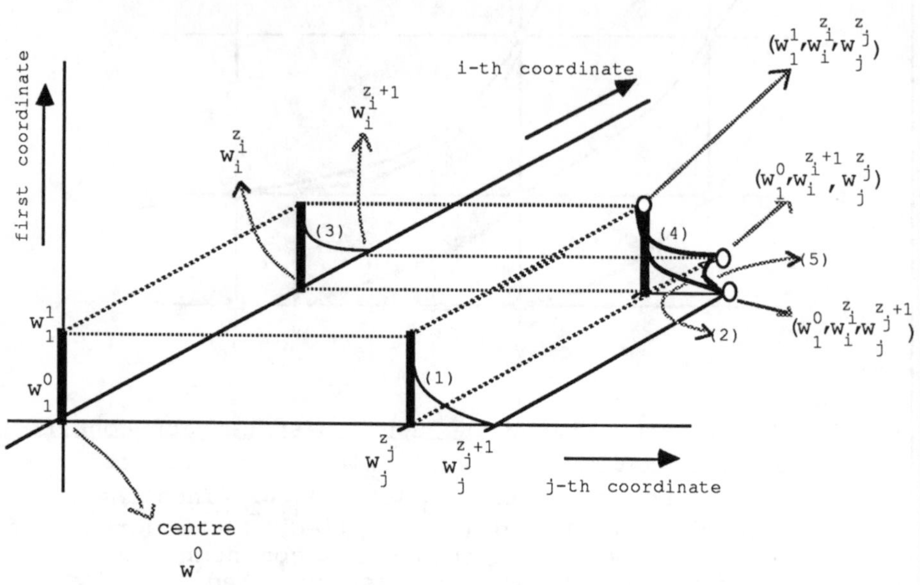

FIGURE III.5.5 (Step 3.2; establishing equivalence (5) in the figure). The equivalence (1) is by definition. The equivalence (2) follows from (1) by CI (compare Figure II.2.1). Analogously the equivalence (4) follows from (3). Finally, equivalence (5) follows from (2) and (4) by transitivity. One may say: the tradeoff between coordinates i and j of $[w_j^{z_j+1}; w_j^{z_j}]$ for $[w_i^{z_i+1}; w_i^{z_i}]$ has been carried out with $[w_1^1; w_1^0]$ as intermediary.

Case 3.2.1. (III.5.3) for the case where $i \neq 1$, $j \neq 1$.

Here we can use the 'measuring rod' $[w_1^1; w_1^0]$ on coordinate 1 as 'intermediary' for the tradeoff between coordinates i and j. Hence we denote coordinates 1, i, j, and suppress all other coordinates w_k^0. Now we have

$$(w_1^0, w^{z_i+1}_i, w^{z_j}_j) \approx (w_1^1, w^{z_i}_i, w^{z_j}_j) \approx (w_1^0, w^{z_i}_i, w^{z_j+1}_j)\ , \qquad \text{(III.5.4)}$$

the first equivalence for the special case $z_j = 0$ by definition, and for $z_j \neq 0$ from the case $z_j = 0$ by CI; the second equivalence for the special case $z_i = 0$ by definition, and for $z_i \neq 0$ from the case $z_i = 0$ by CI.

Case 3.2.2. (III.5.3) for the case where $i = 1$, $j \neq 2$.

Here we use the 'measuring rod' $[w_2^1; w_2^0]$ on coordinate 2 as intermediary for the tradeoff. We denote coordinates 1, 2, j, suppress all other coordinates. We have

$$(w^{z_1+1}_1, w_2^0, w^{z_j}_j) \approx (w^{z_1}_1, w_2^1, w^{z_j}_j) \approx (w^{z_1}_1, w_2^0, w^{z_j+1}_j)\ ,$$

the first equivalence for the special case $z_j = 0$ by definition, and for $z_j \neq 0$ from the case $z_j = 0$ by CI; the second equivalence from the case 3.2.1.

Case 3.2.3. (III.5.3) for the case i = 1, j = 2.

Here we use a 'measuring rod' $[w^1_k;w^0_k]$ for any $k \neq 1$, $k \neq 2$. We denote coordinates 1, 2, k, suppress other coordinates. We have

$$(w^{z_1+1}_1, w^{z_2}_2, w^0_k) \approx (w^{z_1}_1, w^{z_2}_2, w^1_k) \approx (w^{z_1}_1, w^{z_2+1}_2, w^0_k)\ ,$$

the first equivalence by case 3.2.2, the second equivalence by case 3.2.1.

<u>Step 3.3</u>. The grid is O.K.

Comment. We show that $(V_j)_{j=1}^n$ is an array of additive value functions on the grid.

Elaboration. If $\sum_{j=1}^n V_j(v_j) = \sum_{j=1}^n V_j(w_j)$ for two alternatives v,w of the grid, then we can, in the terminology below (III.5.3), say that w can be obtained from v through a number ($\sum_{j=1}^n | V_j(v_j) - V_j(w_j) | /2$ to be precise) of tradeoffs between coordinates, each of size 1; these tradeoffs by repeated application of (III.5.3) never leave the initial equivalence class of v. Obviously, increasing the sum of the additive value functions by one leads to a higher equivalence class, decreasing it by one to a lower equivalence class. Repeated application of this establishes this step.

STAGE 4. GENERAL GRIDS

Comment. Obviously, grids of points as above may by constructed for any v^0 and $v^1_1 \succ_1 v^0_1$ 'close enough to' v^0_1, with v^0 and v^1_1 in the role of w^0 and w^1_1. Step 4.2 presents a general observation. Analogues will be used in Step 6.3.

<u>Step 4.1</u>. The way to construct a general grid.

Elaboration. For any v^0 and $v^1_1 \succ_1 v^0_1$ 'close enough to' v^0_1 (close enough to guarantee, for all j, the existence of v^1_j such that $(v^0_{-1}, v^1_1) \approx (v^0_{-j}, v^1_j)$, we can construct a grid of alternatives of the form $(v^{z_1}_1, \ldots, v^{z_n}_n)$ with v^0 as centre, and $[v^1_1;v^0_1]$ as mesh, analogously as above. Note that any v^1_1 between w^0_1 and w^1_1 is 'close enough to' v^0_1 if $v^0_1 = w^0_1$. In Stage 5 we shall consider grids with higher 'density' than the grid constructed above.

<u>Step 4.2</u>. A general observation concerning grids.

Comment. Let $v^0 = w^0$. If $w^0_1 \prec_1 v^1_1 \prec_1 w^1_1$, then (mainly by weak separability, used without explicit mention) for any w^m_j also v^m_j exists, and $v^m_j \prec_j w^m_j$.

Elaboration. Say j = 1. We use induction. We fix all coordinates j > 2 at w^0_j, and suppress them. Say $w^{m-1}_1 \succ_1 v^{m-1}_1$, and w^m_1 exists. Now $(w^m_1, w^0_2) \approx (w^{m-1}_1, w^1_2) \succ (v^{m-1}_1, v^1_2)$, the latter since $v^1_2 \prec_2 w^1_2$. Hence (see below (III.5.1)) indeed v^m_1 exists, and $v^m_1 \prec_1 w^m_1$ follows straightforwardly.

STAGE 5. DOUBLING THE DENSITY OF THE GRID

Comment. First we shall show that the grid as introduced above can be refined into a grid of double density. This new grid is to include, for every j, the points (denoted $w_j^{z/2}$) in Γ_j with V_j-values z/2, also for z odd. Next, by infinite repetition of this doubling, we shall in Stage 6 obtain a 'dense grid'. The additive value functions can straightforwardly be extended to this 'dense grid'.

We shall double the density of the grid with centre w^0 and mesh $[w_1^1;w_1^0]$, by setting $v^0 := w^0$, and by using a mesh $[v_1^1;v_1^0]$ half as large as $[w_1^1;w_1^0]$. The latter is to be realized by taking v_1^1 so that $v_1^2 = w_1^1$.

Construction of such a v_1^1 (=: $w_1^{1/2}$) is the major problem, and will be established in Steps 5.1 to 5.5. It can be seen that in these steps continuity, with respect to the order-topology-of-$\succcurlyeq_1$, is demonstrated of the map assigning, for fixed w^0, v_1^2 to v_1^1 ($\succ_1 w_1^0$), on the set where this map is defined.

Step 5.1. Measuring rods smaller than half $[w_1^1;w_1^0]$ can be enlarged, still remaining smaller than half $[w_1^1;w_1^0]$ (see Figure III.5.6).

Comment. We shall denote first and second coordinates, suppress remaining coordinates w_k^0. Let v_1^1 be such that $w_1^0 \prec_1 v_1^1 \prec_1 w_1^1$, v_1^2 exists, and $v_1^2 \prec_1 w_1^1$, i.e., $(v_1^1,v_2^1) \prec (w_1^1,w_2^0)$. Then there is $x_1^1 \succ_1 v_1^1$ such that also x_1^2 exists, and $x_1^2 \prec_1 w_1^1$.

Elaboration. Since $(v_1^1,v_2^1) \prec (w_1^1,w_2^0)$, there is an $s_1 \succ_1 v_1^1$ so close to v_1^1 that $(s_1,v_2^1) \prec (w_1^1,w_2^0)$. And there is $s_2 \succ_2 v_2^1$ so close to v_2^1 that $(s_1,s_2) \prec (w_1^1,w_2^0)$.

For guaranteeing $(x_1^1,x_2^1) \prec (w_1^1,w_2^0)$ it suffices to guarantee $(x_1^1,x_2^1) \preccurlyeq (s_1,s_2)$, so it suffices to guarantee $[x_1^1 \preccurlyeq_1 s_1 \;\&\; x_2^1 \preccurlyeq_2 s_2]$. We shall have $(x_1^1,w_2^0) \approx (w_1^0,x_2^1) \preccurlyeq s'$ both for $s' = (s_1,w_2^0)$ and $s' = (w_1^0,s_2)$. This we get by defining $x_1^1 := s_1$ if $(s_1,w_2^0) \preccurlyeq (w_1^0,s_2)$; if $(w_1^0,s_2) \prec (s_1,w_2^0)$, then we first define $x_2^1 := s_2$, next x_1^1 such that $(x_1^1,w_2^0) \approx (w_1^0,x_2^1)$. In either case $[s_1 \succ_1 v_1^1$ and $s_2 \succ_2 v_2^1]$ implies $x_1^1 \succ_1 v_1^1$.

Finally, we have $(x_1^1,x_2^1) \prec (w_1^1,w_2^0)$, from which it follows that x_1^2 exists and that $x_1^2 \prec_1 w_1^1$.

Step 5.2. There exist measuring rods smaller than half $[w_1^1;w_1^0]$.

Elaboration. The comment together with the elaboration of the above step, with w_1^0 in the role of both v_1^1 and v_1^2, w_2^0 in the role of v_2^1, and the second sentence deleted, shows that there is an $x_1^1 \succ_1 w_1^0$ such that $x_1^2 \prec_1 w_1^1$.

Step 5.3. Measuring rods larger than half $[w_1^1;w_1^0]$ can be reduced, still remaining larger than half $[w_1^1;w_1^0]$.

Comment. Suppose that v_1^1 between w_1^0 and w_1^1 is such that either $v_1^2 \succ_1 w_1^1$, or v_1^2 does not exist. In other words, v_1^1 is such that $(v_1^1,v_2^1) \succ (w_1^1,w_2^0)$. Then there exists $x_1^1 \prec_1 v_1^1$ (and $x_1^1 \succ_1 w_1^0$) so close to v_1^1 that $(x_1^1,x_2^1) \succ (w_1^1,w_2^0)$, so that $x_1^2 \succ_1 w_1^1$ or x_1^2 does not exist.

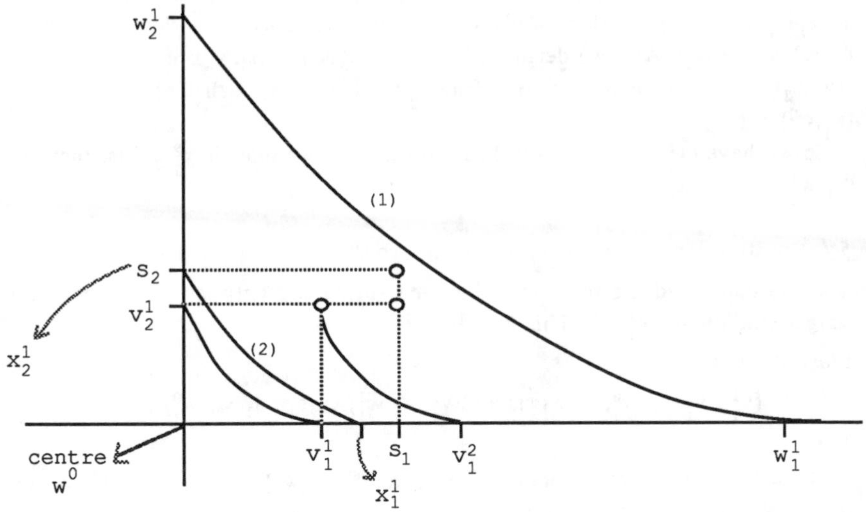

FIGURE III.5.6.a (Step 5.1). The measuring rod $[v_1^1;w_1^0]$ is smaller than 'half' $[w_1^1;w_1^0]$ (since $v_1^2 \prec_1 w_1^1$). First we choose s_1, next s_2, small enough to keep (s_1,s_2) below the equivalence class (1). Say $(w_1^0,s_2) \prec (s_1,w_2^0)$. Then we choose $x_2^1 = s_2$, and choose x_1^1 by the equivalence class (2). Now $x_1^1 \succ_1 v_1^1$, and still $[x_1^1;w_1^0]$ is smallerthan 'half' $[w_1^1;w_1^0]$.

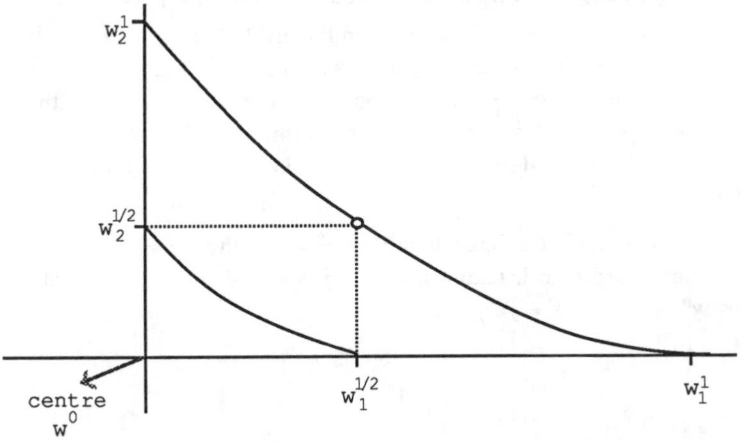

FIGURE III.5.6.b (Step 5.4; the halved measuring rod $[w_1^{1/2};w_1^0]$). The point $w_1^{1/2}$ is the supremum of points like v_1^1 in Figure III.5.6.a.

Elaboration. This is very analogous to the elaboration of Step 5.1. First we take $s_1 \prec_1 v^1_1$ so close to v^1_1 that $(s_1,v^1_2) \succ (w^1_1,w^0_2)$, next $s_2 \prec_2 v^1_2$ so close to v^1_2 that $(s_1,s_2) \succ (w^1_1,w^0_2)$. And we define $x^1_1 := s_1$ if $(w^0_1,s_2) \preccurlyeq (s_1,w^0_2)$; if $(w^0_1,s_2) \succ (s_1,w^0_2)$, then we first define $x^1_2 := s_2$, next x^1_1 such that $(x^1_1,w^0_2) \approx (w^0_1,x^1_2)$.

So we have $(x^1_1,x^1_2) \succ (w^1_1,w^0_2)$. From this it follows that, if x^2_1 exists, then it is $\succ_1 w^1_1$.

Step 5.4. Construction of the halved measuring rod.

Comment. By connectedness there must be a measuring rod between those smaller, and those larger, than half $[w^1_1;w^0_1]$. This is $[w^{1/2}_1;w^0_1]$.

Elaboration. Define

$$G^- := \{v^1_1 : v^1_1 \succ_1 w^0_1, v^2_1 \text{ exists and } v^2_1 \prec_1 w^1_1\} \cup \{s_1 : s_1 \preccurlyeq_1 w^0_1\} ,$$

and

$$G^+ := \{v^1_1 : v^1_1 \succ_1 w^0_1, v^2_1 \text{ does not exists or } v^2_1 \succ_1 w^1_1\} .$$

If $x_1 \in G^-$, then any $x_1' \prec_1 x^1_1$ can be seen to be in G^-; by Steps 5.1 and 5.2 there exists $x_1' \succ_1 x_1$ in G^-. Hence G^- is open. Analogously, if $x_1 \in G^+$, then any $x_1' \succ_1 x_1$ is in G^+ too, and there is $x_1' \prec_1 x_1$ in G^+, so that G^+ is open too. Also G^- and G^+ are disjoint, and nonempty, one containing w^0_1, the other w^1_1. By connectedness there must exist an element v^1_1 of Γ_1 neither contained in G^- nor in G^+. It follows that $w^0_1 \prec_1 v^1_1 \prec_1 w^1_1$, v^2_1 exists, and $v^2_1 \approx w^1_1$. We define $w^{1/2}_1 := v^1_1$.

Step 5.5. Doubling the density of the grid by means of the halved measuring rod.

Comment. We construct the grid with centre w^0, and mesh $[w^{1/2}_1;w^0_1]$.

Elaboration. We have obtained a 'measuring rod' $[v^1_1;v^0_1]$ of 'length half' $[w^1_1;w^0_1]$ ($v^0_1 = w^0_1$, $v^1_1 = w^{1/2}_1$). By restricted solvability we find, for all j, v^1_j such that (denoting all coordinates) $w^0_{-j}v^1_j \approx w^0_{-1}v^1_1$. So we can construct a grid with centre $v^0 = w^0$ and mesh $[v^1_1;v^0_1]$, of alternatives of the form $(v^{z_1}_1,v^{z_2}_2,...,v^{z_n}_n)$. Question is if this fits into the original grid as it should be; i.e., if, for all j and z_j,

$$v^{2z_j}_j = w^{z_j}_j .$$

From the definition of v^1_1 it is immediate that $v^2_1 = w^1_1$, thus $v^2_j = w^1_j$ for all j. But then for any coordinate j, taking some $i \neq j$, we find that (omitting all coordinates w^0_k for $k \neq i$, $k \neq j$)

$$(v^{2z_j}_j,v^0_i) \approx (v^{2z_j-2}_j,v^2_i) ;$$

i.e.,

$$(v^{2z_j}_j,w^0_i) \approx (v^{2z_j-2}_j,w^1_i) .$$

By induction with respect to z_j, $v^{2z_j}_j = w^{z_j}_j$ for all j.

Note that, if on some coordinate j the original grid was bounded, say from the left (right is analogous), so that for some z_j, $w^{z_j}_j$ has been defined, but not $w^{z_j-1}_j$, then $v^{2z_j}_j$ obviously also exists, but $v^{2z_j-2}_j$ does not; $v^{2z_j-1}_j$ may or may not exist.

We define $w^{z_j/2}_j := v^{z_j}_j$ for all j and odd z_j.

We conclude that indeed the 'density of the grid has been doubled'.

STAGE 6. CONSTRUCTING A 'DENSE GRID' BY AN INFINITE REPETITION OF THE DOUBLING OF DENSITY

Comment. In Step 6.1 we shall construct the dense grid; in following steps we establish several properties concerning the 'reach' of the grid.

Step 6.1. Construction of the dense grid, and additive value functions on it.

Comment. The refinement procedure can be repeated, constructing $w^{1/4}_1$, etc., to end up with an 'infinitely fine' grid of alternatives of the form

$$(w^{z_1.2^{-m_1}}_1,\dots,w^{z_n.2^{-m_n}}_n) ,$$

where $m_1,\dots,m_n$ can be any natural numbers, and where

$$V_j : w^{z_j.2^{-m_j}}_j \mapsto z_j.2^{-m_j}$$

gives additive value functions for $\succcurlyeq$ on these alternatives (as elucidated in a moment).

Elaboration. The infinitely fine grid is not a grid in the sense of Stages 2,3 and 4 because there is no 'minimal distance' to serve as mesh. Hence we call it a **dense grid**; it can (but need not) be seen that this dense grid is dense with respect to the product topology of the order topologies with respect to the $\succcurlyeq_i$ relations, which explains its name. That above we indeed have defined additive value functions follows since for every pair of alternatives from the dense grid there is a grid (obtained after *finitely* many refinements) containing the both alternatives, and on this grid it has been established that the functions above are additive value functions.

CONVENTION FOR NOTATION. Often we shall use the character b for binary numbers, so we write b_j instead of $z_j.2^{-m_j}$.

Step 6.2. There exist no coordinates infinitely far away from the centre. The dense grid is wide enough to 'catch' all alternatives, no matter how far away from the centre ('Archimedeanity').

Elaboration. Can it happen that w^m_j is defined for all natural m, but that still for some x_j, $x_j \succ_j w^m_j$ for all m? I.e., that x_j is so far away from the centre that w^m_j can be defined for all m, but that the grid is not 'wide enough' to fall over x_j? We might call such coordinates x_j **infinite coordinates**; we shall show that they do not exist. Let $i \neq j$, we only denote coordinates i and j. By restricted solvability there exists y_j between w^0_j and x_j such that

$$(w^1_i,y_j) \approx (w^0_i,x_j) ;$$

i.e., y_j is obtained from x_j by 'walking from x_j one mesh backwards'. Then still y_j is an infinite coordinate, because $y_j \preccurlyeq_j w^m_j$ would imply

$(w_i^0,x_j) \approx (w_i^1,y_j) \preccurlyeq (w_i^1,w_j^m) \approx (w_i^0,w_j^{m+1})$, so that the impossible $x_j \preccurlyeq_j w_j^{m+1}$ would result. So for any infinite x_j there is an open neigbourhood $\{z_j : z_j \succ_j y_j\}$ within the set of all infinite coordinates, containing x_j; the latter set must be open. Also its complement, the set of noninfinite coordinates, is open, since every $x_j \preccurlyeq_j w_j^m$ is contained in the neighbourhood $\{z_j : z_j \prec_j w_j^{m+1}\}$; further this complement is nonempty. By connectedness of Γ_j the set of infinite coordinates must be empty.

Analogously, if w_j^{-m} is defined for all $m \in \mathbb{N}$, then for every x_j there is m_j such that $w_j^{-m_j} \preccurlyeq_j x_j$, so the grid is wide enough in all directions.

<u>*Step 6.3*</u>. There exist no coordinates infinitely close to the centre. The dense grid is dense in the neighbourhood of w^0; i.e., 'interferes' between every $v_j \neq w_j^0$ and w_j^0.

Elaboration. Say $j = 1$. Say $v_1 \succ_1 w_1^0$ ($v_1 \prec_1 w_1^0$ is analogous). We obtain a w_1^z such that $w_1^0 \prec_1 w_1^z \prec_1 v_1$. Set $v_1^1 := v_1$, and consider the grid with centre $v^0 := w^0$ and mesh $[v_1^1,v_1^0]$. Say $v_1^1 \prec_1 w_1^{1/2}$ (otherwise we would be done). Then, analogously to Step 4.2, whenever v_1^j exists and $v_1^j \prec_1 w_1^{1/2}$, then v_1^{j+1} exists and $v_1^{j+1} \prec_1 w_1^1$. Hence, if there are only finitely many v_1^j's, then $v_1^j \succ_1 w_1^{1/2}$ for some j. If there are infinitely many v_1^j's, then also $v_1^j \succ_1 w_1^{1/2}$ for some j, by Step 6.2. So let j be such that $v_1^j \succ_1 w_1^{1/2}$. Let m be so large that $j.2^{-m} < 1/2$. Analogously to Step 4.2, $w_1^0 \prec_1 w_1^{2^{-m}} \prec_1 v_1^1 = v_1$.

<u>*Step 6.4*</u>. The dense grid is dense enough to 'interfere' everywhere.

Elaboration. Let $x_j \succ_j y_j$. We show that there must be a $w_j^{b_j}$ (b_j binary) such that $x_j \succ_j w_j^{b_j} \succ_j y_j$.

Say $j = 1$. We denote only coordinates 1 and 2. Say $w_1^0 \preccurlyeq_1 y_1$ ($w_1^0 \succcurlyeq_1 x_1$ is analogous). First we consider the case where there is an m such that 'the measuring rod $[x_1;y_1]$ is larger than $[w_1^{2^{-m}};w_1^0]$'; i.e., $(x_1,w_2^0) \succ (y_1,w_2^{2^{-m}})$. Let in this case z_1 be the largest integer such that $w_1^{z_1.2^{-m}} \preccurlyeq_1 y_1$. Then $(w_1^{z_1.2^{-m}},w_2^{2^{-m}}) \preccurlyeq (y_1,w_2^{2^{-m}}) \prec (x_1,w_2^0)$, from which it straightforwardly follows that $w_1^{(z_1+1)2^{-m}}$ exists, and that $w_1^{(z_1+1)2^{-m}} \prec_1 x_1$. So $b_1 := (z_1+1)2^{-m}$ establishes the desired result.

Remains the case where $(x_1,w_2^0) \preccurlyeq (y_1,w_2^{2^{-m}})$ for all m. In that case there must exist a v_2 between w_2^0 and $w_2^{2^{-m}}$ such that $(x_1,w_2^0) \approx (y_1,v_2)$. Apparently $w_2^0 \prec_2 v_2 \prec_2 w_2^{2^{-m}}$ for all m. Step 6.3 shows that such v_2's do not exist.

STAGE 7. DEFINING THE V_j'S OUTSIDE THE GRID

Comment. In this stage we extend the definition of the V_j's outside the grid and check that the V_j's satisfy all desired properties. From the fact that V_j represents $\succcurlyeq_j$ on the dense grid one will easily see that the definition of V_j below indeed extends V_j as already defined on the grid.

Step 7.1. Definition of the V_j's.

Comment. Mainly (III.5.5) below will extend the V_j's outside the grid.

Elaboration. If x_j is **minimal** (with respect to $\succcurlyeq_j$; this means that $y_j \prec_j x_j$ for no y_j) then we assign to x_j the minimal V_j-value; i.e., then

$$V_j(x_j) := \inf\{V_j(w_j^{b_j}) : w_j^{b_j} \text{ is a point of the grid}\} .$$

Note that, by Step 6.2, a minimal x_j can occur only if the grid of Stage 2 is bounded from below; i.e., w_j^{z-1} does not exist for some negative integer z. In that case no V_j-value less than $z - 1$ has been assigned, so $-\infty < V_j(x_j) < 0$.

For nonminimal x_j we define

$$V_j(x_j) := \sup\{V_j(w_j^{b_j}) : w_j^{b_j} \preccurlyeq_j x_j\} . \qquad \text{(III.5.5)}$$

For nonminimal x_j there is a $y_j \prec_j x_j$, thus by Step 6.4 a $w_j^{b_j} \prec_j x_j$, so that $V_j(x_j) > -\infty$. That no V_j-value $+\infty$ is assigned is derived analogously, both for maximal (with respect to $\succcurlyeq_j$) and nonmaximal x_j.

Step 7.2. V_j represents $\succcurlyeq_j$, for all j.

Elaboration. It is direct that :

$$x_j \succcurlyeq_j y_j \Rightarrow V_j(x_j) \geq V_j(y_j) . \qquad \text{(III.5.6)}$$

Next suppose that $x_j \succ_j y_j$. In that case $w_j^{b_j}$ can be found such that $x_j \succ_j w_j^{b_j} \succ_j y_j$, next $w_j^{b_j'}$ such that

$$x_j \succ_j w_j^{b_j} \succ_j w_j^{b_j'} \succ_j y_j ,$$

so that

$$V_j(x_j) \geq V_j(w_j^{b_j}) > V_j(w_j^{b_j'}) \geq V_j(y_j) .$$

(the first and third inequality by (III.5.6), the second because on the dense grid V_j represents $\succcurlyeq_j$). It follows that V_j represents $\succcurlyeq_j$.

Step 7.3. V_j is continuous, for all j.

Elaboration. Let $\mu \in \mathbb{R}$. We derive openness of the set $\{x_j : V_j(x_j) < \mu\}$. If $V_j(y_j) = \mu$ for some y_j, then $\{x_j : V_j(x_j) < \mu\} = \{x_j : x_j \prec_j y_j\}$, which is open because of continuity of $\succcurlyeq$. So suppose that $\mu \notin V_j(\Gamma_j)$. Suppose that we are not in the trivial case where the set $\{x_j : V_j(x_j) < \mu\}$ is empty, or is Γ_j. Then $V_j(s_j) < \mu < V_j(t_j)$ for some s_j, t_j from Γ_j. We can then find a sequence of binary $(b_j^k)_{k=1}^{\infty}$ between s_j and μ, approaching μ, and write

$$\{x_j : V_j(x_j) < \mu\} = \cup_{k=1}^{\infty}\{x_j : V_j(x_j) < b_j^k\} = \cup_{k=1}^{\infty}\{x_j : x_j \prec_j w_j^{b_j^k}\} .$$

Openness follows.

Analogously openness of the set $\{x_j : V_j(x_j) > \mu\}$ is derived. Continuity of V_j follows.

Step 7.4. $V : x \mapsto \sum_{j=1}^{n} V_j(x_j)$ represents $\succcurlyeq$.

Elaboration. First we derive, for all $(x_1,\ldots,x_n)$, $(y_1,\ldots,y_n)$:

$$(x_1,...,x_n) \succ (y_1,...,y_n) \Rightarrow V(x) > V(y) . \qquad \text{(III.5.7)}$$

So let $(x_1,...,x_n) \succ (y_1,...,y_n)$. We write $\tilde{x}_i = x_i$ for all minimal x_i, and $\tilde{y}_i = y_i$ for all maximal y_i. All nonminimal coordinates x_j are replaced by new coordinates $\tilde{x}_j := w_j^{b_j} \prec_j x_j$, and all nonmaximal coordinates y_j by new coordinates $\tilde{y}_j := w_j^{b_j} \succ_j y_j$, so that

$$(x_1,...,x_n) \succ (\tilde{x}_1,...,\tilde{x}_n) \succ (\tilde{y}_1,...,\tilde{y}_n) \succ (y_1,...,y_n) ,$$

where the first and third preference follow since not all x_i can be minimal and not all y_i maximal, and the second preference is obtained by choosing all new coordinates close enough to the original ones; i.e., by replacing one by one the old coordinates by new coordinates, applying each time Lemma III.3.5. Since every V_j represents $\succcurlyeq_j$, $\sum_{j=1}^n V_j(\tilde{x}_j) > \sum_{j=1}^n V_j(x_j)$ and $\sum_{j=1}^n V_j(\tilde{y}_j) > \sum_{j=1}^n V_j(y_j)$ follow.

So for (III.5.7) it suffices to show that, for all $(\tilde{x}_1,...,\tilde{x}_n)$, $(\tilde{y}_1,...,\tilde{y}_n)$ with either $\tilde{x}_j$ minimal or $\tilde{x}_j$ in the dense grid, and either $\tilde{y}_j$ maximal or $\tilde{y}_j$ in the dense grid :

$$(\tilde{x}_1,...,\tilde{x}_n) \succ (\tilde{y}_1,...,\tilde{y}_n) \Rightarrow V(\tilde{x}) \geq V(\tilde{y}) . \qquad \text{(III.5.8)}$$

Let us replace every minimal x_j by an arbitrary x_j' from the dense grid, every maximal y_j by an arbitrary y_j' from the dense grid, write $x_j' = \tilde{x}_j$ for all remaining $\tilde{x}_j$, $y_j' = \tilde{y}_j$ for all remaining $\tilde{y}_j$. Then we certainly have :

$$(x_1',...,x_n') \succ (y_1',...,y_n') ,$$

so that $V(x') > V(y')$.

But $V(\tilde{x})$ is the infimum of all $V(x')$ as above, $V(\tilde{y})$ the supremum of all $V(y')$ as above, so that (III.5.8) follows. This also establishes (III.5.7).

Remains to be shown for Step 7.4 that, for all $(x_1,...,x_n)$, $(y_1,...,y_n)$:

$$(x_1,...,x_n) \succcurlyeq (y_1,...,y_n) \Rightarrow V(x) \geq V(y) . \qquad \text{(III.5.9)}$$

So let $(x_1,...,x_n) \succcurlyeq (y_1,...,y_n)$. If all y_j are minimal, then (III.5.9) is immediate. So let y_j be nonminimal for some j. We replace y_j by an arbitrary $w_j^{b_j} =: y_j' \prec_j y_j$, write $y_i' := y_i$ for all remaining i. Then

$$x \succ y', \text{ so } V(x) > V(y').$$

Since $V(y)$ is the supremum of all $V(y')$ obtainable as above, (III.5.9) follows.

STAGE 8. JOINT CARDINALITY

In the construction of the additive value functions above there were n + 1 arbitrary choices: The choice of $V_j(w_j^0) = 0$ for $j = 1,...,n$, and the choice of $V_1(w_1^1) > V_1(w_1^0)$. We could have obtained additive value functions $(W_j)_{j=1}^n$ by choosing any arbitrary values σ_j for $W_j(w_j^0)$, and any arbitrary value $\tau > 0$ such that $W_1(w_1^1) = \tau + W_1(w_1^0)$. After these choices the functions W_j are uniquely determined, and $W_j = \sigma_j + \tau V_j$ for all j, as follows from the construction in the proof. This establishes joint cardinality of the additive value functions.

□

III.6. CORROLLARIES OF THE CENTRAL THEOREM AND EXTENSIONS

In this section we gather corollaries of the central theorem. Let us first introduce the conditions mostly used in the literature to characterize additive representations for the case of two essential coordinates. These conditions are stronger, i.e., imply the hexagon condition. If n = 2, then $\succcurlyeq$ satisfies the **Thomsen condition** if, for all x_1, y_1, v_1, a_2, b_2, c_2,

$$[(y_1,a_2) \approx (x_1,b_2) \ \& \ (x_1,c_2) \approx (v_1,a_2)] \ \Rightarrow \ [(y_1,c_2) \approx (v_1,b_2)] \ .$$

See Figure III.6.1. Interchanging left and right sides of the equivalences, (or Figure

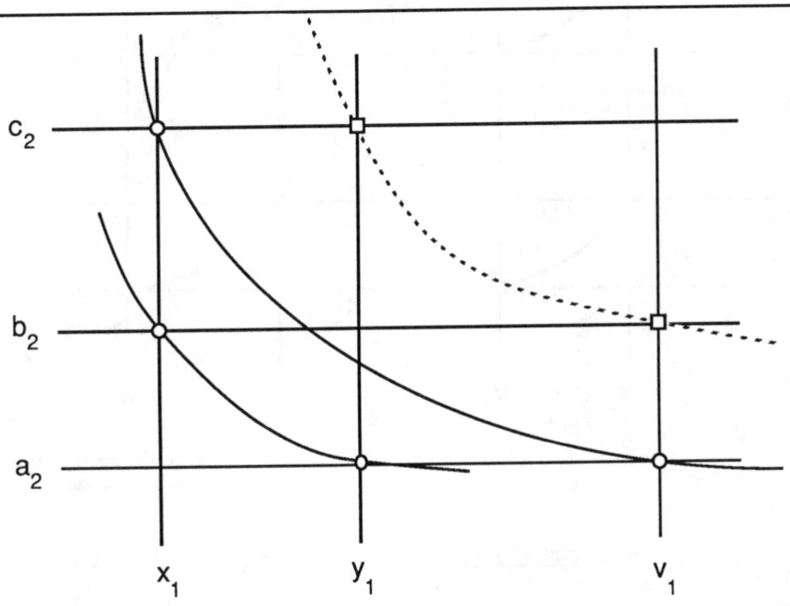

FIGURE III.6.1 (The Thomsen condition). Solid equivalence classes through O-points are presumed, the broken equivalence class through □-points is implied.

III.6.1) shows symmetry in coordinates 1 and 2. We say, again for n = 2, that $\succcurlyeq$ satisfies **triple cancellation** if, for all x_1, y_1, v_1, w_1, a_2, b_2, c_2, d_2 we have :

$$\begin{bmatrix} (x_1,a_2) \preccurlyeq (y_1,b_2) \;\&\; (v_1,a_2) \succcurlyeq (w_1,b_2) \;\& \\ (x_1,c_2) \succcurlyeq (y_1,d_2) \end{bmatrix}$$

$$\Rightarrow \qquad [(v_1,c_2) \succcurlyeq (w_1,d_2)] .$$

The case where all above preferences are equivalences is illustrated in Figure III.6.2.

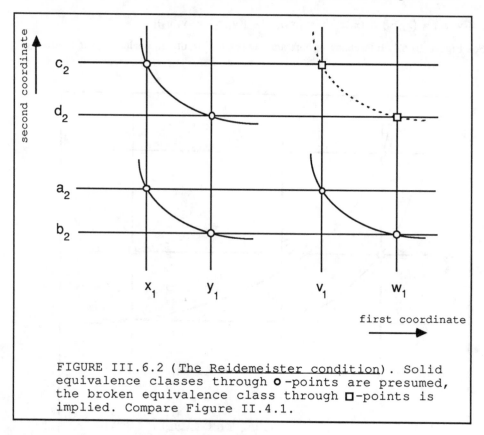

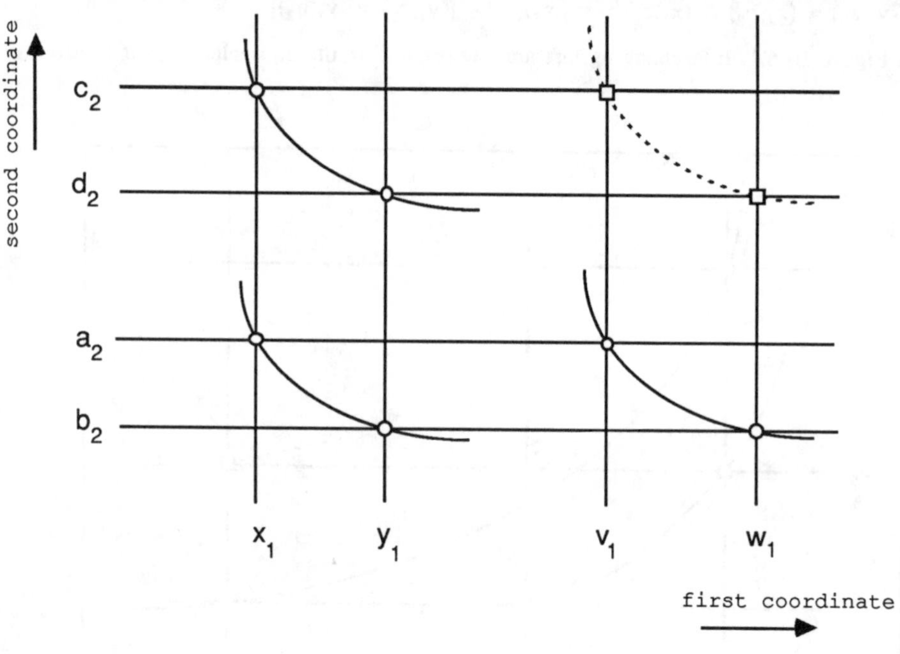

FIGURE III.6.2 (The Reidemeister condition). Solid equivalence classes through o-points are presumed, the broken equivalence class through □-points is implied. Compare Figure II.4.1.

Symmetry of the condition with respect to coordinates 1 and 2 follows from interchanging the second and third preference above. Note that triple cancellation holds if and only if neither coordinate 2, nor coordinate 1, reveals contradictory tradeoffs. (See also Lemma III.6.4 in the sequel.) We think this interpretation in terms of tradeoffs gives the best way to gain intuition for triple cancellation. Finally, the **Reidemeister condition**[rf10] is the condition obtained from triple cancellation by replacing all preferences above by equivalences (See Figure III.6.2). If $n \neq 2$, but there are exactly two essential coordinates, then we say that $\succcurlyeq$ satisfies the **Thomsen condition**, or **triple cancellation**, or the **Reidemeister condition**, whenever the involved condition is satisfied after suppression of the inessential coordinates.

We give the following Lemma and proof because they are characteristic for the way to derive conditions with equivalences from conditions with preferences, when these conditions are special forms of cancellation axioms.

LEMMA III.6.1. *Let exactly two coordinates be essential. Then for any binary relation* $\succcurlyeq$ *the Reidemeister condition is implied by triple cancellation.*

PROOF. Suppose $(x_1,a_2) \approx (y_1,b_2)$ & $(v_1,a_2) \approx (w_1,b_2)$ & $(x_1,c_2) \approx (y_1,d_2)$. To derive is $(v_1,c_2) \approx (w_1,d_2)$. First we replace the first three equivalences by respectively $\preccurlyeq$, $\succcurlyeq$, and $\succcurlyeq$, to obtain $(v_1,c_2) \succcurlyeq (w_1,d_2)$. Next we interchange left and right sides of the preferences, resulting in $(w_1,d_2) \succcurlyeq (v_1,c_2)$.

□

LEMMA III.6.2. *Let exactly two coordinates be essential. Then the Reidemeister condition implies the hexagon condition. If* $\approx$ *is transitive then the Thomsen condition implies the hexagon condition.*[rf11]

PROOF. The hexagon condition is the special case of the Reidemeister condition where, in the notation of the definition of triple cancellation with equivalences instead of preferences, $y_1 = v_1$, and $a_2 = d_2$, compare Figures III.4.1 and III.6.2. A 'typographical' proof is obtained by interchanging left and right sides in the equivalences of the Reidemeister condition, substituting y for y and v, and v for w, and interchanging a_2 ($= d_2$) and b_2. If $\approx$ is transitive, then the hexagon condition is the special case of the Thomsen condition where, in the notation of the definition of the Thomsen condition, further $(x_1,c_2) \approx (y_1,b_2) \approx (v_1,a_2)$ (compare Figures III.4.1 and III.6.1).

□

The following lemma is obtained by substituting additive value functions, and cancelling terms; this is left to the reader.

LEMMA III.6.3. *Let exactly two coordinates be essential. If there exist additive value functions for* $\succcurlyeq$, *then* $\succcurlyeq$ satisfies the Thomsen condition, triple cancellation, the *Reidemeister condition, and the hexagon condition.*

□

The next lemma has been added for the sake of easy reference. It does no more than reformulate, directly in terms of preferences, the nonrevelation of contradictory tradeoffs by coordinates. Hence no proof is given.

LEMMA III.6.4. *No coordinate reveals contradictory tradeoffs if and only if, for all* i, x, y, v, w, a_i, b_i, c_i, d_i :

$$\left[\begin{array}{l} x_{-i}a_i \preccurlyeq y_{-i}b_i \ \ \& \ \ v_{-i}a_i \succcurlyeq w_{-i}b_i \ \ \& \\ x_{-i}c_i \succcurlyeq y_{-i}d_i \end{array}\right]$$

$$\Rightarrow \qquad [v_{-i}c_i \succcurlyeq w_{-i}d_i] .$$

□

Since for n = 2 the above condition is identical with triple cancellation, it is called generalized triple cancellation. There are several alternative ways to generalize triple cancellation, or any of the other conditions introduced above, to the case where not exactly two coordinates are essential. For instance, one may require the conditions to hold in every two-dimensional subspace obtained by keeping all but two coordinates constant. The generalization of triple cancellation that we introduced above is stronger. It is suited as a preparation for the condition of nonrevelation of contradictory tradeoffs, to be introduced in Chapter IV. Further it gives a characterization of additive representations in the main theorem below which does not require separate formulations for different numbers of essential coordinates.

LEMMA III.6.5. *If* $\succcurlyeq$ *is reflexive, then generalized triple cancellation implies CI.*

PROOF. Set, in the definition of generalized triple cancellation, $a_i = b_i$, $c_i = d_i$, and $x = y$.

□

Now we are ready to formulate the main theorem on additive representations.

THEOREM III.6.6. (Main theorem on additive representations). *Let the topological assumption III.3.2 hold. For the binary relation* $\succcurlyeq$ *on* $\prod_{i \in I}\Gamma_i$ *the following four statements are equivalent* :

(i) **There exists a continuous additive representation for $\succcurlyeq$.**

(ii) **The binary relation $\succcurlyeq$ is a continuous CI weak order; if exactly two coordinates are essential then $\succcurlyeq$ furthermore satisfies the hexagon condition.**

(iii) **The binary relation $\succcurlyeq$ is a continuous weak order, satisfying generalized triple cancellation.**

(iv) **The binary relation $\succcurlyeq$ is a continuous weak order, and no coordinate reveals contradictory tradeoffs.**

Furthermore, in (ii) the hexagon condition may be replaced by the Thomsen condition, or the Reidemeister condition.

PROOF. That (i) implies (ii), (iii) and (iv) is straightforward, and is left to the reader (for (iv), see also Lemma II.4.5). Lemma III.6.4 gives the equivalence of (iii) and (iv). (Statement (iv) has been added for the sake of easy reference.) The implication (iii) => (ii) is by Lemmas III.6.5, III.6.1 and III.6.2, and the obvious fact that triple cancellation is implied by generalized triple cancellation. The implication (ii) => (i) has been established in the Central Theorem III.4.1 for two or more essential coordinates, and in Corollary III.3.7 for the case of exactly one or no essential coordinate. The furthermore-statement is by Lemmas III.6.3 and III.6.2.

□

OBSERVATION III.6.6′ (Uniqueness results for Theorem III.6.6). Let us repeat that an additive representation is the sum of additive value functions. The following uniqueness results hold for the additive representation of statement (i) in Theorem III.6.6 :

If two or more coordinates are essential, then the additive representation is cardinal; the additive value functions are then jointly cardinal. (III.6.1)

If exactly one coordinate is essential, then the additive representation is continuously ordinal; also each additive value function is then continuously ordinal. (III.6.2)

If no coordinate is essential, then any additive representation can, and must, be any constant function; also each additive value function can, and must, then be any constant function. (III.6.3)

PROOF. Follows from Corollary III.3.7 and Theorem III.4.1.

□

Let us give an example for the case of exactly two essential coordinates where a continuous CI weak order has no additive representation, so that an additional condition such as the hexagon condition indeed is needed for additive representability.

EXAMPLE III.6.7. Let $\succcurlyeq$ on $\mathbb{R}^2$ be represented be the function $(x_1,x_2) \mapsto x_1 + x_2 + \min\{x_1,x_2\}$. Then $\succcurlyeq$ is a continuous CI weak order, with $\succcurlyeq_1 = \succcurlyeq_2 = \geq$. But $\succcurlyeq$ does not satisfy the hexagon condition. The equivalences $(18,0) \approx (6,6)$, $(30,0) \approx (18,6)$, and $(18,6) \approx (6,18)$, should, according to the hexagon condition with centre $(18,6)$, imply $(30,6) \approx (18,18)$. However, $(30,6) \prec (18,18)$. To show that coordinate 1 reveals contradictory tradeoffs, we set $x_1 = 30$, $y_1 = 17$, $v_1 = 17$, $w_1 = 6$. Then the preferences $(30,0) \succcurlyeq (17,6)$ and $(17,0) \preccurlyeq (6,6)$ reveal $x_1y_1 \succcurlyeq_1^* v_1w_1$, even $x_1y_1 \succ_1^{**} v_1w_1$ since the preferences are strict. The preferences $(17,6) \succcurlyeq (6,17)$ and $(30,6) \prec (17,17)$ reveal $x_1y_1 \prec_1^{**} v_1w_1$. So coordinate 1 reveals contradictory tradeoffs. Even $\succ_1^{**}$ is not asymmetric.

An example that can be dealt with by the approach of KLST, but not by our approach, is provided by the finite 'equally-spaced' case, e.g. $\Gamma_i = \{1,...,m_i\}$ for all i, $m_i \in \mathbb{N}$, with additive value functions V_i = identity for all i. A more interesting example to show that the approach of KLST is more general than the topological approaches such as ours, is case (b) below.

EXAMPLE III.6.8. Let $n = 2$, $\Gamma_1 = \Gamma_2$ are subsets of the reals, specified below. The binary relation $\succcurlyeq$ on $\Gamma_1 \times \Gamma_2$ is represented by $(x_1,x_2) \mapsto x_1 + x_2$, so has additive value functions $V_1 = V_2 =$ identity. Consequently $\succcurlyeq$ is a continuous weak order, and satisfies CI, the hexagon condition, in short, all cancellation axioms. In either case below $\sqrt{3}$ will not be contained in Γ_1, so that the subset $\{x_1 : x_1 > \sqrt{3}\}$ of Γ_1 will be both open and closed with respect to the order topology. This topology consequently is not connected, and the topological assumptions of our approach cannot be satisfied. Still restricted solvability is satisfied, also the 'Archimedean axiom' (see Remark III.7.7), so that the approach of KLST can be used.

Case (a) Γ_1 is Γ_2 is the set of rationals.

Case (b) Γ_1 is Γ_2 is $\{a + b\sqrt{2} : a \text{ and } b \text{ are integers}\}$.

In case (a) the construction of an additive representation as in section III.5 can completely be carried through. This is not so in case (b). The reason is that, for instance between $x_1 = 0$, and $v_1 = \sqrt{2}$, there does not exist a 'midpoint' $(\sqrt{2})/2$, so that Stage 5 in section III.5 does not work.

III.7. FURTHER REMARKS AND EXTENSIONS

It has been our experience that often[rf12] results on additive representations are needed with details which are not exactly available in the literature. Hence, for the sake of easy reference, we list below some possible modifications of the theorems above.

REMARK III.7.1. We needed topological separability only for the case of exactly one essential coordinate; in the Central Theorem III.4.1 the assumption of topological separability (part of the topological assumption III.3.2) may be omitted. It is used nowhere in the proof in section III.5[rf13].

REMARK III.7.2. The only implication of continuity of the preference relation which we used was sectional continuity[rf14]. The only implication of topological connectedness which we used was that, for every j and x, the subset $\{x_{-j}v_j : v_j \in \Gamma_j\}$ of $\prod_{i\in I}\Gamma_i$ is connected with respect to the restriction of the order topology.

REMARK III.7.3. The only implications of CI that we used in the proofs were weak separability, and the version of independence of equal subalternatives with subalternatives of length $n - 2$ and with equivalences instead of preferences; i.e., the version which requires for all i, j, x, y, a_i, b_j, c_i, d_j :

$$[(x_{-i,j}a_i,b_j) \approx (x_{-i,j}c_i,d_j]) \iff [(y_{-i,j}a_i,b_j) \approx (y_{-i,j}c_i,d_j)] .$$

That CI with equivalences is implied by CI with preferences, is proved analogously to Lemma III.6.1. Independence of equal alternatives with subalternatives of length n - 2 implies weak separability, so that this can fully replace CI[rf15].

REMARK III.7.4. For the case of exactly two essential coordinates CI is easily seen to be equivalent to weak separability.

REMARK III.7.5. In the Central Theorem it would have sufficed to weaken the hexagon condition to the North-East hexagon condition, since the South-West hexagon condition can be derived from the North-East hexagon condition by a reasoning analogous to the derivation of the South-East hexagon condition from the hexagon condition, be it somewhat more complicated (suggested in Figure III.5.4.b). Analogously any other of the four versions of the hexagon condition would have sufficed.

The following remark indicates that the intuitive conditions for additive representability are special versions of cancellation axioms :

REMARK III.7.6. For a complete binary relation $\succcurlyeq$ the following things can be seen, with π_j as on page 33. Triple cancellation (for n = 2) and generalized triple cancellation (for arbitrary n) are the version of third-order cancellation with, for some i, $\pi_i(1) = 2$, $\pi_i(2) = 1$, $\pi_i(0) = 3$, $\pi_i(3) = 0$, and with $\pi_j(1) = 0$, $\pi_j(0) = 1$, $\pi_j(2) = 3$, and $\pi_j(3) = 2$ for all $j \neq i$. Analogously to the derivation of the Reidemeister condition from triple cancellation, the Thomsen condition can be derived from the special version of second-order cancellation where $\pi_1(0) = 1$, $\pi_1(1) = 2$, $\pi_1(2) = 0$, $\pi_2(0) = 2$, $\pi_2(1) = 0$, $\pi_2(2) = 1$. The hexagon condition can analogously be derived from the same version of third-order cancellation as involved in triple cancellation above, with i = 1, j = 2, now restricted to the case where $x_1^2 = x_1^3$ and $x_2^0 = x_2^3$.

REMARK III.7.7. Step 6.2 in the proof in section III.3.5 deals in fact with the <u>Archimedean axiom</u>. One way to define it is as follows: For any $i \neq j$, $w_i^1 \succ_i w_i^0$, and infinite sequence $w_j^0, w_j^1, w_j^2, \ldots$ such that (keeping all other coordinates fixed and suppressing them) $(w_i^1, w_j^{m-1}) \approx (w_i^0, w_j^m)$ for all m, there should not exist an x_j such that $x_j \succ_j w_j^m$ for all m. Analogously, if $w_i^1 \prec_i w_i^0$, then no x_j should exist such that $x_j \prec_j w_j^m$ for all m.

REMARK III.7.8. Contrary to what has sometimes been thought, the Cartesian product structure in Theorem III.4.1 is essential. We show that on an arbitrary connected subset of $\mathbb{R}^3$ with nonempty interior a result like Theorem III.4.1 does not have to hold. This will also show that the step of local additive representability to global additive representability is not so self-evident as has sometimes been thought.

Let $E^1 := \{x \in \mathbb{R}^3\colon x_1+x_2+x_3 \leq 0\}$, $E^2 := \{x \in \mathbb{R}^3\colon x_1+x_2+x_3 \geq 0, -2\leq x_1\leq -1, -2\leq x_2\leq -1, 2\leq x_3\leq 4\}$, $E^3 := \{x \in \mathbb{R}^3\colon x_1+x_2+x_3 \geq 0, 1\leq x_1\leq 2, 1\leq x_2\leq 2, -4\leq x_3\leq -2\}$. Let $E := E_1 \cup E_2 \cup E_3$.

Then E is connected, even arcwise connected, it is topologically separable, and has nonempty interior.

Let $\succcurlyeq$ on E be represented by $V : E \to \mathbb{R}$, where $V : x \mapsto (x_1+x_2+x_3)/2$ for all x in E_2, and $V : x \mapsto x_1+x_2+x_3$ for all $x \in E_1 \cup E_3$. Then $\succcurlyeq$ and V are continuous. V is strictly increasing in each variable, so all coordinates are essential (and $\succcurlyeq$ satisfies weak separability). On $E_1 \cup E_2$ $\succcurlyeq$ is additively representable by $x \mapsto x_1+x_2+x_3$. Also on $E_1 \cup E_3$ $\succcurlyeq$ is additively representable by $x \mapsto x_1+x_2+x_3$. (So for every element of E there is an open neighbourhood on which $\succcurlyeq$ is additively representable). The equivalence $[x \succcurlyeq y \Leftrightarrow x_1+x_2+x_3 \geq y_1+y_2+y_3]$ is violated only if one alternative is from E_2, and the other from E_3.

Also $\succcurlyeq$ satisfies coordinate independence. The only violation of coordinate independence might be expected if there are involved elements both from E_2 and from E_3. Since such elements have no coordinate in common, a straightforward elaboration of cases shows that coordinate independence cannot be violated. Also independence of equal subalternatives, on nonCartesian products not always implied by coordinate independence, is satisfied; in this three-dimensional case it is implied by coordinate independence and weak separability.

If an additive representation W of $\succcurlyeq$ would exist, then the elements of E_1 can be seen to imply that W is (a positive affine transform of) $x \mapsto x_1+x_2+x_3$; however $(-1,-1,4) \prec (2,2,-2)$. So no additive representation exists for $\succcurlyeq$.

One possible way to extend the additive representation results is by requiring the involved cancellation axioms such as CI and the hexagon condition to hold only locally; i.e., for each alternative there is a neighbourhood where the involved cancellation axiom holds[rf16]. The above Remark has shown that this is less trivial than is sometimes thought, and on subsets of Cartesian products does not have to hold.

Also the question has been raised whether it will suffice to require additive representability only on every two-dimensional subspace, obtained by keeping all but two coordinates fixed at any level. The following example, communicated to the author by A. Tversky in 1985, shows that this does not suffice: Let $\Gamma = \mathbb{R}_{++}$, n = 3. Let $\succcurlyeq$ be represented by

$$x \mapsto x_1x_2 + x_2x_3 + x_3x_1 = (x_1 + x_3)(x_2 + x_3) - x_3^2.$$

Clearly, with x_3 fixed, $\succcurlyeq$ is represented by $x \mapsto \ln(x_1+x_3) + \ln(x_2+x_3)$, so is additively representable. Analogously $\succcurlyeq$ is additively representable in any two-dimensional subspace. But $\succcurlyeq$ is not additively representable; it does not satisfy CI, as can be seen from $[(1,7,1) \approx (3,3,1)$ & $(1,7,2) \succ (3,3,2)]$. Probably additive representability on every three-dimensional subspace will suffice to guarantee additive representability on the entire space[rf17].

Analogously to the way in which triple cancellation can be obtained from the Reidemeister condition, the hexagon condition can be transformed into a condition with preferences instead of equivalences. Whether in Theorem III.4.1, in the case of exactly two essential coordinates, this condition instead of CI and the hexagon condition will suffice for additive representability, we presently do not know.

III.8. HISTORY AND LITERATURE OF ADDITIVE REPRESENTATIONS, AND FURTHER COMMENTS

Some remarks on literature about additive representations were already given in subsection III.4.1. This section concentrates on the history of additive representations.

The work of Blaschke&Bol(1938) on the mathematical 'web theory' was an important preparation. Suppose F_1, F_2, F_3 are three families of curves in the plane, such that through every point of the plane, for every family F_j, exactly on curve from F_j goes through this point. When is it possible to apply continuous transformations V_1 and V_2 to the first and second coordinates so that the three families of curves are transformed into three families of parallel straight lines? In the special case where F_1 corresponds to 'lines' with constant first coordinate, F_2 to lines with constant second coordinate, and F_3 to equivalence classes of the preference relation, the problem reduces to the problem of additive representation for the case $n = 2$, $\Gamma_1 = \Gamma_2 = \mathbb{R}$. Blaschke&Bol(1938) already presented the hexagon condition, the Thomsen condition, and the Reidemeister condition, and gave earlier references.

Debreu(1960) showed the way, with Theorem III.3.6 as starting point, to use web theory to obtain additive representations. For the case of three or more essential coordinates he showed that CI was the necessary and sufficient condition for continuous weak orders on connected separable topological spaces to be additively representable. First he derived, 'locally', from CI the Thomsen condition in the two-dimensional subspace with third to n-th coordinate kept constant. By the results from web-theory this gave an additive representation on the two-dimensional subspace. Next inductively the dimension on which an additive representation applies was increased up to n. By this Debreu extended earlier work of Leontief(1947a,b), who considered Euclidean spaces, presupposing the existence of 'smooth' representing functions, and then obtained conditions requiring that rates of substitution of pairs of coordinates be independent of other coordinates. Results as those of Leontief had earlier been obtained by Sono(1945, 1961), but this had not been well-known. See also Samuelson(1947, pp. 174-180). Already Fleming(1952) had obtained an informal derivation of additive representations. Fleming's characterizing condition is already formulated without use of derivatives; see his Postulate E. Many parts in the discussion in Fleming(1957), comparing Harsanyi's lottery-approach with Fleming's 'certain-outcome' approach, are relevant for this book, which has as a main aim to derive representations without using lotteries as tool.

Gorman(1968) showed, for Cartesian products of topologically separable arcwise connected spaces, how CI can be weakened, still remaining strong enough in the presence of the other assumptions to imply CI. His weakening requires independence of equal subalternatives only for certain subsets A of I, and implies for instance that it is sufficient to require this for all subsets A containing $n - 2$ elements, as in our Remark III.7.3. In Vind(1971) the extendability of Gorman's result to connected (instead of arcwise connected) separable spaces is indicated. See also Gorman(1971) and Murphy

(1981). We conjecture that, analogously to Remark III.7.1, Gorman's result does not need the assumption of topological separability.

Pfanzagl(1968) also obtains additive representations, in Theorems 9.4.2 and 9.4.4, under topological restrictions like ours (see Remark III.7.2). His working with 'distances' resembles our approach with derived tradeoffs. The assumed existence of the functions in Definitions 8.5.4 and 8.6.8, and their role in the 'solution conditions' are restrictive though, and less suited for being tested.

Another approach can be found in KLST(Chapter 6). They use an algebraic approach, employing a theorem of Hölder(1901) on the embeddability of Archimedean ordered groups into the reals. First KLST use reasonings such as below Figure II.4.1 to obtain subtraction- or addition-like operations on factor sets; next they use this and the Theorem of Hölder to obtain the additive value functions on the coordinates. Instead of our restrictive topological assumption KLST use the restrictive assumption of restricted solvability, and the (not-restrictive) Archimedean axiom. These are less restrictive than the topological assumptions (see Example III.6.8), but still allow the derivation of the results of this monograph. A further advantage of the assumptions of KLST is that there is more clarity about their empirical status, see for instance Adams,Fagot&Robinson(1970). We have chosen the topological approach because this has been more customary in the literature, hence will be more easily accessible to the readers. KLST did not provide continuity of their representation. Wakker(1988d) gave a direct derivation of continuity of additive representations which does not require a full restatement of the derivation of additive representations, and which may serve to supply the result of KLST. For the case of two essential coordinates KLST used the Thomsen condition, or triple cancellation, which are both somewhat stronger than the hexagon condition. Narens (1985) gives algebraic results, more recent and advanced than those of KLST, and in Chapter 3 uses these to derive additive representations for the case of two coordinates. He uses a restrictive 'ab-condition' implying unboundedness of the additive value functions.

Necessary and sufficient conditions for additive representability in full generality, without any restrictive assumption whatsoever, are given in Jaffray(1974a), and in Jaffray(1974b, mainly for the case $n = 2$). He strengthens the cancellation axioms, shown to be necessary and sufficient for the finite case in Scott(1964), in a way to include an Archimedean-like condition. The latter excludes, in a loose-hand way of speaking, infinitely small or large tradeoffs in the sense of section II.4. Using this as a starting point, Jaffray(1974a) derived several versions of additive representations, already dispensing with topological separability. Also Fuhrken&Richter(1988) use the cancellation axioms to obtain additive representations. They do use the same topological assumptions as used in this monograph, in particular they do not need topological separability. Their approach is not so general as other approaches in using all, rather than just one or two, cancellation axioms. An advantage of their approach is that it very clearly separates the empirically meaningful ('proper') axioms from the continuity axioms (which in this approach indeed become purely technical); compare the end of section II.3.

Vind(1986a) deals with additive representations by means of a 'mean groupoid operation', i.e., an operation which assigns to each pair of points a midpoint. His topological assumptions are like those in our Remark III.7.2, and do not need topological separability. Example III.6.8 (b) shows that Vind's approach, like ours, is less general than that of KLST. Further, in Vind(1986b) the following problem, more general than the problem of additive representability, is considered (see also Scott,1964, Theorem 1.1). Let E be a subset of $\prod_{i=1}^{m}\Gamma'_i$. When do there exist functions $(V_i)_{i=1}^{m}$ such that $(x_1,\ldots,x_m) \in E$ if and only if $\sum_{i=1}^{m} V_i(x_i) > 0$? The problem of additive representations is the special case where $m = 2n$, $\Gamma_j = \Gamma'_j = \Gamma'_{j+n}$ for all $j \leq n$, $E = \{(x_1,\ldots,x_{2n}) : (x_1,\ldots,x_n) \succ (x_{n+1},\ldots,x_{2n})\}$, and $V_{j+n} = -V_j$ for all $j \leq n$. Here the main characterizing condition, called independence condition, is close to triple cancellation, generalized to the more general context. Now more general representations can be considered of the form

$$[(x_1,\ldots,x_n) \succ (y_1,\ldots,y_n) \iff \sum_{j=1}^{n} V_j(x_j,y_j) > 0] .$$

Thus additive representations can be studied of certain nontransitive and noncomplete binary relations.

Further remarks on (the history of) additive representations are given in KLST (section 6.2.5) and Vind(1986a, Note 1 at section IV.3).

Experimental tests of additivity are described in Adams&Fagot(1959; a variation on the Thomsen condition is tested), Coombs,Bezembinder,&Goode(1967; in their Table 3 triple cancellation is tested), Tversky(1967b), Tversky&Krantz(1969), and Lukas(1987). Falmagne(1976,1985) introduces probabilistic choices in additive conjoint measurement, a desirable thing for the dealing with error in measurement.

CHAPTER IV

CONTINUOUS SUBJECTIVE EXPECTED UTILITY

IV.1. INTRODUCTION

In this chapter we assume that all factor sets Γ_i in the Cartesian product $\prod_{i\in I}\Gamma_i$ are equal; i.e., $\Gamma_1 = ... = \Gamma_n = \Gamma$ for some connected topological space Γ. We study representations of the form

$$x \mapsto \sum_{j=1}^{n} p_j U(x_j) .$$

The main application lies in decision making under uncertainty. Hence we use the terminology of decision making under uncertainty in this chapter (with the exception of the end of section IV.4), and in chapters V and VI. For finite state spaces Theorem IV.2.7, the central result of this and following chapters, shows that a person with a continuous weak order as preference relation maximizes subjective expected utility if and only if he does not reveal contradictory tradeoffs on consequences. The more complicated conditions for infinite state spaces will be given in Chapter V. Thus we shall characterize subjective expected utility maximization under only one restriction: Continuity of the utility function, with respect to a connected topology (e.g. the usual Euclidean topology). Like Savage(1954) we derive probabilities and utilities simultaneously, without supposing any of them known in advance. One of the motivations for this research was to give a behavioural foundation to subjective probabilities which does not use objective probabilities, and which is suited for economic theory because it uses restrictive assumptions common in economic theory.

We refer to Chapter I and the end of section II.1 for intuitive assumptions underlying our work on decision making under uncertainty.

IV.2. NONCONTRADICTORY TRADEOFFS ON CONSEQUENCES

Let us first repeat the terminology of decision making under uncertainty. We have a set Γ of consequences, and a set $I = \{1,...,n\}$ of (possible) states (of nature). Exactly one state is the true state, the other states are not true. A decision maker is uncertain about which state is the true state, and has *no influence whatsoever* on the truth of the states. Γ^n is the set of acts. An act $x = (x_1,...,x_n)$ can be considered to be a function from I to Γ, assigning consequence x_j to each state j. The interpretation is that, if the decision maker chooses act x, then consequence x_j will result if state j is true. Since the decision maker is uncertain about which state is true, he is uncertain about which consequence will result from the choice of an act x. The binary relation $\succcurlyeq$ on Γ^n denotes the preferences of the decision maker on Γ^n. An <u>event</u> is a subset of I. (This definition will be adapted to infinite state spaces in Chapter V.)

If we do not want to fix the state of nature which a consequence is to be associated with, then we denote the consequence by a small Greek character, $\alpha,\beta,\gamma,\delta$ etc. (Sometimes λ,μ,ν, and also σ,τ, are used to denote real numbers.) The following definition gives the most-used and most-discussed approach to decision making under uncertainty.

DEFINITION IV.2.1. We call $[\Gamma^n, \succcurlyeq, (p_j)_{j=1}^n, U]$ a <u>subjective expected utility (SEU) model (for</u> $\succcurlyeq$) if the p_j's are nonnegative real numbers that sum to one, and $U : \Gamma \to \mathbb{R}$ is a function, such that for all acts x,y,

$$x \succcurlyeq y \iff \sum_{j=1}^n p_j U(x_j) \geq \sum_{j=1}^n p_j U(y_j) .$$

Then p_j is called the <u>subjective probability</u> for state j, U the <u>(subjective) utility function</u>, and $\sum_{j=1}^n p_j U(x_j)$ the <u>subjective expected utility</u> of act x.

In this monograph we follow the conventions of decision science, hence we use the term 'subjective', the most common term. It is an unfortunate term, and terms such as 'personalistic', or 'epistemic', would be preferable.

Since in this chapter all factor sets Γ_i are the same, we can introduce the following notations. They are built upon the notations $\succ_i^{**}$ (Definition II.4.1) and $\succcurlyeq_i^*$ (Definition II.4.2).

DEFINITION IV.2.2. We write $\alpha\beta \succ^{**} \gamma\delta$ if *there exists* a state i such that $\alpha\beta \succ_i^{**} \gamma\delta$, and we write $\alpha\beta \succcurlyeq^{*} \gamma\delta$ if *there exists* an essential state i such that $\alpha\beta \succcurlyeq_i^{*} \gamma\delta$.

Note that, if a state k is inessential, then $\alpha\beta \succcurlyeq_k^{*} \gamma\delta$ for all consequences $\alpha,\beta,\gamma,\delta$. Hence such a state will not reveal useful information about tradeoffs. This motivates the restriction to essential states i in the definition of $\succcurlyeq^*$. For the definition of $\succ^{**}$ no essentiality condition had to be added since $\alpha\beta \succ_i^{**} \gamma\delta$ implies essentiality of state i. As compared to 'contradictory tradeoffs revealed by coordinates', (Definition II.4.4), the definition introduced below also considers comparisons of tradeoffs when derived from different (coordinates =) states of nature. There have been many arguments in the literature that strengths of preferences (under certainty) cannot be derived from decision making under uncertainty (or risk). Hence especially in the present context some readers may prefer the term tradeoff to the term strength of preference.

DEFINITION IV.2.3 (see Figure IV.2.1). The binary relation $\succcurlyeq$ reveals **contradictory tradeoffs (on consequences)** if there exist consequences $\alpha,\beta,\gamma,\delta$, such that both $\alpha\beta \succ^{**} \gamma\delta$ and $\gamma\delta \succcurlyeq^{*} \alpha\beta$.

First we show that the above condition indeed implies that no coordinate reveals contradictory tradeoffs.

LEMMA IV.2.4. *Suppose $\succcurlyeq$ does not reveal contradictory tradeoffs (on consequences). Then no coordinate reveals contradictory tradeoffs.*

PROOF. If $\succcurlyeq$ does not reveal contradictory tradeoffs, then obviously no essential coordinates will reveal contradictory tradeoffs. An inessential coordinate i will never reveal $x_iy_i \succ_i^{**} v_iw_i$, so will neither reveal contradictory tradeoffs.

□

If the binary relation $\succcurlyeq$ is reflexive, then by the above lemma and Lemma III.6.5, CI is implied by the nonrevelation of contradictory tradeoffs by $\succcurlyeq$. In statement (ii) in Theorem IV.2.7 we shall use the characterizing condition that $\succcurlyeq$ should not reveal contradictory tradeoffs, to characterize subjective expected utility maximization. It has been our experience that many feel that this characterizing condition reflects two separate ideas: Firstly, the idea that for any fixed state of nature tradeoffs can be compared (without contradictions) independent of the other states; secondly, the idea that these comparisons are the same (at least, free from contradictions) across different states. We prefer to consider the characterizing condition as one idea, the idea that *tradeoffs of consequences have meaning independent from the choice situation from which they have been revealed;* independent both from the involved essential state of nature, and from the involved quadruple of acts (see Definitions IV.2.2, II.4.1, and II.4.2).

The following lemma is given for the sake of easy reference. It does no more than reformulate the above definition directly in terms of preferences. Hence no proof will be given. The reformulated condition is called **cardinal coordinate independence**, and was published in earlier works of the author, with a minor difference concerning the trivial case of inessentiality of state j^{rf1}.

LEMMA IV.2.5. *The binary relation $\succcurlyeq$ does not reveal contradictory tradeoffs if and only if, for all essential* i,j, *and* $x,\ldots,\delta$ *we have* :

$$\begin{bmatrix} x_{-i}\alpha \preccurlyeq y_{-i}\beta \;\;\&\;\; v_{-j}\alpha \succcurlyeq w_{-j}\beta \;\;\& \\ x_{-i}\gamma \succcurlyeq y_{-i}\delta \end{bmatrix}$$

$$\Rightarrow \qquad [v_{-j}\gamma \succcurlyeq w_{-j}\delta]\,.$$

□

The following lemma is needed for the proof of Theorem IV.2.7, and is analogous to Lemma II.4.5. It is given already here, with a fully elaborated proof, because it may serve as illustration of the condition of nonrevelation of contradictory tradeoffs.

Suppose

$\alpha\beta \preccurlyeq^{*} \gamma\delta$ **and** $\alpha\beta \succ^{**} \gamma\delta$.

Then there exist essential states i and j such that

$\alpha\beta \preccurlyeq_i^{*} \gamma\delta$ *and* $\alpha\beta \succ_j^{**} \gamma\delta$.

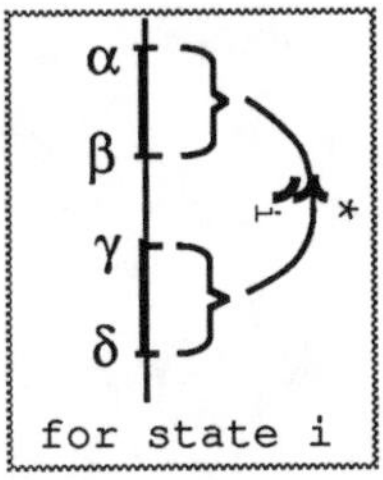

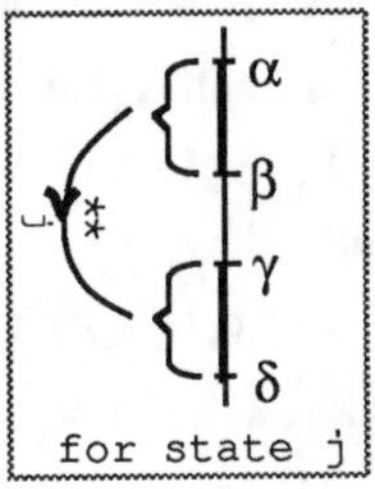

I.e., there exists a 'measuring rod' $[y_{-i}; x_{-i}]$ *to establish the 'revealed comparison of tradeoffs'* $\alpha\beta \preccurlyeq_i^{*} \gamma\delta$.

and

there exists a 'measuring rod' $[w_{-j}; v_{-j}]$ *to establish the 'revealed comparison of tradeoffs'* $\alpha\beta \succ_j^{**} \gamma\delta$.

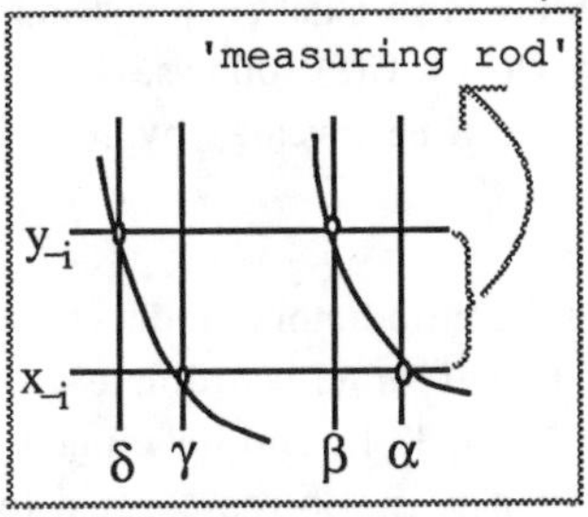

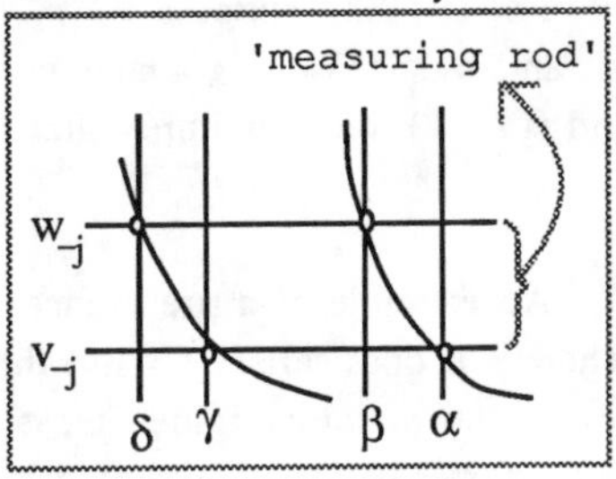

I.e., there are preferences $x_{-i}\alpha \preccurlyeq y_{-i}\beta$ *and* $x_{-i}\gamma \succcurlyeq y_{-i}\delta$

and

there are preferences $v_{-j}\alpha \succcurlyeq w_{-j}\beta$ *and* $v_{-j}\gamma \prec w_{-j}\delta$.

FIGURE IV.2.1 (<u>The revelation of contradictory tradeoffs (on consequences) by the preference relation</u>). Expected utility is falsified if and only if the illustrated revelation occurs, given continuity and weak ordering.

LEMMA IV.2.6. *If an SEU model* $[\Gamma^n, \succcurlyeq, (p_j)_{j=1}^n, U]$ *exists for* $\succcurlyeq$, *then :*

$$\alpha\beta \succ^{**} \gamma\delta \;\Rightarrow\; U(\alpha) - U(\beta) > U(\gamma) - U(\delta) \,, \tag{IV.2.1}$$

$$\alpha\beta \succcurlyeq^{*} \gamma\delta \;\Rightarrow\; U(\alpha) - U(\beta) \geq U(\gamma) - U(\delta) \,. \tag{IV.2.2}$$

Consequently, if an SEU model exists, then $\succcurlyeq$ *does not reveal contradictory tradeoffs.*

PROOF. Let an SEU model as above exist for $\succcurlyeq$. We derive (IV.2.1). Suppose that $\alpha\beta \succ^{**} \gamma\delta$. Let i be such that $\alpha\beta \succ_i^{**} \gamma\delta$. By the definition of $\succ_i^{**}$ there exist alternatives x and y such that

$$[x_{-i}\alpha \succcurlyeq y_{-i}\beta] \text{ and } [\text{not } x_{-i}\gamma \succcurlyeq y_{-i}\delta] \,. \tag{IV.2.3}$$

This implies that

$$\textstyle\sum_{k\neq i} p_k U(x_k) + p_i U(\alpha) \;\geq\; \sum_{k\neq i} p_k U(y_k) + p_i U(\beta)$$

and

$$\textstyle\sum_{k\neq i} p_k U(x_k) + p_i U(\gamma) \;<\; \sum_{k\neq i} p_k U(y_k) + p_i U(\delta) \,.$$

We rewrite these two inequalities as

$$p_i[U(\alpha) - U(\beta)] \;\geq\; \textstyle\sum_{k\neq i} p_k [U(y_k) - U(x_k)]$$

and

$$p_i[U(\gamma) - U(\delta)] \;<\; \textstyle\sum_{k\neq i} p_k [U(y_k) - U(x_k)] \,,$$

which implies

$$p_i[U(\alpha) - U(\beta)] \;>\; p_i[U(\gamma) - U(\delta)] \,.$$

So p_i is positive, and $U(\alpha) - U(\beta) > U(\gamma) - U(\delta)$ follows. (IV.2.1) is established.

For (IV.2.2), suppose $\alpha\beta \succcurlyeq^{*} \gamma\delta$. Then an essential state j must exist such that $\alpha\beta \succcurlyeq_j^{*} \gamma\delta$, and by a reasoning analogous to above $U(\alpha) - U(\beta) \geq U(\gamma) - U(\delta)$ follows. (IV.2.1) and (IV.2.2) together imply that no contradictory tradeoffs can be revealed by $\succcurlyeq$.

□

An example of a preference relation which does reveal contradictory tradeoffs, whereas it does satisfy CI and the hexagon condition, and whereas no coordinate does reveal contradictory tradeoffs, is obtained by taking $n = 2$, $\Gamma =]0,1[$, and defining $\succcurlyeq$ as the binary relation represented by $(x_1,x_2) \mapsto x_1 - x_1x_2$. Then $\succcurlyeq$ is also represented by $(x_1,x_2) \mapsto \ln(x_1) + \ln(1-x_2)$, so that by Theorem III.6.6, $\succcurlyeq$ is a continuous weak order which satisfies CI and the hexagon condition, and no coordinate reveals contradictory tradeoffs. Let us set $\alpha = 1/8$, $\beta = 1/4$, $\gamma = 1/3$, $\delta = 2/3$. We have $(1/8,1/2) \succcurlyeq (1/4,3/4)$ and $(1/3,1/2) \preccurlyeq (2/3,3/4)$, which reveals that $\alpha\beta \succcurlyeq_1^{*} \gamma\delta$; further $(1/5,1/3) \succcurlyeq (2/5,2/3)$ and $(1/5,1/8) \prec (2/5,1/4)$, which reveals that $\gamma\delta \succ_2^{**} \alpha\beta$. Hence $\succcurlyeq$ does reveal contradictory tradeoffs.

An example of a preference relation which does not reveal contradictory tradeoffs, is the preference relation represented by the 'Cobb-Douglas' function on $\mathbb{R}^n_{++}$, $(x_1,\ldots,x_n) \mapsto \prod_{j=1}^n x_j^{\alpha_j}$, with positive α_j's, and $n \in \mathbb{N}$ arbitrary. Then, with

$p_j := \alpha_j/\sum_{i=1}^{n}\alpha_i$, $j = 1,...,n$, and $U : \mu \mapsto \ln(\mu)$, $\succcurlyeq$ is also represented by $x \mapsto \sum_{j=1}^{n} p_j U(x_j)$. By Lemma IV.2.6 indeed $\succcurlyeq$ does not reveal contradictory tradeoffs.

Next we give the central theorem of this monograph. It obtains subjective probabilities without using objective probabilities as a tool. The characterizing condition (ii) below adds to condition (iv) of Theorem III.6.6 (which characterized additive representability) the requirement that revealed comparisons of tradeoffs on consequences should neither give contradictions when derived from different states of nature. Let us repeat that the topological assumption III.3.2 entails that Γ (= Γ_i for all i) is a connected separable topological space, and that Γ^n is endowed with the product topology; for example, this is all satisfied if $\Gamma = \mathbb{R}$, $\Gamma^n = \mathbb{R}^n$.

THEOREM IV.2.7 (Central Theorem). *Under the topological assumption III.3.2, the following two statements are equivalent for the binary relation* $\succcurlyeq$ *on* Γ^n :

(i) **There exists an SEU model $[\Gamma^n, \succcurlyeq, (p_j)_{j=1}^{n}, U]$ for $\succcurlyeq$, with U continuous.**

(ii) **The binary relation $\succcurlyeq$ is a continuous weak order on Γ^n which does not reveal contradictory tradeoffs.**

SKETCH OF PROOF (Section IV.3 gives a full proof). First suppose (i) holds. To derive is (ii). That no contradictory tradeoffs are revealed by $\succcurlyeq$ has been demonstrated in Lemma IV.2.6. The remainder of (ii) is straightforward, e.g. see Theorem III.6.6.

Next suppose (ii) holds. Lemma IV.2.4, together with Theorem III.6.6, show that there exist additive value functions $(V_j)_{j=1}^{n}$ for $\succcurlyeq$. If states are inessential they will have zero probability, and may be suppressed. Hence suppose all states are essential. Now, for every $j \geq 2$, and $\eta \in \Gamma$, there exists an open neighbourhood of η on which V_j can be seen to order differences as V_{j-1} does it (this, and remainder of the proof, will be elaborated in section IV.3). Hence locally V_j can be seen to be a positive affine transform of V_{j-1}. Then it must also be globally. Set $V_j(\theta) = 0$ for arbitrary fixed θ, and all j; take $U := V_1$, and $p_j := V_j(\xi)/\sum V_i(\xi)$ for all j, with ξ any consequence such that $V_j(\xi) \neq 0$.

□

Let us next give uniqueness results applying to the above theorem.

OBSERVATION IV.2.7′ (Uniqueness results for Theorem IV.2.7). The following uniqueness results hold for $(p_j)_{j=1}^{n}$ and U of statement (i) in Theorem IV.2.7 :

If two or more states are essential, then U *is cardinal, and the* p_j*'s are uniquely determined.* (IV.2.4)

If exactly one state i *is essential, then* U *is continuously ordinal,* $p_i = 1$, *and* $p_j = 0$ *for all* $j \neq i$. (IV.2.5)

If no state is essential, then U *can, and must be, any arbitrary constant function, and the* p_j*'s are arbitrary.* (IV.2.6)

□

REMARK IV.2.8. Let us finally consider the special case of statement (i) in Theorem IV.2.7 where $p_j = 1/n$ for all j. The characterization of this case is simple, and does not need Theorem IV.2.7. It is obtained by means of a symmetry condition requiring that $(x_1,...,x_n) \approx (x_{\pi(1)},...,x_{\pi(n)})$ for all x and permutations π on $\{1,...,n\}$, in addition to conditions to characterize additive representability. Now if $(V_1,...,V_n)$ is an array of additive value functions, then so is $(V_2,...,V_n,V_1)$, $(V_3,...,V_n,V_1,V_2)$, ..., as well as $(V_n,V_1,...V_{n-1})$, as well as the sums of all these, i.e., $(\sum_{i=1}^n V_i,...,\sum_{i=1}^n V_i)$. The latter shows that all additive value functions can be chosen identical. Then one chooses U equal to any of these additive value functions, and $p_j = 1/n$ for all j. The symmetry condition can further be used to simplify the characterization of additive representability.

IV.3. PROOF OF THEOREM IV.2.7

In this section we shall prove Theorem IV.2.7. The following definitions are applicable only in the present context, where all factor sets Γ_i are equal, and are denoted as Γ :

DEFINITIONS IV.3.1. For $\alpha \in \Gamma$, $\overline{\alpha} \in \Gamma^n$ is the act with all coordinates equal to α. We write $\alpha \succcurlyeq \beta$ if $\overline{\alpha} \succcurlyeq \overline{\beta}$.

The 'constant' act $\overline{\alpha}$ yields consequence α with certainty. Note that, by the above definition, the binary relation $\succcurlyeq$ on Γ^n induces a binary relation on Γ, also denoted by $\succcurlyeq$. This notation will not cause confusion.

PROOF OF THEOREM IV.2.7, AND OBSERVATION IV.2.7′

First we assume (i) in Theorem IV.2.7, and derive (ii) there. The function, assigning to every act x its expected utility, represents $\succcurlyeq$. So $\succcurlyeq$ is a weak order. This function is also continuous, hence for every act y the set $\{x : x \succcurlyeq y\} = \{x : \sum p_j U(x_j) \geq \sum p_j U(y_j)\}$ is closed; so is the set $\{x : x \preccurlyeq y\}$. Continuity of $\succcurlyeq$ follows. By Lemma IV.2.6, $\succcurlyeq$ does not reveal contradictory tradeoffs. Statement (ii) is established.

Next we suppose that (ii) in Theorem IV.2.7 holds, and derive (i) there, and Observation IV.2.7′. First we deal with the case that no essential state i exists. By Lemma II.2.1 $\succcurlyeq$ is trivial. Then the function U can be any constant function; also U must be constant, since $U(\alpha) > U(\beta)$ would imply $\overline{\alpha} \succ \overline{\beta}$. The numbers (p_j) can be chosen completely arbitrary, as long as they are nonnegative and sum to one. For the case of no essential state everything has been demonstrated.

Next we consider the case of exactly one essential state i. By Corollary III.3.7 there exists a continuous additive representation $V : x \mapsto \sum_{j=1}^n V_j(x_j)$ for $\succcurlyeq$. This essentially needs the assumption of topological separability. From $[x_{-j}\alpha \succ x_{-j}\beta \Leftrightarrow V_j(\alpha) > V_j(\beta)]$ we see that V_i must be nonconstant, and that V_k is constant for all $k \neq i$. Whatever the function U of (i) will be, by the uniqueness result at the end of Corollary III.3.7, for p_iU and hence for U of (i), there exists a continuous strictly increasing transformation φ such that $U = \varphi \circ V_i$. So U will have to be nonconstant. For every $k \neq i$, p_kU must be constant, so p_k must be zero. It follows that $p_i = 1$. Further, any continuous strictly increasing transformation U of V_i, together with $p_i = 1$, $p_k = 0$ for all $k \neq i$, gives an additive representation $x : \mapsto \sum_{k=1}^{n} p_k U(x_k)$ for $\succcurlyeq$, so makes (i) valid. So U can, and must, be any strictly increasing transformation of V_i. For the case of exactly one essential state, (i) and (IV.2.5) follow.

Finally we consider the case of two or more essential states. By Lemma IV.2.4, and Theorem III.6.6, there exists a continuous additive representation $V : x \mapsto \sum_{j=1}^{n} V_j(x_j)$ for $\succcurlyeq$. **Now suppose that state i is essential.** We first show :

For all states j, $V_j = \varphi_j \circ V_i$, for a continuous nondecreasing transformation φ_j. (IV.3.1)

Suppose $V_i(\alpha) \geq V_i(\beta)$. Then, for arbitrary x, the preferences $[x_{-i}\alpha \succcurlyeq x_{-i}\beta]$ and $[x_{-i}\beta \preccurlyeq x_{-i}\beta]$ reveal $\alpha\beta \succcurlyeq_i^* \beta\beta$. Hence not $\beta\beta \succ_j^{**} \alpha\beta$; this, and $[v_{-j}\beta \succcurlyeq v_{-j}\beta]$ for any v, imply $[v_{-j}\alpha \succcurlyeq v_{-j}\beta]$. Consequently $V_j(\alpha) \geq V_j(\beta)$. By Lemma A1.5, (IV.3.1) follows, where we may assume that φ_j is defined only on $V_i(\Gamma)$. Our next step is to show :

Every φ_j is affine. (IV.3.2)

If j is inessential, then V_j is constant, so φ_j is affine. Of course, if $j = i$, then φ_j is identity, so is affine too. So let j be essential, and let $j \neq i$. Let $V_i(\varsigma)$ be an arbitrary element of $V_i(\Gamma)$, the domain of φ_j. There exists an open interval S around $V_i(\varsigma)$ so small that, for all $V_i(\alpha)$, $V_i(\beta)$ in S (thus in $S \cap V_i(\Gamma)$) there are x and y (e.g., $V_j(\Gamma)$ being a nondegenerate interval, $x=z_{-j}x_j$, $y=z_{-j}y_j$ for some z, x_j, y_j) for which

$$V_i(\alpha) - V_i(\beta) = \sum_{k\neq i}[V_k(y_k) - V_k(x_k)] . \tag{IV.3.3}$$

Since φ_j is continuous and $V_i(\Gamma)$ is nondegenerate, we can take the interval S so small that furthermore for all $V_i(\alpha)$, $V_i(\beta)$ in S there are v and w for which

$$\varphi_j(V_i(\alpha)) - \varphi_j(V_i(\beta)) = V_j(\alpha) - V_j(\beta) = \sum_{k\neq j}[V_k(w_k) - V_k(v_k)] . \tag{IV.3.4}$$

To derive 'Jensen's equality' for φ_j, we suppose that $V_i(\alpha)$, $V_i(\beta)$, $V_i(\gamma)$ in S are such that

$$V_i(\gamma) - V_i(\beta) = V_i(\beta) - V_i(\alpha) . \tag{IV.3.5}$$

We show that

$$\varphi_j(V_i(\gamma)) - \varphi_j(V_i(\beta)) = \varphi_j(V_i(\beta)) - \varphi_j(V_i(\alpha)) . \tag{IV.3.6}$$

We take x,y as in (IV.3.3), and conclude from (IV.3.5) that not only $x_{-i}\alpha \approx y_{-i}\beta$, but also $x_{-i}\beta \approx y_{-i}\gamma$. Hence, by $x_{-i}\beta \succcurlyeq y_{-i}\gamma$ and $x_{-i}\alpha \preccurlyeq y_{-i}\beta$:

$$\beta\gamma \succcurlyeq_i^* \alpha\beta . \tag{IV.3.7}$$

Next we take v,w as in (IV.3.4), to obtain

$$v_{-j}\alpha \approx w_{-j}\beta . \tag{IV.3.8}$$

Then, since $v_{-j}\alpha \succcurlyeq w_{-j}\beta$, $v_{-j}\beta \prec w_{-j}\gamma$ cannot be because this would give $\alpha\beta \succ_j^{**} \beta\gamma$, which together with (IV.3.7) would reveal contradictory tradeoffs, i and j being essential.

Analogously we show that $w_{-j}\gamma \prec v_{-j}\beta$ cannot be: By $y_{-i}\gamma \succcurlyeq x_{-i}\beta$ and $y_{-i}\beta \preccurlyeq x_{-i}\alpha$, we have $\gamma\beta \succcurlyeq_i^{*} \beta\alpha$. Since $w_{-j}\beta \succcurlyeq v_{-j}\alpha$, $w_{-j}\gamma \prec v_{-j}\beta$ implies $\beta\alpha \succ_j^{**} \gamma\beta$, which would again reveal contradictory tradeoffs, i and j being essential. The last two paragraphs show :

$$v_{-j}\beta \approx w_{-j}\gamma \, . \qquad \text{(IV.3.9)}$$

Substituting the additive representation gives

$$\varphi_j(V_i(\beta)) - \varphi_j(V_i(\gamma)) = V_j(\beta) - V_j(\gamma) = \textstyle\sum_{k \neq j}[V_k(w_k)-V_k(v_k)] \, .$$

This and (IV.3.4) imply (IV.3.6). So, on S, φ_j satisfies Jensen's equality : $\varphi_j((\sigma+\tau)/2) = [\varphi_j(\sigma) + \varphi_j(\tau)]/2$. By Corollary A1.3[rf2] with $V_i(\varsigma)$ for ν, and $p = 1/2$, affinity of φ_j follows, and (IV.3.2) is established.

So there exist nonnegative $(\sigma_j)_{j=1}^n$, and real $(\tau_j)_{j=1}^n$, such that $V_j = \tau_j + \sigma_j V_i$ for all j. We define :

$$U := V_i \, ; \; p_j := \sigma_j/(\textstyle\sum_{k=1}^n \sigma_k) \text{ for all j.} \qquad \text{(IV.3.10)}$$

Note that $\sigma_i = 1$, so that the denominator $\sum_{k=1}^n \sigma_k$ is positive. Because of joint cardinality, we get additive value functions $(p_j U)_{j=1}^n$ for $\succcurlyeq$. Continuity of $\sum V_j$ implies continuity of U. Statement (i) of Theorem IV.2.7 is established.

For the result of Observation IV.2.7′, for the case of at least two essential states, let $[\Gamma^n, \succcurlyeq, (p'_j)_{j=1}^n, U']$ be another SEU model. Then $(p'_j U')_{j=1}^n$ are additive value functions for $\succcurlyeq$ too. By joint cardinality, $(\tau_j)_{j=1}^n$ and $\sigma > 0$ exist such that $p'_j U' = \sigma p_j U + \tau_j$ for all j; i.e., with α arbitrarily fixed :

$$p'_j[U'(\beta) - U'(\alpha)] = \sigma p_j[U(\beta) - U(\alpha)] \text{ for all } \beta. \qquad \text{(IV.3.11)}$$

Since U is not constant, we can take β such that $U(\beta) \neq U(\alpha)$. Then

$$p_j = p'_j[U'(\beta)-U'(\alpha)] \, / \, (\sigma[U(\beta)-U(\alpha)] \text{ for all j.}$$

Since $\sum p_j = \sum p'_j$, $p_j = p'_j$ for all j follows. Uniqueness of probabilities is established. For $p_j > 0$, (IV.3.11) now shows that $[U'(\beta) - U'(\alpha)] = \sigma[U(\beta)-U(\alpha)]$. Hence $U'(.) = \sigma[U(.)-U(\alpha)] + U'(\alpha)$ must hold: U' is derived from U by multiplication with a positive σ, and addition of a constant (i.e., $U'(\alpha) - \sigma U(\alpha)$) as is required in (IV.2.4). Conversely, that every U' as such instead of U verifies (i), is straightforward.

□

IV.4. AN APPLICATION TO DYNAMIC DECISION MAKING

In this section we sketch several modifications of the condition that $\succcurlyeq$ should not reveal contradictory tradeoffs. For consistency of terminology we shall in the beginning of this section maintain the terminology of decision making under uncertainty, with states of nature, acts, etc. In the final result of this section, Corollary IV.4.4, an application to dynamic contexts will be given. For any $A \subset I$

$x_{-A}\alpha$ is (x with, for all $i \in A$, x_i replaced by α) . (IV.4.1)

The above notation is similar to the notations in section II.2. The definitions given below will be extended to infinite state spaces in Definitions V.2.2.

DEFINITIONS IV.4.1. For event $A \subset I$ and consequences $\alpha,\beta,\gamma,\delta$ we write $\alpha\beta \succcurlyeq^*_A \gamma\delta$ if there exist acts x,y such that both

$$x_{-A}\alpha \succcurlyeq y_{-A}\beta \text{ and} \qquad \text{(IV.4.2)}$$
$$x_{-A}\gamma \preccurlyeq y_{-A}\delta.$$

We write $\alpha\beta \succ^{**}_A \gamma\delta$ if there exist acts x,y such that both

$$x_{-A}\alpha \succcurlyeq y_{-A}\beta \text{ and} \qquad \text{(IV.4.3)}$$
$$\text{not} \quad x_{-A}\gamma \succcurlyeq y_{-A}\delta.$$

DEFINITION IV.4.2. Events A,B <u>(mutually) reveal contradictory tradeoffs (on consequences) (with respect to</u> $\succcurlyeq$) if A and B are essential, and there exist consequences $\alpha,\beta,\gamma,\delta$ such that

$$\alpha\beta \succcurlyeq^*_A \gamma\delta \text{ and } \gamma\delta \succ^{**}_B \alpha\beta .$$

As usual, to avoid cumbersome terminology the parts between brackets in the above definition will mostly be left out; confusion (e.g. if A and B contain exactly one element) is not likely to arise from this. Note that formally the definition is asymmetric in A and B (under usual conditions it can be seen to be symmetric though). The binary relation $\succcurlyeq$ reveals contradictory tradeoffs if and only if there are (essential) *states* i,j which mutually reveal contradictory tradeoffs. It is verified analogously to Lemma IV.2.6 that under expected utility maximization there are no events which reveal contradictory tradeoffs. Theorem IV.2.7 shows that under the assumptions there, such as continuity, no *events* will mutually reveal contradictory tradeoffs if and only if no *states* will mutually do.

THEOREM IV.4.3. *Suppose the topological assumption III.3.2 holds. Let* $n \geq 3$, *and let all states be essential. For the binary relation* $\succcurlyeq$ *on* Γ^n, *the following two statements are equivalent* :

(i) **There exists an SEU model $[\Gamma^n, \succcurlyeq, (p_j)_{j=1}^n, U]$ for $\succcurlyeq$, with U continuous.**

(ii) **The binary relation $\succcurlyeq$ is a continuous weak order on Γ^n; for no $i \geq 2$ the states i-1,i mutually reveal contradictory tradeoffs; neither do 1,j for some j.**

PROOF. The implication (i) => (ii) is straightforward as usually, so we assume (ii), and derive (i). By reflexivity of $\succcurlyeq$ we have $x_{-i}\alpha \succcurlyeq x_{-i}\alpha$ and $x_{-i}\beta \preccurlyeq x_{-i}\beta$ for all x, so $\alpha\alpha \succcurlyeq^*_i \beta\beta$, for all i. Since for every j there is an i such that i,j mutually do not reveal contradictory tradeoffs, $\beta\beta \succ_j^{**} \alpha\alpha$ cannot be, as this and $\alpha\alpha \succcurlyeq_i^{*} \beta\beta$ would reveal contradictory tradeoffs. By Lemma II.4.3 $\succcurlyeq$ satisfies CI. By Theorem III.6.6 there exist additive value functions $(V_j)_{j=1}^n$ for $\succcurlyeq$. The proof that V_{i+1} is an affine nondecreasing transformation of V_i, for i = 1,...,n−1, is exactly as the derivation of (IV.3.1) and (IV.3.2); take j = i + 1 there. We can give all V_i's a common zero. For all $i \geq 2$ it follows that, for some $\mu_i \geq 0$, $V_i = \mu_i V_{i-1}$. Consequently, for all $i \geq 1$ there is a $\lambda_i \geq 0$ such that $V_i = \lambda_i V_1$. By essentiality of all states, $\lambda_i > 0$ for all i. We take $U = V_1$, $p_j = \lambda_j/(\sum_{i=1}^n \lambda_i)$ for all j.

□

The above theorem can also be derived for n = 2, but then a more complicated proof is needed. The main complication is that only a weak version of triple cancellation can be derived, so that the additive value functions cannot be obtained directly from Theorem III.6.6. Further the assumption of essentiality of all states can be omitted, if in (ii) we require that the first *essential* state together with any arbitrary other essential state mutually do not reveal contradictory tradeoffs, and that every subsequent essential state together with its preceding essential state mutually do not reveal contradictory tradeoffs. Also we could have assumed in (ii) above that every essential state together with state 1 mutually did not reveal contradictory tradeoffs, or that, for any appropriately chosen sequence of events $(A_1,\ldots,Am)$, A_{k+1} and A_k mutually do not reveal contradictory tradeoffs, for all $k \leq m-1$. We do not elaborate these matters.

The next corollary gives a characterization of a representation, characterized before by Koopmans(1972) for the context of dynamic decision situations (Example II.1.4). In dynamic contexts coordinates designate points of time. The corollary considers finitely many points of time, whereas Koopmans considered the case where every natural number is a point of time[rf3]. We shall formulate the corollary for the case where $\Gamma = \mathbb{R}$, designating money. The main requirements will be that every point of time and its immediate predecessor mutually do not reveal contradictory tradeoffs on money, and that the amount of money (α in the theorem), equivalent to \$1 on the next point of time, is independent of the particular point of time. Note that, by strong monotonicity, U below will be strictly increasing. **In λ^j below, j is an exponent, not a superscript.**

COROLLARY IV.4.4. *Suppose* $n \geq 3$. *Let the binary relation* $\succcurlyeq$ *on* $\mathbb{R}^n$ *be strongly monotonic. Then the following two statements are equivalent* :

(i) **There exists $0 < \lambda \leq 1$, and a continuous $U : \mathbb{R} \to \mathbb{R}$, such that $x \mapsto \sum_{j=1}^n \lambda^j U(x_j)$ represents $\succcurlyeq$.**

(ii) **The binary relation $\succcurlyeq$ is a continuous weak order, for every $i \geq 2$ i and i−1 mutually do not reveal contradictory tradeoffs, neither do 1 and j for some j; further there exists $\alpha \leq 1$ such that, for all points of time $i \leq n-1$,**

[receiving \$1 at point of time i + 1, \$0 at all other points of time]

$\approx$

[receiving \$$\alpha$ at point of time i and \$0 at all other points of time].

PROOF. The implication (i) => (ii) is straightforward. So let (ii) hold. All conditions in (ii) of Theorem IV.4.3 hold, so a representation $x \mapsto \sum_{i=1}^{n} p_i U(x_i)$ exists for $\succcurlyeq$. By strong monotonicity, positivity of the p_i's and strict increasingness of U can be derived. Now set $\lambda = [U(\alpha)]/U(1)$.

□

The factor λ in (i) above is interpreted as a 'discount factor'. Koopmans(1972) used a stationarity condition which requires invariance, with respect to the point of time, of $\approx$-equivalences as in (ii) above, for all streams of income. We required it only for one 'unit' stream of income. As a price to pay for this, the noncontradictory tradeoffs condition, together with CI as implied by it (see directly below Lemma IV.2.4), is stronger than what Koopmans required besides his stationarity assumption.

IV.5. FURTHER EXTENSIONS AND APPLICATIONS

In Wakker(1988a), and Wakker(1986c, section IV.4 and Theorem IV.4.3), a condition, called equivalence cardinal coordinate independence, is studied. This condition results from cardinal coordinate independence as given in Lemma IV.2.5 by replacing all preferences $\succcurlyeq$ and $\preccurlyeq$ by equivalences $\approx$. It is then shown that, mainly, the above condition together with weak separability instead of the condition that $\succcurlyeq$ does not reveal contradictory tradeoffs, characterizes the representation $x \mapsto \sum_{j=1}^{n} \lambda_j U(x_j)$, with now the λ_j's arbitrary real numbers, possibly negative.

For the case of two coordinates, the representation $(x_1,x_2) \mapsto U(x_1) - U(x_2)$ has received interest in the literature[rf4]. The interpretation is that the strength of preference of x_1 over x_2 is measured. The representation can be characterized by adding to the conditions of weak separability and equivalence cardinal coordinate independence a condition such as $\overline{\alpha} \approx \overline{\beta}$ for all α,β, see Wakker(1986c, Corollary IV.4.5.c).

A way to weaken the condition in Theorem IV.2.7(ii) that $\succcurlyeq$ should not reveal contradictory tradeoffs, is to require this only 'locally'; i.e., for every act x there is an open neigbourhood of x on which this is satisfied. The main problem then is to strengthen the results on additive representations of Chapter III by considering the local versions of the involved characterizing conditions. See below Remark III.7.7. Finally, global proportionality of the additive value functions is derived from local proportionality in neighbourhoods of constant acts.

Also one may weaken in statement (ii) in Theorem IV.2.7 the requirement that for all consequences $\alpha,\beta,\gamma,\delta$, no contradictory tradeoffs should be revealed. It will suffice to require it for only one α. This does not complicate the derivation of CI, so, for more than two essential states, an additive representation must exist. For the case of two essential states matters are more complicated because triple cancellation then no longer directly follows. Once additive value functions have been obtained, the derivation of their proportionality is as in Theorem IV.2.7. Analogously one may restrict the β's, or γ's, or δ's, in Lemma IV.2.5. Whether the restriction there to those $\alpha,\beta,\gamma,\delta$, for which $\beta = \gamma$ (or $\alpha = \delta$) will suffice, is an open question. For such cases no results on additive representations are readily available in the literature.

Also the conjecture has been considered whether in Theorem IV.2.7(ii) it would suffice to require that $\succcurlyeq$ should not reveal contradictory tradeoffs within every two-dimensional subspace, obtained by keeping all but two coordinates fixed. The example of Tversky (see end of section III.7) was also given to serve as a counterexample to this conjecture. Again, requiring that $\succcurlyeq$ should not reveal contradictory tradeoffs within every three-dimensional subspace will probably suffice.

IV.6. COMPARISON OF OUR RESULT TO OTHER DERIVATIONS OF SUBJECTIVE EXPECTED UTILITY MAXIMIZATION

A fully satisfactory characterization, with appealing conditions that are both necessary and sufficient, for subjective expected utility maximization in the context of decision making under uncertainty is not yet available in the literature. Shapiro(1979)[rf5] indicates how difficult this may be. Subjective expected utility provides however the most used (and criticized) approach in decision making under uncertainty. Hence derivations (giving sufficient conditions) are useful.

The best known derivation of subjective expected utility maximization, like ours not presupposing any probabilities or utilities, is the one given in Savage(1954); see our Theorem A2.3. We shall not comment on Savage's Postulate P1 ($\succcurlyeq$ is a weak order), P5 (nontriviality), and P7 (avoiding phenomena resembling the 'St. Petersburg's paradox'). Savage's postulate P4 allows the derivation of a 'qualitative probability relation' ('more probable than') on the set of events, from the preference relation on the set of acts. Mainly Savage's Postulate P2 (the major part of the 'sure-thing principle'; see section 2.7 there) guarantees 'additivity' (condition 2 at the top of page 32 there) of this qualitative probability relation. The main restrictive assumption in Savage's approach is postulate P6, some sort of continuity condition, requiring structure for the state space. For example, the state space must be infinite (though not necessarily uncountable, contrary to what is sometimes thought). The major step in the proof of Savage is to use the obtained qualitative probability relation, and the structure on the state space, to derive the probability measure[rf6]. Once the probability measure has been obtained, the utility function is derived analogously as this was done in von Neumann&Morgenstern(1947, 1953, Chapter 3 and Appendix; see our Theorem A2.2). For the consequence space Savage hardly needs restrictions. Mainly must the utility function be bounded[rf7]. While Savage is mostly referred to in economic analyses for justification of the use of subjective expected utility, we are not aware of an analysis where actually the conditions of Savage have been satisfied and taken as point of departure.

In economic contexts the consequence space is usually assumed to be endowed with topological structure; for example, it is $\mathbb{R}^m_+$. Hence in economic contexts derivations of subjective expected utility maximization, employing this structure, such as our Theorem IV.2.7, and Theorem V.6.1 in the sequel, will be of use. Note that we did not use a qualitative probability relation as intermediate in the derivation of the probability measure. Our probabilities resulted from the 'scale parameters' σ_j in the proof of Theorem IV.2.7, see (IV.3.10); they are proportional to the scales of the additive value functions $(V_j)_{j=1}^n$ there. Another derivation of the same representation as ours, also with a continuity assumption, is given in Grodal(1978). Her derivation is in terms of a derived 'mean groupoid operation' on the consequence space which by means of continuity is derived from the preference relation.

An early derivation of subjective expected utility maximization may be recognized in de Finetti(1930, sections 4 and 5; 1937, Chapter I; the best presentation is given in de Finetti, 1974, Chapter 3; see our Theorem A2.1). De Finetti assumed that consequences were real numbers (amounts of money). His main requirement was the impossibility to make a 'Dutch book' against the decision maker; i.e., no positive linear combination of bets which are all 'fair' (at least as good as not betting) in the view of the decision maker, should result in a bet giving with certainty a negative yield. This entails linearity of the utility function. An advantage of de Finetti's result above other results is that, once his conditions are satisfied, receipt or loss of additional money (certain or uncertain) will not alter the preference relation, so that a preference relation can actually be revealed from choices, *irrespective* of what choices, consequences etc. the decision maker is faced with outside, before, or after, the observed choices. The linearity of utility as resulting from de Finetti's approach has limited the impact on economic science (see for instance Arrow,1971, p.36).

Other approaches assume that not only consequences are available as result from a decision situation, but also all simple lotteries (with known probability distributions) over consequences; or more generally elements of 'mixture spaces' are used, instead of lotteries. See Anscombe&Aumann(1963), presented in our Theorem A2.4, and Fishburn (1982)[rf8]. Also Ramsey(1931) can be placed under the lottery-approach, if his 'ethically neutral event' is considered as a $\frac{1}{2}$-$\frac{1}{2}$ lottery. Pfanzagl(1968, Chapter 12) interprets Ramsey's work like we do, and extends it. All these approaches used linear ('affine'; 'von Neumann-Morgenstern') utility, with respect to the lotteries. The involved mathematics can be related to that of de Finetti. Compared to these, our approach does not need linearity of the utility functions, or the availability of lotteries on the consequence spaces. In many economic applications the introduction of lotteries with known probability distributions on consequences will be felt as an artificial construct. This has motivated our work. Further there will be advantages in philosophical discussions on the objective/subjective nature of probability, to have available foundations of subjective probabilities which do not need objective probabilities.

Extensive surveys of expected utility are provided in Fishburn(1981), Schoemaker (1982), and Machina(1982a). Recent developments are surveyed in Machina(1987); the latter survey shows that the popularity of expected utility in decision theory has been decreasing these last years.

CHAPTER V

CONTINUOUS SUBJECTIVE EXPECTED UTILITY FOR ARBITRARY STATE SPACES

V.1. INTRODUCTION

In this chapter[rf1] terminology will be as in decision making under uncertainty. We extend the characterization of continuous subjective expected utility maximization, given only for finite state spaces in Theorem IV.2.7, to arbitrary state spaces. This is the only chapter where the index set (= state space) I is not assumed finite. Contrary to Savage (1954)'s approach, our approach can deal with unbounded utility functions. We shall give an example (Example V.6.2) where our approach deals with a set of acts, rich enough to generate *every* probability distribution (over utility) with finite mean.

The strategy in this chapter is to first, as much as possible, assume conditions and derive results for $\succcurlyeq$ on the **simple acts**, i.e., acts which are **simple functions** (simple functions have finite image). Next the results are extended to acts with infinite image, by the conditions of 'pointwise monotonicity', 'constant continuity', and 'truncation continuity'.

V.2. MEASURE THEORY AND SIMPLE ACTS

Acts, consequences, and states of nature are as in Example II.1.1 (decision making under uncertainty). To stay close to the tradition in probability theory we generalize our set-up by introducing 'measure-theoretic' structure. A reader not interested in that may simply assume that the 'algebra' Σ, to be introduced in a moment, is 2^I. Then all functions from I to Γ are 'measurable', and all measure-theoretical conditions in the sequel will be trivially satisfied, so can be ignored. This also shows that the introduction of measure-theoretic structure indeed is a generalization.

We assume that an algebra Σ on I is given. Elements A,B of Σ are called events (this generalizes the definition of section IV.2). Further we assume that an algebra Δ on Γ is given. Let Φ denote the set of acts x which are (Δ-Σ-) **measurable**, i.e., for every set $E \in \Delta$, the set $\{i \in I: x_i \in E\}$ is in Σ. Note that $x_{-A}\alpha$ is in Φ whenever A is an event and x is in Φ.

Let $\pi = (A_j)_{j=1}^m$ be a partition of I, consisting of events. By Σ^π we denote the algebra of the subsets of I which are a union of events from π. We write $\sum_{j=1}^m \alpha_j 1_{A_j}$ for the act in Φ which assigns α_j to every i in A_j, j = 1,...,m. Obviously this act is simple. The notation for the simple act above is just suggestive. It does not designate any addition or multiplication operation, these not even being defined for general Γ. The notation has been chosen for being of maximal convenience for the special case where $\Gamma \subset \mathbb{R}$. In that case, with 1_{A_j} the 'indicator function' of A_j assigning 1 to every state in A_j and zero to all other states, the above notation may indeed be taken to designate addition and multiplication operations. For a partition π as above, Φ^π is the set of acts writable as $\sum_{j=1}^m \alpha_j 1_{A_j}$ for some $\alpha_1,...,\alpha_m$. Let $\Phi^s := \{x \in \Phi: x \text{ is simple}\}$, so Φ^s is the union of all sets Φ^π. Note that $x_{-A}\alpha \in \Phi^s$ whenever $x \in \Phi^s$ and $A \in \Sigma$.

The following topological condition is of a finite-dimensional character, thus is weaker than most of the other continuity conditions, used in the literature.

DEFINITION V.2.1. The binary relation $\succcurlyeq$ is **simple-continuous**, or **s-continuous**, if for any partition $(A_j)_{j=1}^m$ consisting of events, and any act $x = \sum_{j=1}^m \alpha_j 1_{A_j}$, the sets $\{(\beta_1,...,\beta_m) \in \Gamma^m : \sum_{j=1}^m \beta_j 1_{A_j} \succcurlyeq x\}$ and $\{(\beta_1,...,\beta_m) \in \Gamma^m : \sum_{j=1}^m \beta_j 1_{A_j} \preccurlyeq x\}$ are closed with respect to the product topology on Γ^m.

S-continuity is equivalent to continuity, with respect to the product topology on Γ^m, for any partition $(A_j)_{j=1}^m$ as above, of the binary relation $\succcurlyeq'$ on Γ^m, defined by :

$$(\alpha_1,...,\alpha_m) \succcurlyeq' (\beta_1,...,\beta_m) \text{ if and only if } \sum_{j=1}^m \alpha_j 1_{A_j} \succcurlyeq \sum_{j=1}^m \beta_j 1_{A_j} . \quad \text{(V.2.1)}$$

This 'finite-dimensional' continuity is not unusually strong since in a finite-dimensional space the product topology is not coarser than other usual topologies. If Γ is a metric space, for example the Euclidean space, then the finite-dimensional product topology is equal to the sup-metric topology, which for Euclidean spaces is equal to the usual Euclidean topology[rf2].

The main topological complications occur for infinite dimensions. Then the product topology is coarser than other usual topologies, and continuity with respect to the product topology is too strong for our purposes. It would imply σ-additivity of the probability measure P, to be derived in the sequel. Further it would quickly lead to boundedness of the utility function U derived in the sequel, if not $\succcurlyeq$ is restricted to an appropriately chosen subset of $\prod_{i \in I}\Gamma$. Our approach will keep the infinite-dimensional complications to a minimum, by restricting conditions as much as possible to simple acts.

There are several ways to extend the definition of contradictory tradeoffs from finite Cartesian products to infinite Cartesian products. As the strategy in this chapter is to work as much as possible with simple acts, we shall derive comparisons of tradeoffs only from simple (measurable) acts. For finite state spaces I it is usually assumed, without further mention, that $\Sigma = 2^I$. Then the following definitions coincide with the definitions given in section IV.4.

DEFINITIONS V.2.2. For event $A \subset I$ and consequences $\alpha,\beta,\gamma,\delta$ we write $\alpha\beta \succcurlyeq_A^* \gamma\delta$ if there exist simple acts x,y such that both

$$x_{-A}\alpha \succcurlyeq y_{-A}\beta \text{ and} \tag{V.2.2}$$
$$x_{-A}\gamma \preccurlyeq y_{-A}\delta.$$

We write $\alpha\beta \succ_A^{**} \gamma\delta$ if there exist simple acts $x,y \in \Phi^s$ such that both

$$x_{-A}\alpha \succcurlyeq y_{-A}\beta \text{ and} \tag{V.2.3}$$
$$\text{not } x_{-A}\gamma \succcurlyeq y_{-A}\delta.$$

We write s-(in)essential as an abbreviation of '(in)essential on Φ^s '. So here again attention is restricted to simple acts.

DEFINITION V.2.3. Events A,B (mutually) reveal contradictory tradeoffs (on consequences) (with respect to $\succcurlyeq$) if A and B are s-essential, and there exist consequences $\alpha,\beta,\gamma,\delta$ such that

$$\alpha\beta \succcurlyeq_A^* \gamma\delta \text{ and } \gamma\delta \succ_B^{**} \alpha\beta .$$

Let us repeat the structural assumptions made so far. **These will be assumed throughout this chapter :**

ASSUMPTION V.2.4. (Structural Assumption, for this Chapter). **I is a non-empty set, endowed with an algebra Σ. Γ is a connected separable topological space, endowed with an algebra Δ containing all open subsets of Γ.**

V.3. RESULTS FOR SIMPLE ACTS

First we deal with the 'degenerate' case where one state, or an 'ultrafilter' of states (see proof below) is 'certainly true'.

LEMMA V.3.1. *Let there not exist two disjoint events which are s-essential. Under Assumption V.2.4 the following two statements are equivalent :*

(i) **There exists a finitely additive probability measure P on Σ, and a continuous function $U : \Gamma \to \mathbb{R}$, such that, for all $\alpha_1,\ldots,B_t$,**
$\sum_{j=1}^{s}\alpha_j 1_{A_j} \succcurlyeq \sum_{k=1}^{t}\beta_k 1_{B_k} \iff \sum_{j=1}^{s}P(A_j)U(\alpha_j) \geq \sum_{k=1}^{t}P(B_k)U(\beta_k)$.

(ii) **The binary relation $\succcurlyeq$ is an s-continuous weak order on Φ^s.**

Furthermore, if (i) holds, then no events mutually reveal contradictory tradeoffs.

OBSERVATION V.3.1′. The following uniqueness results hold for U,P of statement (i) in Lemma V.3.1 :

If $\succcurlyeq$ *is not trivial on* Φ^s, *then* P(A) = 1 *for all s-essential events* A, P(A) = 0 *for all s-inessential events* A, *and* U *is continuously ordinal.* (V.3.1)

If $\succcurlyeq$ *is trivial on* Φ^s, *then* U *can, and must, be any constant function, and* P *is arbitrary.* (V.3.2)

PROOF of Lemma V.3.1 and Observation V.3.1′. The implication (i) => (ii) in Lemma V.3.1 is straightforward. So we suppose (ii), and derive (i), the result below (ii), and the uniqueness results in Observation V.3.1′. Analogously to Lemma II.2.1 one sees that there is no s-essential event if and only if $x \approx y$ for all $x,y \in \Phi^s$; i.e., if and only if $\succcurlyeq$ is trivial on Φ^s. In this case all of (V.3.2), and (i), follows.
So from now on we assume :

There exists an s-essential event. (V.3.3)

To obtain P, we show :

The collection of all s-essential events is an **ultrafilter**; i.e.,

(a) I is s-essential.
(b) Event A is s-essential if and only if A^c is s-inessential.
(c) If events A and B are s-essential, then so is $A \cap B$.

If I would be s-inessential, then $\succcurlyeq$ would be trivial on Φ^s, contradicting (V.3.3). So (a) above follows. If, for an event A, both A and A^c would be s-inessential, then $x \approx x_A y_{A^c} \approx y$ would follow for all $x,y \in \Phi^s$, and $\succcurlyeq$ would be trivial on Φ^s. This cannot hold, and (b) now follows from the assumption that no two disjoint s-essential events can exist. If events A and B are s-inessential, then so is $A \cup B$, since for all $x,y \in \Phi^s$ with $x_{A^c \cap B^c} = y_{A^c \cap B^c}$ we have $x \approx x_{A^c} y_A \approx y$. This and (b) imply (c).

We define P(A) = 1 for all s-essential events A, and P(A) = 0 for all remaining events A. One easily checks that this gives a finitely additive probability measure P.

Let U represent $\succcurlyeq$ on Γ, as defined in Definition IV.3.1. By Theorem III.3.6 such a U indeed exists, by Observation III.3.6′ it is continuously ordinal. Statement (i) is established if we show that :

$$(x =)\sum_{j=1}^{s} \alpha_j 1_{A_j} \succcurlyeq \sum_{k=1}^{t} \beta_k 1_{B_k} (= y) \iff \sum_{j=1}^{s} P(A_j)U(\alpha_j) \geq \sum_{k=1}^{t} P(B_k)U(\beta_k) . \quad \text{(V.3.4)}$$

Of the mutually disjoint events $(A_j \cap B_k)_{j=1,k=1}^{s \quad t}$ exactly one is s-essential, say $A_1 \cap B_1$. Then $x \approx \overline{\alpha}_1$, $y \approx \overline{\beta}_1$, $P(A_1) = 1 = P(B_1)$, and (V.3.4) follows.

Now (V.3.1) follows from the observation that a function U as in (i) must represent $\succcurlyeq$ on Γ, and that P as in (i) must assign probability 0 to every s-inessential event, thus 1 to every s-essential event. The 'furthermore-statement' in the lemma is by simple substitution in (i).

□

The next lemma shows how, for an arbitrary fixed partition $(A_1,...,A_m)$ consisting of events, on the 'finite-dimensional' subspace of the form $\{x \in \Gamma^I : \alpha_1,...,\alpha_m \in \Gamma, x = \sum_{j=1}^m \alpha_j 1_{A_j}\}$, the results for finite Cartesian products can be applied.

LEMMA V.3.2. *Suppose Assumption V.2.4 holds. Let $\succcurlyeq$ be an s-continuous weak order on Φ^s. Let no events mutually reveal contradictory tradeoffs. Let $\pi^1 = (A_1,...,A_s)$ be a partition which consists of events and which contains at least two events which are s-essential. Then there exist nonnegative $(p_j^1)_{j=1}^s$, summing to 1, and a continuous $U^1 : \Gamma \to \mathbb{R}$, such that the function $x \mapsto \sum_{j=1}^s p_j^1 U^1(x_j)$ represents $\succcurlyeq$ on Φ^{π^1}. The p_j^1's are uniquely determined, and U^1 is cardinal.*

PROOF. Define $\succcurlyeq'$ on Γ^s as in (V.2.1), and apply Theorem IV.2.7 and formula (IV.2.4).

□

Next we show that for two finite partitions π^1 and π^2 consisting of events, each with at least two s-essential events, the representations resulting from the previous lemma 'fit together'; i.e., the utility functions can be taken the same, and events occurring in both partitions have the same probability in each representation. This we do by comparing π^1 and π^2 to a partition π^3 consisting of events, with π^3 finer than π^1 and π^2, and by showing that the representations of π^1 and π^2 'fit together' with that of π^3.

LEMMA V.3.3. *Let, under the assumptions and notations of Lemma V.3.2, $\pi^2 = (B_1,...,B_t)$ be another partition which consists of events and which contains at least two s-essential events. Let application of Lemma V.3.2 to π^2 give $(p_j^2)_{j=1}^t$ and U^2. Then $U^2 = \varphi \circ U^1$ for a positive affine φ, and if $A_i = B_j$ for some i,j, then also $p_i^1 = p_j^2$.*

PROOF. Define

$$\pi^3 := (A_1 \cap B_1,...,A_1 \cap B_t, A_2 \cap B_1,...A_2 \cap B_t,...,A_s \cap B_1,...,A_s \cap B_t).$$

First we show that π^3 must have two or more s-essential events. Say A_1 and A_2 are s-essential. Now s-inessentiality of all $A_1 \cap B_k$, $k = 1,...,s$, by a reasoning as used to derive (c) below (V.3.3), implies s-inessentiality of A_1. So of the $A_1 \cap B_k$'s at least one is s-essential. Analogously of the $A_2 \cap B_k$'s at least one is s-essential.

So we can apply Lemma V.3.2 to π^3 instead of π^1, yielding $((p_{jk})_{k=1}^t)_{j=1}^s$ and U^3. Now, defining $p_j := \sum_{k=1}^t p_{jk}$ for all j, and $U := U^3$, we obtain an array $(p_j)_{j=1}^n$ and a U that satisfy all requirements for $(p_j^1)_{j=1}^n$ and U^1 in Lemma V.3.2. The uniqueness results of that lemma imply $p_j = p_j^1$ for all j, and $U^1 = \varphi^1 \circ U^3$ for a positive affine φ^1.

Analogously $p_i^2 = \sum_{j=1}^s p_{ji}$ for all i, and $U^2 = \varphi^2 \circ U^3$ for a positive affine φ^2. So $U^2 = \varphi \circ U^1$ for a positive affine φ. And if $A_i = B_j$ for some i,j, then $p_{ik} = p_{\ell j} = 0$ for all $k \neq j$, $\ell \neq i$; $p_i^1 = p_j^2 = p_{ij}$ follows.

□

Now we are ready for the main result of this section, a characterization of a subjective expected utility representation on Φ^s.

THEOREM V.3.4. *Under Assumption V.2.4, for the binary relation $\succcurlyeq$ on Γ^I the following two statements are equivalent :*

(i) **There exist a finitely additive probability measure P and a continuous function $U : \Gamma \to \mathbb{R}$, such that $\sum_{j=1}^m \alpha_j 1_{A_j} \mapsto \sum_{j=1}^m P(A_j)U(\alpha_j)$ represents $\succcurlyeq$ on Φ^s .**

(ii) **The binary relation $\succcurlyeq$ is an s-continuous weak order on Φ^s, and no events mutually reveal contradictory tradeoffs.**

OBSERVATION V.3.4′. The following uniqueness results hold for U, P of statement (i) in Theorem V.3.4 :

If two disjoint s-essential events exist, then P *is uniquely determined, and* U *is cardinal.* (V.3.5)

If I *is s-essential, but no two disjoint s-essential events exists, then* P *assigns* 1 *to every s-essential event,* 0 *to every s-inessential event, and* U *is continuously ordinal.* (V.3.6)

If I *is s-inessential, then* P *is arbitrary, and* U *can, and must, be any constant function.* (V.3.7)

PROOF of Theorem V.3.4 and Observation V.3.4′. As always, the implication (i) => (ii) is straightforward. So in the sequel we assume (ii), and derive (i) and Observation V.3.4′. The case where I is s-inessential, described in (V.3.7), and the case described in (V.3.6) have been treated in Lemma V.3.1 and Observation V.3.1′. So we assume that there exist two disjoint s-essential events. By Lemma V.3.2 there exist, for every partition $\pi = (A_1,...,A_t)$ consisting of events with at least two s-essential events, a probability measure P_π on the algebra of events consisting of unions of events from π, and a continuous utility function $U_\pi : \Gamma \to \mathbb{R}$, such that $\sum_{j=1}^t \alpha_j 1_{A_j} \mapsto \sum_{j=1}^t P_\pi(A_j)U_\pi(\alpha_j)$ represents $\succcurlyeq$ on the elements of Φ^s that can be written as $\sum_{j=1}^t \alpha_j 1_{A_j}$. By Lemma V.3.3, P_π and U_π can be taken independent of π. That we do, and we leave out indexes π.

First we show that P is a probability measure. $P(\emptyset) = 0$, $P(I) = 1$ are obvious. Let A,B be disjoint. To show is: $P(A \cup B) = P(A) + P(B)$. We define $A_1 := A$, $A_2 := B$, $A_3 := A^c \cap B^c$. Let C,D be two disjoint s-essential events. Define $B_1 := C$, $B_2 := D$, $B_3 := C^c \cap D^c$. Let $\pi = (((A_i \cap B_j)_{i=1}^3)_{j=1}^3)$. This π has, by a reasoning as in the proof of Lemma V.3.3, at least two s-essential events. Let $(p_{ij})_{i=1,j=1}^{3\ \ 3}$ and U be as resulting from Lemma V.3.2. Now $P(A) = \sum_{j=1}^3 p_{1j}$, $P(B) = \sum_{j=1}^3 p_{2j}$, and $P(A \cup B) = \sum_{j=1}^3 (p_{1j} + p_{2j})$. $P(A \cup B) = P(A) + P(B)$ has been shown.

Now [$\sum_{j=1}^s \alpha_j 1_{A_j} \succcurlyeq \sum_{k=1}^t \beta_k 1_{B_k} \iff \sum_{j=1}^s P(A_j)U(\alpha_j) \geq \sum_{k=1}^t P(B_k)U(\beta_k)$] follows from consideration of a π, both finer than $(A_j)_{j=1}^s$ and $(B_k)_{k=1}^t$. The uniqueness result (V.3.5) follows from Lemma V.3.2. □

The following Corollary, a simple consequence of the above theorem, gives properties which $\succcurlyeq$ has on Φ^s, but in general not on larger subsets of Φ, as we shall see in the following section.

COROLLARY V.3.5. *Let* $\succcurlyeq$ *satisfy (i) of Theorem V.3.4. Then, for all* $x,y \in \Phi^s$, $[\overline{x}_i \succcurlyeq \overline{y}_i$ *for all* $i \in I \Rightarrow x \succcurlyeq y]$. *Further* $\succcurlyeq$ *is independent of equal subalternatives on* Φ^s.

V.4. INCLUDING NONSIMPLE ACTS WITH BOUNDED EXPECTED UTILITY

In this section the representation of Theorem V.3.4 (i) will be extended to nonsimple acts. We have in mind an expected utility representation by means of some sort of integral of U with respect to P, and will use the 'Stieltjes type integral' as explicated in section 4.5 of Bhaskara Rao&Bhaskara Rao(1983)[rf3]. In this an integral, notation EU(x), of a bounded measurable function $U \circ x$ on I is obtained as a 'lower integral', equal to

$$\sup\{EU(f^s) : f^s \text{ is a simple measurable function from I to } \mathbb{R},\ f^s \leq^P U \circ x\},$$

with $\leq^P$ **pointwise dominance**; i.e., $f^s \leq^P U \circ x$ whenever $f^s(i) \leq U(x_i)$ for all $i \in I$; the integral may also be obtained as an 'upper integral', which is analogous and yields the same result for bounded functions. If $U \circ x$ is bounded below (above) but unbounded above (below), one may still define the lower (upper) integral, which then may be $+\infty$ ($-\infty$), and one may see if this is useful. Finally, if $U \circ x$ is neither bounded above nor below, one may proceed as follows. First one 'splits up' $U \circ x$ into $U \circ x^+$ and $U \circ x^-$, with $U \circ x^+ : i \mapsto \max\{U \circ x(i),0\}$ and $U \circ x^- : i \mapsto \min\{U \circ x(i),0\}$. Next one sets $\int(U \circ x)dP = \int(U \circ x^+)dP + \int(U \circ x^-)dP$ (first term upper integral, second term lower integral). This is defined whenever not simultaneously the first term is $+\infty$ and the second term $-\infty$. Of course, we have in mind to let functions f^s above be of the form $U \circ x^s$ for $x^s \in \Phi^s$. We handle pointwise dominance by the following definition.

DEFINITION V.4.1. The binary relation $\succcurlyeq$ is **pointwise monotone** on $E \subset \Gamma^I$ if $x \succcurlyeq y$ for all $x, y \in E$ for which $\overline{x}_i \succcurlyeq \overline{y}_i$ for all $i \in I$.

The above condition is the version of weak monotonicity where for every $\geq_i$ the $\succcurlyeq$-relation on the constant acts is taken. Note that in Corollary V.3.5 we established pointwise monotonicity on Φ^s [rf4]. Note that pointwise monotonicity uses comparisons of consequences x_i to consequences y_i, only if these consequences are assigned to the same state of nature; such a comparison can therefore be considered a comparison of acts x and y 'conditional on a state of nature'. This differs from assumption P7 in Savage (1954). The latter requires (see section A2): $x \succcurlyeq y$ whenever $\overline{x}_i \succ y$ for all i, or $x \succ \overline{y}_i$ for all i. We think pointwise monotonicity is both intuitively preferable, and mathematically more suited. Our results allow for unboundedness of utility, whereas in Savage's set-up utility must be bounded, see section 14.1 in Fishburn(1970).

The following example illustrates that pointwise monotonicity is not implied by the other conditions, introduced so far. Some terminology: An act x is **strongly bounded from below** if there exists a consequence ν such that $\nu \preccurlyeq x_i$ for all states i; x is **strongly bounded from above** if there exists a consequence μ such that $\mu \succcurlyeq x_i$ for all i; finally, x is **strongly bounded** if it is both strongly bounded from above and from below. By Φ^b we denote the set of all strongly bounded acts in Φ.

EXAMPLE V.4.2. Let $I =]0,1]$, $\Gamma = \mathbb{R}$, Σ the Borel σ-algebra on $]0,1]$, Δ the Borel σ-algebra on $\mathbb{R}$, U identity, and let P be the Lebesgue measure. Let $\succcurlyeq$ on Φ^b be represented by a linear function ('functional') V from Φ to $\mathbb{R}$, to be defined below. We start setting $V(1_A+0_{A^c}) := P(A)$ for all events A. By linearity of V, this determines V on the linear space generated by the acts $1_A+0_{A^c}$, i.e., on Φ^s; V is the usual integral there. This already suffices to decide that $\succcurlyeq$ is an s-continuous weak order. Linearity of V implies independence of equal subalternatives. (Also $\succcurlyeq$ is 'constant-continuous', see below.) Further no events mutually reveal contradictory tradeoffs. However, outside the linear subspace Φ^s we still have freedom in defining V. For example we may define V such that V assigns to x, with $x_i = i$ for all i, any real number, such as -1, since x is not in the linear subspace generated by the indicator functions. Then $\overline{x_i} \succcurlyeq 0$ for all i, but not $x \succcurlyeq \overline{0}$, so pointwise monotonicity is violated. (The possibility to extend the V as above to the entire space of acts can for instance be guaranteed by the theorem of Hahn-Banach, see Dunford&Schwartz(1958).)

We shall characterize expected utility maximization only for acts with finite expected utility. Finiteness of expected utility will be guaranteed by requiring, for any considered act x, that there exist consequences μ, ν such that $\overline{\mu} \succcurlyeq x \succcurlyeq \overline{\nu}$. For such acts x we shall obtain 'certainty equivalents' in Lemma V.4.3. First we must however introduce an infinite-dimensional topological condition. For the finite-dimensional case this condition is implied by the other conditions of Theorem IV.2.7; this can be formulated as a corollary of Theorem IV.2.7, or proved directly as in Lemma VI.6.1 in the sequel.

DEFINITION V.4.3. The preference relation $\succcurlyeq$ is **constant-continuous** on $E \subset \Gamma^I$ if $\{\alpha \in \Gamma : \overline{\alpha} \succcurlyeq x\}$ and $\{\alpha \in \Gamma : \overline{\alpha} \preccurlyeq x\}$ are closed for all $x \in E$.

As s-continuity, constant-continuity is implied by product-topology-continuity, and by Koopmans' sup-metric-continuity. The only consequence of constant-continuity that we shall use is the following lemma, giving 'certainty-equivalents'.

LEMMA V.4.4. *Suppose* $\succcurlyeq$ *is a constant-continuous pointwise monotone weak order on a set* $E \subset \Phi$ which contains all constant acts. *Let, for* $x \in E$, *there exist* μ, ν *such that* $\overline{\mu} \succcurlyeq x \succcurlyeq \overline{\nu}$. *Then there exists a consequence* α *such that* $x \approx \overline{\alpha}$.

PROOF. The sets $\{\beta \in \Gamma : \overline{\beta} \succcurlyeq x\}$ and $\{\beta \in \Gamma : \overline{\beta} \preccurlyeq x\}$ are closed by constant-continuity, and are nonempty. Their union is Γ, so by connectedness of Γ they must have nonempty intersection. Let α be an element of this intersection.

□

Integrals for unbounded functions $U \circ x$ are undefined when both $U \circ x^+$ and $U \circ x^-$ have infinite integrals. This is even conceivable if $x \approx \overline{\alpha}$ for some α. To exclude such acts x we introduce 'truncation continuity'. A preparatory notation:

For $\alpha,\beta \in \Gamma$, $\alpha \vee \beta$ [respectively $\alpha \wedge \beta$] is α if $\alpha \succcurlyeq \beta$ [respectively $\alpha \preccurlyeq \beta$], β otherwise.

Now, for an act x and a consequence μ, the **above truncation** $t(x \wedge \mu)$ is the act which assigns $x_i \wedge \mu$ to every state i. The **below truncation** $t(x \vee \mu)$ is the act which assigns $x_i \vee \mu$ to every state i. We call a set of acts E **truncation-closed** if, for every consequence μ, and act $x \in E$, the truncations $x \wedge \mu$ and $x \vee \mu$ are also contained in E.

DEFINITION V.4.5. The preference relation $\succcurlyeq$ is **truncation-continuous** on a set $E \subset \Phi$ if for every $x \succ y$ in E there exist μ and ν such that $t(x \wedge \mu) \succ y$ and $x \succ t(y \vee \nu)$.

Note that truncation-continuity is of a nontopological nature, i.e., does not involve a topology. We can now, for any act x with $x \approx \overline{\alpha}$ for some consequence α, define $EU(x) := U(\alpha)$, with U as in Theorem V.3.4, under the appropriate assumptions for $\succcurlyeq$. Then $[x \succcurlyeq y \Leftrightarrow EU(x) \geq EU(y)]$, and for any $x = \sum_{j=1}^{m} \alpha_j 1_{A_j}$, $EU(x) = \sum_{j=1}^{m} P(A_j)U(\alpha_j)$. Question remains whether EU can be considered a (Stieltjes-type) integral outside Φ^s. Below we shall guarantee that it can be.

THEOREM V.4.6. *Suppose $\succcurlyeq$ is a binary relation on Γ^I. Let E be a truncation-closed set of acts, let $\Phi^s \subset E \subset \Phi$, and let for every act $x \in E$ there exist consequences μ,ν such that $\overline{\mu} \succcurlyeq x \succcurlyeq \overline{\nu}$. Then, under Assumption V.2.4, the following two statements are equivalent :*

(i) **There exists a finitely additive probability measure P on Σ, and a continuous function $U : \Gamma \to \mathbb{R}$, such that, on E, $x \mapsto \int (U \circ x)dP$ represents $\succcurlyeq$, with the integral well-defined.**

(ii) **The binary relation $\succcurlyeq$ is a constant- and s-continuous, pointwise monotone, truncation-continuous weak order on E, and no events mutually reveal contradictory tradeoffs.**

PROOF. For (i) => (ii), suppose (i) holds. We shall only derive truncation-continuity, the other conditions in (ii) being established in Theorem V.3.4 or being straightforward. Say $x \succ y$. Then $\int (U \circ x)dP > \int (U \circ y)dP$. Because of connectedness of $U(\Gamma)$, any value between $\inf(U(\Gamma))$ and $\sup(U(\Gamma))$ is in $U(\Gamma)$, hence according to the theory of the Stieltjes-integrals, $\int (U \circ x)dP$ is the supremum of $\int (U \circ x^*)dP$ over the above truncations x^* of x. So there must be such an above truncation x^* such that $\int (U \circ x^*)dP > \int (U \circ y)dP$.

Consequently $x^* \succ y$. Analogously a below truncation y^* of y is found such that $x \succ y^*$.

Next we derive (ii) => (i). Implicit in several places in the sequel is that any simple (i.e., with finite range) measurable function $f : \Gamma \rightarrow \mathbb{R}$ with maximum and minimum in $U(\Gamma)$ can, by connectedness of $U(\Gamma)$, be obtained as $U \circ x^s$ for a simple act x^s; hence for approximations by simple functions as involved in the Stieltjes integral, we can restrict attention to the simple functions $U \circ x^s$. Now suppose (ii) holds. Let P, U be as provided by Theorem V.3.4. Throughout the sequel let α be such that $\overline{\alpha} \approx x$, such an α exists by Lemma V.4.4. Let $EU(x) := U(\alpha)$. We have to show that EU is an integral. This will be done in three stages. First we derive the expected utility representation for strongly bounded acts. Next we extend it to 'one-sided' strongly bounded acts. Finally, we obtain it for the remaining acts x in E.

STAGE 1. Let x be strongly bounded.

Say $\overline{\mu} \succcurlyeq \overline{x_i} \succcurlyeq \overline{\nu}$ for all $i \in I$. If $\overline{\mu} \approx \overline{\nu}$ then by pointwise monotonicity $x \approx \overline{\mu}$, so $\overline{\alpha} \approx \overline{\mu}$, $U \circ x$ is constant, and $EU(x) = \int (U \circ x) dP$. So we suppose in the sequel that $\overline{\mu} \succ \overline{\nu}$. For notational convenience we shall assume that $U(\mu) = 1$, $U(\nu) = 0$. (One may replace U by $U^* : \alpha \mapsto [U(\alpha) - U(\nu)]/[U(\mu) - U(\nu)]$.) We shall construct a sequence of pairs of simple functions $(x^m, y^m)_{m=1}^{\infty}$ such that, for all i,m :

$$U(x_i) - 1/m \leq U(x_i^m) \leq U(x_i) \leq U(y_i^m) \leq U(x_i) + 1/m. \tag{V.4.1}$$

For any m, and $0 \leq k \leq m-1$,

$$A_k := \{i \in I : k/m \leq U(x_i) < (k+1)/m\}$$

is an event, as follows from continuity of U, the fact that Δ contains also all closed sets, and measurability of x. Since $U(\Gamma)$ is an interval, there exists, for any $0 \leq k \leq m$, an α_k such that $U(\alpha_k) = k/m$. Let

$$x^m := \sum_{k=0}^{m-1} \alpha_k 1_{A_k} + \alpha_{m-1} 1_{\{i:\, U(x_i) = 1\}}$$

and

$$y^m := \sum_{k=0}^{m-1} \alpha_{k+1} 1_{A_k} + \alpha_m 1_{\{i:\, U(x_i) = 1\}} \cdot$$

We have $U(y_i^m) \geq U(x_i) \geq U(x_i^m)$ so $y_i^m \succcurlyeq x_i \succcurlyeq x_i^m$ for all i. By pointwise monotonicity $y^m \succcurlyeq x \succcurlyeq x^m$. Hence $EU(y^m) \geq U(\alpha) \geq EU(x^m)$. But also $EU(y^m) - EU(x^m) = 1/m$ for all m, as follows from the representation as already obtained for simple acts, and simpleness of x^m and y^m. We conclude that $EU(x) = U(\alpha) = \lim_{m \to \infty} EU(x^m) = \lim_{m \to \infty} EU(y^m)$. Indeed EU(x) can be considered to be an integral of U with respect to P.

STAGE 2. Let x be strongly bounded 'from one side'.

Suppose that $x_i \succcurlyeq \nu$ for all i. For notational convenience let $U(\nu) = 0$. For any $U(\beta) < U(\alpha) = EU(x)$ there exists, by truncation-continuity, an above truncation x^* of x such that $x^* \succ \overline{\beta}$. By truncation-closedness x^* is in E, so $EU(x^*) > U(\beta)$. It follows that EU(x) is not greater than the supremum of $\{EU(x^*) : x^*$ is an above truncation of x$\}$; EU(x) is in fact equal to this supremum since, by pointwise monotonicity, $EU(x) \geq EU(x^*)$ for any above truncation x^*.

Each above truncation x^* is strongly bounded so, by Stage 1, has $EU(x^*) = \int(U \circ x^*)dP$. By the definition of the Stieltjes-integral for positive functions $U \circ x^*$, $\int(U \circ x^*)dP$ is the supremum of $\int(U \circ x^s)dP$ for simple x^s pointwisely dominated by x^*.

It follows from the above two paragraphs that also EU(x) is the supremum of $\int(U \circ x^s)dP$ for simple x^s pointwisely dominated by x. So EU(x) is the Stieltjes-integral $\int(U \circ x)dP$.

Analogous arguments apply to acts which are strongly bounded above.

STAGE 3. Let x be neither strongly bounded above, nor below.

In this case no maximal or minimal consequences can exist. Now say $U(\beta) < U(\alpha) = EU(x)$. By truncation-continuity there exists an above truncation x^* such that $EU(x^*) > U(\beta)$. By this, and pointwise monotonicity, it follows that EU(x) is the supremum of $\{EU(x^*) : x^* \text{ is an above truncation of } x\}$. It suffices to show that also $\int(U \circ x)dP$ is equal to this supremum.

We may suppose $U(\alpha) > 0$. We consider, for an arbitrary consequence $\mu \succ \alpha$, the above truncation of x at μ, i.e., $t(x \wedge \mu)$. By the previous stage, $EU(t(x \wedge \mu))$ is equal to the Stieltjes integral $\int[U \circ t(x \wedge \mu)]dP$. The latter integral equals $\int[U \circ t(x \wedge \mu)]^- dP + \int[U \circ t(x \wedge \mu)]^+ dP$. The left term is identical to $\int[U \circ x]^- dP$. The right term is the supremum of integrals of pointwisely dominated simple functions; the supremum over all μ of the right side consequently is $\int(U \circ x)^+ dP$.

□

The following observation is obvious from Observation V.3.4′.

OBSERVATION V.4.6′. The uniqueness results for U,P of statement (i) in Theorem V.4.6 are as (V.3.5), (V.3.6), and (V.3.7) in Observation V.3.4′.

□

In Wakker(1985) and Wakker(1986c, Chapter V), the weaker version of Theorem V.4.6 is given where E is the set of all strongly bounded acts. In this weaker version the restrictions for E, and truncation-continuity, are trivially satisfied. The utility function may already be unbounded; however, only acts with bounded utility can be considered. The present result also deals with acts with unbounded utility. This is a desirable result for theoretical applications, such as Bayesian statistics. There one wants to be able to deal with the many usual distributions (on utilities) which have unbounded 'support', such as the 'normal distributions'[rf5]. In the case where $U(\Gamma) = \mathbb{R}$, any act with finite expected utility can be included in the set E above (see Example V.6.2). The next example shows that there are exceptional cases where the above theorem does not deal with all acts with bounded expected utility.

EXAMPLE V.4.7[rf6]. $I = \mathbb{N}$, Σ is 2^I, $\Gamma = [0,1[$, Δ is any algebra on Γ containing all open sets. The utility function U is identity. Let there be given an ultrafilter on $\mathbb{N}$

which does not contain any finite set. The probability measure P assigns probability 1 to any event in the ultrafilter, probability 0 to all other events. Consider the act x which assigns 1 - 1/i to all i. Then P[U(x) > 1-1/i] = 1 for all i, and x has expected utility 1. For all consequences μ we have x $\succ \overline{\mu}$. (This may seem paradoxical: Whatever will be the true state of nature, it will be a disappointment; x is strictly preferred to any of its consequences.) The act x is not strongly bounded. Still the utility function U is bounded.

The above example is rather exceptional. Theorem V.4.6 handles all acts with bounded expected utility if U(Γ) is unbounded from both sides, or is closed from the side(s) where it is bounded, or if the probability measure is σ-additive. Hence we do not complicate the formulations as would be needed to be able to say that also for the above example and its variations our approach can deal with all acts with finite expected utility.

Obviously we could extend the preference relation to an act with expected utility $+\infty$, and let this act be superior to all other acts. In a same trivial way we could have included a few acts with infinite expected utility. Nontrivial (contradiction-free) ways to extend the preference relation to acts with infinite expected utility are not known to us.

V.5. COUNTABLE ADDITIVITY

In this section we give a continuity condition which is necessary and sufficient for countable additivity of the probability measure P of Theorems V.3.4 and V.4.6[rf7].

The following definition will be used only in the definition thereafter. A set of acts E is **uniformly strongly bounded** if there exist $\mu,\nu \in \Gamma$ such that $\mu \succcurlyeq x_i \succcurlyeq \nu$ for all $i \in I$, $x \in E$. With this we define the condition, characterizing σ-additivity of P. Without any difficulty we could below have restricted attention to all simple x^j's, and even to all acts with only two consequences in their image. No more is needed in the proof of Theorem V.5.2.

DEFINITION V.5.1. The binary relation $\succcurlyeq$ is **boundedly strictly continuous** if for any uniformly bounded sequence of acts $(x_j)_{j=1}^{\infty}$, and any pair of acts x,y for which $x^j \succcurlyeq y$ [respectively $x^j \preccurlyeq y$] for all j and $\lim_{j\to\infty} x_i^j = x_i$ for all i, we have $x \succcurlyeq y$ [respectively $x \preccurlyeq y$].

Note that the above definition is weaker than continuity with respect to the product topology, i.e., pointwise convergence. One reason is that we consider only *uniformly strongly bounded* converging sequences (and no uncountable converging 'nets').

THEOREM V.5.2. *Let (i) in Theorem V.4.6 hold. Then* P *can be chosen σ-additive if and only if $\succcurlyeq$ is boundedly strictly continuous.*

PROOF. First we assume bounded strict continuity, and derive σ-additivity. If I is s-inessential, then U is constant, and we can let P be any σ-additive probability measure, e.g. let P(A) = 1 if and only if A contains some fixed $i \in I$. So we suppose that I is s-essential. Then α,β exist such that $\alpha \succ \beta$, otherwise pointwise monotonicity (or the nonrevelation of contradictory tradeoffs) would imply s-inessentiality of I. Now let $(A_m)_{m=1}^{\infty}$ be a sequence of events so that $A_m \supset A_{m+1}$ for all m, and $\cap A_m = \emptyset$. Define $x^m := \alpha 1_{A_m} + \beta 1_{A_m^c}$, $x := \overline{\beta}$. By pointwise monotonicity $x^m \succcurlyeq x^{m+1} \succcurlyeq \overline{\beta}$ for all m, so $\lim_{m\to\infty} EU(x^m) \geq U(\beta)$. (EU has been defined above Theorem V.4.6. The limit of a nonincreasing sequence is defined.) We first show that the last inequality in fact is an equality.

Suppose $\lim_{m\to\infty} EU(x^m) > U(\beta)$. We have $U(\alpha) > U(\beta)$, so $U(\beta)$ is not maximal in $U(\Gamma)$. Since $U(\Gamma)$ is connected, a γ must exist with $\lim_{m\to\infty} EU(x^m) > U(\gamma) > U(\beta)$. Now $x^m \succcurlyeq \overline{\gamma}$ for all m, so $\overline{\beta} = x \succcurlyeq \overline{\gamma}$ by bounded strict continuity. This contradicts $U(\gamma) > U(\beta)$. It follows that :

$$\lim_{m\to\infty} EU(x^m) = U(\beta).$$

The last equality, and the equality $EU(x^m) = P(A_m)U(\alpha) + (1-P(A_m))U(\beta)$, imply $\lim_{m\to\infty} P(A_m) = 0$; as required for σ-additivity of P.

Conversely, let P be σ-additive. Then bounded strict continuity follows from continuity of U and the dominated convergence theorem of Lebesgue (e.g. see Corollary 16 in section I.III.6.16 of Dunford and Schwartz, 1958). This theorem is usually formulated for σ-algebras. It can be applied to our context by taking the smallest σ-algebra containing Σ, and taking the unique σ-additive extension of P to this (guaranteed by the Hahn extension theorem, see Dunford&Schwartz,1958). The values of the involved integrals of $U \circ x_m$ and $U \circ x$ are not affected by this extension of Σ and P.

□

V.6. THE MAIN RESULT, CONCLUSIONS AND FURTHER COMMENTS

The next theorem combines the results obtained so far in this chapter. *Let us repeat* that the structural assumption V.2.4 entails that I is a nonempty set, Σ an algebra on I, elements of Σ are events, Γ is a connected separable topological space, and Δ an algebra of subsets of Γ that contains all open subsets of Γ. Further $\Phi \subset \Gamma^I$ is the set of acts that are Σ-Δ measurable.

THEOREM V.6.1. *Suppose* $\succcurlyeq$ *is a binary relation on* Γ^I. *Let* E *be a truncation-closed set of acts, let* $\Phi^s \subset E \subset \Phi$, *and let for every act* $x \in E$ *there exist consequences* μ,ν *such that* $\overline{\mu} \succcurlyeq x \succcurlyeq \overline{\nu}$. *Then, under the structural Assumption V.2.4, the following two statements are equivalent :*

(i) **There exists a finitely additive probability measure P on Σ, and a continuous function $U : \Gamma \to \mathbb{R}$, such that, on E, $x \mapsto \int(U \circ x)dP$ represents $\succcurlyeq$, with the integral well-defined.**

(ii) **The binary relation $\succcurlyeq$ is a constant- and s-continuous, pointwise monotone, truncation-continuous weak order on E, and no events mutually reveal contradictory tradeoffs.**

Furthermore, in (i) we may replace 'finitely' by 'σ-', if we add in (ii) the requirement that $\succcurlyeq$ is boundedly strictly continuous. The uniqueness results of Observation V.3.4′ also hold here.

PROOF. See Theorem V.3.4, Observation V.3.4′, and Theorems V.4.6, and V.5.2. □

To our knowledge this is the most general characterization of subjective expected utility maximization with continuous utility, now available[rf8].

The above result can be considered an extension of Theorem IV.2.7 to arbitrary state spaces. For the case where the state space is finite the theorem above is not identical with Theorem IV.2.7, because of one (nontrivial) difference. That is the fact that in (ii) above we require that no two events should mutually reveal contradictory tradeoffs. In Theorem IV.2.7 it can be seen that we required the mutual nonrevelation of contradictory tradeoffs only for *single-state* events. This requirement by itself is somewhat weaker, but in the presence of the other assumptions in Theorem IV.2.7 turns out to have the same implications.

We have defined the revealed tradeoffs, and the nonrevelation of contradictory tradeoffs, so that these conditions apply only to simple acts. As a corollary of the above theorem it can now be seen that the straightforward extensions of these notions to nonsimple acts are implied by statement (ii). Hence also independence of equal subalternatives, in full generality, is implied by statement (ii).

Conditions for $\succcurlyeq$, strong enough to guarantee that $\succcurlyeq$ can be represented by an integral for all acts, are usually undesirably strong; for instance, they may simply imply boundedness of U, as turned out to be the case in Savage(1954) (see Fishburn, 1970, section 14.1, and the second edition (1972) of the 'Foundations of Statistics', footnote on page 80). They may even lead to impossibility results, for instance if $\Gamma = [0,1[= I$, $\succcurlyeq$ maximizes Lebesgue integral, and one would let $\Sigma = 2^I$ and require continuity of $\succcurlyeq$ with respect to the product topology on Γ^I. Then this would require a σ-additive extension of the Lebesgue measure to $2^{[0,1[}$, which is known not to exist[rf9]. Finally, such conditions for $\succcurlyeq$ may strongly restrict the set of considered acts.

A major application of Theorem V.6.1 lies in dynamic contexts. The theorem is general enough to apply both to continuous and discrete time. One may characterize 'constantness' of the 'discount factor' ρ, where P corresponds to weights of a form $k \times \exp(-\rho t)$, by the addition of a stationarity assumption[rf10].

Let us now give two conjectures. The first conjecture is that in statement (ii) of Theorem V.6.1 s-continuity of $\succcurlyeq$ is implied by the other conditions for $\succcurlyeq$. The second conjecture is that in statement (ii) of Theorem V.6.1 the condition of pointwise monotonicity can be weakened to the condition that, for all $x,y \in \Phi^b$:

$[\overline{x}_i \succ \overline{y}_i$ for all i] => $[x \succcurlyeq y]$.[rf11]

Finally we give an example showing that our conditions do not imply (in a 'hidden way') boundedness of utility :

EXAMPLE V.6.2. Let $I = [0,1]$, $\Gamma = \mathbb{R}$. Σ and Δ are the Borel-σ-algebra's (i.e., the smallest σ-algebras containing all intervals; they contain all sets one will find in any application). The utility function U is identity. The probability measure P is the Lebesgue measure; i.e., P assigns to each interval its length (this P generates the 'uniform distribution'). Let $E \subset \Gamma^I$ be the set of all acts which generate a probability distribution over $\Gamma = \mathbb{R}$ with finite mean; i.e., E is the set of all acts with finite (expected value =) expected utility. Obviously the preference relation on E is defined as the one represented by expected utility. All conditions in Theorem V.6.1 are satisfied, statements (i) and (ii) there are true; furthermore P is σ-additive. Any probability-distribution over $\Gamma = \mathbb{R}$ can be generated by an act x, for instance by letting x be the properly-defined 'inverse' of the involved distribution function. Hence every distribution with finite mean (over the utility space $\Gamma = \mathbb{R}$) is generated by an act in E

CHAPTER VI

SUBJECTIVE EXPECTED UTILITY WITH NONADDITIVE PROBABILITIES[rf1]

VI.1. INTRODUCTION

In this chapter we shall adopt the terminology of decision making under uncertainty. We shall characterize, in Theorem VI.5.1, subjective expected utility maximization with continuous utility for the case where the probability measure no longer has to be additive. The main characterizing condition will be the 'nonrevelation of comonotonic-contradictory tradeoffs'. The 'nonadditive probability measures' will be called capacities. Choquet(1953-54, 48.1) has indicated, for a special class of capacities, a way to extend the Lebesgue integral to this class of capacities. We shall adopt Choquet's way of integration[rf2]. Capacities play a role in cooperative game theory with side payments, where I is a set of 'players', subsets S of I are 'coalitions', and the capacity is a 'characteristic function', or 'game', indicating productivity, power etc.[rf3] Capacities also play a role in the study of robustness in statistics[rf4].

Schmeidler(1984a,b,c) introduces capacities in decision making under uncertainty. One motive is to avoid paradoxes such as the 'Ellsberg paradox' (see Ellsberg,1961) or the 'Allais paradox' (see Allais,1953a)[rf5], the most well-known paradoxes to criticize or falsify expected utility maximization. Another motive is the applicability in welfare theory. In Schmeidler's approach consequences are lotteries. Thus Schmeidler can start with an application of the theorem of Herstein&Milnor(1953), and immediately obtain a cardinal representing function for the preference relation on the set of acts. This induces 'linear' utility for the consequences. Next he can apply to this representing function the characterization, as given in Schmeidler(1984c), of functionals that can be considered Choquet-integrals[rf6]. We adapt, under the simplifying assumption that the state space is finite, the work of Schmeidler to the case where the consequence space is a connected separable topological space, and utility is continuous, not necessarily linear. In our work a (cardinal) representing function is not easily available, and a derivation of it will be the main mathematical difficulty.

One can consider Schmeidler's work the adaptation of Anscombe&Aumann(1963; see our Theorem A2.4)'s characterization of subjective expected utility, to the case of nonadditive probability. The results of this chapter can be considered the adaptation of the characterization of subjective expected utility, given in Theorem IV.2.7, to nonadditive probabilities. Analogously Gilboa(1987) adapts Savage(1954).

Schmeidler's approach still deals with risk in an additive way. The nonadditive treatment of uncertainty is intended to express the decision maker's aversion of uncertainty. The more confidence a person has in his subjective probabilities, the more these will be additive. Risk is an extreme case in which there is full confidence in the correctness of the probabilities. Our approach to the contrary does not require an additive treatment of risk. If 'true' probabilities are given a decision maker may still continue to behave in a nonadditive way, e.g. as in the 'rank-order approach', developped in Quiggin(1982) and Yaari(1987a). The characterization in our set-up of 'sub-' and 'super-additivity' of the capacities, without any restriction for utility other than continuity, and the characterization of concavity and convexity of utility without any restriction for the capacity, is planned for future research.

VI.2. CAPACITIES AND THE CHOQUET INTEGRAL

Throughout this, and the following, chapter I is the finite set $\{1,\ldots,n\}$.

DEFINITION VI.2.1. A function $v : 2^I \to \mathbb{R}$ is a **capacity** if :

$$v(\emptyset) = 0 \tag{VI.2.1}$$

$$v(I) = 1 \tag{VI.2.2}$$

$$A \subset B \Rightarrow v(A) \leq v(B) \quad (\textbf{monotonicity}) . \tag{VI.2.3}$$

Note that the image of v must be a subset of [0,1]. In the literature capacities are also defined when I is infinite; then usually continuity with respect to increasing and decreasing sequences of events is required. For our finite I this is trivially satisfied. Also the domain of the capacity in the literature is often taken to be the collection of compact subsets of I, with I a (Hausdorff) topological space, or it is taken to be an algebra on I. To follow this, we could of course endow I with the trivial topology, and trivial algebra, 2^I. Finally, the normalization (VI.2.2) is sometimes left out.

The following definition was essentially first given by Choquet(1953-54, 48.1).

DEFINITION VI.2.2 (see Figure VI.2.1). Let $v : 2^I \to \mathbb{R}$ be a capacity. Then, for any function $f : I \to \mathbb{R}$, the **Choquet integral** of f with respect to v, denoted as $\int_I f dv$, or as $\int f dv$, is

$$\int_0^{\infty} v(\{i \in I: f(i) \geq \tau\}) d\tau + \int_{-\infty}^{0} [v(\{i \in I: f(i) \geq \tau\}) - 1] d\tau . \tag{VI.2.4}$$

Note that for nonnegative f the second term vanishes. And note that for additive capacities the Choquet integral coincides with the usual integral (i.e., expectation), as follows from integration by parts. Hence the above notation will not cause confusion. I being finite, (VI.2.4) can be rewritten as a sum. To this end let π be a permutation on $\{1,...,n\}$, dependent on f, such that $f(\pi(1)) \geq f(\pi(2)) \geq ... \geq f(\pi(n))$. So, if the states of nature are ranked in accordance with the values of f, then π assigns to every i, considered as a ranking number, the state of nature with this ranking number. States with equal f-value can be ranked in any arbitrary way. Now (VI.2.4) can be seen to equal (see Figure VI.2.1, (a) and (b)) :

$$(\sum_{j=1}^{n-1}[f(\pi(j))-f(\pi(j+1))]) \times v(\{\pi(1),...,\pi(j)\}) + f(\pi(n)). \tag{VI.2.5}$$

Note from this expression that the mutual ranking of states with equal f-value is immaterial. After a reordering of terms, (VI.2.5) becomes (see Figure VI.2.1 (c)) :

$$\sum_{j=1}^{n} f(\pi(j))[v(\{\pi(1),...,\pi(j)\}) - v(\{\pi(1),...,\pi(j-1)\}]. \tag{VI.2.6}$$

And this will lead to the expression that will be most useful for our work in the sequel. For this a new definition is needed :

DEFINITION VI.2.3. For a capacity v, a permutation π on $\{1,...,n\}$, and $1 \leq j \leq n$,

$$P^{\pi}(j) := v(\{i \in I: \pi^{-1}(i) \leq \pi^{-1}(j)\}) - v(\{i \in I: \pi^{-1}(i) < \pi^{-1}(j)\}).$$

Dependency of $P^{\pi}(j)$ on v is not expressed in this notation. One may interpret $P^{\pi}(j)$ as the marginal contribution in capacity of j to those states of nature which are ranked before j by π. By this we can (with π as described above formula (VI.2.5)) rewrite (VI.2.6) as :

$$\sum_{j=1}^{n} P^{\pi}(j)f(j) . \tag{VI.2.7}$$

Note that, for fixed π (and v), the $P^{\pi}(j)$'s above are nonnegative and sum to one. One may consider $\int f dv$ as the integral of f over I with respect to the (additive) probability measure P^{π}, induced by the $P^{\pi}(j)$'s. This will lead to the main strategy of our approach to derive Theorem VI.5.1 : We shall consider subsets of acts, that induce a same 'ranking' permutation π. On such subsets we can proceed as if we were dealing with additive probabilities as given by P^{π}, and we can apply well-known techniques there.

Let us now give two elementary properties of the Choquet-integral, that follow from the above expressions.

$\int \lambda f dv = \lambda \int f dv$ for all $\lambda \geq 0$ (<u>**positive homogeneity**</u>). (VI.2.8)

$\int (\lambda + f) dv = \lambda + \int f dv$ for all $\lambda \in \mathbb{R}$ (<u>**translation invariance**</u>). (VI.2.9)

Another elementary property is :

If $f(i) \geq g(i)$ for all i, then $\int f dv \geq \int g dv$ (<u>**monotonicity**</u>) . (VI.2.10)

For nonnegative f and g this easily follows from (VI.2.4), where the second term then vanishes. For general f and g this is most easily obtained by taking $\lambda + f$ and $\lambda + g$ with λ so large that $\lambda + f$ and $\lambda + g$ are positive, and by applying (VI.2.9). Finally, if we consider the Choquet integral as a function ('functional') from $\mathbb{R}^n$ to $\mathbb{R}$, with $(\lambda_1,...,\lambda_n) \in \mathbb{R}^n$ interpreted as the function assigning λ_j to every j, then we obtain the well-known :

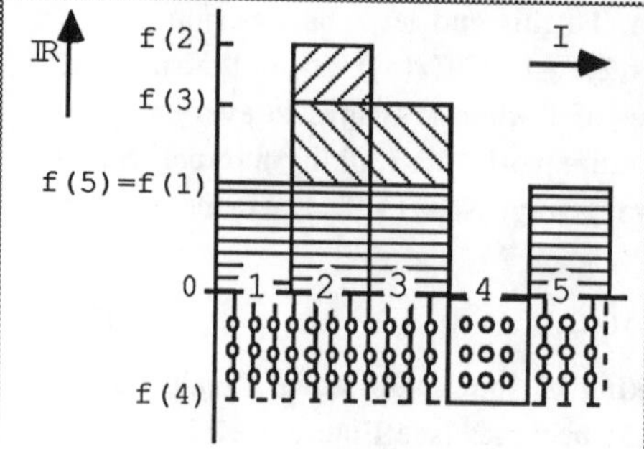

Figure VI.2.1.a. $\int_I f dv$ = (VI.2.4)
= A(///) + A(\\\)+A(≡)+ [A(|||) - A(ooo)].

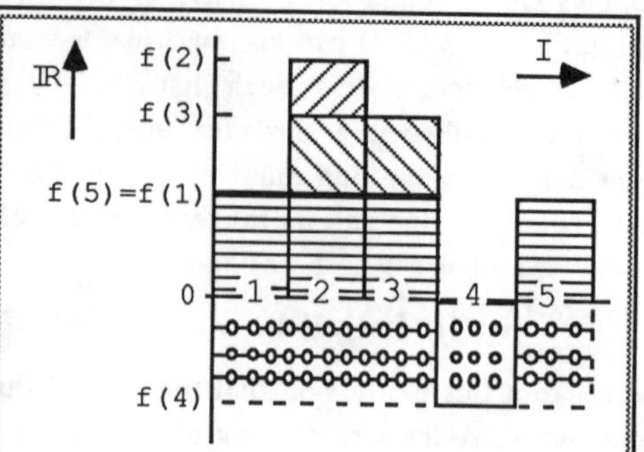

Figure VI.2.1.b. $\int_I f dv$ = (VI.2.5)
= A(///) + A(\\\)+ A(—) + A(≡) - A(ooo).

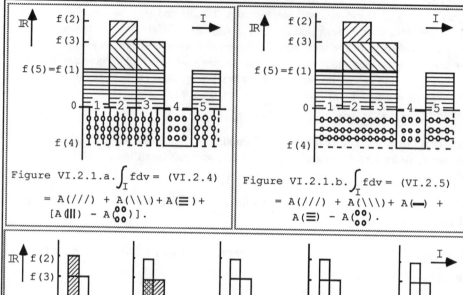

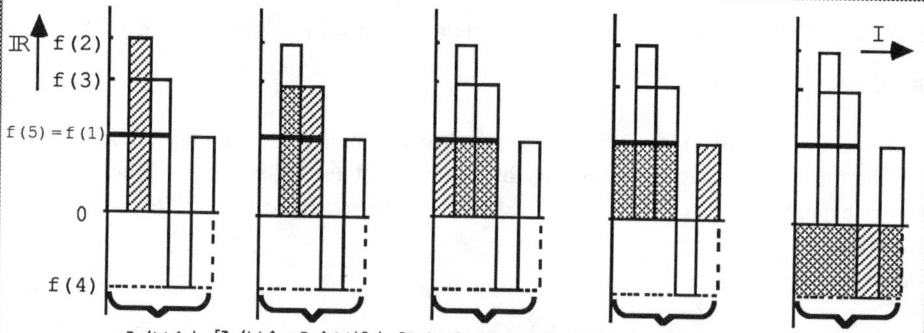

A(///)+ [A(///)-A(\\\)]+ [A(///)-A(\\\)]+[A(///)-A(\\\)] - [A(///)-A(\\\)]

FIGURE VI.2.1.c. $\int_I f dv$ = (VI.2.6) (Rewritten in (VI.2.7)).

FIGURE VI.2.1 (<u>The Choquet integral</u>). I = {1,2,3,4,5}, f:I -> ℝ, f(2) > f(3) > f(1) = f(5) > 0 > f(4). $\pi(1)=2, \pi(2)=3, \pi(3)=1, \pi(4)=5, \pi(5)=4$. We could also have taken $\pi(3)=5, \pi(4)=1$.

A doubly marked part belongs to two areas. For example ⦚⦚⦚ in Figure a belongs both to ||| and to ooo.

A = 'area'. We always take area positive. In Figure a, A(///) = [f(2)-f(3)].v({2}); A(\\\) = [f(3)-f(5)].v({2,3}); f(1) = f(5) hence — is an empty set, A(—) = 0.

Area is additive in the ℝ-axis, so in Figure a, A(≡ ∪ |||) = A(≡) + A(|||). Area does not have to be additive in the I-axis, so in Figure a, A(≡) ≠ f(1).[v({1,2,3}) + v({5})] may very well hold.

PROPOSITION VI.2.4. *The Choquet-integral is continuous.*

PROOF. First we derive continuity in each variable. Let $1 \leq i \leq n$. By (VI.2.10), the Choquet-integral is nondecreasing in its i-th variable. Let $x \in \mathbb{R}^n$, and $\varepsilon > 0$. Let π be as above (VI.2.5). Since the mutual ranking, by π, of states j with value x_j equal to x_i, can be chosen arbitrarily, we may assume that of these states, i is ranked first; i.e., $\pi^{-1}(i)$ is smallest. That will guarantee positivity of the quantity δ, introduced hereafter. Let $\delta = \min\{\varepsilon, x_k - x_i\}$ where k is such that $\pi^{-1}(k) = \pi^{-1}(i) - 1$, if the latter is positive; otherwise $\pi^{-1}(i) = 1$, in which case we let $\delta = \varepsilon$. Then for all $x_{-i}(x_i+\lambda)$ with $0 \leq \lambda \leq \delta$, in the calculation of the Choquet-integral through (VI.2.7), we can use the π of above, and thus the same $P^{\pi}(j)$'s, as for x. So $\int x_{-i}(x_i+\lambda)dv - \int x dv \leq P^{\pi}(i)\delta \leq \delta \leq \varepsilon$.

Analogously one shows that $\delta > 0$ exists such that for all $0 \leq \lambda \leq \delta$, every $x_{-i}(x_i-\lambda)$ gets assigned Choquet-integral, not more than ε less than x. (This time let $\pi^{-1}(i)$ be as large as possible.) The Choquet-integral is nondecreasing and continuous in each variable. It must be continuous. □

We shall need the following observation (VI.2.11) in the proof of Theorem VI.8.8. First note that the $P^{\pi}(i)$'s of Definition VI.2.3 uniquely determine v: For any $A \subset I$, we take a π such that $A = \{\pi(1),...,\pi(i)\}$; then we have $v(A) = \sum_{j=1}^{i} P^{\pi}(\pi(j))$. This also shows that if one takes an arbitrary collection of real numbers $P^{\pi}(j)$, one $P^{\pi}(j)$ for every permutation π on $\{1,...,n\}$ and $1 \leq j \leq n$, then: There exists a (necessarily unique) capacity v such that any $P^{\pi}(j)$ can be derived from it as in Definition VI.2.3, if and only if for all i,π,π' :

$$P^{\pi}(i) \geq 0; \ \sum_{j=1}^{n} P^{\pi}(j) = 1; \qquad \text{(VI.2.11)}$$
$$[\{\pi(1),...,\pi(i)\} = \{\pi'(1),...,\pi'(i)\}] \Rightarrow [\sum_{j=1}^{i} P^{\pi}(\pi(j)) = \sum_{j=1}^{i} P^{\pi'}(\pi'(j))] \ .$$

VI.3. COMONOTONICITY

In the previous section we saw that for the Choquet-integral an ordering on the states of nature, by the 'ranking' permutation π, plays a central role. Hence, with $\succcurlyeq$ on Γ as in Definition IV.3.1, we introduce the following definition: For $x \in \Gamma^n$, $\succcurlyeq_x$ is the binary relation on I defined by $i \succcurlyeq_x j$ whenever $x_i \succcurlyeq x_j$. So $\succcurlyeq_x$ orders the states as regards 'favourability', given act x. If $\succcurlyeq$ is a weak order, then so is $\succcurlyeq_x$. Further, for $S \subset \Gamma^n$,

$$\succcurlyeq_S := \cap_{x \in S} \succcurlyeq_x \ .$$

So $i \succcurlyeq_S j$ if and only if $x_i \succcurlyeq x_j$ for all $x \in S$. The following notion is central[rf7].

DEFINITION VI.3.1. A set $C \subset \Gamma^n$ is **comonotonic** if no $x,y \in C$, $i,j \in I$ exist such that simultaneously $x_i \succ x_j$ and $y_j \succ y_i$.

Loosely spoken, C is comonotonic if no acts in it order the states, as regards favourability, in a contradictory way.

The following sets are 'maximal' comonotonic sets, as will follow.

DEFINITION VI.3.2. For a permutation π on I,
$C^\pi := \{x \in \Gamma^n : x_{\pi(1)} \succcurlyeq x_{\pi(2)} \succcurlyeq \dots \succcurlyeq x_{\pi(n)}\}$.
$C^{id} = C^\pi$ with π identity.

We now obtain, with an <u>ordering</u> a weak order for which no different elements are equivalent, the following lemma. We shall use only (i) and (iv) of it. Statement (iii) has been added because it shows the way to proceed in case I is infinite, a case for further study, and because it may be clarifying. Statement (ii) has been added because it is used in the proof, and because it may also be clarifying.

LEMMA VI.3.3. *Suppose* $S \subset \Gamma^n$. *Let* $\succcurlyeq$ *be a weak order. The following four statements are equivalent* :

(i) **S is comonotonic.**

(ii) **$\succcurlyeq_S$ is a weak order.**

(iii) **There exists an ordering $\succcurlyeq'$ on the state space I such that :**
$[i \succcurlyeq' j] \Rightarrow [x_i \succcurlyeq x_j]$ for all i,j, $\in$ I, $x \in S$.

(iv) **$S \subset C^\pi$ for some permutation π on I.**

PROOF. Statement (iii) follows from (ii) by letting $\succcurlyeq'$ be any ordering such that $i \succcurlyeq' j \Rightarrow i \succcurlyeq_S j$. Such an ordering exists by Szpilrajn(1930)[rf8]. The implication (iii) => (iv) follows by taking π such that $\pi(1) \succcurlyeq' \pi(2) \succcurlyeq' \dots \succcurlyeq' \pi(n)$.

If (iv) holds, then for $x,y \in S$, $x_i \succ x_j$ and $y_j \succ y_i$ would imply $\pi^{-1}(i) > \pi^{-1}(j)$ and $\pi^{-1}(j) > \pi^{-1}(i)$, which cannot hold. So (i) follows. Finally, (i) is assumed, and (ii) will be derived. Transitivity of $\succcurlyeq_S$ is by transitivity of $\succcurlyeq$. So completeness of $\succcurlyeq_S$ remains to be derived. If not $j \succcurlyeq_S i$, then there must be $x \in S$ with $x_i \succ x_j$. By comonotonicity $y_i \succcurlyeq y_j$ for all $y \in S$. So $i \succcurlyeq_S j$.

□

If state i is inessential on C^π, then we also call i <u>π-inessential</u>. If π is the identity, we write <u>id-inessential</u>. The opposite of 'inessential' always is <u>essential</u>.

The proof of the following lemma is more complicated than that of its 'additive' analogue, Lemma II.2.1. The reason is, loosely spoken, that now we are no longer 'free to cross borders' from one C^π to another. This is the main complication in the work of this chapter. A preparatory notation :

For $\alpha,\beta \in \Gamma$, $\alpha \vee \beta$ [respectively $\alpha \wedge \beta$] is α if $\alpha \succcurlyeq \beta$ [respectively $\alpha \preccurlyeq \beta$], β otherwise.

Note that $\alpha \vee \beta$ and $\beta \vee \alpha$ are not identical if $\alpha \approx \beta$ and $\alpha \neq \beta$. They are $\approx$-equivalent if $\succcurlyeq$ is a weak order. Same things hold for $\wedge$.

LEMMA VI.3.4. *Let* $\succcurlyeq$ *be a weak order. Let* $x,y \in C^\pi$, *and* $x_j = y_j$ *for all π-essential* j. *Then* $x \approx y$.

PROOF. Suppose $x,y \in C^{id}$. Define $x^0 := x$, $y^0 := y$, and inductively, for $j = 1,...,n$, $x^j := x^{j-1}{}_{-j}(x_j \vee y_j)$, $y^j := y^{j-1}{}_{-j}(x_j \vee y_j)$. Note that, for all id-essential j, $x_j = y_j = x_j \vee y_j$. Also note that, for all $j > 1$, $x_j \vee y_j \preccurlyeq x^{j-1}_{j-1}$, and $x_j \vee y_j \preccurlyeq y^{j-1}_{j-1}$, so that $x^j,y^j \in C^{id}$ for all j. We conclude: $x = x^0 \approx x^1 \approx ... \approx x^n = y^n \approx y^{n-1} \approx ... \approx y^0 = y$.

□

LEMMA VI.3.5. *Suppose* $\succcurlyeq$ *is a weak order. Let, for all* i,π, i *be* π*-inessential. Then* $\succcurlyeq$ *is trivial.*

PROOF. Let $x,y \in \Gamma^n$. Take any $\alpha \in C$. Since $\overline{\alpha} \in C^\pi$ for all π, there are π,π' such that $x,\overline{\alpha} \in C^\pi$, and $y,\overline{\alpha} \in C^{\pi'}$. By the previous Lemma, $x \approx \overline{\alpha} \approx y$.

□

VI.4. COMONOTONIC-CONTRADICTORY TRADEOFFS

Let us repeat, for the definition of $\succcurlyeq_c^*$ below, that by Lemma VI.3.3.iv four acts $x_{-i}\alpha$, $y_{-i}\beta$, $x_{-i}\gamma$, and $y_{-i}\delta$ are comonotonic if and only if there exists a permutation π on I such that C^π contains all four acts. In this chapter we do not deal with additive contexts, hence we introduce, with the subscript c indicating 'comonotonic' :

DEFINITIONS VI.4.1. We write, for consequences $\alpha,\beta,\gamma,\delta$,

$$\alpha\beta \succ_c^{**} \gamma\delta \qquad \text{(VI.4.1)}$$

if there exist a state i, and <u>comonotonic</u> acts $x_{-i}\alpha$, $y_{-i}\beta$, $x_{-i}\gamma$, and $y_{-i}\delta$, such that

$x_{-i}\alpha \succcurlyeq y_{-i}\beta$ and

not $x_{-i}\gamma \succcurlyeq y_{-i}\delta$.

We write $\succcurlyeq_c^*$ instead of $\succ_c^{**}$ in (VI.4.1) if above we have $\preccurlyeq$ instead of [not $\succcurlyeq$] and if furthermore i is π-essential for a π such that the four involved acts are in C^π.

□

Obviously $\alpha\beta \succ_c^{**} \gamma\delta$ implies $\alpha\beta \succ^{**} \gamma\delta$, and $\alpha\beta \succcurlyeq_c^* \gamma\delta$ implies $\alpha\beta \succcurlyeq^* \gamma\delta$.

DEFINITION VI.4.2. The preference relation $\succcurlyeq$ **<u>reveals comonotonic-contradictory tradeoffs (on consequences</u>**) if there exist consequences $\alpha,\beta,\gamma,\delta$ such that

[both $\alpha\beta \succcurlyeq_c^* \gamma\delta$ and $\gamma\delta \succ_c^{**} \alpha\beta$] .

If the preference relation reveals comonotonic-contradictory tradeoffs then it obviously reveals contradictory tradeoffs. The elementary proof of the implication (i) => (ii) in Theorem VI.5.1, given directly below Theorem VI.5.1, has been elaborated because it is clarifying for the above definition. The remainder of this section gives implications of the above definition.

ASSUMPTION VI.4.3. (For this section). **The binary relation $\succcurlyeq$ is a weak order that does not reveal comonotonic-contradictory tradeoffs.**

It is straightforwardly verified that the preference relation $\succcurlyeq$ does not reveal comonotonic-contradictory tradeoffs if and only if :

> The displayed implication of Lemma IV.2.5 is satisfied whenever there exist permutations π and ρ on I such that $x_{-i}\alpha$, $y_{-i}\beta$, $x_{-i}\gamma$, and $y_{-i}\delta$ are in C^{π}, further $v_{-j}\alpha$, $w_{-j}\beta$, $v_{-j}\gamma$, and $w_{-j}\delta$ are in C^{ρ}, i is π-essential, and j is ρ-essential. (VI.4.2)

The formulation of (VI.4.2) was used, under the name 'comonotonic cardinal coordinate independence', in Wakker(1986c, 1987b). The following is the analogue of coordinate independence. It is more convenient to formulate it now in the spirit of independence of equal subalternatives.

DEFINITION VI.4.4. The binary relation $\succcurlyeq$ satisfies **comonotonic coordinate independence** (**Com.CI**) if for all comonotonic $\{x_{-A}s_A, y_{-A}s_A, x_{-A}t_A, y_{-A}t_A\}$ we have

$$[x_{-A}s_A \succcurlyeq y_{-A}s_A] \Leftrightarrow [x_{-A}t_A \succcurlyeq y_{-A}t_A].$$

LEMMA VI.4.5. *The binary relation $\succcurlyeq$ satisfies comonotonic coordinate independence.*

PROOF. First we consider the special case that A contains one element, say A = {k}. Let $x_{-k}s_k, y_{-k}s_k, x_{-k}t_k, y_{-k}t_k \in C^{\pi}$. If k is π-inessential, then $x_{-k}s_k \approx x_{-k}t_k$, and $y_{-k}s_k \approx y_{-k}t_k$, and everything follows. So let k be π-essential. Then $[x_{-k}s_k \preccurlyeq x_{-k}s_k$ & $x_{-k}t_k \succcurlyeq x_{-k}t_k]$ imply $t_kt_k \succcurlyeq_c^* s_ks_k$. Since $[x_{-k}t_k \prec y_{-k}t_k$ together with $x_{-k}s_k \succcurlyeq y_{-k}s_k]$ would lead to $s_ks_k \succ_c^* t_kt_k$, thus to a revelation of comonotonic-contradictory tradeoffs, we conclude that $x_{-k}t_k \succcurlyeq y_{-k}t_k$.

Next we consider the general case. Say $x_{-A}s_A, y_{-A}s_A, x_{-A}t_A, y_{-A}t_A \in C^{id}$. Define :

$$a^0 := x_{-A}s_A,\ b^0 := y_{-A}s_A,\ c^0 := x_{-A}t_A,\ d^0 := y_{-A}t_A.$$

Then, analogously to Lemma VI.3.4, define inductively, for j = 1,...,n :

If $j \notin A$, then $(a^j,b^j,c^j,d^j) := (a^{j-1},b^{j-1},c^{j-1},d^{j-1})$.

If $j \in A$, then set $\alpha = s_jvt_j$ and define

$$(a^j,b^j,c^j,d^j) := (a^{j-1}_{-j}\alpha,\ b^{j-1}_{-j}\alpha,\ c^{j-1}_{-j}\alpha,\ d^{j-1}_{-j}\alpha).$$

The above construction has been such that $a^j_k = c^j_k$ and $b^j_k = d^j_k$ for all $k \leq j$, and such that all new acts are in C^{id}. For instance, if $j \in A$, then $a^{j-1},b^{j-1},c^{j-1},d^{j-1} \in C^{id}$ imply, by simple manipulations, $\alpha \preccurlyeq a^j_{j-1}$, $\alpha \preccurlyeq b^j_{j-1}$, $\alpha \preccurlyeq c^j_{j-1}$, $\alpha \preccurlyeq d^j_{j-1}$. Further $a^n = c^n$, $b^n = d^n$. By repeated application of the already handled case where A contains exactly one element, we conclude that each of the following preferences holds if and only if its predecessor and successor hold: $x_{-A}s_A \succcurlyeq y_{-A}s_A$, $a^0 \succcurlyeq b^0$, $a^1 \succcurlyeq b^1$, ..., $a^n \succcurlyeq b^n$, $c^n \succcurlyeq d^n$, $c^{n-1} \succcurlyeq d^{n-1}$, ..., $c^0 \succcurlyeq d^0$, $x_{-A}t_A \succcurlyeq y_{-A}t_A$.

□

As can be seen from the above lemma, under Assumption VI.4.3 the following definition is useful.

DEFINITION VI.4.6. We write $x_A \succcurlyeq^{\pi}_{A} y_A$ if :

[There exists s such that: $s_{-A}x_A \succcurlyeq s_{-A}y_A$ and $s_{-A}x_A$, $s_{-A}y_A \in C^{\pi}$].

LEMMA VI.4.7. *If* $x_A \succcurlyeq^{\pi}_{A} y_A$, *then* $s_{-A}x_A \succcurlyeq s_{-A}y_A$ *for all* s *for which* $s_{-A}x_A$, $s_{-A}y_A \in C^{\pi}$.

PROOF. Direct from Lemma VI.4.5.

□

The second and third consequence of the nonrevelation of comonotonic-contradictory tradeoffs are :

DEFINITION VI.4.8. The binary relation $\succcurlyeq$ satisfies <u>pointwise monotonicity</u> (<u>p.mon.</u>) if $x \succcurlyeq y$ whenever $x_i \succcurlyeq y_i$ for all i.

DEFINITION VI.4.9. The binary relation $\succcurlyeq$ satisfies <u>comonotonic strong monotonicity</u> (<u>com.s.mon.</u>) if for all comonotonic $\{x,y\} \subset C^{\pi}$ with $x_i \succcurlyeq y_i$ for all i, and $x_i \succ y_i$ for a π-essential i, we have $x \succ y$.

LEMMA VI.4.10. *The binary relation* $\succcurlyeq$ *satisfies pointwise, and comonotonic strong, monotonicity.*

PROOF. <u>First we derive pointwise monotonicity</u>. In three steps :

Step 1. Let $y = x_{-k}\alpha$, let $\{x,y\}$ be comonotonic, say $x,y \in C^{id}$, and let $x_k \succcurlyeq \alpha$. We show that $x \succcurlyeq x_{-k}\alpha$.

Suppose $x \prec x_{-k}\alpha$. Contradiction will follow.

Define, for $j = 0,\ldots,n$:

$$z^j \text{ has } z^j_1 = .. = z^j_j = x_k,\ z^j_{j+1} = ..= z^j_n = \alpha. \tag{VI.4.3}$$

Then all z^j are in C^{id}. By com.CI, $x \prec x_{-k}\alpha$ implies $z^k_{-k}x_k \prec z^k_{-k}\alpha$; i.e., $z^k \prec z^{k-1}$. Each of the last three preferences implies id-essentiality of k. Thus, by the nonrevelation of comonotonic-contradictory tradeoffs,

$[z^k_{-k}\alpha \preccurlyeq z^k_{-k}\alpha \ \&\ z^k_{-k}\alpha \succcurlyeq z^k_{-k}x_k \ \&\ z^j_{-j}\alpha \succcurlyeq z^j_{-j}\alpha]$ implies

$z^j_{-j}\alpha \succcurlyeq z^j_{-j}x_k$; i.e., $z^{j-1} \succcurlyeq z^j$, for all $j \geq 1$.

Apparently $\overline{\alpha} = z^0 \succcurlyeq z^1 \succcurlyeq \ldots \succcurlyeq z^{k-1}$, $z^{k-1} \succ z^k$, $z^k \succcurlyeq \ldots \succcurlyeq z^n = \overline{x_k}$. This, finally, contradicts $x_k \succcurlyeq \alpha$. Step 1 is established.

Step 2. Let again $y = x_{-k}\alpha$, and $x_k \succcurlyeq \alpha$. Now we do not assume that $\{x,y\}$ is comonotonic. Let us assume that $x \in C^{id}$. We show that $x \succcurlyeq x_{-k}\alpha$.

Let ℓ be such that $x_\ell \succcurlyeq \alpha$, $x_j \prec \alpha$ for all $j > \ell$. Then, by repeated application of the result of step 1, $x \succcurlyeq x_{-k}x_{k+1} \succcurlyeq x_{-k}x_{k+2} \succcurlyeq \dots \succcurlyeq x_{-k}x_\ell \succcurlyeq x_{-k}\alpha$, since every two consecutive acts are comonotonic (e.g. $x_{-k}x_{k+2}$ and $x_{-k}x_{k+3}$ are in C^π for a π with $\pi(k+2) = k$). Step 2 is established.

Step 3. Now let $x_i \succcurlyeq y_i$ for all i; further x and y are general. We show that $x \succcurlyeq y$.

By repeated application of the above result,

$$x \succcurlyeq x_{-1}y_1 \succcurlyeq ((x_{-1}y_1)_{-2}y_2) \succcurlyeq \dots \succcurlyeq (((x_{-1}y_1)_{-2}y_2)\dots_{-n}y_n) = y.$$

<u>Pointwise monotonicity is established</u>.

<u>Next we derive com.s.mon</u>. Suppose that $\{x,y\}$ is comonotonic, say $\{x,y\} \subset C^{id}$, and that $x_j \succcurlyeq y_j$ for all j. Let further $x_k \succ y_k$ for an id-essential k. To derive is $x \succ y$. Define :

z has $z_j = x_j$ for all $j \le k$, $z_j = y_j$ for all $j > k$.

Both (z =) $z_{-k}x_k$ and $z_{-k}y_k$ are in C^{id}. By p.mon. $x \succcurlyeq z_{-k}x_k \succcurlyeq z_{-k}y_k \succcurlyeq y$. It is sufficient for com.s.mon. to show that $z_{-k}x_k \succ z_{-k}y_k$. Suppose to the contrary that we have $z_{-k}x_k \preccurlyeq z_{-k}y_k$. We derive a contradiction.

Define $z^0,\dots,z^n$ as in (VI.4.3), with $\alpha = y_k$. Since k is id-essential, by the nonrevelation of comonotonic-contradictory tradeoffs $[z^k{}_{-k}y_k \preccurlyeq z^k{}_{-k}y_k \;\&\; z^k{}_{-k}y_k \succcurlyeq z^k{}_{-k}x_k \;\&\; z^j{}_{-j}y_k \succcurlyeq z^j{}_{-j}y_k]$ implies $z^j{}_{-j}y_k \succcurlyeq z^j{}_{-j}x_k$; i.e., $z^{j-1} \succcurlyeq z^j$, for all $j \ge 1$. So $\overline{y_k} = z^0 \succcurlyeq z^n = \overline{x_k}$. This contradicts $x_k \succ y_k$.

□

COROLLARY VI.4.11. *The binary relation $\succcurlyeq$ is trivial if and only if $\alpha \succcurlyeq \beta$ for all $\alpha,\beta \in \Gamma$.*

PROOF. If $\succcurlyeq$ is trivial, then $\overline{\alpha} \succcurlyeq \overline{\beta}$, so $\alpha \succcurlyeq \beta$, for all α,β. Next assume $\alpha \succcurlyeq \beta$ for all α,β. Then for any x in any C^π, and any $\alpha \in \Gamma$, $x_i \succcurlyeq \overline{\alpha}_i$ for all i, and $\overline{\alpha} \in C^\pi$, hence by p.mon. $x \succcurlyeq \overline{\alpha}$. Analogously $x \preccurlyeq \overline{\alpha}$. So $x \approx \overline{\alpha}$. Also $x \approx \overline{\alpha} \approx y$ for all x,y,α : $\succcurlyeq$ is trivial.

□

COROLLARY VI.4.12. *One π has a π-essential state if and only if every π has a π-essential state.*

PROOF. If one π has a π-essential state, then $\succcurlyeq$ is not trivial. By Corollary VI.4.11 we have $\overline{\alpha} \prec \overline{\beta}$ for some $\alpha,\beta \in \Gamma$. Since $\overline{\alpha}$, $\overline{\beta} \in C^\pi$ for every π, Lemma VI.3.4 implies that every π must have a π-essential state.

□

VI.5. THE MAIN THEOREM

In this section we give the main theorem of this chapter. After the theorem the simplest implication (i) => (ii) will be proved. The proof of (ii) => (i), and of the uniqueness results of the observation below, will be carried out in the following sections, and completed in section VI.9. A survey will be given in section VI.10.

THEOREM VI.5.1. *Suppose* $n \in \mathbb{N}$. *Let* Γ *be a connected separable topological space. For the binary relation* $\succcurlyeq$ *on* Γ^n, *the following two statements are equivalent* :

(i) **There exist a capacity** v **on** $2^{\{1,\ldots,n\}}$ **and a continuous function** $U : \Gamma \to \mathbb{R}$ **such that** $x \mapsto \int(U \circ x)dv$ **(Choquet integral) represents** $\succcurlyeq$**.**

(ii) **The binary relation** $\succcurlyeq$ **is a continuous weak order that does not reveal comonotonic-contradictory tradeoffs.**

□

PROOF OF (i) => (ii) ABOVE. Suppose (i) holds. Obviously $\succcurlyeq$ is a weak order. Further, the map $x \mapsto (U(x_1),\ldots,U(x_n))$ is continuous; so is, by Proposition VI.2.4, the map $(U(x_1),\ldots,U(x_n)) \mapsto \int(U \circ x)dv$. Consequently the map $x \mapsto \int(U \circ x)dv$ is continuous. This implies continuity of $\succcurlyeq$.

All that remains is the nonrevelation of comonotonic-contradictory tradeoffs. For this, we first derive the analogue of (IV.2.2); i.e., we suppose:

$$\alpha\beta \succcurlyeq_c^* \gamma\delta \, , \tag{VI.5.1}$$

and derive (VI.5.5) below. There exists a permutation π on I, a π-essential state i, and four acts $x_{-i}\alpha$, $y_{-i}\beta$, $x_{-i}\gamma$, $y_{-i}\delta \in C^\pi$, such that

$$x_{-i}\alpha \succcurlyeq y_{-i}\beta, \; x_{-i}\gamma \preccurlyeq y_{-i}\delta \, . \tag{VI.5.2}$$

The two preferences give, by (VI.2.7), with the π in (VI.2.7) identical with our present π since $x_i \succcurlyeq x_j \Rightarrow U(x_i) \geq U(x_j)$:

$$\sum_{k\neq i} P^\pi(k)U(x_k) + P^\pi(i)U(\alpha) \;\geq\; \sum_{k\neq i} P^\pi(k)U(y_k) + P^\pi(i)U(\beta)$$

and

$$\sum_{k\neq i} P^\pi(k)U(x_k) + P^\pi(i)U(\gamma) \;\leq\; \sum_{k\neq i} P^\pi(k)U(y_k) + P^\pi(i)U(\delta).$$

These two inequalities imply :

$$P^\pi(i)[U(\alpha)-U(\beta)] \geq P^\pi(i)[U(\gamma)-U(\delta)]. \tag{VI.5.3}$$

Were $P^\pi(i) = 0$, then by (VI.2.7) and the representation of $\succcurlyeq$ by $x \mapsto \int(U \circ x)dv$, i would be π-inessential. So :

$$P^\pi(i) > 0. \tag{VI.5.4}$$

The last two numbered results imply :

$$U(\alpha) - U(\beta) \geq U(\gamma) - U(\delta) . \tag{VI.5.5}$$

Analogously one derives:

$$\gamma\delta \succ_c^{**} \alpha\beta \Rightarrow U(\gamma) - U(\delta) > U(\alpha) - U(\beta) . \tag{VI.5.6}$$

Hence no comonotonic-contradictory tradeoffs can be revealed.

□

OBSERVATION VI.5.1′. The following uniqueness results hold for U,v of statement (i) in Theorem VI.5.1 :

If some π has two or more π-essential states, then U *is cardinal, and* v *is uniquely determined.* (VI.5.7)

If $\succcurlyeq$ is not trivial, and no π has two or more π-essential states, then U *is continuously ordinal, and* v *is uniquely determined.* (VI.5.8)

If $\succcurlyeq$ is trivial, then U *can, and must, be any constant function, and* v *is arbitrary.* (VI.5.9)

□

The following examples[rf9] have no expected utility representation with additive probability measures, but they can be represented by (i) in the above theorem.

EXAMPLE VI.5.2. Suppose $1 \leq k \leq n$. Let $v(A) = 0$ if $|A| < k$, $v(A) = 1$ if $|A| \geq k$. Then $\int (U \circ x) dv = U(x_j)$, with $U(x_j)$ the k-th highest value in $U(x_1),...,U(x_n)$; $P^{\pi}(\pi(k)) = 1$, for all π. The preference relation belongs to a 'maximin'-decision maker if $k = n$, and to a 'maximax'-decision maker if $k = 1$.

EXAMPLE VI.5.3. Let $0 \leq \lambda \leq 1$, $n \geq 2$, $v(\emptyset) = 0$, $v(I) = 1$, $v(A) = \lambda$ for all remaining A. Here, for all π, $P^{\pi}(\pi(1)) = \lambda$ and $P^{\pi}(\pi(n)) = (1-\lambda)$, and $\int (U \circ x) dv = \lambda \max\{U(x_j) : 1 \leq j \leq n\} + (1-\lambda)\min\{U(x_j) : 1 \leq j \leq n\}$. The preference relation belongs to a decision maker, adopting the 'Hurwicz criterion' with 'pessimism-optimism index' $1-\lambda$[rf10].

VI.6. PREPARATIONS FOR THE PROOF

LEMMA VI.6.1. *Let Γ be a topological space, $\succcurlyeq$ a weak order on Γ^n, continuous with respect to the product topology. Then for all $x \in \Gamma^n$, $\{\alpha \in \Gamma : \overline{\alpha} \succ x\}$ and $\{\alpha \in \Gamma : \overline{\alpha} \prec x\}$ are open subsets of Γ.*

PROOF. Let $\overline{\alpha} \succ x$. Then an open neighbourhood $V \subset \Gamma^n$ of $\overline{\alpha}$ exists such that $y \succ x$ for all $y \in V$. We may assume that V is of the form $A_1 \times ... \times A_n$, with all A_j open subsets of Γ. Now $A := \cap_{j=1}^n A_j$ gives an open neighbourhood of α within

$\{\alpha \in \Gamma : \overline{\alpha} \succ x\}$. The latter must be open.

Analogously $\{\alpha \in \Gamma : \overline{\alpha} \prec x\}$ is open.

□

LEMMA VI.6.2. *Suppose no π has two or more π-essential states. Let the assumptions in Theorem VI.5.1, and also (ii) there, hold. Then also (i), and (VI.5.8) and (VI.5.9), hold. If $\succcurlyeq$ is nontrivial, then* v *only assigns values* 0 *and* 1.

PROOF. If there is a π with no π-essential state, then by Lemma VI.3.4, for all $\alpha,\beta \in \Gamma$, $\overline{\alpha} \approx \overline{\beta}$. By Corollary VI.4.11, $\succcurlyeq$ is trivial. Now (VI.5.9), and (i), follow straightforwardly.

So we assume :

Every π has exactly one π-essential state. (VI.6.1)

The binary relation on Γ, also denoted by $\succcurlyeq$, and defined by $\alpha \succcurlyeq \beta$ if $\overline{\alpha} \succcurlyeq \overline{\beta}$, obviously is a weak order. By Lemma VI.6.1 it is continuous. By Theorem III.3.6 there exists a $\varphi : \Gamma \rightarrow \mathbb{R}$ which represents $\succcurlyeq$ on Γ. By Observation III.3.6′ φ is continuously ordinal. We can set U := φ, as we shall see; so any continuous strictly increasing transformation of U can be used.

Next we define v. Let $A \subset I$ be arbitrary. By nontriviality, we can take some α and β such that $\alpha \succ \beta$. If $\overline{\beta}_{-A}\alpha \succ \overline{\beta}$, then we define v(A) := 1, otherwise v(A) := 0. By com.s.mon. and Lemma VI.3.4 we see that v(A) = 1, if and only if for any π with $\{\pi(1),...,\pi(k)\}$ = A, A contains the π-essential state. This shows that v is independent of the particular choice of α and β above. Also it follows that $P^{\pi}(j) = 0$ for all π-inessential j, and $P^{\pi}(j) = 1$ for the π-essential j.

Now we show that with these constructions, (i) in Theorem VI.5.1 holds. Let x and y be two acts. Let $x \in C^{\pi}$, $y \in C^{\pi'}$. Let i be the π-essential state, j the π'-essential state. Then, by Lemma VI.3.4, $x \approx \overline{x_i}$, $y \approx \overline{y_j}$. There follows: $x \succcurlyeq y \Leftrightarrow \overline{x_i} \succcurlyeq \overline{y_i} \Leftrightarrow$ $U(x_i) \geq U(y_j) \Leftrightarrow \sum P^{\pi}(k)U(x_k) \geq \sum P^{\pi'}(k)U(y_k) \Leftrightarrow \int(U\circ x)dv \geq \int(U\circ y)dv$.

Finally we derive the uniqueness result (VI.5.8). We saw above that U can be any continuous strictly increasing transform of φ. Since, obviously, U has to represent $\succcurlyeq$ on Γ, no other kind of U can be taken: U is continuously ordinal.

For uniqueness of v we consider an arbitrary π, and show that $P^{\pi}(i) = 0$ for all π-inessential i. Then $P^{\pi}(j)$ must be 1 for the π-essential j; these values $P^{\cdot}(\cdot)$ uniquely determine v. So let, finally, $i = \pi(k)$ be π-inessential. Let $\alpha \succ \beta$. Let x assign α to $\pi(1),...,\pi(k)$, β to $\pi(k+1),...,\pi(n)$. Then x and $x_{-i}\beta$ are in C^{π}. By π-inessentiality of i, $x \approx x_{-i}\beta$. Since $U(\alpha) > U(\beta)$, by (VI.2.7) we obtain $P^{\pi}(i) = 0$.

□

In cooperative game theory with side payments functions v as above are called (monotonic) simple games[rf11]. We conclude this section with some terminology: Whenever we call a consequence **maximal** or **minimal**, that is with respect to the preference relation $\succcurlyeq$ on Γ introduced in Definition IV.3.1.

VI.7. ADDITIVE VALUE FUNCTIONS ON C^{id}

In this section we derive results for C^{id}. Of course, analogous results hold for any C^{π}. Without further mention, we assume throughout this section :

ASSUMPTION VI.7.1 (for this section). **The assumptions, and statement (ii), of Theorem VI.5.1 hold. There are at least two id-essential states. Moreover, we assume that all states are id-essential. No maximal or minimal consequences exist.**

The assumption of the existence of at least two id-essential states is essential for the sequel. The assumption that all states are id-essential is only made for convenience. By Lemma VI.3.4 id-inessential states do not affect the preference relation on C^{id}, and may just as well be suppressed. They will simply get assigned additive value functions V_j^{id} that are constant, say zero. The next subsection derives additive value functions on subsets which are Cartesian products and which are comonotonic.

VI.7.1. ADDITIVE VALUE FUNCTIONS $(V_j^z)_{j=1}^n$ ON SETS E^z

NOTATION VI.7.2. For $z \in C^{id}$, $E^z := E_1^z \times ... \times E_n^z$, with $E_1^z := \{\alpha \in \Gamma : \alpha \succcurlyeq z_1\}$, $E_n^z := \{\alpha \in \Gamma : z_{n-1} \succcurlyeq \alpha\}$, and for all $1 < j < n$, $E_j^z := \{\alpha \in \Gamma : z_{j-1} \succcurlyeq \alpha \succcurlyeq z_j\}$.

Note that z_n plays no role in the above notation. Further $z \in E^z$ and $E^z \subset C^{id}$. The E^z's are Cartesian products and are comonotonic, so that on them the conditions of this chapter hold without the comonotonicity premise. That enables us to apply the theorems of Chapter III. Before that, we still have to take care of a problem concerning the topological assumption III.3.2. The problem is that, if we simply use the restriction to E_j^z of the topology on Γ, then possibly E_j^z will no longer be connected. For instance, let (i) of Theorem VI.5.1 hold, where $\Gamma = \mathbb{R}$ with the usual Euclidean topology, n = 2, v is the additive probability measure assigning $|A|/2$ to every $A \subset I$, and $U : \alpha \mapsto \alpha\sin\alpha$. Let $z = (0,0)$. Then $E_1^z = \{\alpha : U(\alpha) \geq 0\}$ is not connected. Hence, for preserving connectedness, a coarser topology will have to be taken.

NOTATION VI.7.3. The topology on Γ is denoted as T. By $T(\succcurlyeq)$ we denote the coarsest topology on Γ with respect to which $\succcurlyeq$ on Γ is continuous. By $...|E$ we denote: 'Restricted to E'.

By Lemma VI.6.1, $T(\succcurlyeq)$ is coarser than T, so is connected too.

LEMMA VI.7.4. *Any* $E \subset \Gamma$ *of the form* $\{\alpha \in \Gamma : \sigma \succcurlyeq \alpha \succcurlyeq \tau\}$, $\{\alpha \in \Gamma : \sigma \succcurlyeq \alpha \succ \tau\}$, $\{\alpha \in \Gamma : \sigma \succ \alpha \succcurlyeq \tau\}$, $\{\alpha \in \Gamma : \sigma \succ \alpha \succ \tau\}$, $\{\alpha \in \Gamma : \sigma \succcurlyeq \alpha\}$, $\{\alpha \in \Gamma : \sigma \succ \alpha\}$, $\{\alpha \in \Gamma : \alpha \succcurlyeq \tau\}$, *or* $\{\alpha \in \Gamma : \alpha \succ \tau\}$, *is connected with respect to* $T(\succcurlyeq)|E$.

PROOF. **Throughout this proof, 'open' always refers to the topology** $T(\succcurlyeq)$. Let E have a form as above. Let F_1,F_2 be open subsets of Γ. Let $E_1 = E \cap F_1$, $E_2 = E \cap F_2$. Suppose $E_1 \neq \emptyset \neq E_2$, $E_1 \cap E_2 = \emptyset$, $E_1 \cup E_2 = E$. We derive a contradiction.

Let $\alpha_1 \in E_1$, $\alpha_2 \in E_2$. $T(\succcurlyeq)$ does not 'separate between' $\approx$-equivalent consequences, so $\alpha_1 \approx \alpha_2$ does not hold. Say $\alpha_1 \prec \alpha_2$. Define :

$$G_1 := [F_1 \cap \{\alpha : \alpha_1 \prec \alpha \prec \alpha_2\}] \cup [\{\alpha : \alpha \preccurlyeq \alpha_1\}], \text{ and}$$

$$G_2 := [F_2 \cap \{\alpha : \alpha_1 \prec \alpha \prec \alpha_2\}] \cup [\{\alpha : \alpha \succcurlyeq \alpha_2\}].$$

Then $G_1 \cap G_2 = \emptyset$, $G_1 \neq \emptyset \neq G_2$, and $G_1 \cup G_2 = \Gamma$ since $\{\alpha : \alpha_1 \prec \alpha \prec \alpha_2\} \subset E$.

First we derive openness of G_1. For any element of G_1, an open neighbourhood H of it within G_1 must be found. Let $\delta \in G_1$. If $\delta \prec \alpha_1$, take $H = \{\alpha : \alpha \prec \alpha_1\}$; if $\delta \succ \alpha_1$, $H = F_1 \cap \{\alpha : \alpha_1 \prec \alpha \prec \alpha_2\}$ is taken.
So finally let $\delta \approx \alpha_1$. There must be an open neighbourhood H' of δ within F_1 of the form $\{\alpha : \alpha \succ \mu\}$, or $\{\alpha : \nu \succ \alpha \succ \mu\}$, or $\{\alpha : \nu \succ \alpha\}$ for some $\mu,\nu \in \Gamma$. The first case is impossible since $\alpha_2 \notin F_1$. So, finally, $H = \{\alpha : \nu \succ \alpha\}$ can be taken, in both remaining cases, as the open neighbourhood of δ within G_1.

Analogously openness of G_2 is derived. Openness of G_1 and G_2 contradicts connectedness of Γ.

□

The above lemma shows that, if we use $T(\succcurlyeq)$ instead of T, then every E_j^z is connected. For completeness we give the following lemma. Since we deal here with the case of more than one essential state, by Remarks A3.1 and III.7.1 topological separability is inessential. Hence the following lemma could have been dispensed with, and is proved concisely.

LEMMA VI.7.5. *Every* E_j^z *is separable with respect to* $T(\succcurlyeq) \mid E_j^z$.

PROOF. This is obvious if E_j^z contains exactly one $\approx$-equivalence class. If it contains more, then the intersection with E_j^z of any countable dense subset of Γ is dense in E_j^z with respect to $T(\succcurlyeq) \mid E_j^z$, since every subset H of E_j^z, open with respect to $T(\succcurlyeq) \mid E_j^z$, has, by connectedness, nonempty intersection with $H \cap \{\alpha : z_{j-1} \succ \alpha \succ z_j\}$, open in Γ.

□

Next we show :

LEMMA VI.7.6. *For any* $z \in C^{id}$, $\succcurlyeq$, *restricted to* E^z, *is continuous with respect to the product topology of the* $T(\succcurlyeq) \mid E_j^z$*'s.*

PROOF. Let $x,y \in E^z$, $x \succ y$. We construct an auxiliary $\tilde{x}$ such that $\tilde{x} \succ y$, and by means of this a subset $F_1 \times ... \times F_n$ of $\{v \in E^z : v \succ y\}$, containing x, and with every $F_j \subset E_j^z$ open with respect to $T(\succcurlyeq) \mid E_j^z$. For the construction of $\tilde{x}_1$, consider :

$$G := \{\alpha \in \Gamma : (\alpha,x_2,...,x_n) \succ y\}.$$

By Lemma 0.2.1 this is open with respect to T. G contains x_1 so is nonempty. If G contains z_1, then $\tilde{x}_1 = z_1$ and $F_1 = E_1^z$ is taken. If G does not contain z_1, then by connectedness of Γ with respect to T, G cannot be closed with respect to T, so not of the form $\{\alpha : \alpha \succcurlyeq x_1\}$, as follows from continuity of $\succcurlyeq$ on Γ (Lemma VI.6.1) with respect to T. Since G, by p.mon., contains all $\alpha \succcurlyeq x_1$, G must contain an $\alpha \prec x_1$. This α cannot be $\preccurlyeq z_1$ (that, by p.mon., would imply $z_1 \in G$). So $z_1 \prec \alpha \prec x_1 : \alpha \in E_1^z$. Take $\tilde{x}_1 = \alpha$, $F_1 = E_1^z \cap \{\beta \in \Gamma : \beta \succ \alpha\}$.

Anyway, $(\tilde{x}_1, x_2, ..., x_n) \succ y$, and F_1 is open with respect to $T(\succcurlyeq) \mid E_1^z$. By analogous constructions we obtain $\tilde{x}_2, F_2, ..., \tilde{x}_n, F_n$, such that: $(\tilde{x}_1, \tilde{x}_2, ..., \tilde{x}_j, x_{j+1}, ..., x_n) \succ y$ for all j, $F_j = E_j^z$ if $\tilde{x}_j = z_j$, otherwise $z_j \prec \tilde{x}_j \prec x_j$ and $F_j = E_j^z \cap \{\beta : \beta \succ \tilde{x}_j\}$. Finally, $(\tilde{x}_1, ..., \tilde{x}_n) \succ y$. For every $w \in F_1 \times ... \times F_n$, in particular $w = x$, $w_j \succcurlyeq \tilde{x}_j$ for all j. By p.mon. : $w \succcurlyeq \tilde{x} \succ y$.

So indeed, if $x \succ y$, we can construct $F_1 \times ... \times F_n \subset [E^z \cap \{w : w \succ y\}]$, containing x, and open with respect to the product topology of $T(\succcurlyeq) \mid E_j^z$, j = 1,...,n. Hence $\{x \in E^z : x \succ y\}$ is open with respect to the latter product topology, for all $y \in E^z$. Analogously $\{x \in E^z : x \prec y\}$ is open, for all y. Continuity of $\succcurlyeq$ with respect to the product topology of the $T(\succcurlyeq) \mid E_j^z$'s follows.

□

We can now take care of the topological assumption III.3.2 for Proposition VI.7.7. On every E_j^z we take $T(\succcurlyeq) \mid E_j^z$. By Lemma VI.7.4, E_j^z is connected, by Lemma VI.7.5 it is separable. On E^z we take the product topology. By Lemma VI.7.6, $\succcurlyeq$ on E^z is continuous with respect to this topology. So indeed we can apply the Theorems of Chapter III:

PROPOSITION VI.7.7. *For any* $z \in C^{id}$ *there exist continuous jointly cardinal additive value functions* $(V_j^z)_{j=1}^n$ *for* $\succcurlyeq$ *on* E^z.

PROOF. Since no maximal consequences exist, there is $\alpha \succ z_1$ in E_1^z. Since no minimal consequences exist, there is $\beta \prec z_{n-1}$ in E_n^z. Hence, by id-essentiality of 1,n, and by com.s.mon., $z_{-1}\alpha \succ z \succ z_{-n}\beta$. This shows that 1 and n are essential on E^z. Since E^z, and any subset of it, is comonotonic, Com.CI and the nonrevelation of comonotonic-contradictory tradeoffs hold without the comonotonicity restrictions. From this the nonrevelation of contradictory tradeoffs *by coordinates* follows. The topological assumption III.3.2 on E^z has been guaranteed above the Proposition. Theorem III.6.6 and Observation III.6.6′ yield jointly cardinal additive value functions, continuous with respect to the $T(\succcurlyeq)E_j^z$'s, so certainly with respect to the $T \mid E_j^z$'s.

□

VI.7.2. FITTING THE FUNCTIONS V_j^z TOGETHER ON C^{id}

Our next step is to show that there exist $V_j^{id} : \Gamma \to \mathbb{R}$, j = 1,...,n, such that for every z and j, V_j^z can be taken to be the restriction of V_j^{id} to E_j^z. This of course could never be done if there were $A \subset I$, and $s,t \in C^{id}$, such that $(V_j^s)_{j \in A}$ and $(V_j^t)_{j \in A}$ would be additive value functions for different binary relations on the 'common domain' $\prod_{j\in A}(E_j^s \cap E_j^t)$. By Lemma VI.4.5, the implication of the nonrevelation of comonotonic-contradictory tradeoffs, that never happens. Both $(V_j^s)_{j\in A}$ and $(V_j^t)_{j\in A}$ are additive value functions for the binary relation $\succcurlyeq^{id}_A$, on appropriate domains. The remainder of this subsection is devoted to the following lemma, and its proof.

LEMMA VI.7.8. *There exists a continuous cardinal additive function* $V : x \mapsto \sum_{j=1}^{n} V_j(x_j)$ *on* C^{id} *which represents* $\succcurlyeq$ *on every* E^z.

PROOF. On every E^z we are given an additive representation $V^h : x \mapsto \sum_{j=1}^{n} V_j^h(x_j)$ which is cardinal. This cardinality will be frequently used in the sequel, without explicit mentioning. We may add to every V_j^z an arbitrary 'location' constant $\tau_j(z)$, and multiply the V_j^z's by one positive 'scale' constant $\sigma(z)$, to obtain an additive representation again. The plan in the sequel is to choose, in five stages, scales and locations so that all V_j^z's will 'fit together', i.e., will be the same on common domains. They can then be considered the restriction of one array $(V_j^{id})_{j=1}^{n}$.

There must exist $\beta^1, \beta^0 \in \Gamma$ such that $\beta^1 \succ \beta^0$. We shall set $V_j^{id}(\beta^0) = 0$ for all j, and $V_1^{id}(\beta^1) = 1$. (In section VI.8, Assumption VI.8.1 the scale will be changed.)

STAGE 1. Choice of scale and location on E^r with $r = \overline{\beta^0}$.

Let r ('reference point') = $\overline{\beta^0}$. $E_1^r = \{\alpha : \alpha \succcurlyeq \beta^0\}$, it contains β^1. $E_n^r = \{\alpha : \alpha \preccurlyeq \beta^0\}$. For all $1 \neq j \neq n$, $E_j^r = \{\alpha : \alpha \approx \beta^0\}$. Of course we choose scale and locations so that :

$$V_j^r(\beta^0) = 0 \text{ for all j, } V_1^r(\beta^1) = 1. \tag{VI.7.1}$$

STAGE 2. Choice of scale on every E^z, and location for every V_1^z, V_n^z .

Let $z \in C^{id}$ be arbitrary. By com.CI, (V_1^r, V_n^r) and (V_1^z, V_n^z) are additive value functions for the same $\succcurlyeq^{id}_{\{1,n\}}$ on $(E_1^r \cap E_1^z) \times (E_n^r \cap E_n^z)$. Note that both 1 and n are essential on $(E_1^r \cap E_1^z) \times (E_n^r \cap E_n^z)$ with respect to $\succcurlyeq^{id}_{\{1,n\}}$. This will be used several times, without explicit mentioning, in the sequel. By Lemmas VI.7.4 and VI.7.5, $E_1^r \cap E_1^z$ and $E_n^r \cap E_n^z$ are connected and separable with respect to the restrictions of $\mathcal{T}(\succcurlyeq)$, and by subsection VI.7.1 we may use the uniqueness result of Observation III.6.6′. So we can choose the scale for (V_1^z, V_n^z), (and hence for all $(V_j^z)_{j=1}^{n}$,) and the locations for (V_1^z, V_n^z), such that $V_1^r = V_1^z$ on $E_1^r \cap E_1^z$, and $V_n^r = V_n^z$ on $E_n^r \cap E_n^z$. We get (as we shall see), even stronger:

$$V_1^s = V_1^t \text{ and } V_n^s = V_n^t \text{ on common domain for all } s,t \in C^{id}. \tag{VI.7.2}$$

This follows since, on $(E_1^s \cap E_1^t) \times (E_n^s \cap E_n^t)$, (V_1^s, V_n^s) and (V_1^t, V_n^t) are additive value functions for the same $\succcurlyeq^{id}_{\{1,n\}}$, so that they can differ only with respect to their locations, and a common scale. However, for j = 1,n, V_j^s and V_j^t coincide (with V_j^r) on $E_j^s \cap E_j^t \cap E_j^r$; hence they coincide on common domains.

STAGE 3. Intermediate observation .

For all s,t,j, V_j^s and V_j^t now have the same scale, and differ only with respect to their location, as we shall show :

For all s,t $\in C^{id}$ and $1 \le j \le n$ there exist constants $\tau_j(s,t)$ such that on $E_j^s \cap E_j^t$, $V_j^s = \tau_j(s,t) + V_j^t$. (VI.7.3)

For j = 1 or j = n, by (VI.7.2), $\tau_j(s,t) = 0$. So let $1 \neq j \neq n$. Then (V_1^s, V_j^s, V_n^s) and (V_1^t, V_j^t, V_n^t) are additive value functions for the same $\succcurlyeq^{id}_{\{1,j,n\}}$ on $(E_1^s \cap E_1^t) \times (E_j^s \cap E_j^t) \times (E_n^s \cap E_n^t)$. So they can differ only by location, and common scale. However, V_1^s and V_1^t, and V_n^s and V_n^t, coincide on their common domain (which contains more than one element). The common scales must be the same.

STAGE 4. Choice of location for all V_j^z's ($j \neq 1,n$), having β^0 in their domain .

Of course for all V_j^z's as above we choose location such that $V_j^z(\beta^0) = 0$. Now we have not only (VI.7.1) to (VI.7.3), but also :

If V_j^s and V_1^t have β^0 in their domain then they coincide on common domain. (VI.7.4)

This follows directly from (VI.7.3).

STAGE 5. Choice of location for remaining V_j^z's .

Now let z $\in C^{id}$ and j be such that $1 \neq j \neq n$, $\beta^0 \notin E_j^z = \{\alpha : z_{j-1} \succcurlyeq \alpha \succcurlyeq z_j\}$. Say $z_j \succ \beta^0$ ($z_{j-1} \prec \beta^0$ is analogous). Let $r(z) \in C^{id}$ be such that $(r(z))_i = z_{j-1}$ for all i < j, $(r(z))_i = \beta^0$ for all $i \ge j$. Then $E_j^h \subset E_j^{r(z)} = \{\alpha : z_{j-1} \succcurlyeq \alpha \succcurlyeq \beta^0\}$. By Stage 4, $V_j^{r(z)}(\beta^0) = 0$. We now choose the location of V_j^z such that $V_j^z = V_j^{r(z)}$ on E_j^z. We shall show :

For all s,t $\in C^{id}$, $1 \le j \le n$, V_j^s and V_j^t coincide on common domain . (VI.7.5)

We check this only for the case where $1 \neq j \neq n$, β^0 is neither in the domain of V_j^s, nor in that of V_j^t (other cases have been dealt with before, or are analogous), and $s_j \succ \beta^0$. Here E_j^s is of the form $\{\alpha : s_{j-1} \succcurlyeq \alpha \succcurlyeq s_j\}$. For E_j^t to have nonempty intersection with E_j^s, we must have $t_j \succ \beta^0$. Now V_j^s and $V_j^{r(s)}$ coincide on $E_j^s \cap E_j^{r(s)}$, so do V_j^t and $V_j^{r(t)}$ on $E_j^t \cap E_j^{r(t)}$; so do, by (VI.7.4), $V_j^{r(s)}$ and $V_j^{r(t)}$ on $E_j^{r(s)} \cap E_j^{r(t)}$. The latter contains $E_j^s \cap E_j^t$. So (VI.7.5) follows.

We can now define $(V_j^{id})_{j=1}^n$. For any $\alpha \in \Gamma$, and $1 \le j \le n$, we take any z $\in C^{id}$ such that $\alpha \in E_j^z$, $z_j = \alpha$ suffices for that. Then we define $V_j^{id}(\alpha) := V_j^z(\alpha)$. By (VI.7.5), this does not depend on the particular choice of z; and every V_j^z is now the restriction of V_j^{id} to E_j^z.

For continuity, let $\sup(V_j^{id}(\Gamma)) > \mu > \nu > \inf(V_j^{id}(\Gamma))$. Openness of $\{x_j : \mu > V_j^{id}(x_j) > \nu\}$ follows from Proposition VI.7.7, with z such that $V_j^{id}(z_{j-1}) > \mu$ (if $j > 1$), $\nu > V_j^{id}(z_j)$. Continuity of V_j follows.

Finally the uniqueness result. Any $(W_j^{id})_{j=1}^n$, for which real τ_j, j = 1,...,n, and positive σ exist such that $W_j^{id} = \tau_j + \sigma V_j^{id}$ for all j, satisfy the requirements of the Lemma. Conversely, if $(W_j^{id})_{j=1}^n$ satisfy all the requirements of the lemma, then so do

$$Z_j^{id} := [W_j^{id} - W_j^{id}(\beta^0)]/[W_1^{id}(\beta^1) - W_1^{id}(\beta^0)] .$$

From $Z_j^{id}(\beta^0) = 0$, $Z_1^{id}(\beta^1) = 1$, and from rereading the proof, the reader can see that this uniquely determines Z_j^{id}, $Z_j^{id} = V_j^{id}$ must hold for all j.

□

Note that we may not yet conclude that $(V_j^{id})_{j=1}^n$ are additive value functions on *the entire* C^{id}. Only for alternatives x,y from a same E^h the equivalence $[x \succcurlyeq y \iff \sum V_j(x_j) \geq \sum V_j(y_j)]$ has been established so far. (Recall that, by Remark III.7.8, an additive function which is 'locally' representing, does not have to be 'globally' representing.)

VI.7.3. THE FUNCTIONS $(V_j^{id})_{j=1}^n$ ARE ADDITIVE VALUE FUNCTIONS ON C^{id}

LEMMA VI.7.9. *For all (*id*-essential)* k: $[\alpha \succcurlyeq \beta \iff V_k^{id}(\alpha) \geq V_k^{id}(\beta)]$. *Hence* $[\overline{\alpha} \succcurlyeq \overline{\beta} \iff \sum_{j=1}^n V_j^{id}(\alpha) \geq \sum_{j=1}^n V_j^{id}(\beta)]$.

PROOF. Let α,β,k be arbitrary. Say $\alpha \succcurlyeq \beta$. Let $x_j = \alpha$ for all j < k, $x_j = \beta$ for all $j \geq k$. Then (x =) $x_{-k}\beta$ and $x_{-k}\alpha \in C^{id}$, and $x_{-k}\beta$ and $x_{-k}\alpha \in E^x$. By p.mon. and Lemma VI.7.8 :

$$[\alpha \approx \beta] \Rightarrow [\alpha \succcurlyeq \beta \text{ and } \beta \succcurlyeq \alpha] \Rightarrow [x_{-k}\alpha \approx x_{-k}\beta] \Rightarrow V_k^{id}(\alpha) = V_k^{id}(\beta).$$

By com.s.mon. and Lemma VI.7.8 :

$$\alpha \succ \beta \Rightarrow x_{-k}\alpha \succ x_{-k}\beta \Rightarrow V_k^{id}(\alpha) > V_k^{id}(\beta).$$

Analogously :

$$\alpha \prec \beta \Rightarrow V_k^{id}(\alpha) < V_k^{id}(\beta).$$

All of this together implies that V_k^{id} represents $\succcurlyeq$ on Γ.

□

LEMMA VI.7.10. *Let* $x \in C^{id}$, $x \approx \overline{\alpha}$. *Then* $\sum_{j=1}^n V_j^{id}(x_j) = \sum_{j=1}^n V_j^{id}(\alpha)$.

PROOF. The case $x_j \approx \alpha$ for all j is direct. The case $x_j \succ \alpha$ for some j and $x_j \prec \alpha$ for no j, and the case $x_j \prec \alpha$ for some j and $x_j \succ \alpha$ for no j, are excluded by com.s.mon. So suppose j < i exist such that $x_j \succ \alpha$, $x_{j+1} \approx ... \approx x_{i-1} \approx \alpha$, $x_i \prec \alpha$. We define x^0 such that $x_k^0 = x_k$ for all $x_k \not\approx \alpha$, and $x_k^0 = \alpha$ for all $x_k \approx \alpha$. By (twice) p.mon. $x^0 \approx \overline{\alpha}$.

Now suppose, for some $0 \leq \ell \leq n-2$, $x^\ell \in C^{id}$ has been defined such that $x^\ell \approx \overline{\alpha}$, and $\sum V_k^{id}(x_k^\ell) = \sum V_k^{id}(x_k)$, with at least ℓ coordinates of x^ℓ equal to α, and no coordinate of x^ℓ equivalent but unequal to α. If x^ℓ has $\ell+1$ or more coordinates equal to α, define $x^{\ell+1} := x^\ell$. If not, then, say :

$$x_a^\ell \succ \alpha,\ x_{a+1}^\ell = .. = x_{b-1}^\ell = \alpha,\ x_b^\ell \prec \alpha, \text{ with } b = a + \ell + 1.$$

If now $x^\ell_{-a,b}\alpha,\alpha \approx \overline{\alpha}$, define $x^{\ell+1} := x^\ell_{-a,b}\alpha,\alpha$. If $x^\ell_{-a,b}\alpha,\alpha \prec \overline{\alpha}$, define (by restricted solvability, established in Lemma III.3.3) $\alpha \prec x_a^{\ell+1} \preccurlyeq x_a^\ell$ such that :

$$x^{\ell+1} := x^\ell_{-b,a}\alpha,x_a^{\ell+1} \approx \overline{\alpha}.$$

If $x^\ell_{-a,b}\alpha,\alpha \succ \overline{\alpha}$, define $\alpha \succ x_b^{\ell+1} \succcurlyeq x_b^\ell$ such that :

$$x^{\ell+1} := x^\ell_{-a,b}\alpha,\ x_b^{\ell+1} \approx \overline{\alpha}.$$

In any case, for $z = x^\ell_{-a}\alpha$, both $x^{\ell+1}$ and x^ℓ are in E^z, their a-th coordinate being 'between' x_{a-1}^ℓ and α, their b-th coordinate 'between' α and x_b^ℓ. Hence by Lemma VI.7.8, $x^\ell\ (\approx\overline{\alpha}) \approx x^{\ell+1}$ implies $\sum V_k^{id}(x_k^{\ell+1}) = \sum V_k^{id}(x_k^\ell)$.

Finally we end up with $x^{n-1} \approx \overline{\alpha}$, with n−1 coordinates equal to α. Then by com.s.mon. the remaining coordinate of x^{n-1} must also be equivalent, so equal, to α. And :

$$\textstyle\sum_k V_k^{id}(x_k) = \sum_k V_k^{id}(x_k^0) = \ldots = \sum_k V_k^{id}(x_k^{n-1}) = \sum_k V_k^{id}(\alpha) \text{ follows.}$$

□

Finally we show that the $(V_j^{id})_{j=1}^n$ are additive value functions on C^{id}.

THEOREM VI.7.11. *There exists a continuous cardinal additive representation* $V : x \mapsto \sum_{j=1}^n V_j(x_j)$ *for* $\succcurlyeq$ *on* C^{id}.

PROOF. Let $x,y \in C^{id}$ be arbitrary. Let $(V_j^{id})_{j=1}^n$ be as constructed above. Let α,β be such that $x \approx \overline{\alpha}$, $y \approx \overline{\beta}$ (Lemma V.4.4). Then $x \succcurlyeq y$ iff $\overline{\alpha} \succcurlyeq \overline{\beta}$, which by Lemma VI.7.9 is iff $\sum_k V_k^{id}(\alpha) \geq \sum_k V_k^{id}(\beta)$. The latter by Lemma VI.7.10 holds iff $\sum_k V_k^{id}(x_k) \geq \sum_k V_k^{id}(y_k)$.

□

The following corollary is not needed for the sequel, but has interest of its own. It considers, as all of this section does, an example of an additive representation on a set that is not a Cartesian product, but only a subset of that[rf12].

COROLLARY VI.7.12. *Suppose* $X := \{x \in \mathbb{R}^n_{++} : x_1 \geq x_2 \geq \ldots \geq x_n\}$. *Let* $\succcurlyeq$ *be a strongly monotonic continuous weak order on* X. *Let* $n \geq 3$. *Then the following two statements are equivalent* :

(i) **There exists a continuous cardinal additive representation for $\succcurlyeq$ on X.**

(ii) **The binary relation does not reveal comonotonic-contradictory tradeoffs.**

PROOF. This result is derived in the same way as Theorem VI.7.11. Pointwise, and (comonotonic) strong, monotonicity are easily verified. All, so certainly three of more, states are essential. For this case the only consequence of the nonrevelation of comonotonic-contradictory tradeoffs, (apart from the monotonicities,) used in the proof of Theorem VI.7.11, is Com.CI. Theorem VI.7.11 considered only C^{id}, and did not need any assumption 'outside' C^{id}.

□

VI.8. COMPLETION OF THE PROOF OF THEOREM VI.5.1 UNDER ABSENCE OF MAXIMAL AND MINIMAL CONSEQUENCES

Throughout this section, with Theorem VI.8.8 excepted, we shall assume :

ASSUMPTION VI.8.1 (for this section, except Theorem VI.8.8). **The assumptions, and statement (ii), of Theorem VI.5.1 hold. There exists a π with two π-essential states, say π = identity. Throughout this section m is an id-essential state. No maximal or minimal consequences exist. Let $\beta^1 \succ \beta^0$ be two fixed consequences. For every π with two or more π-essential states, the continuous cardinal additive representation $V : x \mapsto \sum_{j=1}^{n} V_j(x_j)$ of $\succcurlyeq$ on C^π (which exists according to the previous section) is chosen such that $V_j^\pi(\beta^0) = 0$ for all j, and $\sum_{j=1}^{n} V_j^\pi(\beta^1) = 1$.**

Note that we have changed 'scale', as compared to the previous section. There we had $V_1^{id}(\beta^1) = 1$, now $\sum_{j=1}^{n} V_j^{id}(\beta^1) = 1$. Note also that, at present, we may not yet conclude for different π, π', and $x \in C^\pi$, $y \in C^{\pi'}$, that $x \succcurlyeq y \Leftrightarrow \sum_{j=1}^{n} V_j^\pi(x_j) \geq \sum_{j=1}^{n} V_j^{\pi'}(y_j)$. The only consequences of the nonrevelation of comonotonic-contradictory tradeoffs that we used in the previous section, i.e., comonotonic coordinate independence, pointwise monotonicity, and comonotonic strong monotonicity, probably do not suffice for this purpose. We shall essentially use :

LEMMA VI.8.2. *Suppose there are at least two π-essential, and two π'-essential, states. Let* k *be π'-essential. Then for all $\ell \in I$, $V_\ell^\pi = \varphi_\ell \circ V_k^{\pi'}$ for a constant or positive affine φ_ℓ.*

PROOF. Say π' is the identity. We write φ for φ_ℓ. If ℓ is π-inessential, then V_ℓ^π is constant, and φ is the same constant. So assume :

ℓ is π-essential.

By Lemma VI.7.9, (which applies to all essential k) V_ℓ^π and V_k^{id} represent the same $\succcurlyeq$, hence $V_\ell^\pi = \varphi \circ V_k^{id}$ for a continuous strictly increasing φ.

First note that the nonrevelation of comonotonic-contradictory tradeoffs implies the condition in (VI.4.2) with all preferences replaced by equivalences. (Apply (VI.4.2) twice, the second time with left and right sides of preferences interchanged.) This we write out in terms of additive value functions, and with $\varphi \circ V_k^{id}$ for V_ℓ^π everywhere :

For all $x_{-k}\alpha$, $y_{-k}\beta$, $x_{-k}\gamma$, $y_{-k}\delta \in C^{id}$, *and* $s_{-\ell}\alpha$, $t_{-\ell}\beta$, $s_{-\ell}\gamma$, $t_{-\ell}\delta \in C^\pi$,

$$V_k^{id}(\alpha) - V_k^{id}(\beta) =^{(1)} \sum_{j\neq k}[V_j^{id}(y_j)-V_j^{id}(x_j)] =^{(2)} V_k^{id}(\gamma) - V_k^{id}(\delta) \qquad \text{(VI.8.1)}$$

and

$$\varphi \circ V_k^{id}(\alpha) - \varphi \circ V_k^{id}(\beta) =^{(3)} \sum_{j\neq \ell}[V_j^\pi(t_j)-V_j^\pi(s_j)] \qquad \text{(VI.8.2)}$$

imply

$$\sum_{j\neq \ell}[V_j^\pi(t_j)-V_j^\pi(s_j)] =^{(4)} \varphi \circ V_k^{id}(\gamma) - \varphi \circ V_k^{id}(\delta) . \qquad \text{(VI.8.3)}$$

Now let $V_k^{id}(\mu)$ be an arbitrary element of $\text{int}(V_k^{id}(\Gamma))$. There can be seen to be an interval S around $V_k^{id}(\mu)$, so small that for all $V_k^{id}(\alpha)$, $V_k^{id}(\beta)$, $V_k^{id}(\gamma)$, and $V_k^{id}(\delta) \in S$, there exist x,y such that $x_{-k}\alpha$, $y_{-k}\beta$, $x_{-k}\gamma$, $y_{-k}\delta$ are in C^{id}, and such that $=^{(1)}$ is satisfied. For this we use the existence of a state $i \neq k$ which is id-essential so that the interval $V_i^{id}(\Gamma)$ is nondegenerate. Of course, if $i < k$, then $x_i \succcurlyeq \alpha$, $x_i \succcurlyeq \gamma$, $y_i \succcurlyeq \beta$, $y_i \succcurlyeq \delta$ will have to hold. If $i > k$, the reverse has to hold. Furthermore, by continuity of φ, S can be taken so small that $\varphi(S)$ is small enough to guarantee existence of s and t such that $s_{-\ell}\alpha$, $t_{-\ell}\beta$, $s_{-\ell}\gamma$, $t_{-\ell}\delta$ are in C^π, and such that $=^{(3)}$ holds.

We conclude for all $V_k^{id}(\alpha)$, $V_k^{id}(\beta)$, $V_k^{id}(\gamma)$, $V_k^{id}(\delta) \in S$:

$$V_k^{id}(\alpha) - V_k^{id}(\beta) = V_k^{id}(\gamma) - V_k^{id}(\delta) \Rightarrow \qquad \text{(VI.8.4)}$$
$$\varphi \circ V_k^{id}(\alpha) - \varphi \circ V_k^{id}(\beta) = \varphi \circ V_k^{id}(\gamma) - \varphi \circ V_k^{id}(\delta) .$$

This is now shown by choosing x,y,s,t as above, and combining $=^{(3)}$ and $=^{(4)}$. (VI.8.4), only for the case where $\beta = \gamma$, already suffices to show that on S, φ satisfies: $\varphi((\tilde{\alpha} + \tilde{\delta})/2) = [\varphi((\tilde{\alpha}) + \varphi(\tilde{\delta})]/2$. Corollary A1.3 gives affinity of φ.

□

For all π with two or more π-essential states, we can, by Lemma VI.8.2, and the fact that all $V_j^\pi(\beta^0)$ are 0, define $\lambda_j^\pi \in \mathbb{R}_+$ such that, with m id-essential :

$$V_j^\pi = \lambda_j^\pi V_m^{id}. \qquad \text{(VI.8.5)}$$

We define for all these π :

$$p_j^\pi := \lambda_j^\pi / \sum_{i=1}^n \lambda_i^{id} . \qquad \text{(VI.8.6)}$$

For π with exactly one π-essential state, say ℓ, we define :

$$p_\ell^\pi := 1,\ p_i^\pi := 0 \text{ for all } i \neq \ell . \qquad \text{(VI.8.7)}$$

We now proceed to define $U : \Gamma \to \mathbb{R}$.

DEFINITION VI.8.3. For all $\alpha \in \Gamma$, $U : \alpha \mapsto \sum_{j=1}^n V_j^{id}(\alpha)$.

LEMMA VI.8.4. *For all π with two or more π-essential states, and all α,* $V_j^{\pi}(\alpha) = p_j^{\pi}U(\alpha)$. *For all π,* $\sum p_j^{\pi} = 1$.

PROOF. Let π have two π-essential states. Then $P_j^{\pi}U(\alpha) = [\lambda_j^{\pi}/\sum_{i=1}^{n}\lambda_i^{id}][\sum_{i=1}^{n}V_i^{id}(\alpha)]$ $= [\lambda_j^{\pi}/\sum_{i=1}^{n}\lambda_i^{id}][\sum_{j=1}^{n}\lambda_i^{id}V_m^{id}(\alpha)] = V_j^{\pi}(\alpha)$. For such π, $\sum p_j^{\pi} = \sum\lambda_j^{\pi}/\sum\lambda_i^{id} = \sum V_j^{\pi}(\beta^1)/\sum V_i^{id}(\beta^1) = 1/1 = 1$.

For other π, with only one π-essential state, $[\sum p_j^{\pi} = 1]$ is direct.

□

LEMMA VI.8.5. *Let* $x \in C^{\pi}$, $x \approx \overline{\alpha}$. *Then* $\sum p_j^{\pi}U(x_j) = U(\alpha)$.

PROOF. If there are two or more π-essential states, then by Lemma VI.7.10, adapted to C^{π}, $\sum V_j^{\pi}(x_j) = \sum V_j^{\pi}(\alpha)$. Hence then $\sum p_j^{\pi}U(x_j) = \sum p_j^{\pi}U(\alpha) = U(\alpha)$.

If π has exactly one π-essential state, say k, then by Lemma VI.3.4, $x \approx \overline{x_k}$. Hence by Lemma VI.7.9, $U(\overline{x_k}) = U(\alpha)$; i.e., $\sum p_j^{\pi}U(x_j) = U(\alpha)$.

□

LEMMA VI.8.6. *Let* $x \in C^{\pi}$, $y \in C^{\pi'}$. *Then*

$$x \succcurlyeq y \iff \sum_{j=1}^{n} p_j^{\pi}U(x_j) \geq \sum_{j=1}^{n} p_j^{\pi'}U(y_j).$$

PROOF. Let (Lemma V.4.4) $x \approx \overline{\alpha}$, $y \approx \overline{\beta}$. Then $x \succcurlyeq y$ iff $\overline{\alpha} \succcurlyeq \overline{\beta}$, which by Lemma VI.7.9 holds iff $U(\alpha) \geq U(\beta)$. By Lemma VI.8.5 the latter holds iff $\sum p_j^{\pi}U(x_j) \geq \sum p_j^{\pi}U(y_j)$.

□

LEMMA VI.8.7. *Let* $A \subset I$. *Let* $A = \{\pi(1),...,\pi(k)\} = \{\pi'(1),...,\pi'(k)\}$. *Then* $\sum_{j=1}^{k} p_j^{\pi} = \sum_{j=1}^{k} p_j^{\pi'}$.

PROOF. Let $x_j = \beta^1$ for all $j \in A$, $x_j = \beta^0$ for all $j \notin A$. Then $x \in C^{\pi}$ and $x \in C^{\pi'}$. Apply the above Lemma with $y = x$.

□

The purpose of the last two sections has been to derive the following result, which holds in generality without Assumption VI.8.1 presumed.

THEOREM VI.8.8. *Suppose the assumptions of Theorem VI.5.1 hold. Let (ii) there hold. Furthermore, let no maximal or minimal consequences exist, and let there be a π with two or more π-essential states. Then (i) of Theorem VI.5.1, and the uniqueness result (VI.5.7), hold.*

PROOF. According to Lemma VI.8.7, and formula (VI.2.11), with $P^{\pi}(j) := p_j^{\pi}$ for all π,j, there exists a unique capacity v in accordance with Definition VI.2.3. Note that the U in Definition VI.8.3 is continuous. Lemma VI.8.6 and formula (VI.2.7) now give (i) of Theorem VI.5.1.

To derive (VI.5.7), say there are two or more id-essential states. Then the fact that $(P^{id}(j)U)_{j=1}^{n}$ are additive value functions for $\succcurlyeq$ on C^{id}, and joint cardinality of $(V_j^{id})_{j=1}^{n}$ in Theorem VI.7.11 (follows from cardinality of V), give cardinality of U, and together with $[\sum P^{id}(j) = 1]$ uniquely determine $(P^{id}(j))_{j=1}^{n}$. Analogously $(P^{\pi}(j))_{j=1}^{n}$ are uniquely determined for any π with two or more π-essential states. If π has exactly one π-essential state k, then $P^{\pi}(k) = 1$ must hold, and $P^{\pi}(j) = 0$ for all $j \neq k$. Anyway, the $P^{\pi}(j)$ uniquely determine the capacity v.

□

VI.9. MAXIMAL AND/OR MINIMAL CONSEQUENCES

In this section we derive the implication (ii) => (i) in Theorem VI.5.1, and the uniqueness result (VI.5.7), for the case where maximal and/or minimal consequences may exist, and where furthermore, as will be assumed throughout this section without further mention :

ASSUMPTION VI.9.1 (for this section). **The assumptions of Theorem VI.5.1 hold. Also statement (ii) there holds. There exists a permutation π with two or more π-essential states, say π =** identity.

The following lemma could have been obtained as a corollary of Lemma III.3.5.

LEMMA VI.9.2. *Let $\alpha,\gamma \in \Gamma$ be such that $\alpha \succ \gamma$. Then there exists $\beta \in \Gamma$ such that $\alpha \succ \beta \succ \gamma$.*

PROOF. $E := \{\beta : \beta \succ \gamma\}$ and $F := \{\beta : \beta \prec \alpha\}$ are open (by Lemma VI.6.1) and nonempty. Their union is Γ, for if $\delta \in F^c$ then $\delta \succcurlyeq \alpha$ so $\delta \succ \gamma$. Hence by connectedness of Γ, E and F must have nonempty intersection.

□

NOTATION VI.9.3. $\Gamma^* := \{\alpha \in \Gamma : \alpha$ is neither maximal nor minimal$\}$. $\Gamma^{\pi*} := \Gamma^{\pi} \cap (\Gamma^*)^n$.

Since π = id has a π-essential state (even more than one), there exists $\alpha \succ \beta$. By Lemma VI.9.2, Γ^* is nonempty, and has no ('new') maximal or minimal consequences itself.

LEMMA VI.9.4. *If* i *is essential on Γ^{π} (i.e., π-essential), then it is on $\Gamma^{\pi*}$.*

PROOF. Say π is identity. There exist $\alpha,\beta \in \Gamma$ such that $\alpha \succ \beta$. By Lemma VI.9.2, there exists γ such that $\alpha \succ \gamma \succ \beta$; again Lemma VI.9.2 gives δ such that $\gamma \succ \delta \succ \beta$. Let $x \in C^{id}$

have $x_k = \gamma$ for all $k \leq i$, $x_k = \delta$ for all $k > i$. Then $x_{-i}\gamma$, $x_{-i}\delta$ are in C^{id}, even in C^{id*}. By com.s.mon. $x_{-i}\gamma \succ x_{-i}\delta$.

□

Next we show that, on $(\Gamma^*)^n$, (i) in Theorem VI.5.1 is satisfied.

PROPOSITION VI.9.5. *There exist a capacity* v, *and a continuous function* $U^* : \Gamma^* \to \mathbb{R}$, *such that* $x \mapsto \int(U^* \circ x)dv$ *represents* $\succcurlyeq$ *on* $(\Gamma^*)^n$.

PROOF. By Lemma VI.9.2, Γ^* itself has no maximal or minimal consequences. By Lemma VI.9.4, essentiality of states on $(\Gamma^*)^n$ is as on Γ^n. The proposition now follows from Theorem VI.8.8, if the required topological conditions can be guaranteed. This is done analogously to subsection VI.7.1: $T(\succcurlyeq) \mid \Gamma^*$ is taken as topology on Γ^*. Mainly by Lemma VI.7.4 this preserves connectedness. Continuity of $\succcurlyeq$ on $(\Gamma^*)^n$ with respect to the product topology of the $T(\succcurlyeq) \mid \Gamma^*$'s, differs only in details from Lemma VI.7.6 :

Let again $x \succ y$, for $x,y \in (\Gamma^*)^n$. We construct $\tilde{x} \succ y$, and by means of this a subset $F_1 \times \ldots \times F_n$ of $\{w \in (\Gamma^*)^n : w \succ y\}$ which contains x and which has every $F_j \subset \Gamma^*$ open with respect to $T(\succcurlyeq) \mid \Gamma^*$. For the construction of $\tilde{x}_1$, consider :

$$V := \{\alpha \in \Gamma : (\alpha,x_2,\ldots,x_n) \succ y\}.$$

By Lemma 0.2.1 this is open with respect to T, the 'old' topology on Γ. V contains x_1 so is nonempty. If V = Γ, then $x_1 \in \Gamma^*$ not being minimal, we take $\tilde{x}_1 = \alpha$ for any $\alpha \in \Gamma^*$ with $\alpha \prec x_1$. If V ≠ Γ, then by connectedness of Γ with respect to T, V is not closed with respect to T. By continuity of $\succcurlyeq$ on Γ (Lemma VI.6.1) with respect to T, V is not of the form $\{\alpha : \alpha \succcurlyeq x_1\}$. And since, by p.mon., V contains all $\alpha \succcurlyeq x_1$, V must contain an $\alpha \prec x_1$. Now take (Lemma VI.9.2) $\tilde{x}_1 = \beta$ for any $\alpha \prec \beta \prec x_1$. Then $\tilde{x}_1 \in \Gamma^*$.

So always $\tilde{x}_1 \in \Gamma^*$ is found with $\tilde{x}_1 \prec x_1$, $(\tilde{x}_1,x_2,\ldots,x_n) \succ y$. Let $F_1 := \{\alpha : \alpha \succ \tilde{x}_1\}$. Further we proceed as in the proof of Lemma VI.7.6.

□

We plan to define $U : \alpha \mapsto \sup(U^*(\Gamma^*))$ [respectively $\inf(U^*(\Gamma^*))$] for maximal [respectively minimal] α. Hence :

LEMMA VI.9.6. *If* α *is maximal [respectively minimal], then* $U^*(\Gamma^*)$ *is bounded above [respectively below].*

PROOF. The proof will be given only for the case of a maximal α. Let i < j be two id-essential states. Let, only in this proof, $(\overline{\beta},\overline{\gamma})$ denote the act z with $z_k = \beta$ for $k \leq i$, $z_k = \gamma$ for $k > i$, for all $\beta,\gamma \in \Gamma$. By com.s.mon., for all $\gamma \in \Gamma^*$, $\overline{\alpha} \succ (\overline{\alpha},\overline{\gamma})$.

Let $\gamma \in \Gamma^*$ be fixed, let β (by Lemma V.4.4) be such that $(\overline{\alpha},\overline{\gamma}) \approx \overline{\beta}$ (so $\beta \in \Gamma^*$). Now for all $\mu \in \Gamma^*$ with $\mu \succcurlyeq \gamma$, $(\overline{\mu},\overline{\gamma})$ is in Γ^{id*}, and $(\overline{\mu},\overline{\gamma}) \prec (\overline{\alpha},\overline{\gamma}) \approx \overline{\beta}$, so :

$$v(\{1,\ldots,i\})U^*(\mu) + [v(S) - v(\{1,\ldots,i\})]U^*(\gamma) < U^*(\beta). \qquad \text{(VI.9.1)}$$

Since i is essential on Γ^{id*}, $v(\{1,\ldots,i\})$ is positive, and (VI.9.1) induces an upper bound for $\{U^*(\mu) : \mu \in \Gamma^*, \mu \succcurlyeq \gamma\}$, thus for $U^*(\Gamma^*)$.

□

DEFINITION VI.9.7. If $\alpha \in \Gamma$ is maximal, then $U(\alpha) := \sup(U^*(\Gamma^*))$. If $\alpha \in \Gamma$ is minimal, then $U(\alpha) := \inf(U^*(\Gamma^*))$. If $\alpha \in \Gamma^*$, then $U(\alpha) := U^*(\alpha)$.

As we saw above, $U(\alpha) \in \mathbb{R}$ for all α. We denote :

NOTATION VI.9.8. $\Gamma^+ := \Gamma^* \cup \{\alpha \in \Gamma : \alpha \text{ is maximal}\}$.

With this we obtain :

LEMMA VI.9.9. *For all* $x \in (\Gamma^+)^n$, *and* $\theta \in \Gamma$ *with* $x \approx \overline{\theta}$, $\int(U\circ x)dv = U(\theta)$.

PROOF. Say $x \in \Gamma^{id}$. By com.s.mon., θ is not minimal, so $\theta \in \Gamma^+$. If no maximal α exists, Proposition VI.9.5 gives the desired result. So let α be maximal. Let $0 \le k \le n$ be such that $x_1 \approx \alpha,...,x_k \approx \alpha$, $x_{k+1} \prec \alpha$, ...,$x_n \prec \alpha$. If θ is maximal, then $\theta \approx \alpha$, and by com.s.mon. k+1,...,n must be id-inessential. Then $\int(U\circ x)dv = U(\theta)$ follows.

There remains the most complicated case, where θ is not maximal, so, neither being minimal, is in Γ^*. First we show that $\int(U\circ x)dv \le U(\theta)$. By p.mon., for all $\mu \in \Gamma^*$ with $(\alpha \succ)\mu \succcurlyeq x_{k+1}$, we have

$(\mu,...,\mu,x_{k+1},...,x_n) \preccurlyeq \overline{\theta}$; i.e.,

$\int(U\circ(\mu,...,\mu,x_{k+1},...,x_n))dv \le U(\theta)$.

Writing, for all $1 \le j \le k$, $U(x_j) = U(\alpha) = \sup\{U(\mu) : \mu \in \Gamma^*, \mu \succcurlyeq x_{k+1}\}$ shows that $\int(U\circ x)dv \le U(\theta)$.

To see that $\int(U\circ x)dv \ge U(\theta)$, we consider δ such that $\theta \succ \delta$, so $x \succ \overline{\delta}$. By standard arguments continuity of $\succcurlyeq$, Lemma 0.2.1, and connectedness of Γ, imply existence of μ_k such that $x_k \succ \mu_k \succcurlyeq x_{k+1}$, and $x_{-k}\mu_k \succ \overline{\delta}$. Also, μ_{k-1} exists such that $x_{k-1} \succ \mu_{k-1} \succcurlyeq \mu_k$ and $(x_{-(k-1),k}\mu_{k-1},\mu_k) \succ \overline{\delta}$. Finally we end up with $\alpha \succ \mu_1 \succcurlyeq \mu_2 \succcurlyeq ... \succcurlyeq \mu_k$ such that $(\mu_1,...,\mu_k,x_{k+1},...,x_n) \succ \overline{\delta}$. Hence, for all $\mu \in \Gamma$ such that $\alpha \succ \mu \succcurlyeq \mu_1(\succcurlyeq ... \succcurlyeq \mu_k)$, we obtain $\int(U\circ(\mu,...,\mu,x_{k+1},...,x_n))dv > U(\delta)$.

Substituting, for $1 \le j \le k$, $U(x_j) = U(\alpha) = \sup\{U(\mu) : \mu \in \Gamma^*, \mu \succcurlyeq \mu_1\}$, shows that $\int(U\circ x)dv \ge U(\delta)$. This holds for all $\delta \prec \theta$. Hence $\int(U\circ x)dv \ge U(\theta)$.

□

LEMMA VI.9.10. *The map* $x \mapsto \int(U\circ x)dv$ *represents* $\succcurlyeq$ *on* $(\Gamma^+)^n$.

PROOF. First for constant acts. Suppose $\gamma \succ \delta$, with γ maximal. Then, by Lemma VI.9.2, $\gamma \succ \alpha \succ \delta$ for some $\alpha \in \Gamma$. So $U(\gamma) \ge U(\alpha) > U(\delta)$ follows, the latter strict inequality follows from Proposition VI.9.5. All other cases of $\gamma \succcurlyeq \delta \Leftrightarrow U(\gamma) \ge U(\delta)$ are straightforward.

Next let $x,y \in (\Gamma^+)^n$ be arbitrary. Let $x \approx \overline{\theta}$, $y \approx \overline{\delta}$ (by Lemma V.4.4). Then $x \succcurlyeq y \Leftrightarrow \overline{\theta} \succcurlyeq \overline{\delta} \Leftrightarrow U(\theta) \ge U(\delta) \Leftrightarrow \int(U\circ x)dv \ge \int(U\circ y)dv$, the latter by Lemma VI.9.9.

□

Next it must be shown that $x \mapsto \int(U \circ x)dv$ represents $\succcurlyeq$ also on $(\Gamma^+ \cup \{\alpha \in \Gamma : \alpha \text{ is minimal}\})^n = \Gamma^n$. This is very analogous to the above, hence elaboration is left out. We conclude that the implication (ii) => (i) in Theorem VI.5.1 is also established if maximal and/or minimal consequences exist. For the uniqueness result (VI.5.7), we must show that for maximal [respectively minimal] α no other choice for $U(\alpha)$, than $\sup(U(\Gamma^*))$ [or $\inf(U(\Gamma^*))$] can be made. This can be seen for instance from the proof of Lemma VI.9.9. Let $i > j$ be two id-essential states. Then, with α maximal, $x_1 = \ldots = x_i = \alpha$, $\alpha \succ x_{i+1} \succcurlyeq \ldots \succcurlyeq x_n$, the formula $\int(U \circ x)dv = U(\theta)$ there uniquely determines $U(\alpha)$. For minimal consequences matters are analogous.

VI.10. SURVEY OF THE PROOF OF THEOREM VI.5.1

The implication (i) => (ii) in Theorem VI.5.1 has been established directly below the Theorem. The proof of (ii) => (i) for the case where no π has two or more π-essential states, and the proof of the uniqueness results (VI.5.8) and (VI.5.9), have been given in Lemma VI.6.2. There remains the case where at least one π has two or more π-essential states. The case of no maximal or minimal consequences has been handled in Theorem VI.8.8. The existence of maximal consequences has been handled in Lemma VI.9.10. The general case has been handled in the final lines of section VI.9.

CHAPTER VII[rf1]

CONCAVITY ON MIXTURE SPACES AND RISK AVERSION

VII.1. INTRODUCTION

In this chapter we shall assume that $\prod_{i=1}^{n}\Gamma_i$, the set of alternatives, is a Cartesian product of 'mixture spaces', i.e., spaces endowed with some sort of convex combination operation. Two main examples of mixture spaces are, firstly, convex subsets of Euclidean spaces, and secondly, sets of probability distributions, 'lotteries' over a given set of 'certain outcomes'. Mixture spaces have been introduced in von Neumann& Morgenstern(1944), mainly as generalization of lotteries, and have almost exclusively been studied with the purpose to obtain results useful for lotteries[rf2]. We shall study mixture spaces mainly as generalizations of convex subsets of Euclidean spaces, and deal with concavity and convexity of (representing) functions on mixture spaces. To the best of our knowledge concavity and/or convexity of functions on mixture spaces have not yet been studied in the literature, whereas mixture spaces do have the natural structure for the study of these notions.

The first four sections study '(quasi)concave' additive representations. (Quasi)concavity is a prevailing assumption in consumer and producers theory, and optimization theory. It guarantees the existence of equilibria and the solvability of optimization problems[rf3]. Section 5 gives applications to decision making under uncertainty, where concavity is associated with risk aversion. The last two sections consider decision making under uncertainty with monetary consequences, and characterize the prevailing special case of expected utility with risk aversion: The case of nonincreasing risk aversion. We shall see that this further behavioural assumption simplifies the derivation of expected utility maximization, and makes it possible to dispense with the condition of the nonrevelation of contradictory tradeoffs by the preference relation[rf4].

VII.2. PRODUCT TOPOLOGICAL MIXTURE SPACES

Whenever no confusion is likely, we shall use the same notations for mixture spaces as for Euclidean spaces. This will be of most convenience for readers interested only in Euclidean spaces.

DEFINITION VII.2.1. Suppose Γ is a nonempty set, and θ is a map from $(\Gamma \times [0,1] \times \Gamma)$ to Γ. Let $\lambda\alpha + (1-\lambda)\beta$ denote $\theta(\alpha,\lambda,\beta)$. θ is a **mixture operation** if for all α, $\beta \in \Gamma$, λ, $\mu \in [0,1]$:

$$\lambda\alpha + (1-\lambda)\beta \;=\; (1-\lambda)\beta + \lambda\alpha \text{ (\textbf{commutativity})}. \quad \text{(VII.2.1)}$$

$$\mu(\lambda\alpha + (1-\lambda)\beta) + (1-\mu)\beta \;=\; (\mu\lambda)\alpha + (1-\mu\lambda)\beta \text{ (\textbf{associativity})} . \quad \text{(VII.2.2)}$$

$$1\alpha + 0\beta \;=\; \alpha \text{ (\textbf{identity})} . \quad \text{(VII.2.3)}$$

If θ is a mixture operation, then (Γ,θ), or simply Γ, is called a **mixture space**.

We write α/μ for $(1/\mu)\alpha$, and $\lambda\alpha/\mu$ for $(\lambda/\mu)\alpha$. We say that β **is between** α and γ if there exists a $\lambda \in [0,1]$ such that $\beta = \lambda\alpha + (1-\lambda)\gamma$. The following result is well-known[rf5].

LEMMA VII.2.2. *If* Γ *is a mixture space, then for all* $\alpha,\beta \in \Gamma$, $\lambda,\mu,\nu \in [0,1]$:

$$\mu\alpha + (1-\mu)\alpha \;=\; \alpha . \quad \text{(VII.2.4)}$$

$$\lambda(\mu\alpha + (1-\mu)\beta) + (1-\lambda)(\nu\alpha + (1-\nu)\beta) \;= \quad \text{(VII.2.5)}$$
$$[\lambda\mu + (1-\lambda)\nu]\alpha + [\lambda(1-\mu) + (1-\lambda)(1-\nu)]\beta.$$

PROOF. For (VII.2.4), we have $\mu\alpha + (1-\mu)\alpha = \mu(1\alpha + 0\alpha) + (1-\mu)\alpha = \mu(0\alpha + 1\alpha) + (1-\mu)\alpha = 0\alpha + 1\alpha = 1\alpha + 0\alpha = \alpha$, respectively by identity (VII.2.3), commutativity (VII.2.1), associativity (VII.2.2), commutativity, and identity. (VII.2.5) is straightforward if μ or ν is 0 or 1. So, say, $0 < \mu \le \nu < 1$. Then

$$\lambda(\mu\alpha + (1-\mu)\beta) + (1-\lambda)(\nu\alpha + (1-\nu)\beta) = \lambda[\mu/\nu(\nu\alpha + (1-\nu)\beta) + (1-\mu/\nu)\beta] + (1-\lambda)(\nu\alpha + (1-\nu)\beta)$$
$$= \lambda[(1-\mu/\nu)\beta + \mu/\nu(\nu\alpha + (1-\nu)\beta)] + (1-\lambda)(\nu\alpha + (1-\nu)\beta) =$$
$$(\lambda-\lambda\mu/\nu)\beta + [1-(\lambda-\lambda\mu/\nu)](\nu\alpha + (1-\nu)\beta) = [1-(\lambda-\lambda\mu/\nu)](\nu\alpha + (1-\nu)\beta) + (\lambda-\lambda\mu/\nu)\beta =$$
$$[\lambda\mu + (1-\lambda)\nu]\alpha + [\lambda(1-\mu) + (1-\lambda)(1-\nu)]\beta,$$

respectively by associativity, commutativity, associativity, commutativity, and associativity.

□

Some examples of mixture spaces are :

EXAMPLE VII.2.3. Γ is a convex subset of a linear space over $\mathbb{R}$. θ is the usual convex combination operation.

EXAMPLE VII.2.4. Γ is a set of probability distributions ('lotteries'). For every P_1, $P_2 \in \Gamma$, and $0 \leq \lambda \leq 1$, the probability distribution $\lambda P_1 + (1-\lambda)P_2$, assigning $\lambda P_1(A) + (1-\lambda)P_2(A)$ to every A, must also be contained in Γ.

One can consider Example VII.2.4 as a special case of Example VII.2.3. Mixture spaces do not have to be isomorphic to convex subsets of linear spaces. Stone(1949)[rf6] showed that strengthening of the 'two-dimensional' associativity condition (VII.2.2) to 'three-dimensional' associativity, together with addition of a 'cancellation' axiom are the necessary and sufficient conditions for a mixture space to be isomorphic to a convex subset of a linear space. These conditions are violated by the next example.

EXAMPLE VII.2.5 (see Figure VII.2.1). Let $\Gamma = \{(x_1,x_2) \in \mathbb{R}^2 : -1 \leq x_1 \leq 0, x_2 = 0\} \cup \{(x_1,x_2) \in \mathbb{R}^2 : 0 \leq x_1 \leq 1, -x_1 \leq x_2 \leq x_1\}$. In this example the notation $\lambda\alpha + (1-\lambda)\beta$ is used for the usual convex combination on Euclidean spaces, which here is different from the mixture operation θ; θ is defined as follows :

(i) If $x_1y_1 \geq 0$, then $\theta((x_1,x_2),\lambda,(y_1,y_2)) = (\lambda x_1 + (1-\lambda)y_1, \lambda x_2 + (1-\lambda)y_2)$.

(ii) If $x_1y_1 < 0$, then $\theta((x_1,x_2),\lambda,(y_1,y_2))$ is the unique point in $\{\mu x : 0 \leq \mu \leq 1\} \cup \{\mu y : 0 \leq \mu \leq 1\}$ with first coordinate $\lambda x_1 + (1-\lambda)y_1$.

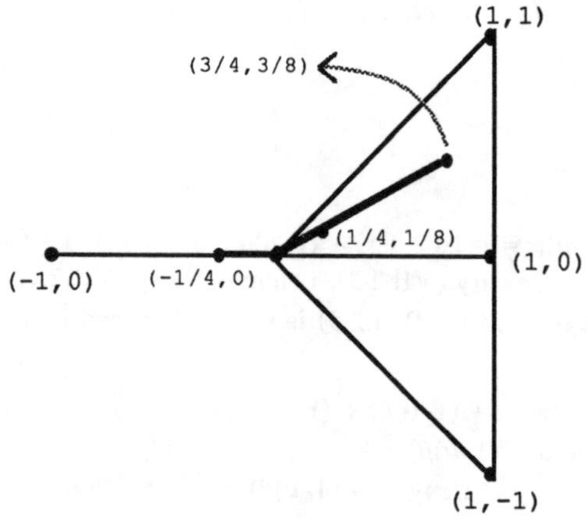

FIGURE VII.2.1 (Example VII.2.5). Within the triangle, and outside the triangle, mixtures are as usual. Mixing a point from within the triangle with a point from outside the triangle deviates; for example (1/4,1/8) results from the mixture $\theta((-1/4,0),1/2,(3/4,3/8))$.

In the above example every 'line segment' {z : z is between x,y} can be considered isomorphic to $\{z_1 \in \mathbb{R} : z_1$ is between x_1 and $y_1\}$. Still Γ is not isomorphic to a convex subset of a linear space as follows from the equality $\theta((-1,0),\frac{1}{2},(1,1)) = (0,0) = \theta((-1,0),\frac{1}{2},(1,-1))$, whereas of course $(1,1) \neq (1,-1)$. The 'triangle' with vertices (-1,0), (1,1), and (-1,1) is not isomorphic to a Euclidean triangle.

EXAMPLE VII.2.6. Suppose Γ = {g,u,b}, where g stands for 'good', u for 'undetermined', and b for 'bad'. Let $\lambda x + (1-\lambda)y :=$

g if: [x = y = g] or [λ = 1 and x = g] or [λ = 0 and y = g];
b if: [x = y = b] or [λ = 1 and x = b] or [λ = 0 and y = b];
u in all remaining cases.

From the above examples one may infer that, contrary to what is sometimes thought, it is not straightforward to define, for an arbitrary set, the notion of 'smallest mixture space' generated by the arbitrary set; e.g., let the set be {(-1,0),(1,1),(1,-1)} and consider Example VII.2.5, or VII.2.6. The following adaptations of well-known notions for linear spaces to mixture spaces are straightforward. Let Γ be a mixture space. A subset E of Γ is **convex** if $\lambda\alpha + (1-\lambda)\beta \in E$ for all $\alpha,\beta \in E$ and $0 \leq \lambda \leq 1$. A function $V : E \to \mathbb{R}$ is **concave** if $V(\lambda\alpha + (1-\lambda)\beta) \geq \lambda V(\alpha) + (1-\lambda)V(\beta)$ for all $\alpha,\beta \in E$, $o \leq \lambda \leq 1$. V is **convex** if -V is concave, and V is **affine** if it is both convex and concave. We prefer the term affine to the often used term linear. Finally, V is **quasiconcave** if $V(\lambda\alpha + (1-\lambda)\beta) \geq \min\{V(\alpha),V(\beta)\}$ for all $\alpha,\beta \in \Gamma$, $0 \leq \lambda \leq 1$. The latter holds if and only if, for every $\mu \in \mathbb{R}$, $\{\alpha \in \Gamma : V(\alpha) \geq \mu\}$ is convex. Every concave function is quasiconcave.

DEFINITION VII.2.7. A triple (Γ,T,θ) is a **topological mixture space** if Γ is a nonempty set, T a topology on Γ, and θ a mixture operation which is continuous with respect to the product topology on $\Gamma \times [0,1] \times \Gamma$.

Often we simply write Γ instead of (Γ,T,θ). Again, any convex subset of a Euclidean space is a topological mixture space. The following lemma will be used for Corollary VII.2.9, and in the proof of Lemma VII.2.10.

LEMMA VII.2.8. *Suppose* Γ *is a topological mixture space. Let* $\alpha,\beta \in \Gamma$. *Then* $\varphi : [0,1] \to \Gamma$, *defined by* $\varphi : \lambda \mapsto \lambda\alpha + (1-\lambda)\beta$, *is continuous.*

PROOF. Let $E \subset \Gamma$ be open. By continuity of θ, $\{(\gamma,\lambda,\delta) \in \Gamma \times [0,1] \times \Gamma : \lambda\gamma + (1-\lambda)\delta \in E\}$ is open. By Lemma 0.2.1, $\{\lambda \in [0,1] : \lambda\alpha + (1-\lambda)\beta \in E\}$ is open. Continuity of φ follows.

□

A direct consequence of Lemma VII.2.8 is :

COROLLARY VII.2.9. *A topological mixture space* Γ *is arcwise connected, hence connected.*

□

The following lemma is the straightforward generalization of related results for linear spaces (compare Lemma A1.2), and will be used in the proof of Theorem VII.3.5.

LEMMA VII.2.10. *Suppose* V *is a continuous function from a mixture space* Γ *to* $\mathbb{R}$. *Let there exist* $\eta > 0$ *such that for all* $\alpha,\beta \in \Gamma$ *with* $0 \le V(\alpha) - V(\beta) \le \eta$ *there exists* $0 < \lambda < 1$ *for which* $V(\lambda\alpha + (1-\lambda)\beta) \ge \lambda V(\alpha) + (1-\lambda)V(\beta)$. *Then* V *is concave.*

PROOF. Let $\gamma,\delta \in \Gamma$ be arbitrary. We must show that $V(\lambda\gamma + (1-\lambda)\delta) \ge \lambda V(\gamma) + (1-\lambda)V(\delta)$ for all $0 \le \lambda \le 1$. By Lemma VII.2.8, $\varphi : \lambda \mapsto \lambda\gamma + (1-\lambda)\delta$ is continuous. So $W = V\circ\varphi$ is also continuous. The proof is complete if we show that W is concave.

Let $\mu \in]0,1[$ be arbitrary. W being continuous, there is an open interval S around μ within [0,1], such that $|W(\sigma) - W(\tau)| \le \eta$ for all σ,τ in S. So for all $\sigma,\tau \in S$ with, say, $W(\sigma) \ge W(\tau)$, we have $0 \le V(\sigma\gamma + (1-\sigma)\delta) - V(\tau\gamma + (1-\tau)\delta) \le \eta$.

Hence $0 < \nu < 1$ exists such that :

$$V(\nu[\sigma\gamma + (1-\sigma)\delta] + (1-\nu)[\tau\gamma + (1-\tau)\delta]) \ge \nu V(\sigma\gamma + (1-\sigma)\delta) + (1-\nu)V(\tau\gamma + (1-\tau)\delta).$$

To the left side of this inequality we apply (VII.2.5), to obtain :

$$V([\nu\sigma + (1-\nu)\tau]\gamma + [\nu(1-\sigma) + (1-\nu)(1-\tau)]\delta) \ge \nu V(\sigma\gamma + (1-\sigma)\delta) + (1-\nu)V(\tau\gamma + (1-\tau)\delta).$$

Next we substitute W :

$$W(\nu\sigma + (1-\nu)\tau) \ge \nu W(\sigma) + (1-\nu)W(\tau).$$

W is concave by Lemma A1.2. (Substitute [0,1] for S, $-W$ for φ, μ for ν, S for W; if $\sigma < \tau$, substitute ν for p; if $\sigma > \tau$, then interchange σ and τ, and substitute $1-\nu$ for p.)

□

As in linear spaces, a binary relation $\succcurlyeq$ on a mixture space Γ is <u>convex</u> if $\{x \in \Gamma : x \succcurlyeq y\}$ is convex for every $y \in \Gamma$. A weak order $\succcurlyeq$ is convex if and only if $[x \succcurlyeq y]$ implies $[\lambda x + (1-\lambda)y \succcurlyeq y]$ for all x,y,λ. This holds if and only if $\lambda x + (1-\lambda)y \succcurlyeq x \wedge y$ ($\wedge$ denotes 'minimum'). If a function V represents $\succcurlyeq$, then $\succcurlyeq$ is convex if and only if V is quasiconcave.

LEMMA VII.2.11. *Suppose* $\succcurlyeq$ *is a continuous weak order on a topological mixture space* Γ. *Let, for all* $x \succcurlyeq y$, $0 < \lambda < 1$ *exist such that* $\lambda x + (1-\lambda)y \succcurlyeq y$. *Then* $\succcurlyeq$ *is convex.*

PROOF. Let $s,t \in \Gamma$ be arbitrary. Let $s \succcurlyeq t$. We shall demonstrate that $S := \{\mu \in [0,1] : \mu s + (1-\mu)t \succcurlyeq t\}$ equals [0,1].

By continuity of $\succcurlyeq$, $\{z \in \Gamma : z \succcurlyeq t\}$ is closed. By continuity of θ, $\{(v,\mu,w) \in \Gamma \times [0,1] \times \Gamma : \mu v + (1-\mu)w \succcurlyeq t\}$ is closed. By Lemma 0.2.1, S is closed. Let $\sigma,\tau \in S$, $\sigma \ne \tau$. Say $\sigma s + (1-\sigma)t \succcurlyeq \tau s + (1-\tau)t \succcurlyeq t$. There exists $0 < \lambda < 1$ such that :

$\lambda[\sigma s + (1-\sigma)t] \;+\; (1-\lambda)[\tau s + (1-\tau)t] \;\succcurlyeq\; \tau s + (1-\tau)t.$

By (VII.2.5) and transitivity this gives :

$[\lambda\sigma + (1-\lambda)\tau]s \;+\; [\lambda(1-\sigma) + (1-\lambda)(1-\tau)]t \;\succcurlyeq\; t.$

So the closed subset S of [0,1], containing 0 and 1, contains for every $\sigma \neq \tau$ in S an element strictly between σ and τ. S must be [0,1].

□

The terminology in the following definition will be justified by Theorem VII.2.13.

DEFINITION VII.2.12. For a sequence of mixture spaces $(\Gamma_i,\theta_i)_{i=1}^n$, the **product mixture operation** $\theta : \prod_{i=1}^n\Gamma_i \times [0,1] \times \prod_{i=1}^n\Gamma_i \to \prod_{i=1}^n\Gamma_i$ is defined by :

$\theta : (x,\lambda,y) \mapsto (\lambda x_1 + (1-\lambda)y_1,\dots,\lambda x_n + (1-\lambda)y_n) =: \lambda x + (1-\lambda)y,$

where $x = (x_1,\dots,x_n)$, $y = (y_1,\dots,y_n)$. We call $(\prod_{i=1}^n\Gamma_i,\theta)$, or simply $\prod_{i=1}^n\Gamma_i$, the **product mixture space**.

If the Γ_i's are topological mixture spaces, then $\prod_{i=1}^n\Gamma_i$, endowed with the product topology, is the **product topological mixture space**.

THEOREM VII.2.13. *A product mixture space is a mixture space. A product topological mixture space is a topological mixture space.*

PROOF. Let $(\Gamma_i,\theta_i)_{i=1}^n$, and θ be as in Definition VII.2.12. It is straightforward that θ is a mixture operation. Now let T_i be a topology on Γ_i, i = 1,...,n, and let every θ_i be continuous. We derive continuity of θ. Let $E_1 \in T_1$. Then $\theta^{-1}(E_1 \times \Gamma_2 \times \dots \times \Gamma_n)$ equals, after a reordering of the coordinates of $(\prod_{i=1}^n\Gamma_i) \times [0,1] \times \prod_{i=1}^n\Gamma_i)$, the set $(\theta_1^{-1}(E_1)) \times (\prod_{i=2}^n\Gamma_i) \times (\prod_{i=2}^n\Gamma_i)$, which is open. This can be shown not only for E_1 but, mutatis mutandis, for any $E_i \in \Gamma_i$. Continuity of θ follows.

□

VII.3. NONINCREASING TRADEOFFS

In this section we shall assume without further mention :

ASSUMPTION VII.3.1 (for this section). **$\prod_{i=1}^n\Gamma_i$ is a product topological mixture space.**

Further, as throughout this monograph, $\succcurlyeq$ is a binary relation on $\prod_{i=1}^n\Gamma_i$. In the following condition[rf7], and in the remainder of this chapter, we shall sometimes use the notation $[\alpha;\beta]$ instead of $\alpha\beta$ when dealing with comparisons of tradeoffs through $\succcurlyeq_i^*$ and $\succ_i^{**}$. For understanding of the following condition it may be useful to realize that

(VII.3.2) in the sequel holds for any concave function $V_i : \mathbb{R} \rightarrow \mathbb{R}$, irrespective of whether $x_i \geq y_i$ or not and irrespective of whether V_i is strictly increasing, strictly decreasing, or neither.

DEFINITION VII.3.2. Coordinate i reveals <u>nonincreasing tradeoffs (with respect to $\succcurlyeq$)</u> if for all x_i, y_i, and λ :

$$\text{Not } [x_i;(\lambda x_i+(1-\lambda)y_i)] \succ_i^{**} [((1-\lambda)x_i+\lambda y_i);y_i] \, .$$

The term nonincreasing tradeoffs (nonincreasing value of tradeoffs would be more accurate, but too long) is best understood from consideration of the case of monetary coordinates with (say, strictly increasing) concave additive value functions $(V_j)_{j=1}^n$. Then (with, say, $v_i > w_i$) the 'value' $V_i(v_i+\varepsilon) - V_i(w_i+\varepsilon)$ of the tradeoff $[v_i+\varepsilon;w_i+\varepsilon]$ is nonincreasing as function of ε. That this is indeed implied by nonincreasing tradeoffs can be inferred from Theorem VII.3.5, and Statement (ii) in Corollary VII.3.7 below. For another elucidation, closer to the above definition, see Figure VII.3.1. Nonincreasing marginal utility is an 'infinitesimal' relative of nonincreasing tradeoffs, which is another motive for the chosen term. In Wakker(1986a) the above condition was called the

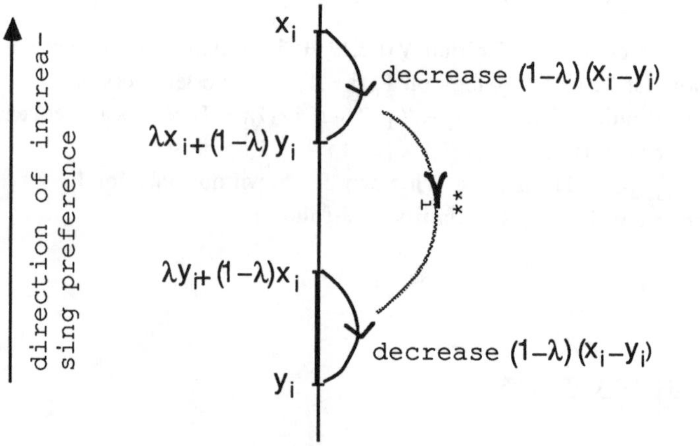

FIGURE VII.3.1 (<u>Increasing (value of) tradeoffs</u>). Coordinate i reveals $[x_i; \lambda x_i+(1-\lambda)y_i] \succ_i^{**} [\lambda y_i+(1-\lambda)x_i; y_i]$; i.e., an increase in tradeoffs.

This violates the idea of nonincreasing marginal utility, according to which a loss can never be more serious if incurred at a higher level of utility.

concavity assumption, and was formulated without use of $\succ_i^{**}$, as follows.

For all i, v, w, x_i, y_i, and λ,

$$v_{-i}x_i \succcurlyeq w_{-i}(\lambda x_i+(1-\lambda)y_i) \Rightarrow v_{-i}(\lambda y_i+(1-\lambda)x_i) \succcurlyeq w_{-i}y_i \,. \tag{VII.3.1}$$

The following lemmas generalize some results of Yaari(1978)[rf8]. Yaari's results were formulated for the special case where $\Gamma_i = \mathbb{R}_+$ for all i; for this case Yaari's 'Axiom Q' can elementarily be seen to be equivalent to (VII.3.1) (see Corollary VII.3.7(ii) below).

LEMMA VII.3.3. *If all coordinates reveal nonincreasing tradeoffs, then* $\succcurlyeq$ *is coordinate independent.*

PROOF. Let $\lambda = 1$ in Definition VII.3.2, and apply Lemma II.4.3.

□

LEMMA VII.3.4. *Suppose* $\succcurlyeq$ *is a continuous weak order. Let all coordinates reveal nonincreasing tradeoffs. Then* $\succcurlyeq$ *is convex.*

PROOF. By Lemma VII.2.11, it suffices to prove that $v \succcurlyeq w$ implies $v/2 + w/2 \succcurlyeq w$. For this it suffices to prove that, under the assumption $v/2 + w/2 \preccurlyeq w \preccurlyeq v$, we have $v/2 + w/2 \succcurlyeq v$. We define, inductively, for $0 \le j \le n$:

$$v^0 := v/2 + w/2,\ v^j := v^{j-1}{}_{-j}v_j;\ w^0 := w,\ w^j := w^{j-1}{}_{-j}(v_j/2 + w_j/2).$$

This gives $v^n = v$, $w^n = v/2 + w/2$. For $j = 0$ we have, by assumption, $w^0 \succcurlyeq v^0$. Now suppose $w^{j-1} \succcurlyeq v^{j-1}$ for some $1 \le j \le n$; i.e.,

$$(w^{j-1} =)\ w^j{}_{-j}w_j \succcurlyeq v^j{}_{-j}(v_j/2 + w_j/2)\ (= v^{j-1}).$$

By (VII.3.1) with $\lambda = 1/2$, this implies

$$w^j{}_{-j}(v_j/2 + w_j/2) \succcurlyeq v^j{}_{-j}v_j, \text{ i.e., } w^j \succcurlyeq v^j.$$

By induction $w^n \succcurlyeq v^n$ follows; i.e., $v/2 + w/2 \succcurlyeq v$.

□

If three or more coordinates are essential, the above lemma can also be obtained as a corollary of Theorem VII.3.5 below. The following theorem is the main result of this section.

THEOREM VII.3.5[rf9]. *Let the binary relation* $\succcurlyeq$ *on the product topological mixture space* $\prod_{i=1}^n \Gamma_i$ *have at least two essential coordinates. The following two statements are equivalent* :

(i) **There exist continuous concave additive value functions $(V_j)_{j=1}^n$ for $\succcurlyeq$.**

(ii) **The binary relation $\succcurlyeq$ is a continuous weak order for which all coordinates reveal nonincreasing tradeoffs; further, if exactly two coordinates are essential, then $\succcurlyeq$ satisfies the hexagon condition.**

□

OBSERVATION VII.3.5′. *The functions* $(V_j)_{j=1}^n$ *of statement (i) in Theorem VII.3.5 are jointly cardinal.*

□

PROOF of Theorem VII.3.5 and Observation VII.3.5′. Suppose (i) above holds. Then all of (ii), except the revelation of nonincreasing tradeoffs, follows straightforwardly from Theorem III.6.6. For the revelation of nonincreasing tradeoffs first note that twofold application of concavity of V_i, and adding up of inequalities, gives :

$$V_i(\lambda x_i+(1-\lambda)y_i) + V_i(\lambda y_i+(1-\lambda)x_i) \geq V_i(x_i) + V_i(y_i) . \qquad \text{(VII.3.2)}$$

If we would have a violation of (VII.3.1), i.e.,

$$v_{-i}x_i \succcurlyeq w_{-i}(\lambda x_i+(1-\lambda)y_i) \text{ and } w_{-i}y_i \succ v_{-i}(\lambda y_i+(1-\lambda)x_i),$$

then we could express these two preferences in inequalities of sums of additive value functions, add up these two inequalities, cancel all terms $V_j(v_j)$ and $V_j(w_j)$ $(j \neq i)$, and end up with formula (VII.3.2) with '<' instead of '≥'. So then a contradiction would result. Hence the concavity assumption must hold, and all coordinates reveal nonincreasing tradeoffs.

Next we suppose that (ii) holds. To derive is (i), and Observation VII.3.5′. The existence of continuous additive value functions $(V_j)_{j=1}^n$, jointly cardinal, follows from Corollary VII.2.9, Remark III.7.1, Lemma VII.3.3, and Theorem III.4.1. So only concavity of the V_j's remains to be proved. Rewriting the definition of the concavity assumption in terms of additive value functions, with $\lambda = 1/2$, gives :

$$\begin{aligned} &V_i(x_i) - V_i(x_i/2 + y_i/2) \geq^{(1)} \textstyle\sum_{j\neq i}[V_j(w_j) - V_j(v_j)] \Rightarrow \\ &\textstyle\sum_{j\neq i}[V_j(w_j) - V_j(v_j)] \leq^{(2)} V_i(x_i/2 + y_i/2) - V_i(y_i). \end{aligned} \qquad \text{(VII.3.3)}$$

This means that, for all x_i, y_i, for which v,w can be found to make $\geq^{(1)}$ hold with equality, we have :

$$[V_i(x_i) + V_i(y_i)]/2 \leq V_i(x_i/2 + y_i/2). \qquad \text{(VII.3.4)}$$

At least one coordinate $j \neq i$ is essential, so $V_j(\Gamma_j)$ (which by connectedness of Γ_j and continuity of V_j is an interval) must have length greater than η for some $\eta > 0$. For any x_i and y_i with $0 \leq V_i(x_i) - V_i(y_i) \leq \eta$, we can find v_j, w_j with $V_j(w_j) - V_j(v_j) = V_i(x_i) - V_i(y_i)$. Taking $v_k = w_k$ for all $k \neq i$, $k \neq j$ gives $\geq^{(1)}$ with equality. Now concavity of V_i, analogously of any V_j, follows from Lemma VII.2.10.

□

Statement (i) above is equivalent to the statement that there exists a cardinal, continuous, and additive representing function $V : \prod_{i=1}^n \Gamma_i \to \mathbb{R}$ which is concave, as mainly follows from the following result.

PROPOSITION VII.3.6. *Suppose* $V_j : \Gamma_j \to \mathbb{R}$ *for all* $1 \leq j \leq n$. *Let* $V : x \mapsto \sum_{j=1}^n V_j(x_j)$. *Then V is concave if and only if every* V_j *is concave.*

PROOF. Let V be concave. We derive concavity of V_1. $V_1(\lambda x_1 + (1-\lambda)y_1)$ equals, for an arbitrary z, $V(\lambda(z_{-1}x_1) + (1-\lambda)(z_{-1}y_1)) - \sum_{j\neq 1} V_j(z_j)$. By concavity of V this is greater than or equal to $\lambda V(z_{-1}x_1) + (1-\lambda)V(z_{-1}y_1)) - \sum_{j\neq 1} V_j(z_j)$. The latter equals $\lambda V_1(x_1) + (1-\lambda)V_1(y_1)$. So V_1 is concave. Analogously concavity of any V_j follows.

Next suppose that every V_j is concave. Then every V_j', assigning $V_j(x_j)$ to every x, is concave. V is a sum of concave functions V_j', so V itself is concave. □

The following Corollary applies Theorem VII.3.5 to the case where $\Gamma_i = \mathbb{R}_{++}$ for all i, and $\succcurlyeq$ is weakly monotonic. The condition after 'furthermore' in (ii) below is a reformulation of the revelation of nonincreasing tradeoffs. In statement (i) below we use Theorem 10.1 of Rockafellar, saying that a concave function on $\mathbb{R}_{++}$ is continuous.

COROLLARY VII.3.7. *Let* $n \geq 3$, *and let* $\succcurlyeq$ *be a binary relation on* $\mathbb{R}^n_{++}$. *The following two statements are equivalent* :

(i) **There exist concave (so continuous) nondecreasing nonconstant additive value functions** $(V_j)_{j=1}^n$.

(ii) **The binary relation** $\succcurlyeq$ **is a continuous weak order, weakly monotonic, every coordinate is essential, and furthermore, for all i,** $[(\alpha-\varepsilon);(\beta-\varepsilon)] \succcurlyeq_i^* [\alpha;\beta]$ **whenever** $(\alpha-\beta)\varepsilon \geq 0$. □

Of course the results of this section can easily be adapted to deal with convex additive value functions; e.g. by replacing everywhere $\succcurlyeq$ by $\preccurlyeq$, and V_j by $-V_j$. Also results on concavity and convexity can be combined to obtain results for affine additive value functions[rf10].

VII.4. SOME COUNTEREXAMPLES

In this section we give all logical relations between the statements (VII.4.1) through (VII.4.4) in Figure VII.4.1. Throughout we assume :

ASSUMPTION VII.4.1 (for this section). **The binary relation** $\succcurlyeq$ **is a continuous weak order on a product topological mixture space** $\prod_{i=1}^n \Gamma_i$. **Further** $m \leq n$ **is the number of essential coordinates.**

In the sequel of this section we shall give elucidations to the seven counterexamples of Figure VII.4.1.

Counterexample (1). For m = 1, statement (VII.4.2) does not imply (VII.4.1), even if a representing function V exists. This follows from Kannai(1977, p.17), or from f^5 in the

There exist continuous concave additive value functions. (VII.4.1)

⇑ : { m=1: counterexample (1), $V=f^5$; m=2: counterexample (2), $V=f^2$; m≥3: correct by Thm.VII.3.5 }

⇓ : { Trivial for m=1; By Thm.VII.3.5 for m≥2 }

All coordinates reveal nonincreasing tradeoffs. (VII.4.2)

⇑ : { m=1: counterexample (3), $V=f^1$; m=2: counterexample (4), $V=f^3$; m≥3: counterexample (5), $V=f^3$ }

⇓ : { By Lemmas VII.3.3 and VII.3.4 }

The preference relation is convex and CI. (VII.4.3)

⇑ : { m=1: correct; m=2: counterexample (6), $V=f^4$; m≥3: counterexample (7), $V=f^2$ }

⇓ : { direct }

The preference relation is convex. (VII.4.4)

FIGURE VII.4.1 (<u>Counterexamples for additivity and convexity</u>). *The preference relation is a continuous weak order on* $\mathbb{R}^n_{++}$, *with* m *essential coordinates. In the counterexamples the function* V *represents the preference relation. The solid arrows downwards indicate implications that hold, the broken arrows upwards indicate implications that do not always hold. For all* $1 \le k \le 5$, f^k *is a function from* $\mathbb{R}^n_{++}$ *to* $\mathbb{R}$:

$f^1(x) = 1$ if $x_1 \le 1$, $f^1(x) = x_1$ if $x_1 \ge 1$;

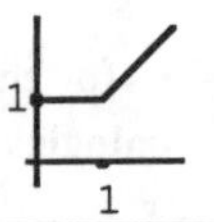

$f^2(x) = \Sigma_{j=1}^n x_j + \min(\{x_1, \ldots, x_n\})$;

$f^3(x) = (n-1)e^{x_1} + \Sigma_{j=2}^n \log(x_j)$;

$f^4(x) = -(2n - \Sigma_{j=1}^n x_j)^2$;

$f^5(x) = x_1 - 1$ for $0 < x_1 < 1$, $f^5(x) = (x_1 - 1)^2$ for $1 \le x_1 < 2$, $f^5(x) = 3 - x_1$ for $x_1 \ge 2$.

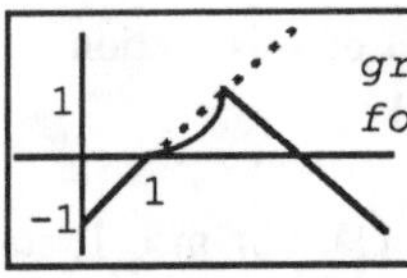

Figure. This function f^5 is straightforwardly seen to represent a binary relation $\succcurlyeq$ with respect to which all coordinates reveal nonincreasing tradeoffs. The function f^5 is a minor variation on the example of Artstein in Kannai(1981, p.562), where it is shown not to be 'concavifiable'; i.e., the binary relation $\succcurlyeq$, represented by f^5, has no concave representation.

Counterexample (2). For m = 2, (VII.4.2) does imply (VII.4.1) if and only if $\succcurlyeq$ satisfies the hexagon condition. That $\succcurlyeq$, represented by f^2, does not satisfy this for (n =) m = 2, hence has no additive value functions, can be inferred from Example III.6.7, (where now all coordinates should simply be increased by 1, since the domain now is $\mathbb{R}^2_{++}$). Still, by elementary but tedious arguments it can be seen that all coordinates reveal nonincreasing tradeoffs.

Counterexample (3). For the binary relation $\succcurlyeq$, represented by f^1, we have $(1/2,1,...,1) \succcurlyeq (1,...,1)$ and $(1,...,1) \prec (3/2,1,...,1)$, from which we derive $[1/2;1] \succ_1^{**} [1;3/2]$. This violates the condition of nonincreasing tradeoffs (set $x_i = 1/2$, $y_i = 3/2$, $\lambda = 1/2$ in Definition VII.3.2). Here the involved tradeoffs are to be considered 'negative'. For intuitive purposes one may prefer to derive, in the spirit of the 'reversibility' mentioned below Definition II.4.2, from the 'directly revealed' tradeoff comparison $[1/2;1] \succ_1^{**} [1;3/2]$, an 'indirectly revealed' tradeoff comparison $[3/2;1] \succ_1^{**} [1;1/2]$. The latter, in dealing with 'positive differences', more clearly reveals the idea of increasing tradeoffs.

Counterexamples (4) and (5). That f^3 is quasiconcave, so represents a convex binary relation $\succcurlyeq$, can be derived from 6.28 of Arrow&Enthoven(1961), and is not elaborated. For (n =) m ≥ 2, $\ln(v_j) = e^2$ and $\ln(w_j) = e^3$ for all j ≥ 2, the preferences $v_{-1}3 \succcurlyeq w_{-1}2$ and $v_{-1}2 \prec w_{-1}1$ reveal $[3;2] \succ_1^{**} [2;1]$; i.e., coordinate 1 has revealed an increase in tradeoff. Note that f^3 is a sum of additive value functions of which the first is not concave[rf11].

Counterexample (6). That, for m ≥ 2, the binary relation $\succcurlyeq$ as represented by f^4 is not coordinate independent, follows from the preferences $(2,...,2) \succ (2,3,2,...,2)$ and $(1,2,...,2) \prec (1,3,2,...,2)$.

Counterexample (7). That, for m ≥ 3, the binary relation $\succcurlyeq$ as represented by f^2 is not coordinate independent, follows from $(1,6,1,...,1) \succ (3,3,1,...,1)$, $(1,6,3,...,3) \prec (3,3,...,3)$.

VII.5. SUBJECTIVE EXPECTED UTILITY WITH RISK AVERSION

This and the following two sections show that classical results concerning risk aversion can be adapted to the case where no lotteries or objective probabilities are given. As in Chapters IV to VI, we assume $\Gamma_i = \Gamma$ for all i.

ASSUMPTION VII.5.1 (for this section). **Γ^n is a product topological mixture space.**

In this section we adopt again the terminology of decision making under uncertainty. We combine the nonrevelation of contradictory tradeoffs on consequences with the revelation of nonincreasing tradeoffs by coordinates, to obtain a characterization of subjective expected utility maximization with 'risk aversion'. Here risk aversion is simply taken to mean concavity of the utility function (the traditional definition, equivalent to it, will be given in Definition VII.6.2). While mathematically not very surprising, the conciseness of the provided characterization of expected utility with risk aversion motivated our presentation of the condition.

DEFINITION VII.5.2 (see Figure VII.5.1). The binary relation $\succcurlyeq$ reveals <u>nonincreasing noncontradictory tradeoffs (on consequences)</u> if for all consequences $\alpha,\beta,\gamma,\delta$, and all essential states i and j :

$$[\alpha;(\lambda\alpha+(1-\lambda)\beta)] \succcurlyeq_i^* [\gamma;\delta] \Rightarrow \text{not } [\gamma;\delta] \succ_j^{**} [(\lambda\beta+(1-\lambda)\alpha);\beta] .$$

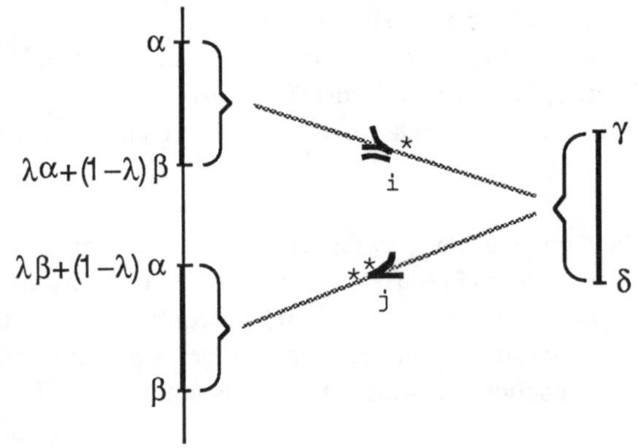

FIGURE VII.5.1.(<u>Nonincreasing noncontradictory tradeoffs</u>). Revealed tradeoffs as indicated in the Figure are excluded by the condition of nonincreasing noncontradictory tradeoffs on consequences. Compare Figure VII.3.1.

The following lemma motivates the above terminology.

LEMMA VII.5.3. *Suppose $\succcurlyeq$ is a continuous weak order. Let $\succcurlyeq$ reveal nonincreasing noncontradictory tradeoffs. Then $\succcurlyeq$ does not reveal contradictory tradeoffs, and all coordinates reveal nonincreasing tradeoffs.*

PROOF. That no contradictory tradeoffs are revealed by $\succcurlyeq$ can be seen by setting $\lambda = 0$ in Definition VII.5.2. So only the revelation of nonincreasing tradeoffs remains to be derived. Let, for i essential :

$$x_{-i}\gamma \succcurlyeq y_{-i}(\lambda\gamma + (1-\lambda)\delta) . \tag{VII.5.1}$$

It suffices to prove :

$$x_{-i}(\lambda\delta+(1-\lambda)\gamma) \succcurlyeq y_{-i}\delta . \tag{VII.5.2}$$

because then it is guaranteed that never $[\gamma;(\lambda\gamma+(1-\lambda)\delta)] \succ_i^{**} [(\lambda\delta+(1-\lambda)\gamma);\delta]$ will be revealed. Suppose there exist $\eta, \xi \in \Gamma$ with $x_{-i}\eta \prec y_{-i}\xi$; if no such η, ξ would exist then (VII.5.2) would follow immediately. Our plan is to find α,β in Γ such that :

$$x_{-i}\alpha \approx y_{-i}\beta . \tag{VII.5.3}$$

If we succeed in this then (VII.5.1) and (VII.5.3) give $[\gamma;(\lambda\gamma+(1-\lambda)\delta)] \succcurlyeq_i^* [\alpha;\beta]$. This by the nonincreasing noncontradictory tradeoffs, with i = j, excludes $[\alpha;\beta] \succ_i^{**} [(\lambda\delta+(1-\lambda)\gamma);\delta]$, so that (VII.5.2) follows. So finally, by means of η, ξ as above, we derive (VII.5.3) for some α,β.

First suppose that $y_{-i}(\lambda\gamma+(1-\lambda)\delta) \succcurlyeq x_{-i}\eta$. Then $x_{-i}\gamma \succcurlyeq y_{-i}(\lambda\gamma+(1-\lambda)\delta) \succcurlyeq x_{-i}\eta$. By restricted solvability (Lemma III.3.3), we obtain an α such that (VII.5.3) holds, with $\beta := \lambda\gamma + (1-\lambda)\delta$.

Next suppose $y_{-i}(\lambda\gamma+(1-\lambda)\delta) \prec x_{-i}\eta$. Then $y_{-i}(\lambda\gamma+(1-\lambda)\delta) \prec x_{-i}\eta \prec y_{-i}\xi$. By restricted solvability, we obtain β such that (VII.5.3) holds, with $\alpha := \eta$. □

With the above lemma we obtain :[rf12]

THEOREM VII.5.4. *Let at least two states be essential with respect to the binary relation $\succcurlyeq$ on the product topological mixture space Γ^n. The following three statements are equivalent* :

(i) **There exists an SEU model $[\Gamma^n, \succcurlyeq, (p_j)_{j=1}^n, U]$ for $\succcurlyeq$ with U concave and continuous.**

(ii) **The binary relation $\succcurlyeq$ is a continuous weak order that does not reveal contradictory tradeoffs; further all coordinates reveal nonincreasing tradeoffs.**

(iii) **The binary relation $\succcurlyeq$ is a continuous weak order that reveals nonincreasing noncontradictory tradeoffs.**

PROOF. We derive (i) => (iii) => (ii) => (i). First suppose (i) holds. Obviously $\succcurlyeq$ is a continuous weak order. To show that $\succcurlyeq$ reveals nonincreasing noncontradictory tradeoffs let i,j be essential, and let $[\alpha;(\lambda\alpha+(1-\lambda)\beta)] \succcurlyeq_i^* [\gamma;\delta]$. Then $U(\gamma) - U(\delta) \leq U(\alpha) - U(\lambda\alpha+(1-\lambda)\beta)$, compare (IV.2.2). By concavity of U the latter righthand side is less than or equal to $U(\lambda\beta+(1-\lambda)\alpha) - U(\beta)$. We get $U(\gamma) - U(\delta) \leq U(\lambda\beta+(1-\lambda)\alpha) - U(\beta)$. So $v_{-j}\gamma \succcurlyeq w_{-j}\delta$ implies $v_{-j}(\lambda\beta+(1-\lambda)\alpha) \succcurlyeq w_{-j}\beta$. Thus $[\gamma;\delta] \succ_j^{**} [(\lambda\beta+(1-\lambda)\alpha);\beta]$ cannot occur. Nonincreasing noncontradictory tradeoffs result, and (iii) is established.

The implication (iii) => (ii) follows from Lemma VII.5.3. So finally we assume (ii), and derive (i). We may conclude from Theorem IV.2.7 that there exists an SEU model for $\succcurlyeq$, with U continuous, as soon as we have taken care of the topological assumption III.3.2. This can be taken care of by Corollary VII.2.9, and Remark III.7.1 which applies as well to Theorem IV.2.7. Of course $(p_jU)_{j=1}^{n}$ are additive value functions for $\succcurlyeq$. Concavity of U will now result from Theorem VII.3.5 and its uniqueness result in Observation VII.3.5′. Details are as follows: since all coordinates reveal nonincreasing tradeoffs, and $\succcurlyeq$ satisfies the hexagon condition if exactly two states are essential, by Theorem VII.3.5 there exist jointly cardinal concave additive value functions $(V_j)_{j=1}^{n}$ for $\succcurlyeq$. So for every j, V_j is a positive affine transformation of p_jU. Since at least one p_j is positive, U must share concavity with V_j.

□

VII.6. COMPARISONS OF RISK AVERSION

In this section we consider again the context of decision making under uncertainty, and deal with comparisons of risk aversion of different decision makers. For the context of decision making under risk, with probabilities available as primitives, the classical results concerning comparisons of risk aversion have been established in Pratt(1964) and Arrow(1965, 1971). We shall show that these classical results can be adapted to the context of decision making under uncertainty, where probabilities are not given in advance and should not be used as primitives in the formulations of the behavioural conditions. The only auxiliary condition that we shall use is continuity of utility. Remark VII.6.6 will indicate that Theorem VII.6.5, characterizing comparability of risk aversion, can also be applied to contexts where no quantification of consequences has been obtained yet. This is contrary to the results of Pratt and Arrow, who essentially use the quantitative nature of consequences, and differentiability assumptions[rf13].

In this section, and in section VII.7, the richest structural assumption of this book is made :

ASSUMPTION VII.6.1. (Structural assumption, for this section, and section VII.7). **$\Gamma \subset \mathbb{R}$ is a nondegenerate interval. Further $\Gamma_i = \Gamma$ for all i. The usual Euclidean topology is used.**

First we consider the traditional definition of risk aversion, which uses probabilities as primitives.

DEFINITION VII.6.2. Let $[\Gamma^n, \succcurlyeq, (p_j)_{j=1}^n, U]$ be an SEU model for $\succcurlyeq$. Then $\succcurlyeq$ is <u>risk averse</u> if, for all x and $\alpha = \sum p_j x_j$: $x \preccurlyeq \overline{\alpha}$.

If a decision maker (i.e., his preference relation) is risk averse, then he will never strictly prefer an act x to its 'expected value' $\sum_{j=1}^n p_j x_j$.

We have decided to use the common term risk aversion throughout the sequel, this term being best known. In the present context the term uncertainty aversion might be more appropriate.

The characterizations (i) <=> (ii) and (i) <=> (iv) of risk aversion in the following theorem are well known. Using probabilities as primitive, statement (ii) below does not provide a satisfactory behavioural condition for decision making under uncertainty; statements (iii) and (iv) below do give proper behavioural conditions.

PROPOSITION VII.6.3. *Suppose* $n \geq 2$. *Let* $[\Gamma^n, \succcurlyeq, (p_j)_{j=1}^n, U]$ *be an SEU model for* $\succcurlyeq$, *with all* $p_j > 0$, *and* U *continuous. Then the following four statements are equivalent:*

(i) **U is concave.**

(ii) **The preference relation $\succcurlyeq$ is risk averse.**

(iii) **All states reveal nonincreasing tradeoffs.**

(iv) **The preference relation $\succcurlyeq$ is convex.**

PROOF. The implications (i) <=> (iii) are by Theorem VII.5.4; (i) => (ii) is straightforward. Next suppose (ii) holds. Let $\gamma = p_1\alpha + (1-p_1)\beta$. By risk aversion, $\overline{\gamma} \succcurlyeq (\alpha,\beta,...,\beta)$, consequently $U(p_1\alpha+(1-p_1)\beta) \geq p_1U(\alpha) + (1-p_1)U(\beta)$. By Lemma A1.1, U is concave. The implication (iii) => (iv) has been obtained in Lemma VII.3.4. The implication (iv) => (i) has been pointed out in Debreu&Koopmans(1982, near the end of section 1). The derivation of this is not elementary, and will not be repeated here. □

One may argue that risk aversion as in Definition VII.6.2 rather reflects the decision maker's attitude towards the (linear structure of) money, than his attitude towards risk or uncertainty. Statement (i) above supports this. Inspired by Kahneman&Tversky(1979), some authors have introduced new definitions of 'risk aversion', reflecting the decision maker's attitude towards risk through the modeling of probabilities, rather than utilities. See Quiggin(1982), Yaari(1987a,b), and Chew,Karni,&Safra(1987).

Now let $\succcurlyeq^1$ and $\succcurlyeq^2$ be two preference relations of different decision makers on Γ^n. The usual formulations of 'more risk averse than' employ probabilities as primitive, hence are not suited for us. The following formulation, originating from Yaari(1969)[rf14] does suit our purposes.

DEFINITION VII.6.4. The preference relation $\succcurlyeq^1$ is <u>more risk averse than</u> (<u>MRA</u>) $\succcurlyeq^2$ if, for all acts x, and consequences α:

$$x \succcurlyeq^1 \overline{\alpha} \Rightarrow x \succcurlyeq^2 \overline{\alpha}.$$

So, if the first decision maker is willing to choose a (possibly) risky act x, rather than a certain act $\overline{\alpha}$, then certainly the less risk averse second decision maker is willing to do so. Wakker,Peters&Van Riel(1985) also consider the modification of the above condition, called 'less risk prone', with everywhere $\succ$ instead of $\succcurlyeq$. The next theorem shows that the main result (d) in Theorem 1 in Pratt(1964) can also be characterized in our set-up, without probabilities given as primitives. In Remark VII.6.6 we shall point out that the result in Pratt, where $U^1 = \psi \circ U^2$ for a concave ψ, comes down to (i)(a) below, by setting $\varphi := \psi^{-1}$. The main mathematical complication in the derivation of the following theorem is that we do not have probabilities available as primitives, so that we no longer can use all probability distributions over consequences. We can only use those probabilities that happen to occur as subjective probabilities, and we have no guarantee in advance that these are the same for the different decision makers.

THEOREM VII.6.5. *Suppose* Γ *is a nondegenerate interval. Let* $[\Gamma^n, \succcurlyeq^1, (p_j^1)_{j=1}^n, U^1]$ *and* $[\Gamma^n, \succcurlyeq^2, (p_j^2)_{j=1}^n, U^2]$ *be two SEU-models, with* U^1 *and* U^2 *continuous. Then the following two statements are equivalent :*

(i) **At least one of the following three cases applies :**

(a) (<u>The nondegenerate case</u>). $U^2 = \varphi \circ U^1$ *for a convex nondecreasing continuous transformation* φ, *and* $(p_j^1)_{j=1}^n = (p_j^2)_{j=1}^n$.

(b) (<u>The degenerate case of certainty</u>). $U^2 = \varphi \circ U^1$ *for a nondecreasing continuous transformation* φ, *and there exists a* j *such that* $p_j^1 = p_j^2 = 1$, $p_i^1 = p_i^2 = 0$ *for all* $i \neq j$.

(c) (<u>The degenerate case of triviality</u>). *The preference relation* $\succcurlyeq^2$ *is trivial.*

(ii) **The preference relation $\succcurlyeq^1$ is MRA $\succcurlyeq^2$.**

PROOF. The implications (i)(c) => (ii) and (i)(b) => (ii) are straightforward. Now suppose (i)(a) holds. We derive (ii). In this paragraph we define $p_j := p_j^1$ $(= p_j^2)$. Suppose $x \succcurlyeq^1 \overline{\alpha}$, i.e., $\sum_{j=1}^n p_j U^1(x_j) \geq U^1(\alpha)$. We have $\sum_{j=1}^n p_j U^2(x_j) = \sum_{j=1}^n p_j(\varphi \circ U^1)(x_j) \geq \varphi[\sum_{j=1}^n p_j U^1(x_j)] \geq \varphi(U^1(\alpha)) = U^2(\alpha)$. So $x \succcurlyeq^2 \overline{\alpha}$. (ii), and the implication (i) => (ii), have been proved.

Next suppose (ii) holds. We derive (i). If $\succcurlyeq^2$ is trivial, i.e., U^2 is constant, there remains nothing to prove. So let U^2 be nonconstant. Then, since $\succcurlyeq^1$ is MRA $\succcurlyeq^2$, $\overline{\beta} \succcurlyeq^1 \overline{\alpha} \Rightarrow \overline{\beta} \succcurlyeq^2 \overline{\alpha}$; i.e., $U^1(\beta) \geq U^1(\alpha) \Rightarrow U^2(\beta) \geq U^2(\alpha)$. By Lemma A1.5, $U^2 = \varphi \circ U^1$ for a continuous nondecreasing transformation $\varphi : U^1(\Gamma) \to U^2(\Gamma)$. Like U^2, U^1 and φ must be nonconstant. So we may use throughout the remainder of the proof:

U^2 is nonconstant; $U^2 = \varphi \circ U^1$ with φ nondecreasing and continuous; φ and U^1 are nonconstant.

To derive either case (a), or case (b), first we derive a 'key inequality'. For all $U^1(\alpha)$ and $U^1(\gamma)$ in the connected $U^1(\Gamma)$ also $U^1(\beta) := p_1^1 U^1(\alpha) + (1-p_1^1)U^1(\gamma)$ is contained in $U^1(\Gamma)$. For β, $(\alpha,\gamma,...,\gamma) \approx^1 \overline{\beta}$. By (ii), $(\alpha,\gamma,...,\gamma) \succcurlyeq^2 \overline{\beta}$; i.e., $p_1^2 U^2(\alpha) + (1-p_1^2)U^2(\gamma) \geq U^2(\beta)$. So, for all λ $(=U^1(\alpha))$ and ν $(=U^1(\gamma))$ in $U^1(\Gamma)$ (i.e., the domain of φ) :

(<u>Key inequality</u>) $p_1^2\varphi(\lambda) + (1-p_1^2)\varphi(\nu) \geq \varphi(p_1^1\lambda + (1-p_1^1)\nu)$. (VII.6.1)

Since φ is a continuous nondecreasing nonconstant function on a connected domain, $[p_1^1 = 1 \Leftrightarrow p_1^2 = 1]$ and $[p_1^1 = 0 \Leftrightarrow p_1^2 = 0]$ straightforwardly follow from the key inequality. Analogously for any j :

$$[p_j^1 = 1 \Leftrightarrow p_j^2 = 1] \text{ and } [p_j^1 = 0 \Leftrightarrow p_j^2 = 0] . \qquad \text{(VII.6.2)}$$

Hence, for the case where some $p_j^1 = 1$ or some $p_j^2 = 1$, everything has been proved; we are then in case (b).

Remains the case where $0 < p_j^1 < 1$ for some j. Then by (VII.6.2) also $0 < p_j^2 < 1$. Say j = 1. We show that we are in case (a). First convexity of φ is derived, next equality of the subjective probabilities.

For convexity of φ, let $\sigma > \tau \in U^1(\Gamma)$. If $p_1^1 \geq p_1^2$, then $p_1^1\varphi(\sigma) + (1-p_1^1)\varphi(\tau) \geq p_1^2\varphi(\sigma) + (1-p_1^2)\varphi(\tau) \geq \varphi(p_1^1\sigma+(1-p_1^1)\tau)$, the latter inequality by the key inequality. If $p_1^1 \leq p_1^2$, then $(1-p_1^1)\varphi(\sigma) + p_1^1\varphi(\tau) \geq (1-p_1^2)\varphi(\sigma) + p_1^2\varphi(\tau) \geq \varphi((1-p_1^1)\sigma+p_1^1\tau)$, the latter inequality again by the key inequality. Both if $p_1^1 \geq p_1^2$, and if $p_1^1 \leq p_1^2$, Lemma A1.1 gives convexity of φ.

For equality of the subjective probabilities, we only establish the equality $p_1^1 = p_1^2$. We assume $0 < p_1^1 < 1$; other cases have been dealt with in (VII.6.2). Since φ is convex and nonconstant on a connected domain, there must exist a $\mu \in \text{int}(U^1(\Gamma))$ where φ is differentiable with derivative $\varphi'(\mu) > 0$; this can be seen as follows, with φ_r' right derivative, and φ_ℓ' left derivative, and all observations restricted to $\text{int}(U^1(\Gamma))$: By Rockafellar(1970, Theorem 23.1), φ_r' and φ_ℓ' exist everywhere, and $\varphi_r'(\nu) \leq \varphi_\ell'(\sigma) \leq \varphi_r'(\sigma) \leq \varphi_r'(\tau)$ for all $\nu < \sigma < \tau$. Since φ is nonconstant, φ_r' cannot be zero everywhere; it must be positive in some σ, and then is positive for all $\nu > \sigma$. By its nondecreasingness, the right derivative can be noncontinuous in at most countably many points. In any other point, greater than σ, φ is differentiable, with positive derivative. Let μ be such a point.

Take $\varepsilon \neq 0$ so close to 0 that $\lambda := \mu + (1-p_1^1)\varepsilon$ and $\nu := \mu - p_1^1\varepsilon$ are in $U^1(\Gamma)$. We have $\mu = p_1^1\lambda + (1-p_1^1)\nu$. By the key inequality

$$p_1^2\varphi(\mu+(1-p_1^1)\varepsilon) + (1-p_1^2)\varphi(\mu-p_1^1\varepsilon) \geq \varphi(\mu).$$

Letting ε approach zero, the above inequality can hold only if $(p_1^2(1-p_1^1)\varepsilon)\varphi'(\mu) - (p_1^1(1-p_1^2)\varepsilon)\varphi'(\mu) \geq 0$ for all ε close to zero, both positive and negative. Since $\varphi' > 0$, we conclude that $p_1^2 = p_1^1$.

□

In our set-up of decision making under uncertainty it is very well conceivable that the different decision makers who are to be compared with respect to risk aversion, have different subjective probabilities. This is an essential difference between our set-up and the set-up of decision making under risk. The above theorem shows that in the nontrivial cases the two decision makers, to be comparable concerning risk aversion, must have the same subjective probabilities. In the trivial case (i)(c) where $\succcurlyeq^2$ shows complete indifference, the subjective probabilities $(p_j^2)_{j=1}^n$ can be chosen arbitrarily, so again can be chosen identical with $(p_j^1)_{j=1}^n$. Apparently, whenever two decision makers are comparable concerning risk aversion, they can be thought to have identical subjective probabilities[rf15].

REMARK VII.6.6. *The only structure on* Γ *used in Theorem VII.6.5 and its proof is that* Γ *is a connected topological space. The definition of MRA does not need any structure on* Γ. Hence Theorem VII.6.5 might already have been presented in Chapter IV. Pratt and Arrow formulated their results for the case where consequences are real numbers (amounts of money), and utility is strictly increasing, so that the certain acts $\overline{\alpha}$ are ordered the same way by the different decision makers. Kihlstrom&Mirman(1974) extended the results to multidimensional quantitative consequences[rf16]. The present Remark establishes the extension to any connected topological space, with continuity of utility as only restriction.

In settings more general than that of Pratt and Arrow, it is conceivable that the decision makers order the certain acts differently. As the above theorem shows, that still is possible if the decision makers are comparable concerning risk aversion. It actually happens if $\succcurlyeq^2$ is trivial, and $\succcurlyeq^1$ not (then U^1 is not constant, and $\succcurlyeq^1$ is neither trivial on the set of certain acts). Still, since $U^2 = \varphi \circ U^1$ for a nondecreasing φ, the orderings of the certain acts will not be very different. In the nondegenerate case, case (i)(a) above, φ is convex, so that φ can then be constant and not strictly increasing only where U^2 is minimal. So the certain acts which are not inferior under U^2 are ordered the same way by U^1 and U^2. Under the more stringent conditions of Kihlstrom&Mirman(1974), the certain acts must be ordered the same way by the two decision makers, and φ is strictly increasing. In that case one can write $U^1 = \varphi^{-1} \circ U^2$, where the inverse function φ^{-1} can be seen to be concave. This equivalent presentation, by means of a *concave* transformation, is customary in the literature.

Next we consider dependency of risk aversion on varying levels of wealth. Again, we extend the results of Pratt and Arrow to the case of decision making under uncertainty, so no longer have all probability distributions over consequences readily available. And again, the only auxiliary assumption that we use is continuity of utility. The following results do essentially use the quantitative nature of consequences; they apply to arbitrary nondegenerate intervals, rather than only to $\mathbb{R}$ as do the results of Pratt and Arrow.

DEFINITION VII.6.7. The preference relation $\succcurlyeq$ reveals **nonincreasing** [respectively **nondecreasing**; or **constant**] **(absolute) risk aversion** if for all $\varepsilon \geq 0$ [respectively $\varepsilon \leq 0$; or $\varepsilon \in \mathbb{R}$], and for all x, $x + \overline{\varepsilon}$ in Γ^n, α, $\alpha + \varepsilon \in \Gamma$, we have:
$x \succcurlyeq \overline{\alpha} \Rightarrow x + \overline{\varepsilon} \succcurlyeq \overline{\alpha} + \overline{\varepsilon}$.

So, if a decision maker is willing to choose a (possibly) risky act x instead of a certain amount α, then he certainly is willing to do so if first his level of wealth has increased by a positive amount ε, and only then he has to choose between x (so that in fact he ends up with $x + \overline{\varepsilon}$) or the certain amount α (so that he ends up with $\overline{\alpha} + \overline{\varepsilon}$).

DEFINITION VII.6.8. The preference relation $\succcurlyeq$ reveals <u>constant relative risk aversion</u> if for all $\lambda \in \mathbb{R}_{++}$, x, $\lambda x \in \Gamma^n$, α, $\lambda\alpha \in \Gamma$, we have :

$$x \succcurlyeq \overline{\alpha} \Rightarrow \lambda x \succcurlyeq \lambda\overline{\alpha}.$$

So, suppose a decision maker is willing to invest an amount α into a risky undertaking, instead of keeping amount α for himself; where the risky undertaking gives him in return x_j/α per invested unit, if state of nature j is the true state. Then, if the amount to be invested is $\lambda\alpha$ instead of α, then the decision maker is still willing to invest it in the risky undertaking. In other contexts than decision making under uncertainty, the above condition for preference relations is often called homotheticity.

THEOREM VII.6.9. *Let* $n \geq 2$. *The following three statements are equivalent for the nondegenerate interval* Γ, *and the preference relation* $\succcurlyeq$ *on* Γ^n :

(i) **There exists an SEU model $[\Gamma^n, \succcurlyeq, (p_j)_{j=1}^n, U]$ for $\succcurlyeq$, with all $p_j > 0$, and with U continuous, strictly increasing and concave, such that for all $\alpha > \beta \geq \gamma > \delta$ in Γ, on its domain the function :**

$$\varepsilon \mapsto [U(\alpha+\varepsilon)-U(\beta+\varepsilon)]/[U(\gamma+\varepsilon)-U(\delta+\varepsilon)] \text{ is nondecreasing.} \qquad \text{(VII.6.3)}$$

(ii) **There exists an SEU model $[\Gamma^n, \succcurlyeq, (p_j)_{j=1}^n, U]$ for $\succcurlyeq$, with all $p_j > 0$, U continuous and strictly increasing. Further $\succcurlyeq$ is risk averse, and reveals nonincreasing risk aversion.**

(iii) **The preference relation $\succcurlyeq$ is a continuous strongly monotonic weak order which does not reveal contradictory tradeoffs, all states reveal nonincreasing tradeoffs, and $\succcurlyeq$ reveals nonincreasing risk aversion.**

PROOF. Apart from the statements on nonincreasing risk aversion, and (VII.6.3), everything is straigthforward from Theorem IV.2.7, and Proposition VII.6.3. So let us assume that everything of statement (i), except (possibly) (VII.6.3), holds. We show, concisely, that nonincreasing risk aversion is equivalent to (VII.6.3). Let $\varepsilon > 0$. Let $\Gamma' := \{\mu \in \Gamma : \mu+\varepsilon \in \Gamma\}$. Define $\succcurlyeq'$ on $(\Gamma')^n$ by $x \succcurlyeq' y$ if and only if $x + \overline{\varepsilon} \succcurlyeq y + \overline{\varepsilon}$, and define $U' : \alpha \mapsto U(\alpha+\varepsilon)$ on Γ'. By strict increasingness of U and U′ there exists a strictly increasing transformation φ such that $U' = \varphi \circ U$, by Lemma A1.5 this transformation is continuous. By Theorem VII.6.5 $\succcurlyeq$ reveals nonincreasing risk aversion if and only if (for every positive ε) φ is convex. The continuous φ is convex if and only if its right derivative is defined everywhere in the interior of its domain and is nondecreasing, as can be inferred from Rockafellar(1970, Theorems 24.1 and 24.2). That can be seen (where the fact is useful that a continuous convex function can be written as the integral of its right derivative, see Corollary 24.2.1 of Rockafellar(1970)) to hold if and only if $[\varphi(U(\alpha))-\varphi(U(\beta))]/[U(\alpha)-U(\beta)] \geq [\varphi((U(\gamma))-\varphi(U(\delta))]/[U(\gamma)-U(\delta)]$ for all $U(\alpha) > U(\beta) \geq U(\gamma) > U(\delta)$ in the interior of $U(\Gamma)$; i.e., $[\varphi(U(\alpha))-\varphi(U(\beta))]/[\varphi(U(\gamma))-\varphi(U(\delta))] \geq [U(\alpha)-U(\beta)]/[U(\gamma)-U(\delta)]$ for all such $U(\alpha),\ldots,U(\delta)$. By continuity of φ, the restriction 'in the interior of' can be omitted, and it follows that $[U(\alpha+\varepsilon)-U(\beta+\varepsilon)]/[U(\gamma+\varepsilon)-U(\delta+\varepsilon)] \geq [U(\alpha)-U(\beta)]/[U(\gamma)-U(\delta)]$ for all involved $U(\alpha),\ldots,U(\delta)$. This is straightforwardly seen to be equivalent to (VII.6.3).

□

The equivalence of (VII.6.3) with nonincreasing risk aversion does not follow from, mainly, (e) in Theorem 1 of Pratt(1964), because there U was assumed twice continuously differentiable, Γ was IR there, and all probability distributions were assumed available where we only have a fixed and finite number of probabilities $p_1,...,p_n$.

Statement (iii) has been added to give a 'complete' characterization of (i); i.e., a formulation of necessary and sufficient conditions, completely in terms of conditions for the preference relation. Statement (iii) can be considered to translate the meaning of the theoretical statement (i) fully into empirical terms. Hence we could not use the condition of risk aversion in it, as this needs the probabilities for its definition. In (ii) and (iii) above one can replace nonincreasing risk aversion by nondecreasing risk aversion if one replaces nondecreasingness of the function defined in (VII.6.3) by nonincreasingness. Analogously one can of course substitute 'constant risk aversion' in (ii) and (iii), and constantness of the function, defined in (VII.6.3). In the latter case U is either affine or exponential ($\alpha \mapsto \tau + \lambda e^{\rho\alpha}$, where concavity implies $\lambda < 0$ and $\rho < 0$), as can be derived from Theorem VII.7.6 in the sequel. Finally, if $\Gamma = \mathbb{R}_{++}$, one can replace 'nonincreasing risk aversion' in (ii) and (iii) above by 'constant relative risk aversion' if one replaces the statement concerning the function defined in (VII.6.3) by the statement that $U : \alpha \mapsto \ln(\alpha)$, or $U : \alpha \mapsto \lambda\alpha^\rho$, as can be derived from Theorem VII.7.5 in the sequel.

VII.7. <u>REMOVING THE REQUIREMENT OF NONCONTRADICTORY TRADEOFFS</u>

The major mathematical difficulty of this section is dealt with in the following lemma.

LEMMA VII.7.1. *Suppose* $(V_j)_{j=1}^n$ *are continuous nondecreasing additive value functions for* $\succcurlyeq$, *with* V_1, *and at least one other additive value function, nonconstant. Let, for* $j = 1,...,n$, *there exist* $f_j : \Gamma \to \mathbb{R}$ *such that* $V_j(\alpha) - V_j(\beta) = \int_{]\beta,\alpha[} f_j(\tau)d\tau$ *(Lebesgue integral) for all* $\alpha > \beta$ *in* Γ. *Let* $\succcurlyeq$ *reveal nonincreasing, or nondecreasing, risk aversion. Then there exist* $\tau_j \in \mathbb{R}$, *and* $\sigma_j \in \mathbb{R}_+$, *such that* $V_j = \tau_j + \sigma_j V_1$ *for all* $j \geq 2$.

PROOF. First we consider the case where $\succcurlyeq$ reveals nonincreasing risk aversion. By Theorem 6 of Chapter VI of Hartman&Mikusiński(1961), every function which can be written as an integral, so also every V_j, is Lebesgue almost everywhere differentiable on every interval $[\alpha,\beta] \subset \Gamma$; hence also on Γ. So there is a subset E of Γ, with Lebesgue measure zero, such that for every j, V_j is differentiable on $\Gamma \backslash E$. We may assume that E includes boundary points of Γ, and that f_j vanishes on E; $f_j = V_j'$ on $\Gamma \backslash E$, for every j, by the above-mentioned theorem. Note that V_j', hence f_j, is nonnegative. First we derive an auxiliary result :

$$f_i(\alpha)f_j(\beta) = f_j(\alpha)f_i(\beta) \text{ for all i,j and } \alpha,\beta \in \Gamma . \qquad \text{(VII.7.1)}$$

Because of symmetry in i and j, it suffices to prove :

$$\text{If } i \neq j, \text{ and } \alpha > \beta, \text{ then } f_i(\alpha)f_j(\beta) \geq f_j(\alpha)f_i(\beta) . \qquad \text{(VII.7.2)}$$

The result follows immediately if α or $\beta \in E$, in that case $f_i(\alpha)f_j(\beta) = 0 = f_j(\alpha)f_i(\beta)$. So let $\alpha,\beta \in \Gamma \backslash E$; i.e., the f_k's are derivatives of the V_k's and α,β are in int(Γ). First we derive (VII.7.2) for those β for which $\mu > 0$ exists such that $\beta - \mu \in \Gamma$, and $V_j(\beta-\mu) = V_j(\beta)$. Then V_j is constant on $[\beta-\mu,\beta]$, and $f_j(\beta) = V_j'(\beta) = 0$. Also then $\overline{\beta}_{-j}(\beta-\mu) \approx \overline{\beta}$. We add $\alpha-\beta$, apply nonincreasing risk aversion, and get $\overline{\alpha}_{-j}(\alpha-\mu) \succcurlyeq \overline{\alpha}$. Consequently $V_j(\alpha-\mu) \geq V_j(\alpha)$, so that V_j is constant on $[\alpha-\mu,\alpha]$. Also $f_j(\alpha) = 0$, and $f_i(\alpha)f_j(\beta) = 0 = f_j(\alpha)f_i(\beta)$, in agreement with (VII.7.2).

Next we derive (VII.7.2) for those β for which $\mu > 0$ exists such that $\beta + \mu \in \Gamma$, and $V_i(\beta+\mu) = V_i(\beta)$. We can take μ so small that $\alpha + \mu \in \Gamma$. Now $\overline{\beta} + \overline{\mu} \approx (\overline{\beta + \mu})_{-i}\beta$. By nonincreasing risk aversion $\overline{\alpha} + \overline{\mu} \preccurlyeq (\overline{\alpha + \mu})_{-i}\alpha$. Consequently $V_i(\alpha+\mu) = V_i(\alpha)$, and $f_i(\alpha) = 0 = f_i(\beta)$, again in agreement with (VII.7.2).

Remains the case where $V_j(\gamma) < V_j(\beta)$ for all $\gamma < \beta$, and $V_i(\gamma) > V_i(\beta)$ for all $\gamma > \beta$. For this case we first take $(\mu^k)_{k=1}^{\infty}, (\nu^k)_{k=1}^{\infty} \in \mathbb{R}_{++}$ such that

$$\mu^k \downarrow 0, \ \nu^k \downarrow 0, \ V_i(\beta+\nu^k) - V_i(\beta) = V_j(\beta) - V_j(\beta-\mu^k) \qquad \text{(VII.7.3)}$$

for all k. By continuity of V_i, V_j indeed such μ^k, ν^k exist. Now, for all k, $(\overline{\beta}_{-i,j}(\beta+\nu^k),(\beta-\mu^k)) \approx \overline{\beta}$ follows. We can take ν^1 so small that $\alpha + \nu^1 \in \Gamma$, so that $\alpha + \nu^k \in \Gamma$ for all k. Then, by nonincreasing risk aversion, $(\overline{\alpha}_{-i,j}(\alpha+\nu^k),(\alpha-\mu^k)) \succcurlyeq \overline{\alpha}$, hence for all k :

$$V_i(\alpha+\nu^k) - V_i(\alpha) \geq V_j(\alpha) - V_j(\alpha-\mu^k) . \qquad \text{(VII.7.4)}$$

From (VII.7.3) and (VII.7.2) the following inequality follows :

$$f_i(\alpha)f_j(\beta) = \lim_{k\to\infty}[V_i(\alpha+\nu^k)-V_i(\alpha)][V_j(\beta)-V_j(\beta-\mu^k)]/\nu^k\mu^k \geq$$
$$\lim_{k\to\infty}[V_j(\alpha)-V_j(\alpha-\mu^k)][V_i(\beta+\nu^k)-V_i(\beta)]/\mu^k\nu^k = f_j(\alpha)f_i(\beta).$$

So (VII.7.2) always holds, thence (VII.7.1) holds. Now we use this, with j = 1. Since V_1 is not constant, $f_1(\eta) > 0$ for some η. We define $\sigma_i := f_i(\eta)/f_1(\eta)$ for all i. By (VII.7.1), with $\beta = \eta$, j = 1, we have $f_i(\alpha) = \sigma_i f_1(\alpha)$ for all $\alpha \in \Gamma$. So

$$V_i(\alpha) - V_i(\beta) = \int_{]\beta,\alpha[} f_i(\tau)d\tau = \int_{]\beta,\alpha[} \sigma_i f_1(\tau)d\tau = \sigma_i[V_1(\alpha) - V_1(\beta)]$$

follows. Now $\tau_i := V_i(\eta) - \sigma_i V_1(\eta)$.

For the case where $\succcurlyeq$ reveals nondecreasing, instead of nonincreasing, risk aversion, the proof is like above, with minor changes, mainly reversals of inequalities and preferences. One lets $\alpha < \beta$ in (VII.7.2), next lets μ always be negative, etc. □

With this we obtain the main mathematical result of this section :

THEOREM VII.7.2. *Suppose* $\succcurlyeq$ *has continuous nondecreasing additive value functions* $(V_j)_{j=1}^n$ *such that, for* $j = 1,\dots,n$, *there exist* f_j *with* $V_j(\alpha) - V_j(\beta) = \int_{]\beta,\alpha[} f_j(\tau)d\tau$, *for all* $\alpha > \beta$. *Let at least two states be essential, and let* $\succcurlyeq$ *either reveal nonincreasing, or nondecreasing, absolute risk aversion. Then there exists an SEU model* $(\Gamma^n, \succcurlyeq, (p_j)_{j=1}^n, U)$ *for* $\succcurlyeq$.

PROOF. Say state 1 is essential, so that V_1 is not constant. Apply Lemma VII.7.1, let $U := V_1$, $\sigma_1 := 1$, and $p_j := \sigma_j/\sum_{i=1}^n \sigma_i$ for all j.

□

In all characterization theorems of this monograph after Chapter II it has been our aim to use in the characterizing statements (mostly numbered (ii)) only conditions formulated fully in empirical terms, i.e., in terms of the preference relation. The above theorem as such is not well suited to be considered a characterization theorem, because the assumption about the existence of the f_j's has, to the author's knowledge, no equivalent formulation in terms of simple appealing conditions for the preference relation. The theorem does however serve as a starting point to derive characterization results.

COROLLARY VII.7.3. *In statement (iii) of Theorem VII.6.9, for* $n \geq 3$ *the condition of noncontradictory tradeoffs may be omitted.*

PROOF. The condition of strong monotonicity in statement (iii) of Theorem VII.6.9 implies that every state is essential; so at least three states are essential. By Theorem VII.3.5 the revelation of nonincreasing tradeoffs implies the existence of continuous concave additive value functions $(V_j)_{j=1}^n$. Strong monotonicity implies nondecreasingness, even strict increasingness, of every function V_j. By concavity of the V_j's and Corollary 24.2.1 of Rockafellar(1970) there exist f_j's such that $V_j(\alpha) - V_j(\beta) = \int_{]\beta,\alpha[} f_j(\tau)d\tau$ for all $\alpha > \beta$ in int(Γ); e.g., f_j may be the right or left derivative of V_j. By continuity of V_j this also holds if α and/or β are boundary points of Γ, e.g. let $f_j := 0$ in boundary points. Theorem VII.7.2 gives existence of an SEU model, which implies the nonrevelation of contradictory tradeoffs.

□

Of course, the same result as in the above Corollary holds for the version of Theorem VII.6.9 which deals with nondecreasing, instead of nonincreasing, risk aversion. For the case of exactly two essential coordinates the hexagon condition should be added in Corollary VII.7.3. For characterization purposes, the following conjecture, if true, would be useful. It would, for $n \geq 3$, show equivalence of (i) and (iii) in Theorem VII.6.9, if concavity of U in (i) was left out, the condition of nonincreasing tradeoffs in (iii) was left out, and in (iii) the condition of nonincreasing tradeoffs was replaced by coordinate independence.

CONJECTURE VII.7.4. In Theorem VII.7.2 existence of the f_j's can be left out.

We do not need the 'f_j-condition' in Theorem VII.7.2 if $\Gamma = \mathbb{R}$ and we have constant absolute risk aversion, or if $\Gamma = \mathbb{R}_{++}$ and we have constant relative risk aversion. First we give the latter result, this being directly derivable from Stehling(1975).

THEOREM VII.7.5. *Let* $\Gamma = \mathbb{R}_{++}$. *The following two statements are equivalent for the preference relation* $\succcurlyeq$ *on* Γ^n *:*

(i) **There exists an SEU model** $[\Gamma^n, \succcurlyeq, (p_j)_{j=1}^n, U]$ **for** $\succcurlyeq$**, with all** $p_j > 0$**, and either** $U : \alpha \mapsto \lambda\alpha^\rho$ **for some** $\lambda,\rho \in \mathbb{R}$ **with** $\lambda\rho > 0$**, or** $U : \alpha \mapsto \ln(\alpha)$**.**

(ii) **The preference relation** $\succcurlyeq$ **is a strongly monotonic continuous coordinate independent weak order, satisfying the hexagon condition if** $n = 2$**;** $\succcurlyeq$ **reveals constant relative risk aversion.**

PROOF. Suppose (i) holds. Then, for any $\mu > 0$, $x \in \Gamma^n$, for the expected utility EU, $EU(\mu x) = \mu^\rho EU(x)$ or $EU(\mu x) = \ln(\mu) + EU(x)$. Constant relative risk aversion, and the rest of (ii), follow straightforwardly.

Next we suppose that (ii) holds, and we derive (i). If $n = 1$ then the choice $p_1 = 1$ and U = identity, by strong monotonicity, gives (i). So let $n \geq 2$. By strong monotonicity every state is essential. By Theorems III.6.6 there exist continuous additive value functions $(V_j)_{j=1}^n$ for $\succcurlyeq$. By strong monotonicity every V_j is strictly increasing. Define $V : \Gamma^n \to \mathbb{R}$, $\varphi : \Gamma \to \mathbb{R}$, $W : \Gamma^n \to \mathbb{R}$ by :

$$V : x \mapsto \sum V_j(x_j),\ \varphi : \alpha \mapsto V(\overline{\alpha}),\ W : x \mapsto \varphi^{-1} \circ V(x).$$

Then V and W represent $\succcurlyeq$, $W(\overline{\alpha}) = \alpha$, $[W(x) = \alpha \Rightarrow x \approx \overline{\alpha}]$, $W(\mu x) = \mu W(x)$ for $\mu > 0$ (W is 'linearly homogeneous', so V is 'homothetic'). By Stehling(1975, Theorem 2)[rf17], either there exist a continuous strictly increasing function ψ, a positive constant μ, and nonzero $p_1,\ldots,p_n$ summing to one, such that :

$$V : x \mapsto \psi[\mu(\prod_{j=1}^n x_j^{p_j})] \, , \tag{VII.7.5}$$

or there exist a continuous strictly increasing function ψ, a nonzero constant ρ, and positive $\sigma_1,\ldots,\sigma_n$ such that :

$$V : x \mapsto \psi[(\sum_{j=1}^n \sigma_j x_j^\rho)^{1/\rho}] \, . \tag{VII.7.6}$$

In the case of (VII.7.5), V is a strictly increasing transformation of $x \mapsto \prod x_j^{p_j}$, so, by taking logarithms, of $x \mapsto \sum p_j \ln(x_j)$. By strict increasingness of every V_j, every p_j is positive. So indeed we have an SEU model for $\succcurlyeq$, with $U : \alpha \mapsto \ln(\alpha)$. Next suppose we are in the case of (VII.7.6), and first suppose that $\rho > 0$. Then V is a strictly increasing transform of $\sum \sigma_j x_j^\rho$. So we have an SEU model for $\succcurlyeq$, with $p_j := \sigma_j / \sum_{i=1}^n \sigma_i$ for every j, and $U : \alpha \mapsto \alpha^\rho$, so $\lambda = 1$ in (i) above. We are left with one case: (VII.7.6) holds, with $\rho < 0$. Then V is a *strictly decreasing* transformation of $x \mapsto \sum \sigma_j x_j^\rho$, so a strictly increasing transformation of $x \mapsto \sum \sigma_j(-(x_j^\rho))$. Again we have an SEU model for $\succcurlyeq$, with $p_j := \sigma_j / \sum_{i=1}^n \sigma_i$ for every j, and $U : \alpha \mapsto -(\alpha^\rho)$, so in (i) above, $\lambda = -1$.

□

From this we derive :

THEOREM VII.7.6. *Let* $\Gamma = \mathbb{R}$. *The following two statements are equivalent for the preference relation* $\succcurlyeq$ *on* Γ^n :

(i) **There exists an SEU model** $[\Gamma^n, \succcurlyeq, (p_j)_{j=1}^n, U]$ **for** $\succcurlyeq$**, with all** $p_j > 0$**, and** $U : \alpha \mapsto \lambda e^{\rho\alpha}$ **for some** $\lambda, \rho \in \mathbb{R}$ **with** $\lambda\rho > 0$**, or U identity.**

(ii) **The preference relation** $\succcurlyeq$ **is a continuous strongly monotonic coordinate independent weak order, satisfying the hexagon condition if n = 2;** $\succcurlyeq$ **reveals constant absolute risk aversion.**

PROOF. Suppose that statement (i) holds. Then, for any $\mu > 0$, $x \in \Gamma^n$, the expected utility EU satisfies the equation $EU(x+\mu) = e^{\rho\mu}EU(x)$ or $EU(x+\mu) = \mu + EU(x)$. Constant absolute risk aversion, and the rest of (ii), follow straightforwardly. Next we suppose that statement (ii) holds, and derive (i).

Define $L : \mathbb{R}^n_{++} \to \mathbb{R}^n$ by $L : (x_1,...,x_n) \mapsto (\ln(x_1),...,\ln(x_n))$, and define $\succcurlyeq'$ on $\mathbb{R}^n_{++}$ by $x \succcurlyeq' y$ if and only if $L(x) \succcurlyeq L(y)$. Then it follows straightforwardly that $\succcurlyeq'$ satisfies (ii) of Theorem VII.7.5. We obtain, for all $x,y \in \mathbb{R}^n$, with U, p_j, and also λ, ρ as in (i) of Theorem VII.7.5 :

$$x \succcurlyeq y \iff L^{-1}(x) \succcurlyeq' L^{-1}(y) \iff \sum p_j U(e^{x_j}) \geq \sum p_j U(e^{y_j}).$$

This implies (i) of the Theorem VII.7.6.

□

Most probably the last two theorems also hold for any interval $\Gamma \subset \mathbb{R}_{++}$, respectively $\Gamma \subset \mathbb{R}$, but we do not know of a reference where the analogue of Stehling's theorem, needed to prove this, is readily available[rf18].

APPENDIX

A1. GENERALIZATIONS OF MIDPOINT CONVEXITY

The first two results below give conditions which are sufficient for convexity of a function φ, by means of properties which are variations on 'midpoint-convexity' [i.e., $\varphi((\mu+\nu)/2) \leq \varphi(\mu)/2 + \varphi(\nu)/2)$]. When formulated for $-\varphi$, these conditions are of course sufficient for concavity of φ, and when formulated both for φ and $-\varphi$, they are sufficient for affinity of φ, see for example Corollary A1.3.

LEMMA A1.1. *Suppose* $S \subset \mathbb{R}$ *is a nondegenerate interval. Let* $\varphi : S \rightarrow \mathbb{R}$ *be continuous. Let there exist, for all* $\sigma < \tau \in S$, a $0 < p < 1$ *such that*

$$\varphi(p\sigma+(1-p)\tau) \leq p\varphi(\sigma) + (1-p)\varphi(\tau).$$

Then φ *is convex.*

PROOF[rf1]. Suppose φ would not be convex. Then $\lambda < \mu < \nu$ in S would exist such that the point $(\mu,\varphi(\mu))$ of the graph G of φ lies strictly above the straight line ℓ through $(\lambda,\varphi(\lambda))$ and $(\nu,\varphi(\nu))$. Let $(\sigma,\varphi(\sigma))$ and $(\tau,\varphi(\tau))$ be the points of intersection of G and ℓ, closest to $(\mu,\varphi(\mu))$, with $\sigma < \mu < \tau$. Then $\lambda \leq \sigma < \mu < \tau \leq \nu$. Between σ and τ all of G lies strictly above ℓ, contradicting the existence of the p as in the Lemma.

□

The following lemma shows that it suffices for convexity to require the condition of the above lemma only 'locally'.

LEMMA A1.2. *Suppose* $S \subset \mathbb{R}$ *is a nondegenerate interval. Let* $\varphi : S \rightarrow \mathbb{R}$ *be continuous. Let, for every* $\nu \in \text{int}(S)$, *an open neighbourhood* W *of* ν *within* S *be given such that for all* $\sigma < \tau$ *in* W, *there exists* $0 < p < 1$ *such that* $\varphi(p\sigma+(1-p)\tau) \leq p\varphi(\sigma) + (1-p)\varphi(\tau)$. *Then* φ *is convex.*

PROOF. For every ν in int(S) there must exist an interval $]\nu-\delta,\nu+\delta[$ around ν within S, such that for all σ,τ within this interval, a p as in the Lemma exists. By Lemma A1.1, φ is convex on $]\nu-\delta,\nu+\delta[$. This implies convexity of φ on all of int(S), for instance because φ has a nondecreasing right derivative everywhere. By continuity, φ is convex on all of S.

□

COROLLARY A1.3. *Suppose* $S \subset \mathbb{R}$ *is a nondegenerate interval. Let* $\varphi : S \to \mathbb{R}$ *be continuous. Let, for every* $\nu \in \text{int}(S)$, *an open neighbourhood* W *of* ν *within* S *be given such that for all* $\sigma < \tau$ *in* W, *there exists* $0 < p < 1$ *such that* $\varphi(p\sigma+(1-p)\tau) = p\varphi(\sigma) + (1-p)\varphi(\tau)$. *Then* φ *is affine.*

PROOF. Apply Lemma A1.2 to φ and $-\varphi$.

□

The following results consider transformations φ, with f and g two functions such that $f = \varphi \circ g$.

LEMMA A1.4. *Suppose* Γ *is a connected topological space. Let* $f,g : \Gamma \to \mathbb{R}$ *be continuous, and let* $f = \varphi \circ g$ *for a transformation* $\varphi : g(\Gamma) \to \mathbb{R}$. *If* φ *is nondecreasing or nonincreasing, then it is continuous.*

PROOF. Since φ is a nondecreasing, or nonincreasing, function from a (connected) interval $g(\Gamma)$ *onto* the (connected) interval $f(\Gamma)$, φ cannot make 'jumps', and must be continuous.

□

LEMMA A1.5. *Suppose* Γ *is a connected topological space. Let* $f,g : \Gamma \to \mathbb{R}$ *be continuous. The following three statements are equivalent :*

(i) $f = \varphi \circ g$ **for a nondecreasing transformation** φ.

(ii) $f = \varphi \circ g$ **for a nondecreasing continuous transformation** φ.

(iii) $[g(\alpha) \geq g(\beta)] \Rightarrow [f(\alpha) \geq f(\beta)]$ **for all** $\alpha,\beta \in \Gamma$.

PROOF. The implications (ii) => (i) and (i) => (iii) are obvious. So we assume (iii). To derive is (ii). If $g(\alpha) = g(\beta)$, then $g(\alpha) \geq g(\beta)$ and $g(\alpha) \leq g(\beta)$, so $f(\alpha) \geq f(\beta)$ and $f(\alpha) \leq f(\beta)$, i.e., $f(\alpha) = f(\beta)$. Hence $f = \varphi \circ g$ for some transformation φ. By (iii) φ must be nondecreasing. By Lemma A1.4, φ is continuous.

□

A2. CLASSICAL REPRESENTATIONS OF SEU-MAXIMIZATION

In this section we give a concise formal description of four classical representations of SEU-maximization, without proofs, and adapted to our set-up and definitions. A discussion of these results has been given in section IV.6. One classical result, not given here, is the result of Ramsey(1931). Ramsey did not fully elaborate his result. Neither the approach to decision making under uncertainty of this monograph (see Example II.1.1), nor the approach of Jeffrey(1965; Jeffrey does not distinguish between acts and states of nature), nor any other approach known to us, make it possible to formalize all aspects of Ramsey's work. Fishburn(1982, section 5) succeeds in giving a good 'approximation' of Ramsey's result.

First we give a version of a result of de Finetti. De Finetti's result can be considered to derive the maximization of expected 'value'; i.e., expected utility with linear utility. His set-up is somewhat different from ours[rf2]. The famous 'coherence condition' is a version of monotonicity, in the presence of additivity. In defenses of de Finetti's result often the monotonicity-part of coherence is placed central, and the remaining conditions are given relatively little attention. In our opinion 'additivity' is the most crucial condition[rf3]. A binary relation $\succcurlyeq$ on $\mathbb{R}^n$ is **additive** if $[x \succcurlyeq y \Rightarrow x + v \succcurlyeq y + v]$ for all $x,y,v \in \mathbb{R}^n$.

THEOREM A2.1 (de Finetti; maximization of expected value). *Let $\succcurlyeq$ be a binary relation on $\mathbb{R}^n$. The following two statements are equivalent* :

(i) **There exist positive $(p_j)_{j=1}^n$, summing to one, such that $x \mapsto \sum_{j=1}^n p_j x_j$ represents $\succcurlyeq$.**

(ii) **The binary relation $\succcurlyeq$ is a strongly monotonic, continuous, additive weak order on $\mathbb{R}^n$.**

□

Next we give the theorem of von Neumann and Morgenstern(1944), in the version of Jensen(1967). The main characterizing condition in it is the following. A binary relation $\succcurlyeq$ on a mixture space is **vNM-independent** if, for all $x,y,z \in X$, and $0 < \lambda < 1$, we have :

$$[x \succcurlyeq y] \Leftrightarrow [\lambda x + (1-\lambda)z \succcurlyeq \lambda y + (1-\lambda)z] .$$

Further we say that $\succcurlyeq$ is **Jensen-continuous** if for every $x \succ y$ and z in X there exist $\lambda > 0$ and $\mu > 0$ such that $\lambda z + (1-\lambda)x \succ y$ and $x \succ \mu z + (1-\mu)y$.

THEOREM A2.2 (von Neumann&Morgenstern). *Let $\succcurlyeq$ be a binary relation on a mixture space* X. *The following two statements are equivalent* :

(i) **There exists an affine representing function for $\succcurlyeq$.**

(ii) **The binary relation $\succcurlyeq$ is a weak order, it satisfies vNM-independence and Jensen-continuity.**

□

To relate this result to expected utility, suppose Γ is a set of 'prizes', and X is the set of 'lotteries' on Γ. A **lottery** is a finite probability distribution denoted for instance as $(p_1;\alpha_1,...,p_m;\alpha_m)$ if it assigns probability p_j to prize α_j, for $j = 1,...,m$. (So here probabilities are assumed to be given in advance.) Then according to Example VII.2.4, X is a mixture space, and the above theorem can be applied to X. Say U^* is the affine function of statement (i) above. Define a 'vNM-utility function' U on Γ by

$U : \alpha \mapsto U^*(1;\alpha)$. Then by affinity U^* will assign $\sum_{j=1}^{m} p_j U(\alpha_j)$ to every lottery $(p_1;\alpha_1,\ldots,p_m;\alpha_m)$, so can be considered to be expected utility.

Next we present the theorem of Savage. To this end we take the approach of Chapter V, see the structural assumption V.2.4. For simplicity, Savage assumed that the algebra of events Σ was 2^I. Further, in deviation of Chapter V and the structural assumption V.2.4, there is not assumed any structure on the set Γ of consequences. P2 and P3 together constitute what Savage called the **sure-thing principle**. In the literature the term sure-thing principle is sometimes used for only P2.

THEOREM A2.3 (Savage). *There exists a finitely additive probability measure* P *on* I, *and a bounded utility function* $U : \Gamma \to \mathbb{R}$, *such that* $x \mapsto \int_I (U \circ x) dP$ *represents* $\succcurlyeq$, *whenever the following conditions are satisfied* :

P1. $\succcurlyeq$ is a weak order.

P2. $\succcurlyeq$ satisfies independence of equal subalternatives.

P3. If event A is essential, then $[x_{-A}\alpha \succcurlyeq x_{-A}\beta] \iff [\overline{\alpha} \succcurlyeq \overline{\beta}]$.

P4. If $\overline{\alpha} \succ \overline{\beta}$ and $\overline{\gamma} \succ \overline{\delta}$, then $[\overline{\beta}_{-A}\alpha \succcurlyeq \overline{\beta}_{-B}\alpha] \iff [\overline{\delta}_{-A}\gamma \succcurlyeq \overline{\delta}_{-B}\gamma]$.

P5. $\succcurlyeq$ is nontrivial.

P6. If $x \succ y$ and $\alpha \in \Gamma$, then there exists a partition $(A_1,\ldots,A_m)$ of I such that $x_{-A_j}\alpha \succ y$ and $x \succ y_{-A_j}\alpha$ for all j.

P7. $[z_{-A}x_A \prec z_{-A}(y(i))$ for all $i \in A] \Rightarrow [z_{-A}x_A \preccurlyeq z_{-A}y_A]$;
$[z_{-A}x_A \succ z_{-A}(y(i))$ for all $i \in A] \Rightarrow [z_{-A}x_A \succcurlyeq z_{-A}y_A]$.

□

Next we consider a version of the result of Anscombe&Aumann(1963), adapted to the terminologies of this book.

THEOREM A2.4 (Anscombe&Aumann). *Let* $\succcurlyeq$ *be a binary relation on a product mixture space* Γ^n. *The following two statements are equivalent* :

(i) **There exists an SEU model** $[\Gamma^n, \succcurlyeq, (p_j)_{j=1}^n, U]$ **for** $\succcurlyeq$, **with U affine.**

(ii) **The binary relation** $\succcurlyeq$ **is a weak order on** Γ^n, **it satisfies vNM-independence and Jensen-continuity, and** $\succcurlyeq_i = \succcurlyeq_j$ **for all nontrivial** $\succcurlyeq_i$ **and** $\succcurlyeq_j$.

□

Anscombe&Aumann considered the case where Γ is a set of lotteries. We explicated this below the theorem of von Neumann and Morgenstern. There is a further difference. Anscombe&Aumann also assume that lotteries *on acts* are available, not just lotteries on consequences given states of nature, as we did above. Their Assumption 2 however entails that the only relevant aspect of a lottery over acts is the marginal distribution given any state of nature which will result from that lottery over the acts. Hence our approach may be used as well[rf4].

A3. FURTHER REMARKS

REMARK A3.1 (Topological separability). In the major part of the book we have assumed topological separability. This was done for simplicity of formulation. We could have weakened the topological assumption III.3.2 (and the structural assumption V.2.4) by requiring topological separability only for the case where exactly one coordinate is essential. For that case we need Theorem III.3.6, which essentially uses topological separability. For the case of two or more essential coordinates the results of this book are based on Theorem III.4.1, which according to Remark III.7.1 does not need topological separability. The case of no essential coordinate is trivial, and neither needs topological separability.

In the way as described above, we can strengthen Theorems III.4.1, III.6.6, IV.2.7, IV.4.3, V.3.4, V.4.6, V.6.1, VI.5.1 (Γ should be separable only if every permutation π on $\{1,...,n\}$ has exactly one π-essential state). This way of strengthening was already used in Theorems VII.3.5, and VII.5.4. That topological separability can mostly be dispensed with in additive representations has been observed in KLST(Chapter 6), Jaffray (1974a,b), Vind(1986a), and Fuhrken&Richter(1988).

REMARK A3.2 (Survey of notions of tradeoffs). In Definition II.4.4 we introduced contradictory tradeoffs, revealed by coordinates; we used $\succ_i^{**}$ of Definition II.4.1 and $\succcurlyeq_i^*$ of Definition II.4.2. The end of section II.4 mentions 'tradeoffs between coordinates'.

In Definition IV.2.3 we introduced contradictory tradeoffs (on consequences), revealed by the preference relation $\succcurlyeq$; we used $\succ^{**}$ and $\succcurlyeq^*$ of Definition IV.2.2.

In Definition IV.4.2 we introduced contradictory tradeoffs (on consequences) revealed (mutually) by events; we used $\succcurlyeq_A^*$ and $\succ_A^{**}$ of Definition IV.4.1. These last notions have been extended to infinite state spaces in Definition V.2.3, using Definition V.2.2.

In Definition VI.4.2 we introduced comonotonic-contradictory tradeoffs (on consequences), revealed by the preference relation $\succcurlyeq$; we used $\succcurlyeq_c^*$ and $\succ_c^{**}$ of Definition VI.4.1.

In Definition VII.3.2 we introduced 'nonincreasing tradeoffs'; we used $\succ_i^{**}$ of Definition II.4.1.

Finally, in Definition VII.5.2 we introduced nonincreasing noncontradictory tradeoffs (on consequences), revealed by the preference relation $\succcurlyeq$; we used $\succ_i^{**}$ of Definition II.4.1 and $\succcurlyeq_i^*$ of Definition II.4.2.

REMARK A3.3 (Main representation theorems). Each of the following 'main representation theorems' of this book should be directly understandable through consultation of the Subject Index, and consultation of the text directly above the theorem : III.6.6, IV.2.7, V.6.1, VI.5.1, VII.3.5, VII.6.5, and (Corollary) VII.7.3.

REMARK A3.4 (Incomplete preference relations). The definition of 'representing function' (see section I.2.3) implies that a represented preference relation is complete. In order to deal with incomplete preference relations, the following definition is in order :

$$[\{x \succcurlyeq y \Rightarrow V(x) \geq V(y)\} \text{ and } \{x \succ y \Rightarrow V(x) > V(y)\}].$$

The brief sketch of the characterization of additive representability of section II.3 holds under this more general definition.

REFERENCE-FOOTNOTES

REFERENCE-FOOTNOTES TO CHAPTER I

[rf1] Compare Benson(1987). A discussion of attempts to encompass both freedom and determinism is given in Woolfolk&Sass(1988).

[rf2] See for instance Winterfeldt&Edwards(1986), first paragraph of section 2.1.

[rf3] This use of 'imaginary choices' is one of the central topics in Shafer(1986, e.g. p. 500, fourth paragraph). Ramsey(1931, top of p. 170, and p. 172) is very illuminating on this point.

[rf4] See Sneed(1971, Chapter VI) for a further discussion of classical particle mechanics, many parts of which are relevant to the topics of this monograph. The question as to how far representing notions such as utility may be shown to refer to an a priori specified content and in this sense may be said to be really 'existing', is considered in Bezembinder(1987, section 6).

[rf5] nonphysical in the terminology of Sneed(1971, p.22). For the context of decision making under uncertainty, comments on this are given at several parts in Drèze(1987, for instance at p.7 lines 9–11, or p.91).

[rf6] Krantz,Luce,Suppes&Tversky(1971), hereafter abbreviated KLST, state on page 200/201 that it is not evident why the measurement of probability should have been the focus of more philosophic controversy than that of any other scientifically significant attribute. A same opinion can be found in Freudenthal(1965).

Further work on the implications and relations between choices, preferences, and representations of these, is provided in Bezembinder(1987). Samuels(1988) ascribes a special normative status to economics, economics being involved in 'the complex process through which the economy is made'.

[rf7] C_f is called a selection function in Basu(1980, p.50). See also Richter(1971, page 31, third paragraph).

[rf8] Work like Cooke&Draaisma(1984), comparing numbers of arbitrary preference relations to numbers of preference relations with 'nice' properties, can be of use for this. Also Bezembinder(1981), measuring 'circularity' in preferences, can be applied to this problem. A 'cycle' like $x \succ y \succ z \succ x$ then is to be reinterpreted as $C_f\{x,y\} = x$, $C_f\{y,z\} = y$, $C_f\{z,x\} = z$, revealing that $C(D) = D$ for $D = \{x,y\}, \{y,z\}$, and $\{z,x\}$. Finally, for predictive applications the preliminary choice problem will be a problem, to yield only the prediction that the decision maker will choose an element from C(D), and not the prediction which element that will be.

[rf9] Drèze(1987, Chapter 2, end of section 9.1) gives an appreciation of this.

[rf10] Von Wright(1963) places preference relations between the 'anthropological' (acting) level and the 'axiological' (assessing) level. For more comments and references, see Foxall(1986).

[rf11] There are many other ways to derive binary relations from choice functions, see Sen(1971). Often first a relation analogous to R above is defined, and then P and E are defined as the asymmetric, respectively symmetric, part of R, see for instance Weddepohl(1970). We have chosen the above definitions to achieve maximal operationality. As soon as we observe $x \in C(D)$ and $y \in D\backslash C(D)$ for some $D \in \Delta$, we can now conclude xPy. If we had defined xPy by [xRy and not yRx], then for verification of [not yRx] we would have had to find out the choices from *all* $D \in \Delta$, containing both x and y. This may be an impossible task if most of the involved choice situations are hypothetical (see subsection I.1.3). In the sequel we adapt the results of

literature to our deviating definitions. The equivalence (i) <=> (vi) in Theorem I.2.5 will show that one way to characterize the desired representation in (i) there is, with $\bar{P}$ and $\bar{R}$ as in Definition I.2.3, to require that $\bar{P}$ as derived from our deviating definition of P leads to the same binary relation as the usual *definition* of $\bar{P}$ in the literature: the asymmetric part of $\bar{R}$.

rf12 Richter(1971, Theorems 5 and 8) derived the equivalence of (i), (ii), (iii) and (v).

rf13 A graph-theoretic approach to these matters is presented in Wakker(1988c).

rf14 The WARP-condition has been introduced in Samuelson(1938a; the term was introduced in Samuelson,1950; see also Samuelson,1938b and 1947, pp. 107–117), and SARP in Houthakker(1950) and Ville(1946). These authors studied the special context of consumer demand theory, the origin of revealed preference theory. There the assumption was often made that C(D) contains exactly one element, for every $D \in \Delta$. Then indeed SARP implies WARP. The extension of these notions to choice functions C with not always $|C(D)| = 1$ is not unique, and has been done in several ways in the literature. In the above way SARP does not imply WARP anymore. A characterization of WARP has been provided in Clark(1988, Corollaries I and II). An early reference to IIA is Nash (1950a, Axiom 3); there it is propagated that utility be considered as a 'choice operator, indicating the reaction of an organism to a given set of alternatives', rather than as an 'ordering system'. Nash(1950b), for single-valued choice functions in the context of bargaining game theory, required IIA for every fixed 'disagreement point'. Chernoff (1954) uses in fact IIA to criticize the minimax regret criterion. Luce&Raiffa(1957, section 13.3 and other sections) give a discussion of several versions of the condition. Luce(1959, section I.C.1.c) shows that his 'choice axiom', defined for probabilistic choice making, reduces to IIA for single-valued choice functions when considered for the special case of deterministic choice making. Arrow (1959) refers to condition C4 in the unpublished Arrow(1948) as an occurrence of IIA. Arrow himself uses the term IIA for a *different* condition, in his impossibility theorem for social choice in Arrow(1951a). Ray(1973) and Karni&Schmeidler(1976) comment on the difference between the condition IIA above, and the one from social choice theory.

rf15 For the case where Δ contains all two- and three-point subsets of X, the equivalence of (i) and (iv) above can also be obtained from the proof in Arrow(1959), which was meant only for the case where Δ contains all finite subsets of X. Sen(1971, bottom of page 312), noted that Arrow's proof remains valid in our case. For the case where Δ is union-closed, the equivalence of (i) and (iv) above is given in Fishburn(1973, Theorem 15.4), or Hansson(1968), or Weddepohl(1970, Theorem 3.9.6, without K5 and K7). For the case where Δ contains all finite subsets of X, Bandyopadhyay(1988) shows that the statements of Corollary I.2.12 are equivalent to a 'sequential path independence' condition.

rf16 See page 48 of Richter(1971).

rf17 See Debreu(1954, Lemma II) or KLST,Theorem 2.2, or Jaffray(1975). Further Debreu(1954, 1964) gave simpler *sufficient* topological conditions for $\succcurlyeq$ to guarantee the existence of (continuous) representations (see Theorem III.3.6).

rf18 This approach is common in consumer demand theory, see for instance Chipman,Hurwicz,Richter,&Sonnenschein(1971). See also Lensberg(1987) and Peters& Wakker(1987).

rf19 Luce&Suppes do allow 1/2-1/2 lotteries in algebraic approaches; these may reflect indifference. In our approach neither such lotteries will occur.

rf20 Savage's 'small worlds', intended to avoid the necessity of total formalization of all uncertainty, have often been criticized. A clear account is given in Shafer(1986, section 5).

rf21 For a supplement to the latter, see Wakker(1986b).

[rf22] Bounded rationality is central in Simon(1982).
[rf23] Fishburn(1982) gives many results for the lottery approach.

REFERENCE-FOOTNOTES TO CHAPTER II

[rf1] See for instance von Winterfeldt&Edwards(1986), first paragraph of section 2.1, and section 2.4.
[rf2] Examples like the following ones are also dealt with in 'multicriteria decision making', where index i describes a 'criterion', 'objective', 'attribute', etc.; see Hwang& Yoon(1981), and White(1982).
[rf3] Wakker(1988a, sections 5.1 and 6.3) shows how representation theorems for binary relations can be transformed into representation theorems for (the ordinal character of) functions V, and indicates how such ordinal results can also be of use in the derivation of nonordinal results. Vind(1986a, sections II.5, IV.3, V.4) shows how representation theorems for binary relations can be used to solve functional equations.
[rf4] Numerous other examples can be given. See Montgomery&Svenson,(1976) for 'information processing' techniques, or the 'Analytic Hierarchy Process' of Saaty(1980, 1986). French&Vassiloglou(1986) consider examination assessment. Tversky(1977) considers similarity judgements. Mak(1987) considers continuous systems.
[rf5] The modeling of uncertainty, as in Example II.1.1, has been introduced in economic literature by Savage(1953) and Arrow(1953). It is crucial in Debreu(1959, Chapter 7). In many places in the literature the formal analogy of the above examples plays a special role. The relation, and the differences, between social choice theory, welfare-theory as in Example II.1.5, and multicriteria decision making are central in Arrow&Raynaud(1986), and are studied in Bezembinder&Van Acker(1980, 1987), and Bezembinder(1987). The analogy of social choice theory and multicriteria decision making was already observed in May(1954). To illuminate his approach of welfare theory, Harsanyi(1955, pp. 434-435; see also Dahlby,1987) uses the relatedness of Example II.1.5 to Example II.1.1, in adopting thought experiments where persons are supposed not to know which person in a society they will be. So in these thought experiments persons serve as states of nature. Wakker(1987a) uses the modeling of decision making under uncertainty as above, and the observation, as in Example II.1.5, that coordinates may just as well refer to persons, to connect several results from decision making under uncertainty and game theory. Peters&Wakker(1987) use the analogy between Example II.1.2 and the 'I = set of persons (bargainers)' to derive results which extend both the utility maximization in consumer theory to nonlinear budget sets, and the Nash bargaining solution to 'group utility' functions of more general forms. Also Machina(1982a, section 5.2), Chew(1983, introduction), and many other authors make explicit the analogy of the above examples. The maximization of (what can be seen to be) the 'Choquet-integral', studied in Chapter VI, has been introduced independently by Schmeidler(1984a) for decision making under uncertainty, Ebert(1988) for welfare theory, and Yager(1988) for multicriteria decision making. The latter two add a symmetry ('anonymity') restriction.
[rf6] A clear account of the history and foundations of decision making under uncertainty is given in Drèze(1987, Chapter I). Of course also the first five chapters in Savage(1954) give an excellent account. A survey for economics in the 'pre-Savage-period' is Arrow(1951b).
[rf7] The generality with which this view is held may appear from Drèze(1987, Chapter 2, footnote 8).
[rf8] Hammond(1988) shows how this 'consequentialist' assumption is related to CI and

other conditions for decision making.

rf9 A recent discussion of acts as signals is Rabinowicz(1988).

rf10 This result has been given in Scott(1964), Tversky(1964), KLST(Theorem 9.1), and Narens(1985, Theorems 5.2.1 and 5.2.2). The latter two references also deal with noncomplete binary relations, compare Remark A3.4. Scott very clearly presents the general procedure to prove this, and many analogous, results.

rf11 Compare Savage(1954, p.77, in particular line 16), or Arrow(1971, p. 48, lines 25 etc.).

rf12 Further comments on this are provided in section 9.1 of KLST. Derivations of additive representations, built on the above-mentioned characterization are Jaffray (1974a,b), obtaining necessary and sufficient conditions for additive representability in full generality, and Fuhrken&Richter(1988); these will be further discussed in section III.8. For algorithms to test additive representability, see Nygren(1986) and Roskam (1987). Scott&Suppes(1958) showed that additive representability for all finite models is not axiomatizable by a universal sentence in first order propositional calculus.

rf13 Essentially the same definition occurred in Pfanzagl(1968, Definitions 8.5.13 and 8.6.8), Keeney&Raiffa(1976, beginning of section 3.4.7), KLST(near end of section 6.2.4), Wakker(1984, section 3), French(1986, section 9.3), and Vind(1986b, the relation $\succ_A$); a verbal formulation has already been given in Fleming(1952, p. 374, l. 30-33). The way in which the definition will be used in this book to obtain transparent formal expressions of characterizing conditions has been introduced in Wakker(1988e); in that paper the term strength of preference has been used instead of the term tradeoff as in this book. Pfanzagl(1968, end of Remark 9.4.5) stated that the indirect approach over 'distances' (our tradeoffs) in his opinion is more intuitive.

rf14 These conditions were taken from KLST(Theorem 4.2 and Definition 4.3).

REFERENCE-FOOTNOTES TO CHAPTER III

rf1 Such a view has been expressed in Aumann(1962, p.446). Some further discussions of the 'rationality' of completeness (and other elementary conditions for preferences) can be found in Shafer(1986, p.469), and throughout Hogarth&Reder(1987).

rf2 Wakker(1988d) gives arguments in favour of the algebraic approach. Further comments will be given here in section III.8. More elaborated topological results are provided in Vind(1986a, Chapter III).

rf3 There have been many vivid discussions about ordinal versus cardinal utility. Recent references are Cooter&Rappoport(1984, 1985), and Basu(1982). Hence, to avoid unintended connotations, in the literature often the expression 'unique up to a linear/positive affine transformation' is used instead of cardinal, and 'unique up to a strictly increasing transformation' instead of ordinal. Sometimes ordinal is used instead of continuously ordinal. In psychological literature the terms ordinal scale and interval scale (the latter for cardinal representation) are customary. The reason for our choice of terminology is linguistic. The adjective cardinal is more convenient than the noun (interval) scale, and 'unique up to a positive affine transformation' is inconvenient because of its length.

Other usual scale types are 'nominal scales', for which only the = and ≠ relations are relevant, and 'ratio-scales', where in comparison with cardinal scales also a natural 'zero-point' is given. Also sometimes 'consists of' in section III.2 has been changed into 'is a subset of the set of', or 'is a superset of the set of'. Although in principle many more kinds of scale types could be thought of, in practice mainly the above-mentioned ones occur. Luce&Narens(1987) use 'homogeneity arguments' to explain this.

rf4 Lemma I.3.2 in Vind(1986a) may serve as an illustration of the meaning of topological connectedness.
rf5 Recent proofs are provided in Jaffray(1975) and Richter(1980).
rf6 Fishburn(1970) gives as well the topological approach, as the algebraic approach, as a 'mixture-space-approach'.
rf7 There is mainly one exception concerning generality, and that is the result of Gorman(1968). His generalization falls somewhat outside the scope of this monograph; its derivation will not be given. An efficient derivation of it is provided in Theorem V.2.4 in Vind(1986a). Example III.6.8(b) will show two aspects in which our approach is less general than that of KLST.
rf8 For this mainly Blaschke(1928) and Keeney&Raiffa(1976)) were inspiring to us. Also Fleming(1952) uses this way of constructing a grid; he uses an infinitesimally small mesh.
rf9 and without Keeney&Raiffa(1976, Chapter 3) available
rf10 In Keeney&Raiffa(1976) it is called the corresponding trade-offs condition.
rf11 This result was pointed out in Debreu(1960, introduction).
rf12 e.g. in Wakker(1988a)
rf13 Probably Lemma III.1.5 in Vind(1986a) is the most advanced result to show that topological separability need not be assumed unless exactly one coordinate is essential.
rf14 In this we follow Pfanzagl(1968, Definitions 8.5.12 and 8.6.3), Vind(1986a, condition c3), and Fuhrken&Richter(1988).
rf15 That independence is required only for equal subalternatives of length n - 2, has also been established by Gorman(1968, section 4.4) for the case where his stronger restrictive assumptions are satisfied. The problems of CI with equivalences instead of preferences, and *without* weak separability (or monotonicity) are addressed in Mak(1988).
rf16 Debreu(1960, p.17, lines 2 - 4) suggests that this will suffice, and uses it in his proof. Also Corollary IV.2.6 in Vind(1986a) shows this, for the Thomsen condition.
rf17 A recent reference is Bell(1987).

REFERENCE-FOOTNOTES TO CHAPTER IV

rf1 'Compatibility' in section 8.2.6 in KLST, formulated in a complicated context, is the condition in the literature most similar to cardinal coordinate independence. Also the 'invariance-of-standard-sequences property' in section 6.11.2 in KLST, and 'invariance' in Tversky(1977), are related conditions in making comparisons between 'intervals' on different coordinates.
rf2 or Theorem 1 of section 2.1.4 of Aczél(1966), or by (88) of section 3.7 of Hardy, Littlewood,&Pólya(1934)
rf3 Grodal(1978, Theorem 4) has given a result for continuous time. KLST sketch a result for finitely many points of time by requiring (for the case of three or more essential points of time) CI and a stationarity condition (in Definition 6.15 there) which is not easily compared with our approach. Also Samuelson(1958) considers the case of finitely many points of time. Zilcha(1988) is a recent survey describing approaches for which finiteness of the set of points of time, faced by a consumer, is essential.
rf4 See Frisch(1926), Lange(1934), Alt(1936), Scott&Suppes(1958), Debreu(1958), Suppes&Zinnes(1963), Fishburn(1970, Chapter 6), KLST(Chapter 4), Shapley(1975), Basu(1982).
rf5 See also Richter(1975), Richter&Shapiro(1978), and Tversky(1967a).
rf6 Wakker(1981) pointed out some misunderstandings in the literature about this part of Savage's work.

rf7 This was discovered after publication of Savage(1954). See Fishburn(1970, section 14.1), where also a well-organized proof of Savage's result is given. An original proof of Savage's theorem, bringing in techniques of additive representations as in Chapter III, is given in Arrow(1971, Essay 2; also published as Chapter 2 in McGuire& Radner,1972). Marschak&Radner(1972) give an appealing presentation of Savage's theorem, interpreting Savage's postulates P3 (entailing that the ordering of consequences is the same for all states of nature) and P4 as 'independence of tastes and beliefs'. Shafer(1986) is a recent discussion of Savage's work. Cooper(1987) uses evolutionary considerations to argue for the axioms of Savage.

rf8 Pratt,Raiffa,&Schlaifer(1964), while claiming not to be innovative, give a very appealing approach, in which consequences in a sense are probabilities.

REFERENCE-FOOTNOTES TO CHAPTER V

rf1 This chapter closely follows Wakker(1985). We generalize Wakker(1985) by also dealing with acts with unbounded utility. A further generalization is obtained by leaving out the restriction that Δ, the algebra on the consequence space to be introduced in the sequel, should contain all one-point subsets of Γ. This generalization has been accomplished by a small variation in the definition of 'simple' acts.

rf2 Koopmans(1972) uses a sup-metric topology on a denumerable Cartesian product, which again leads to a stronger continuity-assumption than s-continuity.

rf3 The approach to integration for measures that are only finitely additive, as adopted in section I.III.2 of Dunford&Schwarz(1958) or section 4.4 of Bhaskara Rao&Bhaskara Rao(1983), does not seem to be suited for our purposes. This is because we see no easy way to reformulate the properties of P and $U \circ x$, used there in the definition of an integral, in terms of our primitive, i.e., $\succcurlyeq$. The less general Stieltjes type integral, as in section 4.5 of Bhaskara Rao&Bhaskara Rao(1983) does serve our purposes.

rf4 Suppes(1956, A9) also used such a kind of monotonicity.

rf5 This is also pointed out in DeGroot(1970) end of section 7.9.

rf6 This example is related to Savage(1954, section 5.4, formula (1)).

rf7 This adapts the known results, as presented in de Finetti(1972, section 6.9) to the more general case where $\Gamma \neq \mathbb{R}$; with everything formulated in terms of the preference relation $\succcurlyeq$. Condition F7 in Fishburn(1982, section 10.3), and the 'monotone continuity' assumption of Villegas(1964), also used in Arrow(1971, Essay 2), are analogous.

rf8 The special case where $\Gamma = \mathbb{R}$, and U is identity, has been treated in de Finetti (1972, e.g. Chapter 5), a major source of inspiration for the above Theorem. Theorem 3 of Grodal(1978) derives a representation as in (i) above, so also for a possibly infinite state space, under the supposition that a triple of disjoint s-essential events exists. The conditions used there employ a (presupposed) measure on Σ, and a mean groupoid operation derived from the preference relation by means of continuity. Grodal's condition that the set of acts is a 'mixture', together with the condition that the constant acts are included, implies that all simple acts are included, and that the set of acts is truncation-closed.

rf9 See Banach&Kuratowski(1929), or Ulam(1930).

rf10 Such a thing is done in Theorem 4 of Grodal(1978). Compare also Corollary IV.4.4.

rf11 This condition is closer related to the 'coherence condition' of de Finetti(1974, section 3.3.6).

REFERENCE-FOOTNOTES TO CHAPTER VI

rf1 This chapter closely follows Wakker(1987b). Wakker(1987c) extends these results to arbitrary state spaces, and gives several applications of the Choquet-integral approach.

rf2 Gilboa(1989) considers an alternative way of integration which uses the 'dual' capacity, assigning to an event one minus the value which the original capacity assigned to the complement of that event.

rf3 See von Neumann&Morgenstern(1944), Luce&Raiffa(1957), Driessen(1988).

rf4 See Huber(1981, section 10.2), Huber&Strassen(1973).

rf5 or Allais(1953b, 1979) or Savage(1954, pp.101-103)

rf6 See also Anger(1977, Theorem 3).

rf7 Dellacherie(1970) showed that the Choquet integral is additive for comonotonic functions, thus may have been the first to see the importance of comonotonicity in the presence of the Choquet-integral. Conversely, Schmeidler(1984c) showed that, under some natural conditions, a functional which is additive for comonotonic functions must be a Choquet integral. In fact already Yaari(1969, p.324 and 328) used comonotonicity as 'bets on the same event', however, without relating it to the nonadditive-probability approach to expected utility.

rf8 or Richter(1966, Lemma 2) (applied to $\succ'$)

rf9 discussed in Luce&Raiffa(1957, Chapter 13, for instance page 282)

rf10 See Hurwicz(1951).

rf11 See Driessen(1988, Definition V.3.1).

rf12 The only literature on this subject, known to the author, is KLST(section 6.5.5), and Jaffray(1974b, section 6.4); see also Fishburn(1967, 1971) for the case where factor sets are 'mixture spaces' (see Definition VII.2.1). See also our Example III.7.8.

REFERENCE-FOOTNOTES TO CHAPTER VII

rf1 The first five sections of this chapter closely follow Wakker(1986a). Section 6 closely follows Wakker,Peters&Van Riel(1985, sections 4 and 5). The last section closely follows Wakker(1989).

rf2 Fishburn(1982) contains many results. See also Luce&Suppes(1965). Gudder(1977) and Gudder&Schroeck(1980) mention applicability of mixture spaces in quantum mechanics, and colour perception in psychology.

rf3 Shubik(1975) remarked that, also without risk or uncertainty, the assumption of concavity of the utility function (to be used in expected utility) is important. Without it, in a Walras allocation the risk-loving agents would 'create markets for lotteries'. See also Debreu(1976, footnote 1), Drèze(1971), Raiffa(1968, section 4.13).

rf4 Arrow(1971, Essay 3, page 96) and Machina(1982b, top of page 1069) comment on the universality of the assumption of nonincreasing risk aversion. See also section 3 in Bernoulli(1738). Risk-aversion in the presence of state-dependent utility functions is studied in Karni(1985).

rf5 e.g., see Fishburn(1970, section 8.4)

rf6 The same result is given in Gudder(1977, Theorem 4). A related result is given in Krantz(1975).

rf7 a generalization of 'Axiom Q' in Yaari(1978, p.109)

rf8 i.e., the Remark at section 4, and Lemma 2 of section 5 and, by that, the implication of 'Axiom D' by 'Axiom Q'

rf9 By Lemma VII.3.4, statement (ii) in Theorem VII.3.5 implies convexity of the preference relation. This in turn implies quasiconcavity of the additive representation V, which exists according to section III.6. In Yaari(1977) it is demonstrated that a quasiconcave additive representing function has all but one of its terms concave. See also Debreu&Koopmans(1982, Theorem 2, and end of section 4). Hence one might conjecture that in (ii) above the revelation of nonincreasing tradeoffs might be replaced by three conditions, as follows. First one uses coordinate independence (and the hexagon condition) to guarantee the existence of additive value functions. Next one uses convexity of $\succcurlyeq$ to guarantee quasiconcavity of the sum of the additive value functions, which by the result of Yaari implies concavity of all but one of the additive value functions. Thirdly, one weak condition for $\succcurlyeq$ is added to guarantee concavity of the one remaining additive value function. (Figure VII.4.1 (mainly f^3 there) will show that such a weak condition cannot be dispensed with.) We have not been able to find such a weak condition, hence we have taken an alternative approach, which does not use Yaari's results.

rf10 This, under the addition of continuity conditions, gives characterizations, alternative to those in Fishburn(1965), Pollak(1967), and Keeney&Raiffa(1976, Theorem 6.4).

rf11 The observation that (VII.4.3) does not imply (VII.4.2) for $m \geq 2$, is closely related to the observation that quasiconcavity and additivity of a function V do not imply (VII.4.1), i.e., concavity of V. This latter observation has been made several times in the literature. The earliest reference, given in Debreu&Koopmans(1982), is Slutsky(1915).

rf12 A derivation of the SEU model with concave utility, using differentiability conditions, is given in Stigum(1972).

rf13 Kihlstrom&Mirman(1974) adapted the Pratt-Arrow results to multidimensional quantitative consequences, still using differentiability assumptions. Wakker,Peters&Van Riel(1985, section 3) obtained, for decision making under risk, results for completely general consequence spaces.

rf14 Yaari uses a different, but trivially equivalent, formulation by means of 'acceptance sets'.

rf15 Yaari(1969, Remark 1) obtains a related result, using differentiability tools, for the case n=2.

rf16 Wakker,Peters&Van Riel(1985, section 3) extended the results, for decision making under risk, to completely general consequence spaces, and completely general utility functions.

rf17 or Eichhorn(1978, Theorem 2.5.2)

rf18 For the possibility to extend the above results, for the case of constant risk aversion, to multidimensional consequences, Rothblum(1975) may be useful.

REFERENCE-FOOTNOTES TO THE APPENDIX

rf1 This lemma, and its elegant proof, are due to Hardy,Littlewood,&Pólya(1934, Theorem 88).

rf2 De Finetti(1974, Chapter 3) requires a decision maker to value each act from a set of acts ('random quantities') by a number which is called price, or prevision. Next (section 3.1.5) an additivity condition '(a)' and a weak version of monotonicity '(b)' are added, implying that the prevision assigns expected values. (In the derivation in de Finetti,1974, section 3.3.5, by means of the 'first criterion', in fact also a scalar-multiplication-condition is added.) The special case where all the acts-to-be-valued are indicator functions of events, has been dealt with in de Finetti(1930, sections 4 and 5; 1931; 1937, Chapter I), and in de Finetti(1972, section 1.5 and Chapter 5).

[rf3] Our present version of de Finetti's result comes close to Theorem 4.3.1 in Blackwell&Girshick(1954). All conditions in statement (ii) below can be weakened. Stronger results are available in the literature, see for instance Weibull(1982,1984).

[rf4] A more general result than the above theorem is given in Fishburn(1982, Theorem 10.1).

REFERENCES

Aczél,J.,(1966), '*Lectures on Functional Equations and Their Applications*'. Academic Press, New York.

Adams,E.W.&R.F.Fagot(1959), 'A Model of Riskless Choice', *Behavioral Science* 4, 1-10.

Adams,E.W.,R.F.Fagot,&R.Robinson(1970), 'On the Empirical Status of Axioms in Theories of Fundamental Measurement',*Journal of Mathematical Psychology* 7,379-409.

Allais,M.(1953a), 'Fondements d'une Théorie Positive des Choix Comportant un Risque et Critique des Postulats et Axiomes de l'Ecole Américaine, *Colloques Internationaux du Centre National de la Recherche Scientifique* 40, Econométrie, 257-332. Paris: Centre National de la Recherche Scientifique. Translated into English, with additions, as 'The Foundations of a Positive Theory of Choice Involving Risk and a Criticism of the Postulates and Axioms of the American School', *in* M.Allais&O.Hagen(1979,Eds.), *Expected Utility Hypotheses and the Allais Paradox*, 27-145, Reidel, Dordrecht, The Netherlands.

Allais,M.(1953b), 'Le Comportement de l'Homme Rationnel devant le Risque: Critique des Postulats et Axiomes de l'Ecole Américaine', *Econometrica* 21, 503-546.

Allais,M.(1979), 'The So-Called Allais Paradox and Rational Decisions under Uncertainty'. *In* M.Allais&O.Hagen(1979,Eds.), *Expected Utility Hypotheses and the Allais Paradox*, 437-681, Reidel, Dordrecht, The Netherlands.

Alt,F.(1936), Über die Messbarkeit des Nutzens'. *Zeitschrift für Nationalökonomie* 7, 161-169. Translated into English by S.Schach(1971), 'On the Measurability of Utility', *in* J.S.Chipman,L.Hurwicz,M.K.Richter,&H.F.Sonnenschein(Eds.), *Preferences,Utility, and Demand*, Chapter 20. Hartcourt Brace Jovanovich, New York.

Anger,B.(1977), 'Representations of Capacities', *Mathematische Annalen* 229, 245-258.

Anscombe,F.J.&R.J.Aumann(1963), 'A Definition of Subjective Probability', *Annals of Mathematical Statistics* 34, 199-205.

Archimedes(287-212 B.C.), '*De Aequiponderantibus*', Syracuse.

Arrow,K.J.(1948), 'The Possibility of a Universal Social Welfare Function', Project RAND, RAD(L)-289, 26 October, Santa Monica, California, (hectographed).

Arrow,K.J.(1951a), '*Social Choice and Individual Values*'. Wiley, New York. (Ninth edition 1972, Yale University Press, New Haven.)

Arrow,K.J.(1951b), 'Alternative Approaches to the Theory of Choice in Risk-Taking Situations', *Econometrica* 19, 404-437.

Arrow,K.J.(1953), Le Rôle des Valeurs Boursières pour la Répartition la Meilleure des Risques'. *Colloques Internationaux du Centre National de la Recherche Scientifique (Econométrie)* 40, 41-47. Translated into English as 'The Role of Securities in the Optimal Allocation of Risk-Bearing', *Review of Economic Studies* 31 (1964), 91-96.

Arrow,K.J.(1959), 'Rational Choice Functions and Ordering', *Economica*,N.S., 26, 121-127.

Arrow,K.J.(1965), '*Aspects of the Theory of Risk-Bearing*'. Academic Bookstore, Helsinki.

Arrow,K.J.(1971), '*Essays in the Theory of Risk-Bearing*'. North-Holland, Amsterdam.

Arrow,K.J.&A.C.Enthoven(1961),'Quasi-Concave Programming'. *Econometrica* 29, 779-800.

Arrow,K.J.&H.R.Raynaud(1986), '*Social Choice and Multicriterion Decision Making*'. MIT, Cambridge Massachusetts.

Aumann,R.J.(1962), 'Utility Theory without the Completeness Axiom', *Econometrica* 30, 445-462.

Banach,St.&C.Kuratowski(1929), 'Sur une Généralisation du Problème de la Mesure', *Fundamenta Mathematicae* 14, 127-131.

Bandyopadhyay,T.(1988), 'Revealed Preference Theory, Ordering and the Axiom of Sequential Path Independence', *Review of Economic Studies* 55, 343–351.

Basu,K.(1980), '*Revealed Preference of Government*'. Cambridge University Press, Cambridge.

Basu,K.(1982), 'Determinateness of the Utility Function: Revisiting a Controversy of the Thirties', *Review of Economic Studies* 49, 307–311.

Bell,D.E.(1987), 'Multilinear Representations for Ordinal Utility Functions', *Journal of Mathematical Psychology* 31, 44–59.

Benson,P.(1987), 'Freedom and Value', *The Journal of Philosophy* 84, 465–486.

Berger,J.O.&R.L.Wolpert(1984), '*The Likelihood Principle: A Review, Generalizations and Statistical Implications*'. Lecture Notes, Monograph Series, Volume 6, Institute of Mathematical Statistics, Hayward, California.

Bernoulli,D.(1738), 'Specimen Theoria Novae de Mensura Sortis', *Commentarii Academiae Scientiarum Imperialis Petropolitanae* 5, 175–192. Translated into English by L.Sommer (1954), 'Exposition of a New Theory on the Measurement of Risk', *Econometrica* 12, 23–36; or in A.N.Page(Ed.,1968), '*Utility Theory: A Book of Readings*', Chapter 11, Wiley, New York.

Bezembinder,Th.G.G.(1981), 'Circularity and Consistency in Paired Comparisons', *British Journal of Mathematical and Statistical Psychology* 34, 16–37.

Bezembinder,Th.G.G.(1987), 'Problems of Content and Structure in Utilities for Social Choice'. *In* E.E.Roskam&R.Suck(Eds.), *Progress in Mathematical Psychology* 1, 467–483, Elsevier, North-Holland, Amsterdam.

Bezembinder,Th.G.G.&P.van Acker(1980), 'Intransitivity in Individual and Social Choice'. *In* E.D.Lantermann&H.Feger(Eds.), *Similarity and Choice*, Huber Publishers, Bern.

Bezembinder,Th.G.G.&P.van Acker(1987), 'Factual versus Representational Utilities and their Interdimensional Comparisons', *Social Choice and Welfare* 4, 79–104.

Bhaskara Rao,K.P.S.&M.Bhaskara Rao(1983), '*Theory of Charges*'.Academic Press,London.

Blackorby,C.,D.Primont,&R.R.Russell(1978), '*Duality, Separability and Functional Structure: Theory and Economic Applications*'. North-Holland, Amsterdam.

Blackwell,D.&M.A.Girshick(1954), '*Theory of Games and Statistical Decisions*'. Wiley, New York.

Blaschke,W.(1928), 'Topologische Fragen der Differentialgeometrie, I', *Mathematische Zeitschrift* 28, 150–157.

Blaschke,W.&G.Bol(1938), '*Geometrie der Gewebe*'. Springer, Berlin.

Burks,A.W.(1977), '*Chance, Cause, Reason* (An Inquiry into the Nature of Scientific Evidence)'. The University of Chicago Press, Chicago.

Camacho,A.(1980), 'Approaches to Cardinal Utility', *Theory and Decision* 12, 359–379.

Chernoff,H.(1954), 'Rational Selection of Decision Functions', *Econometrica* 22, 422–443.

Chew,S.H.(1983), 'A Generalization of the Quasilinear Mean with Applications to the Measurement of Income Inequality and Decision Theory Resolving the Allais Paradox', *Econometrica* 51, 1065–1092.

Chew,S.H.,E.Karni,&Z.Safra(1987), 'Risk Aversion in the Theory of Expected Utility with Rank Dependent Probabilities', *Journal of Economic Theory* 42, 370–381.

Chipman,J.S.,L.Hurwicz,M.K.Richter,&H.F.Sonnenschein(1971,Eds.), '*Preferences, Utility, and Demand*'. Hartcourt, New York.

Choquet,G.(1953–4), 'Theory of Capacities', *Annales de l'Institut Fourier* (Grenoble), 131–295.

Clark,S.A.(1988), 'An Extension Theorem for Rational Choice Functions', *Review of Economic Studies* 55, 485–492.

Cooke,R.M.&H.Draaisma(1984), 'A Method of Weighing Qualitative Preference Axioms', *Journal of Mathematical Psychology* 28, 436–447.

Coombs,C.A.,Th.G.G.Bezembinder,&F.M.Goode(1967), 'Testing Expectation Theories without Measuring Utility or Subjective Probability', *Journal of Mathematical Psychology* 4, 72–103.

Cooper,W.S.(1987), 'Decision Theory as a Branch of Evolutionary Theory: A Biological Derivation of the Savage Axioms', *Psychological Review* 94, 395–411.

Cooter,R.D.&P.Rappoport(1984), 'Were the Ordinalists Wrong about Welfare Economics?', *Journal of Economic Literature* 22, 507–530.

Cooter,R.D.&P.Rappoport(1985), 'Reply to I.M.D. Little's Comment', *Journal of Economic Literature* 23, 1189–1191.

Dahlby,B.G.(1987), 'Inequality Measures in a Harsanyi Framework', *Theory and Decision* 22, 187–202.

de Finetti,B.(1930), 'Problemi Determini e Indetermini nel Calcolo delle Probabilità', *Rendiconti della Academia Nazionale dei Lincei* XII, 367–373.

de Finetti,B.(1931), 'Sul Significato Soggettivo della Probabilità', *Fundamenta Mathematicae* 17, 298–329.

de Finetti,B.(1937), 'La Prévision: Ses Lois Logiques, ses Sources Subjectives', *Annales de l'Institut Henri Poincaré* 7, 1–68. Translated into English by H.E.Kyburg, 'Foresight: Its logical Laws, its Subjective Sources', *in* H.E.Kyburg&H.E.Smokler(1964,Eds.), Studies in Subjective Probability, Wiley, New York.

de Finetti,B.(1972), '*Probability, Induction and Statistics*'. Wiley, New York.

de Finetti,B.(1974), '*Theory of Probability*', Vol.I. Wiley, New York.

Debreu,G.(1954), 'Representation of a Preference Ordering by a Numerical Function'. *In* R.M.Thrall,C.H.Coombs,&R.L.Davis(Eds.),*Decision Processes* 159–165,Wiley,New York.

Debreu,G.(1958), 'Stochastic Choice and Cardinal Utility', *Econometrica* 26, 440–444.

Debreu,G.(1959), '*Theory of Value*'. Wiley, New York.

Debreu,G.(1960), 'Topological Methods in Cardinal Utility Theory'. *In* K.J.Arrow,S.Karlin, &P.Suppes(1959,Eds.), *Mathematical Methods in the Social Sciences*, 16–26, Stanford University Press, Stanford.

Debreu,G.(1964), 'Continuity Properties of Paretian Utility', *International Economic Review* 5, 285–293.

Debreu,G.(1976), 'Least Concave Utility Functions', *Journal of Mathematical Economics* 3, 121–129.

Debreu,G.&T.C.Koopmans(1982), 'Additively Decomposed Quasiconvex Functions', *Mathematical Programming* 24, 1–38.

DeGroot,M.H.(1970), '*Optimal Statistical Decisions*'. McGraw-Hill, New York.

Dellacherie,C.(1970), 'Quelques Commentaires sur les Prolongements de Capacités', *Seminaire de Probabilités V Strasbourg*, (Lecture Notes in Mathematics 191), Springer Verlag, Berlin.

Deschamps,R.&L.Gevers(1978), 'Leximin and Utilitarian Rules: A Joint Characterization', *Journal of Economic Theory* 17, 143–163.

Drèze,J.H.(1971), 'Market Allocation under Uncertainty', *European Economic Review* 2, 133–165.

Drèze,J.H.(1987), '*Essays on Economic Decision under Uncertainty*'. Cambridge University Press, London.

Driessen,T.S.H.(1988), '*Cooperative Games, Solutions and Applications*'. Kluwer Academic Publishers, Dordrecht.

Dunford,N.&J.T.Schwartz(1958), '*Linear Operators, Part I*'. Interscience Publishers, New York.

Ebert,U.(1988), 'Rawls and Bentham Reconciled', *Theory and Decision* 24, 215–223.

Edwards,A.W.F.(1972), '*Likelihood*'. Cambridge University Press, London.

Eichhorn,W.(1978), '*Functional Equations in Economics*'. Addison Wesley, London.

Eichhorn,W.(Ed.,1988), '*Measurement in Economics* (Theory and Applications of Economic Indices)'. Physica-Verlag, Heidelberg.

Ellsberg,D.(1961), 'Risk, Ambiguity and the Savage Axioms', *Quarterly Journal of Economics* 75, 643-669.

Falmagne,J.C.(1976), 'Random Conjoint Measurement and Loudness Summation', *Psychological Review* 83, 65-79.

Falmagne,J.C.(1985), '*Elements of Psychophysical Theory*'. Oxford University Press, New York.

Feller,W.(1966), '*An Introduction to Probability Theory*, Vol. II'. Wiley, New York.

Fishburn,P.C.(1965), 'Independence in Utility Theory with Whole Product Sets', *Operations Research* 13, 28-45.

Fishburn,P.C.(1967), 'Additive Utilities with Incomplete Product Sets: Application to Priorities and Assignments', *Operations Research* 15, 537-542.

Fishburn,P.C.(1970), '*Utility Theory for Decision Making*'. Wiley, New York.

Fishburn,P.C.(1971), 'Additive Representations of Real-Valued Functions on Subsets of Product Sets', *Journal of Mathematical Psychology* 8, 382-388.

Fishburn,P.C.(1972), '*Mathematics of Decision Theory*'. Mouton, The Hague.

Fishburn,P.C.(1973), '*The Theory of Social Choice*'. Princeton University Press, Princeton, New Jersey.

Fishburn,P.C.(1981), 'Subjective Expected Utility: A Review of Normative Theories', *Theory and Decision* 13, 139-199.

Fishburn,P.C.(1982), '*The Foundations of Expected Utility*'. Reidel, Dordrecht.

Fisher,I.(1927a), 'A Statistical Method for Measuring "Marginal Utility" and Testing the Justice of a Progressive Income Tax'. *In* J.H.Hollander(Ed.), *Economic Essays Contributed in Honor of John Bates Clark*, 157-193, MacMillan, New York.

Fisher,I.(1927b), '*The Making of Index Numbers*'. Houghton-Mifflin, Boston. (Third edition 1967, Augustus M. Kelley, New York.)

Fleming,J.M.(1952), 'A Cardinal Concept of Welfare', *Quarterly Journal of Economics* 66, 366-384.

Fleming,J.M.(1957), 'Cardinal Welfare and Individualistic Ethics: A Comment', *Journal of Political Economy* 65, 355-357.

Foxall,G.R.(1986), 'Theoretical Progress in Consumer Psychology: The Contribution of a Behavioural Analysis of Choice', *Journal of Economic Psychology* 7, 393-414.

French,S.(1986), '*Decision Theory* (An Introduction to the Mathematics of Rationality)'. Ellis Horwood Limited/Wiley, New York.

French,S.&M.Vassiloglou(1986), 'Strength of Performance and Examination Assessment', *British Journal of Mathematical and Statistical Psychology* 39, 1-14.

Freudenthal,H.(1965), Review of Kyburg&Smokler(1964), *Nieuw Archief voor Wiskunde* 13, 168-173.

Frisch,R.(1926), 'Sur un Problème d'Economie Pure', *Norsk Matematisk Forenings Skrifter Serie I* 16, 1-40. Translated into English by J.S.Chipman, 'On a Problem in Pure Economics', *in* J.S.Chipman,L.Hurwicz,M.K.Richter,&H.F.Sonnenschein(1971,Eds.), *Preferences, Utility, and Demand*, Chapter 19, Hartcourt, New York.

Fuhrken,G.&M.K.Richter(1988), 'Algebra and Topology in Cardinal Utility Theory'. *In* W.Eichhorn(Ed.), '*Measurement in Economics* (Theory and Applications of Economic Indices)', 239-252, Physica-Verlag, Heidelberg.

Gilboa,I.(1987), 'Expected Utility with Purely Subjective Non-Additive Probabilities', *Journal of Mathematical Economics* 16, 65-88.

Gilboa,I.(1989), 'Duality in Non-Additive Expected Utility Theory'. *In* P.C.Fishburn&I.H. LaValle(Eds.), *Choice under Uncertainty*, Annals of Operations Research, J.C.Baltzer AG., Basel, forthcoming.

Gorman,W.M.(1968), 'The Structure of Utility Functions', *Review of Economic Studies* 35, 367-390.

Gorman,W.M.(1971), 'Apologia for a Lemma' and 'Clontarf Revisited', *Review of Economic Studies* 38, 114 and 116.

Gorman,W.M.(1976), 'Tricks with Utility Functions'. *In* M.Artis&R.Nobay(Eds.), *Essays in Economic Analysis*, 211-243, Cambridge University Press, Copenhagen.

Grodal,B.(1978), 'Some Further Results on Integral Representation of Utility Functions', Institute of Economics, University of Copenhagen, Copenhagen. Forthcoming in K.Vind, '*Independent Preferences*'.

Gudder,S.P.(1977), 'Convexity and Mixtures', *SIAM Review* 19, 221-240.

Gudder,S.P.&F.Schroeck(1980), 'Generalized Convexity', *SIAM Journal on Mathematical Analysis* 11, 984-1001.

Halmos,P.R.(1950), '*Measure Theory*'. Van Nostrand, New York.

Hammond,P.J.(1988), 'Consequentialist Foundations for Expected Utility', *Theory and Decision* 25, 25-78.

Hansson,B.(1968), 'Choice Structure and Preference Relations', *Synthese* 18, 443-458.

Hardy,G.H.,J.E.Littlewood,&G.Pólya(1934), '*Inequalities*'. University Press, Cambridge. (Second edition 1952, reprinted 1978.)

Harsanyi,J.C.(1955), 'Cardinal Welfare, Individualistic Ethics, and Interpersonal Comparisons of Utility', *Journal of Political Economy* 63, 309-321.

Hartman,S.&J.Mikusiński(1961), '*The Theory of Lebesgue Measure*'. Pergamon, Oxford.

Herstein,I.N.&J.Milnor(1953), 'An Axiomatic Approach to Measurable Utility', *Econometrica* 21, 291-297.

Hölder,O.(1901), 'Die Axiome der Quantität und die Lehre vom Mass', *Berichte Verhand. König. Sächs. Gesell. Wiss.* (Leipzig), *Math. Phys., Cl.* 53, 1-64.

Hogarth,R.M.&M.W.Reder(1987,Eds.), '*Rational Choice*'. University Press, Chicago.

Houthakker,H.S.(1950), 'Revealed Preference and the Utility Function', *Economica*, N.S. 17, 159-174.

Huber,P.J.(1981), '*Robust Statistics*'. Wiley, New York.

Huber,P.J.&V.Strassen(1973), 'Minimax Tests and the Neyman-Pearson Lemma for Capacities', *The Annals of Statistics* 1, 251-263.

Hurwicz,L.(1951), 'Optimality Criteria for Decision Making under Ignorance', Cowles Commission Discussion Paper, Statistics, No. 370, mimeographed.

Hwang,C.L.&K.Yoon(1981), '*Multiple Attribute Decision Making*'. Springer, Berlin.

Jaffray,J.-Y.(1974a), 'Existence, Propriétés de Continuité, Additivité de Fonctions d'Utilité sur un Espace Partiellement ou Totalement Ordonné'. Ph.D. dissertation, Université de Paris VI, Paris.

Jaffray,J.-Y.(1974b), 'On the Extension of Additive Utilities to Infinite Sets', *Journal of Mathematical Psychology* 11, 431-452.

Jaffray,J.-Y.(1975), 'Existence of a Continuous Utility Function: An Elementary Proof', *Econometrica* 43, 981-983.

Jeffrey,R.C.(1965), '*The Logic of Decision*'. McGraw-Hill, New York. (Second edition 1983, University of Chicago Press, Chicago.)

Jensen,N.E.(1967), 'An Introduction to Bernoullian Utility Theory, I, II', *Swedish Journal of Economics* 69, 163-183, 229-247.

Kahneman,D.&A.Tversky(1979), 'Prospect Theory: An Analysis of Decision under Risk', *Econometrica* 47, 263-291.

Kannai,Y.(1977), 'Concavifiability and Constructions of Concave Utility Functions', *Journal of Mathematical Economics* 4, 1-56.

Kannai,Y.(1981), 'Concave Utility Functions, Existence, Constructions and Cardinality'. *In* S.Schaible&W.T.Ziemba(Eds.), *Generalized Concavity in Optimization and Economics*, 543-611, Academic Press, New York.
Karni,E.(1985), '*Decision-Making under Uncertainty: The Case of State-Dependent Preferences*'. Harvard University Press, Cambridge, Massachussets.
Karni,E.&D.Schmeidler(1976), 'Independence of Nonfeasible Alternatives, and Independence of Nonoptimal Alternatives', *Journal of Economic Theory* 12, 488-493.
Katzner,W.D.(1970), '*Static Demand Theory*'. MacMillan, London.
Keeney,R.L.&H.Raiffa(1976), '*Decisions with Multiple Objectives*'. Wiley, New York.
Kelley,J.L,.(1955), '*General Topology*'. Van Nostrand, London.
Kihlstrom,R.E.&L.J.Mirman(1974), 'Risk Aversion with Many Commodities', *Journal of Economic Theory* 8, 361-388.
KLST: Krantz,Luce,Suppes,&Tversky(1971)
Koopmans,T.C.(1972), 'Representations of Preference Orderings with Independent Components of Consumption', & 'Representations of Preference Orderings over Time'. *In* C.B.McGuire&R.Radner(Eds.), *Decision and Organization*, 57-100, North-Holland, Amsterdam.
Krantz,D.H.(1975), 'Color Measurement and Color Theory. I. Representation Theorem for Grassman Structures', *Journal of Mathematical Psychology* 12, 283-303.
Krantz,D.H.,R.D.Luce,P.Suppes,&A.Tversky(1971) (=KLST), '*Foundations of Measurement*, Vol. I. (Additive and Polynomial Representations)'. Academic Press, New York.
Lange,O.(1934), 'The Determinateness of the Utility Functions', *Review of Economic Studies* 1, 218-224.
LaValle,I.H.&K.R.Wapman(1986), 'Rolling Back Trees Requires the Independence Axiom', *Management Science* 32, 382-385.
Lazimy,R.(1986), 'Solving Multiple Criteria Problems by Interactive Decomposition', *Mathematical Programming* 35, 334-361.
Lensberg,T.(1987), 'Stability and Collective Rationality', *Econometrica* 55, 935-961.
Leontief,W.W.(1947a), 'A Note on the Interrelation of Subsets of Independent Variables of a Continuous Function with Continuous First Derivatives', *Bulletin of the American Mathematical Society* 53, 343-350.
Leontief,W.W.(1947b), 'Introduction to a Theory of the Internal Structure of Functional Relationships', *Econometrica* 51, 361-373.
Luce,R.D.(1959), '*Individual Choice Behavior*'. Wiley, New York.
Luce,R.D.&H.Raiffa(1957), '*Games and Decisions*'. Wiley, New York.
Luce,R.D.&L.Narens(1987), 'Measurement Scales on the Continuum', *Science* 236, 1527-1532.
Luce,R.D.&P.Suppes(1965), 'Preference, Utility, and Subjective Probability'. *In* R.D.Luce, R.R.Bush,&E.Galanter(Eds.), *Handbook of Mathematical Psychology*, III, Wiley, New York.
Lukas,J.(1987), 'Additiv Verbundene Messung der Wahrgenommenen Flächengrösse: Ein Experimentelles Verfahren zur Lösung des Testbarkeitsproblems', *Zeitschrift für Experimentelle und Angewandte Psychologie* 34, 416-430.
McClennen,E.F.(1983), 'Sure-Thing Doubts'. *In* B.P.Stigum&F.Wenstop(Eds.), '*Foundations of Utility and Risk Theory with Applications*', 117-136, Reidel, Dordrecht.
McGuire,C.R.&R.Radner(1972,Eds.), *Decision and Organization*, 57-100, North-Holland, Amsterdam.
Mach,E.(1883), '*Die Mechanik in Ihrer Entwicklung Historisch-Kritisch Dargestellt*'. Translated into English by T.J.McCormack(1893), '*The Science of Mechanics: A Critical and Historical Account of Its Development*', Open Court, La Salle, Illinois. (Sixth Edition 1960.)

Mach,E.(1896), '*Prinzipien der Wärmelehre*', Leipzig.
Machina,M.J.(1982a),"Expected Utility' Analysis without the Independence Axiom', *Econometrica* 50, 277-323.
Machina,M.J.(1982b),'A Stronger Characterization of Declining Risk Aversion', *Econometrica* 50, 1069-1079.
Machina,M.J.(1987), 'Choice under Uncertainty: Problems Solved and Unsolved', *Economic Perspectives* 1, 121-154.
Mak,K.-T.(1987), 'Coherent Continuous Systems and the Generalized Functional Equation of Associativity', *Mathematics of Operations Research* 12, 597-625.
Mak,K.-T.(1988), 'Separability and the Existence of Aggregates'. *In* W.Eichhorn(Ed.), '*Measurement in Economics* (Theory and Applications of Economic Indices)', 649-670, Physica-Verlag, Heidelberg.
Marschak,J.&R.Radner(1972), '*Economic Theory of Teams*'. Yale University Press, New Haven.
May,K.O.(1954), 'Intransitivity, Utility, and the Aggregation of Preference Patterns', *Econometrica* 22, 1-13.
Montgomery,H.&O.Svenson(1976), 'On Decision Rules and Information Processing Strategies for Choices among Multiattribute Alternatives', *Göteborg Psychological Reports* 6, number 3.
Murphy,F.P.(1981), 'A Note on Weak Separability', *Review of Economic Studies* 48, 671-672.
Narens,L.(1985), '*Abstract Measurement Theory*'. MIT Press, Cambridge Massachusets.
Nash,J.F.(1950a), 'Rational Nonlinear Utility'. *In* Shubik,M.(1982), '*Game Theory in the Social Sciences*', Appendix A2, The MIT Press, Cambridge.
Nash,J.F.(1950b), 'The Bargaining Problem', *Econometrica* 18, 155-162.
Nygren,T.E.(1986), 'A Two-Stage Algorithm for Assessing Violations of Additivity via Axiomatic and Numerical Conjoint Analysis', *Psychometrika* 51, 483-491.
Peters,H.J.M.(1986), '*Bargaining Game Theory*'. Ph.D. dissertation, University of Nijmegen, Department of Mathematics.
Peters,H.J.M.&P.P.Wakker(1987), 'Independence of Irrelevant Alternatives and Revealed Group Preferences', WP 87-014, University of Maastricht, Department of Economics, Maastricht, The Netherlands.
Pfanzagl,J.(1968), '*Theory of Measurement*'. Physica-Verlag, Vienna.
Pollak,R.A.(1967), 'Additive von Neumann-Morgenstern Utility Functions', *Econometrica* 35, 485-494.
Praag,B.M.S.van(1975), 'Utility, Welfare and Probability: An Unorthodox Economist's View'. *In* D.Wendt&C.A.J.Vlek(Eds.), *Utility, Probability, and Human Decision Making*, 279-295, Reidel, Dordrecht.
Pratt,J.W.(1964), 'Risk Aversion in the Small and in the Large', *Econometrica* 32, 122-136.
Pratt,J.W.,H.Raiffa,&R.Schlaifer(1964), 'The Foundations of Decision under Uncertainty: An Elementary Exposition', *Journal of American Statistical Association* 59, 353-375.
Quiggin,J.(1982), 'A Theory of Anticipated Utility', *Journal of Economic Behaviour and Organization* 3, 323-343.
Rabinowicz,W.(1988), 'Ratifiability and Stability'. *In* P.Gärdenfors&N.-E.Sahlin(Eds.), *Decision, Probability, and Utility*, 406-427.
Raiffa,H.(1968), '*Decision Analysis*'. Addison-Wesley, London.
Ramsey,F.P.(1931), 'Truth and Probability', *in 'The Foundations of Mathematics and other Logical Essays*', 156-198,Routledge and Kegan Paul,London. Reprinted *in* H.E.Kyburg &H.E.Smokler(1964,Eds.), *Studies in Subjective Probability*, 61-92, Wiley,New York.
Ray,P.(1973), 'Independence of Irrelevant Alternatives', *Econometrica* 41, 987-991.
Richter,M.K.(1966), 'Revealed Preference Theory', *Econometrica* 34, 635-645.

Richter,M.K.(1971), 'Rational Choice'. *In* J.S.Chipman,L.Hurwicz,M.K.Richter,&H.F. Sonnenschein(Eds.), *Preferences, Utility, and Demand*, 29-58, Hartcourt, New York.

Richter,M.K.(1975), 'Rational Choice and Polynomial Measurement Theory', *Journal of Mathematical Psychology* 12, 99-113.

Richter,M.K.(1980), 'Continuous and Semi-continuous Utility', *International Economic Review* 21, 293-299.

Richter,M.K.&L.Shapiro(1978), 'Revelations of a Gambler', *Journal of Mathematical Economics* 5,229-244.

Rockafellar,R.T.(1970), *'Convex Analysis'*. Princeton University Press, Princeton.

Roskam,E.E.(1987), 'ORDMET3: An Improved Algorithm to Find the Maximin Solution to a System of Linear (In)equalities'. Report 87MA06, University of Nijmegen, Department of Mathematical Psychology.

Rothblum,U.G.(1975), 'Multivariate Constant Risk Posture', *Journal of Economic Theory* 10, 309-322.

Saaty,T.L.(1980), *'The Analytic Hierarchy Process'*. McGraw-Hill, New York.

Saaty,T.L.(1986), 'Axiomatic Foundation of the Analytic Hierarchy Process', *Management Science* 32, 841-855.

Samuels,W.J.(1988), 'An Essay on the Nature and Significance of the Normative Nature of Economics', *Journal of Post Keynesian Economics* 10, 347-354.

Samuelson,P.A.(1938a), 'A Note on the Pure Theory of Consumer's Behaviour', *Economica*, N.S. 5, 61-71, 353-354.

Samuelson,P.A.(1938b), 'The Empirical Implications of Utility Analysis', *Econometrica* 6, 344-356.

Samuelson,P.A.(1947), *'Foundations of Economic Analysis'*. Harvard University Press, Cambridge, Massachusets.

Samuelson,P.A.(1950), 'The Problem of Integrability in Utility Theory', *Economica*, N.S. 17, 355-385.

Samuelson,P.A.(1952), 'Probability, Utility, and the Independence Axiom', *Econometrica* 20, 670-679.

Samuelson,P.A.(1958), 'An Exact Consumption-Loan Model of Interest with or without the Social Contrivance of Money', *The Journal of Political Economy* 46, 467-482.

Savage,L.J.(1953), 'Une Axiomatisation du Comportement Raisonnable Face à l'Incertitude'. *Colloques Internationaux du Centre National de la Recherche Scientifique* (Econométrie) 40, 55-67.

Savage,L.J.(1954), *'The Foundations of Statistics'*. Wiley, New York. (Second edition 1972, Dover, New York.)

Schmeidler,D.(1971), 'A Condition for the Completeness of Partial Preference Relations', *Econometrica* 39, 403-404.

Schmeidler,D.(1984a), 'Subjective Probability and Expected Utility without Additivity'. Caress working paper 84-21 (first part), University of Pennsylvania, Center for Analytic Research in Economics and the Social Sciences, Pennsylvania.

Schmeidler,D.(1984b), 'Nonadditive Probabilities and Convex Games'. Caress working paper 84-21 (second part), University of Pennsylvania, Center for Analytic Research in Economics and the Social Sciences, Pennsylvania.

Schmeidler,D.(1984c), 'Integral Representation without Additivity'. Working paper, Tel-Aviv University and IMA University of Minnesota.

Schoemaker,P.H.J.(1982), 'The Expected Utility Model: Its Variations, Purposes, Evidence and Limitations', *Journal of Economic Literature* 20, 529-563.

Scott,D.(1964), 'Measurement Structures and Linear Inequalities', *Journal of Mathematical Psychology* 1, 233-247.

Scott,D.&P.Suppes(1958), 'Foundational Aspects of Theories of Measurement', *Journal of Symbolic Logic* 23, 113-128.

Sen,A.K.(1971), 'Choice Functions and Revealed Preference', *Review of Economic Studies* 38, 307-317.

Shafer,G.(1986), 'Savage Revisited' (including comments), *Satistical Science* 1, 463-501.

Shapiro,L.(1979), 'Necessary and Sufficient Conditions for Expected Utility Maximizations: The Finite Case, with a Partial Order', *Annals of Statistics* 7, 1288-1302.

Shapley,L.S.(1975), 'Cardinal Utility Comparisons from Intensity Comparisons'. Report R-1683-PR, The Rand Corporation, Santa Monica, California.

Shephard,R.W.(1970), '*Theory of Cost and Production Functions*'. Princeton University Press, Princeton, New Jersey.

Shubik,M.(1975), 'Competitive Equilibrium, the Core, Preferences for Risk and Insurance Markets', *Economic Records* 51, 73-83.

Simon,H.A.(1982), '*Models of Bounded Rationality*, Vols 1 and 2'. The MIT Press, London.

Slutsky,E.E.(1915), 'Sulla Teoria del Bilancio del Consumatore', *Giornale degli Economisti* 51, 1-26. Translated into English as: 'On the Theory of the Budget of the Consumer', *in* R.Irwin(1952), *Readings in Price Theory*, 27-56, Americal Economic Association.

Sneed,J.D.(1971), '*The Logical Structure of Mathematical Physics*'. Reidel, Dordrecht.

Sonnenschein,H.F.(1965), 'The Relationship between Transitive Preference and the Structure of the Choice Space', *Econometrica* 33, 624-634.

Sono,M.(1945), 'The Effect of Price Changes on the Demand and Supply of Separable Goods' (in Japanese), *Kokumin Keisai Zasshi* 74, 1-51.

Sono,M.(1961), 'The Effect of Price Changes on the Demand and Supply of Separable Goods', *International Economic Review* 2, 239-271.

Stehling,F.(1975), 'Eine Neue Characterisierung der CD- und ACMS-Produktionsfunktionen', *Operations Research-Verfahren* 21, 222-238.

Stigum,B.P.(1972), 'Finite State Space and Expected Utility Maximization', *Econometrica* 40, 253-259.

Stone,M.H.(1949), 'Postulates for the Barycentric Calculus', *Annali di Matematica Pura ed Applicata* 29, 25-30.

Suppes,P.(1956), 'The Role of Subjective Probability and Utility in Decision Making'. *Proceedings of the Third Berkeley Symposium on Mathematical Statistics and Probability*, 1954-1955, 5, 61-73.

Suppes,P.&J.L.Zinnes(1963), 'Basic Measurement Theory'. *In* R.D.Luce,R.R.Bush,& E.Galanter(Eds.), *Handbook of Mathematical Psychology*, Vol.I, 1-76, Wiley, New York.

Szpilrajn,E.(1930), 'Sur l'Extension de l'Ordre Partiel', *Fundamenta Mathematicae* 16, 386-389.

Tversky,A.(1964), 'Finite Additive Structures', Michigan Mathematical Psychology Program, MMPP 64-6, University of Michigan.

Tversky,A.(1967a), 'A General Theory of Polynomial Conjoint Measurement', *Journal of Mathematical Psychology* 4, 1-20.

Tversky,A.(1967b), 'Additivity, Utility, and Subjective Probability', *Journal of Mathematical Psychology* 4, 175-201.

Tversky,A.(1977), 'Features of Similarity', *Psychological Review* 84, 327-352.

Tversky,A.&D.H.Krantz(1969), 'Similarity of Schematic Faces: A Test of Interdimensional Additivity', *Perception and Psychophysics* 5, 124-128.

Ulam,St.(1930), 'Zur Masstheorie in der Allgemeinen Mengenlehre', *Fundamenta Mathematicae* 16, 140-150.

Ville,J.(1946), 'Sur les Conditions d'Existence d'une Ophélimité Totale et d'un Indice du Niveau des Prix', *Annales de l'Université de Lyon*, 9, Sec. A(3), 32–39. Translated into English by P.K.Newman(1951–52), 'The Existence-Conditions of a Total Utility Function', *Review of Economic Studies* 19, 123–128.

Villegas,C.(1964), 'On Quantitative Probability σ-Algebras', *Annals of Mathematical Statistics* 35, 1787–1796.

Vind,K.(1971), 'The Structure of Utility Functions' and 'Comment', *Review of Economic Studies* 38, 113 and 115.

Vind,K.(1986a), 'Additive Utility Functions and Other Special Functions in Economic Theory' (preliminary version), Institute of Economics, University of Copenhagen, Copenhagen.

Vind,K.(1986b), 'Independent Preferences' (preliminary version), Institute of Economics, University of Copenhagen, Copenhagen.

von Neumann,J.&O.Morgenstern(1944,1947,1953), '*Theory of Games and Economic Behavior*'. Princeton University Press, Princeton NJ.

von Winterfeldt,D.&W.Edwards(1986), '*Decision Analysis and Behavioral Research*'. Cambridge University Press, Cambridge.

von Wright,G.H.(1963), '*The Logic of Preference: An Essay*'. Edinburgh.

Wakker,P.P.(1981), 'Agreeing Probability Measures for Comparative Probability Structures', *The Annals of Statistics* 9, 658-662.

Wakker,P.P.(1984), 'Cardinal Coordinate Independence for Expected Utility', *Journal of Mathematical Psychology* 28, 110-117.

Wakker,P.P.(1985), 'Continuous Expected Utility for Arbitrary State Spaces', *Methods of Operations Research* 50, 113-129.

Wakker,P.P.(1986a), 'Concave Additively Decomposable Representing Functions and Risk Aversion'. *In* L.Daboni, A.Montesano,&M.Lines(Eds.), *Recent Developments in the Foundations of Utility and Risk Theory*, 249-262. Reidel, Dordrecht.

Wakker,P.P.(1986b), 'The Repetitions Approach to Characterize Cardinal Utility', *Theory and Decision* 17, 33-40.

Wakker,P.P.(1986c), 'Representations of Choice Situations'. Ph.D. Dissertation, University of Brabant, Department of Economics, The Netherlands.

Wakker,P.P.(1987a), 'From Decision Making under Uncertainty to Game Theory'. *In* H.J.M. Peters&O.J.Vrieze(Eds.), *Surveys of Game Theory and Related Topics*, 163–180, CWI Tract 39, Centre for Mathematics and Computer Science, Amsterdam.

Wakker,P.P.(1987b), 'Continuous Subjective Expected Utility with Nonadditive Probabilities', *Journal of Mathematical Economics*, forthcoming.

Wakker,P.P.(1987c), 'Nonadditive Probabilities and Derived Strengths of Preferences', Internal report 87 MA 03, University of Nijmegen, Department of Mathematical Psychology, Nijmegen, The Netherlands.

Wakker,P.P.(1988a), 'Characterizations of Quasilinear Representing Functions, and Specified Forms of These'. *In* W.Eichhorn(Ed.), *Measurement in Economics* (Theory and Applications of Economic Indices), 311-326, Physica-Verlag, Heidelberg.

Wakker,P.P.(1988b), 'Nonexpected Utility as Aversion of Information', *Journal of Behavioral Decision Making* 1, 169–175.

Wakker,P.P.(1988c), 'A Graph-Theoretic Approach to Revealed Preference', *Methodology and Science*, forth-coming.

Wakker,P.P.(1988d), 'The Algebraic Versus the Topological Approach to Additive Representations', *Journal of Mathematical Psychology*, forthcoming.

Wakker,P.P.(1988e), 'Derived Strength of Preference Relations on Coordinates', *Economics Letters*, forthcoming.

Wakker,P.P.(1989), 'Subjective Expected Utility for Non-Increasing Risk Aversion'. *In* P.C. Fishburn&I.H.LaValle(Eds.), *Choice under Uncertainty*, Annals of Operations Research, J.C.Baltzer AG., Basel, forthcoming.

Wakker,P.P.,H.J.M.Peters,&T.B.P.L.van Riel(1986), 'Comparisons of Risk Aversion, with an Application to Bargaining', *Methods of Operations Research* 54, 307-320.

Weddepohl,H.N.(1970), '*Axiomatic Choice Models (and Duality)*'. Ph.D. Dissertation, Universitaire Pers Rotterdam, Wolters-Noordhoff, Rotterdam.

Weibull,J.W.(1982), 'A Dual to the von Neumann-Morgenstern Theorem', *Journal of Mathematical Psychology* 26, 191-203.

Weibull,J.W.(1984), 'Continuous Linear Representations of Preference Orderings in Vector Spaces'. *In* H.Hauptmann,W.Krelle,&K.C.Mosler(Eds.), *Operations Research and Economic Theory* 291-305, Springer, Berlin.

White,D.J.(1982), '*Optimality and Efficiency*. Wiley, New York.

Woolfolk,R.L.&L.A.Sass(1988), 'Behaviorism and Existentialism Revisited', *Journal of Humanistic Psychology* 28, 108-119.

Yaari,M.E.(1969), 'Some Remarks on Measures of Risk Aversion and on Their Uses', *Journal of Economic Theory* 1, 315-329.

Yaari,M.E.(1977), 'A Note on Separability and Quasi-Concavity', *Econometrica* 45, 1183-1186.

Yaari,M.E.(1978), 'Separable Concave Utilities or the Principle of Diminishing Eagerness to Trade', *Journal of Economic Theory* 18, 102-118.

Yaari,M.E.(1987a), 'The Dual Theory of Choice under Risk', *Econometrica* 55, 95-115.

Yaari,M.E.(1987b), 'Univariate and Multivatiate Comparisons of Risk Aversion: a New Appraoch', *in* W.P.Heller,R.M.Starr,&D.A.Starrett(Eds.), *Uncertainty, Information and Communication, Essays in honor of Kenneth J. Arrow*, Vol. III, 173-187, Cambridge University Press, Cambridge.

Yager,R.R.(1988), 'On Ordered Weighted Averaging Aggregation Operators in Multicriteria Decisionmaking', *IEEE Transactions on Systems, Man, and Cybernetics* 18, 183-190.

Young,H.P.(1987a), 'Progressive Taxation and the Equal Sacrifice Principle', *Journal of Public Economics* 32, 203-214.

Young,H.P.(1987b), 'On Dividing an Amount According to Individual Claims or Liabilities', *Mathematics of Operations Research* 12, 398-414.

Zilcha,I.(1988), 'Intergenerational Transfers'. *In* J.Eatwell&P.Newman(Eds.), *The New Palgrave: A Dictionary of Economic Theory and Doctrine*, The MacMillan Press, Cambridge, forthcoming.

AUTHOR INDEX

SUBJECT INDEX

NOTATION INDEX

THEORY AND DECISION LIBRARY

SERIES C: GAME THEORY, MATHEMATICAL PROGRAMMING AND OPERATIONS RESEARCH

Already published:

Compromise, Negotiation and Group Decision
Edited by Bertrand R. Munier and Melvin F. Shakun
ISBN 90–277–2625–6

Models of Strategic Rationality
by Reinhard Selten
ISBN 90–277–2663–9

Cooperative Games, Solutions and Applications
by Theo Driessen
ISBN 90–277–2729–5